An Important Notice to PG-EJO-945 Investors

The American Association of Individual Investors conducted an independent real time study of 50 top investment strategies every month from January 1, 1998 to December 31, 2009 and found O'Neil's CAN SLIM® to be the top performing investment strategy.

In AAII's study, CAN SLIM produced a 2,763% result, an average of 35.3% per year versus 3.3% a year for the S&P 500 during the same time period.

Investor's Business Daily's digital edition, eIBD™, and Web site, Investors.com, received these national awards in 2009:

Web Marketing Association's
WebAward

WebAward for Best Investment Website.
Award granted by the Web Marketing Association "for outstanding achievement in web development." Over 2,000 sites were judged in this premier competition.

DPAC Awards.
eIBD was named Best Branded Digital Magazine. The DPAC Award recognizes overall excellence and breakthrough achievement in Digital Publishing and Advertising.

IMA
2009

Interactive Media Awards Outstanding Achievement Award for Financial Information.
Award recognizes "the highest standards of excellence in Web site design and development. It honors organizations for their outstanding achievement."

2009
W3 AWARDS
SILVER WINNER

Silver w3 Award.
Honoring creative excellence on the Web, with over 3,000 sites judged.

How to Make Money in Stocks FOURTH EDITION

A WINNING SYSTEM IN GOOD TIMES OR BAD

WILLIAM J. O'NEIL

New York Chicago San Francisco Lisbon London
Madrid Mexico City Milan New Delhi San Juan
Seoul Singapore Sydney Toronto

13   DOC/DOC   1 5

ISBN-13: 978-0-07-161413-9
MHID: 0-07-161413-3

This publication is designed to provide accurate and authoritative information in regard to the subject matter covered. It is sold with the understanding that neither the author nor the publisher is engaged in rendering legal, accounting, or other professional service. If legal advice or other expert assistance is required, the services of a competent professional person should be sought.

—From a Declaration of Principles jointly adopted
by a Committee of the American Bar
Association and a Committee of Publishers

McGraw-Hill books are available at special quantity discounts to use as premiums and sales promotions, or for use in corporate training programs. To contact a representative please visit the Contact Us pages at www.mhprofessional.com.

This text contains the following, which are trademarks, service marks, or registered trademarks of Investor's Business Daily, Inc., William O'Neil + Co. Incorporated, or their affiliated entities in the United States and/or other countries: *Investor's Business Daily*®, IBD®, CAN SLIM®, *SmartSelect*®, ACC/DIS RTG®, SMR®, Stock Checkup®, Stocks on the Move™, Daily Graphs®, Daily Graphs Online®, O'Neil Database®, and The William O'Neil + Co. 197 Industry Groups®.

This book is printed on acid-free paper.

· CONTENTS ·

Part I:
A Winning System: CAN SLIM®

Part II:
Be Smart from the Start

Part III:
Investing Like a Professional

PART
I

A Winning System: CAN SLIM®

You Must Learn and Benefit from America's 100 Years of Super Winners

After the market debacles of 2000 and 2008, investors now realize they must take charge and learn much more about what they're doing when they save and invest their hard-earned money. However, many investors don't know where to turn, whom to trust, or what they must stop doing in order to achieve true superior investment performance.

You don't have to give your money to a Bernie Madoff, who'll take it but won't tell you exactly what he's doing with it. Instead, you need to read a few of the best investment books, attend some investment classes, or participate in an investment meet-up group so you can learn how to invest with real knowledge and confidence. At the very least, you need to learn and understand well the sound principles, proven rules and methods that can protect and build your investment portfolio over time. Half of all Americans save and invest; now it's time to learn to do it intelligently with critical know-how.

When I started investing, I made most of the same mistakes you've probably made. But here's what I've learned:

- You buy stocks when they're on the way up in price, not on the way down. And when you buy more, you do it *only* after the stock has risen from your purchase price, not after it has fallen below it.

- You buy stocks when they're nearer to their highs for the year, not when they've sunk lower and look cheap. You buy higher-priced, better quality stocks rather than the lowest-priced stocks.

- You learn to always sell stocks quickly when you have a small 7 or 8% loss rather than waiting and hoping they'll come back. Many don't.

- You pay far less attention to a company's book value, dividends, or PE ratio—which for the last 100 years have had little predictive value in spotting America's most successful companies—and focus instead on vital historically proven factors such as strong earnings and sales growth, price and volume action, and whether the company is the number one profit leader in its field with a superior new product.

- You don't subscribe to a bunch of market newsletters or advisory services, and you don't let yourself be influenced by recommendations from analysts, or friends who, after all, are just expressing personal opinions that can frequently be wrong and prove costly.

- You also must acquaint yourself with daily, weekly, and monthly price and volume charts—an invaluable tool the best professionals wouldn't do without but amateurs tend to dismiss as irrelevant.

- Lastly, you must use time-tested sell rules to tell you when to sell a stock and take your worthwhile gains. Plus you'll need buy and sell rules for when it's best to enter the general market or sell and lower your percent invested. Ninety percent of investors have neither of these essential elements.

All these wise actions are totally contrary to human nature! In reality, the stock market is human nature and crowd psychology on daily display, plus the age-old law of supply and demand at work. Because these two factors remain the same over time, it is remarkable but true that chart patterns are just the same today as they were 50 years ago or 100 years ago. Few investors know or understand this. It can be your priceless advantage.

In this fourth edition of *How to Make Money in Stocks*, I'm showing you right up front, in Chapter 1, 100 annotated color charts of 100 of America's greatest winning stocks, covering each decade from the 1880s to the end of 2008—from the Richmond and Danville Railroad in 1885 and Northern Pacific during the famous corner of the stock in 1901, when it raced from $115 to $700 in one week, to Apple and Google in our twenty-first century.

There is an enormous amount you will learn from studying these great historical examples. You'll see chart base patterns that are repeated year after year with huge success. There are 105 examples (among the 100 stocks) of classic chart bases that look like cups with handles. Some are small cups, others large, and others in between.

In addition to cups with handles, we've identified eight other distinctively different, highly successful chart base patterns that occurred in cycle after cycle. Bethlehem Steel in 1915 is our first powerful high, tight flag example and served as a perfect historical precedent for later high, tight flag patterns such as Syntex, Rollins, Simmonds Precision, Yahoo!, and Taser. All of these stocks had spellbinding price moves.

Charts plus earnings will help you tell the best stocks and general markets from the weaker, riskier stocks and markets that you must avoid altogether. That's why I put all these outstanding chart examples in Chapter 1, with notes marked on each chart to help you learn a skill that could just change your whole life and let you live better and far smarter.

A good clear picture is worth a thousand words. These 100 examples are just a small sample of what you've been missing for years. We have models of more than 1,000 great stock market winners over the last 100 years. It takes only one or two to make your year or your future. But you have to get serious and work at really learning and knowing what you're doing when you invest. You can do it if you really want to and it's important to you.

You'll find this an exciting "common sense" new way of viewing America and its stock market. From the railroad to the auto and the airplane, from the radio and TV to computers, from jet airliners to space exploration, from massive discount stores to semiconductors and the Internet, this country has shown rapid, unceasing growth. Living standards for the great majority of Americans have improved materially from 100, 50, or even 30 years ago.

Yes, there will always be problems, and everyone likes to criticize. But America's innovators, entrepreneurs, and inventors have been a major driving force behind its unparalleled growth. They have created the new industries, new technologies, new products, new services, and 80% of the jobs from which we all continually benefit.

Now it's up to you to learn how to intelligently take advantage of the relentless growth opportunities America's freedom makes possible and that entrepreneurs keep presenting for you during every business cycle.

In the following chapters, you will learn how to pick big winners in the stock market and nail down the gains they produce. You will also learn how to substantially reduce your mistakes and losses.

Many people who dabble in stocks either have mediocre results or lose money because of their lack of knowledge. But no one has to continue to lose money. You can definitely learn to invest wisely. This book will provide you with the investment understanding, skills, and methods you need to become a more successful investor, if you're willing to work at it.

I believe most people in this country and throughout the free world, whether young or old, regardless of their profession, education, background, or economic position, should learn to save and invest in common stocks. This book isn't written for the elite, but for the millions of ordinary individuals everywhere who want a chance to be better off financially. You are never too old or too young to start investing intelligently.

● **YOU CAN START SMALL**–If you're a typical working person or a beginning investor, you should know that it doesn't take a lot of money to start. You can begin with as little as $500 to $1,000 and add to it as you earn and save more money. I began with the purchase of just five shares of Procter & Gamble when I was only 21 and fresh out of school.

Mike Webster is one of our in-house managers who also started small. In fact, Mike sold personal belongings, including his music CD collection, to raise cash for investing. Prior to managing money for the firm, he had a gain of over 1,000% in his personal account in 1999, a very unusual year.

Steve Birch, another of our in-house money managers, started managing money earlier. He took advantage of the roaring bull market of the late 1990s and protected most of his gains by going mainly to cash in the bear market. Between 1998 and 2003, he had gained over 1,300%. Both Mike and Steve have had their rough years, but they've learned from their many mistakes, which we all make, and have gone on to achieve significant performance.

You live in a fantastic time of unlimited opportunity, an era of outstanding new ideas, emerging industries, and new frontiers. However, you have to read the rest of this book (probably two or three times) to learn how to recognize and take full advantage of these amazing new situations.

Opportunities are there for everyone. You are in a continually changing and, hopefully, improving New America. We lead the world in high technology, the Internet, medical advancements, computer software, military capability, and innovative new entrepreneurial companies. The communist/socialist system of a centralized "command economy" disintegrated on the ash heap of history. It did not work. Stalin's old Soviet Union killed 20 million of its own people. Our system of freedom and opportunity serves as a model of success for most countries in the world.

Today it's not enough for you to just work and earn a salary. To do the things you want to do, go where you want to go, and have the things you want to have in your life, you must save and invest intelligently. The income from your investments and net gains you can make will, in time, let you reach your goals and provide you real security. This book can change your whole life. No one can hold you back but yourself. Think positive.

● **SECRET TIP**–The first step in learning how to pick big stock market winners is to examine leaders of the past, like those you're about to see, to learn all the characteristics of the most successful stocks. From these observations, you will be able to recognize the types of price and earnings patterns these stocks developed just before their spectacular price advances.

Key factors you'll discover include what the quarterly earnings of these companies were at the time, what the annual earnings histories of these organizations had been in the prior three years, what amount of trading volume was present, what degree of relative strength there was in the prices of the stocks before their enormous success, and how many shares of common stock were outstanding in the capitalization of each company.

You'll also learn many of the greatest winners had significant new products or new management, and many were tied to strong industry group moves caused by important changes occurring in an entire industry.

It's easy to conduct this type of practical, commonsense analysis of all past successful leaders. I have already completed such a comprehensive study. In our historical analysis, we selected the greatest winning stocks in the stock market each year (in terms of percentage increase for the year), spanning the past 125 years.

We call the study "The Model Book of Greatest Stock Market Winners." It's been expanded recently to cover stocks dating back to the 1880s. It now analyzes more than 1,000 of the biggest winning companies in recent market history in detail, super stocks such as

Texas Instruments, whose price soared from $25 to $250 from January 1958 through May 1960

Xerox, which escalated from $160 to the equivalent of $1,340 between March 1963 and June 1966

Syntex, which leaped from $100 to $570 in only six months during the last half of 1963

Dome Petroleum and Prime Computer, which advanced 1,000% and 1,595%, respectively, in the 1978–1980 stock market

Limited Stores, which wildly excited lucky shareowners with a 3,500% increase between 1982 and 1987

Cisco Systems, which between October 1990 and March 2000 advanced from a split-adjusted $0.10 to $82

Home Depot and Microsoft both increased more than 20 times during the 1980s and early 1990s. Home Depot was one of the all-time great performers, jumping 20-fold in less than two years from its initial public offering in September 1981 and then climbing another 10 times from 1988 to 1992. All of these companies offered exciting new entrepreneurial products and concepts. In total, we actually have 10 different model books that cover America's innovative and highly successful companies.

Would you like to know the common characteristics and rules of success we discovered from this intensive study of all past stock market leaders?

They're all covered in the next few chapters and in a simple, easy-to-remember formula we have named CAN SLIM. Each letter in the words CAN SLIM stands for one of the seven chief characteristics of these greatest winning stocks at their early developing stages, just before they made huge profits for their shareholders and our country (companies and employees all pay taxes as well as helping to improve our standard of living). Write this formula down, and repeat it several times so you won't forget it.

The reason CAN SLIM continues to work cycle after cycle and AAII's 11-year independent study, done in real time, rated it the top investment strategy in America is it's based 100% on realistic historical studies of how the stock market has actually worked rather than on our personal opinion or anyone else's, including Wall Street's . . . or academic theorists'. Furthermore, human nature at work in the market simply doesn't change. So CAN SLIM does not get outmoded as fads, fashions, and economic cycles come and go. It will beat big egos, personal opinions, and emotions every time.

You can definitely learn how to pick winners in the stock market, and you can become part owner of the best companies in the world. So, let's get started right now. Here's a sneak preview of CAN SLIM:

C Current Quarterly Earnings and Sales: *The Higher, the Better*

A Annual Earnings Increases: *Look for Significant Growth*

N New Products, New Management, New Highs: *Buying at the Right Time*

S Supply and Demand: *Shares Outstanding Plus Big Volume Demand*

L Leader or Laggard: *Which Is Your Stock?*

I Institutional Sponsorship: *Follow the Leaders*

M Market Direction: *How You Can Learn to Determine It*

Please begin immediately with Chapter 1. Go for it. You can do it.

America's Greatest Stock-Picking Secrets

In this latest revised edition, you'll observe 100 charts of the greatest winners from 1880 to 2009. Study them carefully. You'll discover secret insights into how these companies set the stage for their spectacular price increases.

Don't worry if you're a new investor and don't understand these charts at first. After all, every successful investor was a beginner at some point—and this book will show you how to spot key buying opportunities on the charts, as well as critical signals that a stock should be sold. To succeed you need to learn sound, historically proven buy rules plus sell rules.

As you study these charts you'll see there are specific chart patterns that are repeated over and over again whether in 1900 or 2000. This will give you a huge advantage once you learn to, with practice, recognize these patterns that in effect tell you when a stock is under professional accumulation.

It is the unique combination of your finding stocks with big increases in sales, earnings and return on equity plus strong chart patterns revealing institutional buying that together will materially improve your stock selection and timing. The best professionals use charts.

You too can learn this valuable skill.

This book is all about how America grows and you can too. The American dream can be yours if you have the drive and desire and make up your mind to never give up on yourself or America.

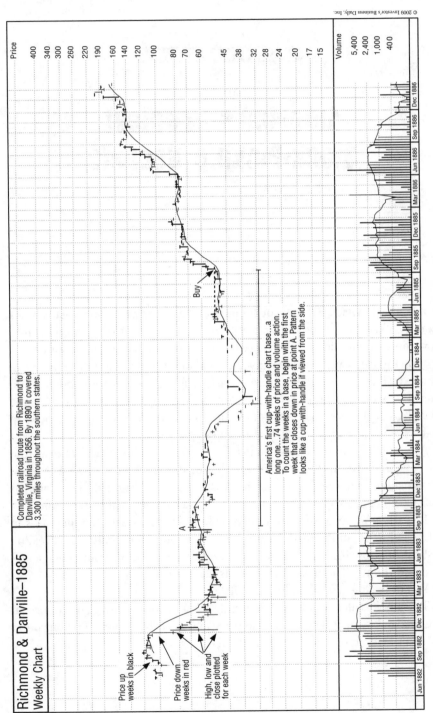

Richmond & Danville—1885
Weekly Chart

Completed railroad route from Richmond to Danville, Virginia in 1856. By 1890 it covered 3,300 miles throughout the southern states.

Price up weeks in black

Price down weeks in red

High, low and close plotted for each week

A

Buy

America's first cup-with-handle chart base...a long one...74 weeks of price and volume action. To count the weeks in a base, begin with the first week that closes down in price at point A. Pattern looks like a cup-with-handle if viewed from the side.

Richmond & Danville increased 257% in 70 weeks.

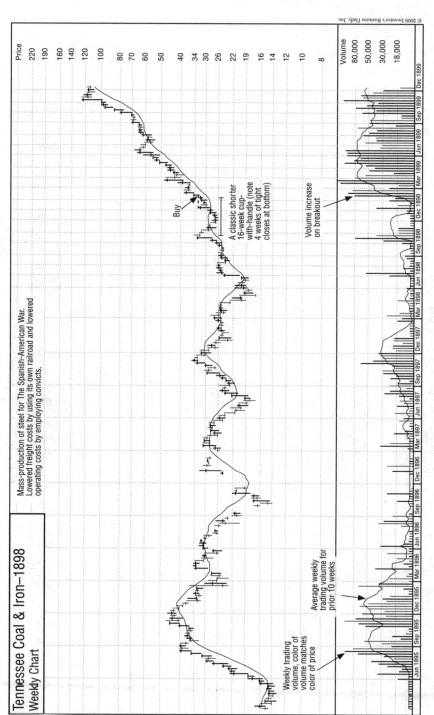

Tennessee Coal & Iron—1898
Weekly Chart

Mass-production of steel for The Spanish-American War. Lowered freight costs by using its own railroad and lowered operating costs by employing convicts.

Buy

A classic shorter 16-week cup-with-handle (note 4 weeks of tight closes at bottom)

Volume increase on breakout

Weekly trading volume, color of volume matches color of price

Average weekly trading volume for prior 10 weeks

Price
220
190
160
140
120
100
80
70
60
50
40
34
30
26
22
19
16
14
12
10
8

Volume
80,000
50,000
30,000
18,000

Jun 1895 Sep 1895 Dec 1895 Mar 1896 Jun 1896 Sep 1896 Dec 1896 Mar 1897 Jun 1897 Sep 1897 Dec 1897 Mar 1898 Jun 1898 Sep 1898 Dec 1898 Mar 1899 Jun 1899 Sep 1899 Dec 1899

© 2009 Investor's Business Daily, Inc.

Tennessee Coal & Iron increased 265% in 39 weeks.

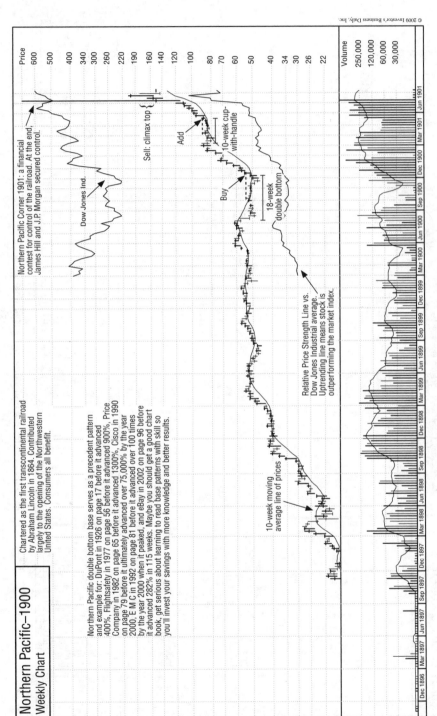

© 2009 Investor's Business Daily, Inc.

Northern Pacific—1900 Weekly Chart

Chartered as the first transcontinental railroad by Abraham Lincoln in 1864. Contributed largely to the opening of the Northwestern United States. Consumers all benefit.

Northern Pacific Corner 1901: a financial contest for control of the railroad. At the end, James Hill and J.P. Morgan secured control.

Northern Pacific double bottom base serves as a precedent pattern and example for: DuPont in 1926 on page 17 before it advanced 400%, Flightsafety in 1977 on page 56 before it advanced 900%, Price Company in 1982 on page 65 before it advanced 1300%, Cisco in 1990 on page 79 before it ultimately advanced over 75,000% by the year 2000, E M C in 1992 on page 81 before it advanced over 100 times by the year 2000 when it peaked, and eBay in 2002 on page 96 before it advanced 282% in 115 weeks. Maybe you should get a good chart book, get serious about learning to read base patterns with skill so you'll invest your savings with more knowledge and better results.

Price
600
500
400
340
300
260
220
190
160
140
120
100
80
70
60
50
40
34
30
26
22

Dow Jones Ind.

Sell: climax top

Add

10-week cup-with-handle

Buy

18-week double bottom

Relative Price Strength Line vs. Dow Jones Industrial average. Uptrending line means stock is outperforming the market index.

10-week moving average line of prices

Volume
250,000
120,000
60,000
30,000

Dec 1896 | Mar 1897 | Jun 1897 | Sep 1897 | Dec 1897 | Mar 1898 | Jun 1898 | Sep 1898 | Dec 1898 | Mar 1899 | Jun 1899 | Sep 1899 | Dec 1899 | Mar 1900 | Jun 1900 | Sep 1900 | Dec 1900 | Mar 1901 | Jun 1901

Northern Pacific increased 1181% in 29 weeks.

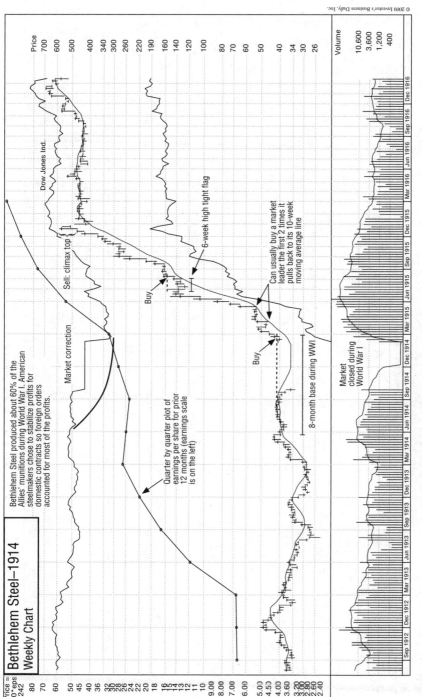

Bethlehem Steel increased 1479% in 99 weeks.

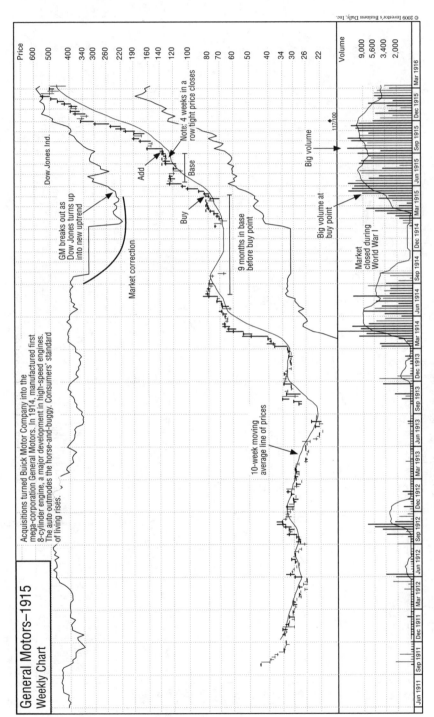

General Motors—1915
Weekly Chart

Acquisitions turned Buick Motor Company into the mega-corporation General Motors. In 1914, manufactured first 8-cylinder engine, a major development in high-speed engines. The auto outmodes the horse-and-buggy. Consumers' standard of living rises.

Dow Jones Ind.

GM breaks out as Dow Jones turns up into new uptrend

Market correction

Add

Base

Buy

Note: 4 weeks in a row tight price closes

9 months in base before buy point

10-week moving average line of prices

Big volume

117.00

Big volume at buy point

Market closed during World War I

General Motors increased 471% in 39 weeks.

Price
600
500
400
340
300
260
220
190
160
140
120
100
80
70
60
50
40
34
30
26
22

Volume
9,000
5,600
3,400
2,000

Jun 1911 | Sep 1911 | Dec 1911 | Mar 1912 | Jun 1912 | Sep 1912 | Dec 1912 | Mar 1913 | Jun 1913 | Sep 1913 | Dec 1913 | Mar 1914 | Jun 1914 | Sep 1914 | Dec 1914 | Mar 1915 | Jun 1915 | Sep 1915 | Dec 1915 | Mar 1916

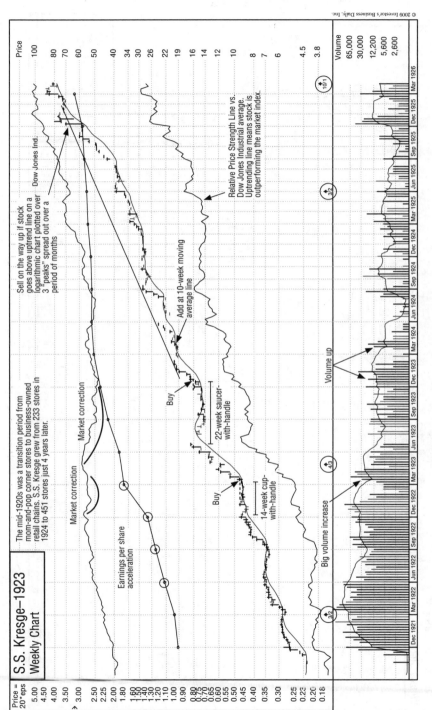

S.S. Kresge—1923
Weekly Chart

Price = 20*eps

	Price
5.00	100
4.50	80
4.00	70
3.50	60
> 3.00	50
2.50	40
2.25	34
2.00	30
1.80	26
1.60	22
1.50	19
1.40	16
1.30	14
1.20	12
1.10	10
1.00	
0.90	
0.80	8
0.75	7
0.70	
0.65	6
0.60	
0.55	
0.50	
0.45	4.5
0.40	3.8
0.35	
0.30	
0.25	
0.23	
0.20	
0.18	

The mid-1920s was a transition period from mom-and-pop corner stores to business-owned retail chains. S.S. Kresge grew from 233 stores in 1924 to 451 stores just 4 years later.

Market correction

Market correction

Market correction

Earnings per share acceleration

Buy

Buy

14-week cup-with-handle

22-week saucer-with-handle

Add at 10-week moving average line

Sell on the way up if stock goes above uptrend line on a logarithmic chart plotted over 3 "peaks" spread out over a period of months

Dow Jones Ind.

Relative Price Strength Line vs. Dow Jones Industrial average. Uptrending line means stock is outperforming the market index.

Big volume increase

Volume up

Volume
65,000
30,000
12,200
5,600
2,600

Dec 1921 | Mar 1922 | Jun 1922 | Sep 1922 | Dec 1922 | Mar 1923 | Jun 1923 | Sep 1923 | Dec 1923 | Mar 1924 | Jun 1924 | Sep 1924 | Dec 1924 | Mar 1925 | Jun 1925 | Sep 1925 | Dec 1925 | Mar 1926

S.S. Kresge increased 836% in 154 weeks.

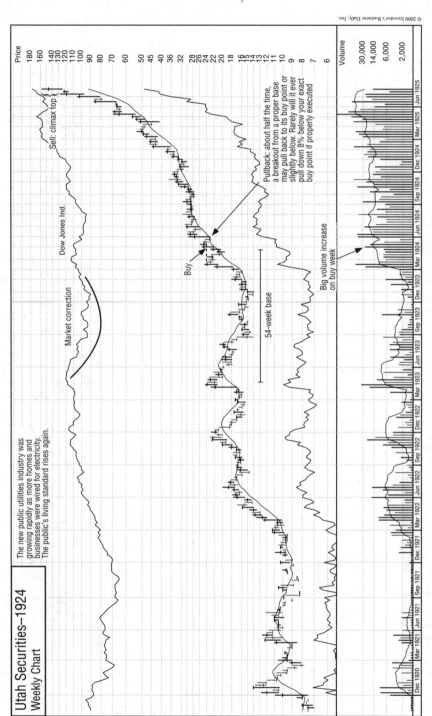

Utah Securities–1924
Weekly Chart

The new public utilities industry was growing rapidly as more homes and businesses were wired for electricity. The public's living standard rises again.

Price
180
160
140
130
120
110
100
90
80
70
60
50
45
40
36
32
28
26
24
22
20
18
16
15
14
13
12
11
10
9
8
7
6

Sell: climax top

Dow Jones Ind.

Market correction

Pullback: about half the time, a breakout from a proper base may pull back to its buy point or slightly below. Rarely will it ever pull down 8% below your exact buy point if properly executed

Buy

54-week base

Big volume increase on buy week

Volume
30,000
14,000
6,000
2,000

Dec 1920
Mar 1921
Jun 1921
Sep 1921
Dec 1921
Mar 1922
Jun 1922
Sep 1922
Dec 1922
Mar 1923
Jun 1923
Sep 1923
Dec 1923
Mar 1924
Jun 1924
Sep 1924
Dec 1924
Mar 1925
Jun 1925

Utah Securities increased 538% in 63 weeks.

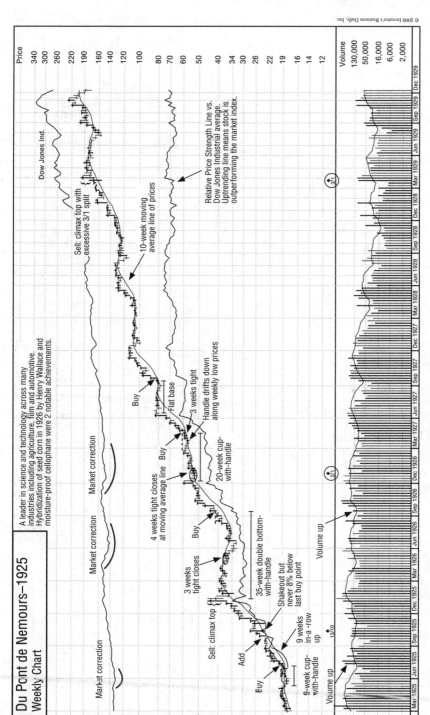

Du Pont de Nemours—1925
Weekly Chart

A leader in science and technology across many industries including agriculture, film and automotive. Hybridization of seed corn in 1926 by Henry Wallace and moisture-proof cellophane were 2 notable achievements.

Dow Jones Ind.

Market correction

Market correction

Market correction

Sell: climax top with excessive 3/1 split

10-week moving average line of prices

Relative Price Strength Line vs. Dow Jones Industrial average. Uptrending line means stock is outperforming the market index.

Buy

Flat base

3 weeks tight

Handle drifts down along weekly low prices

4 weeks tight closes at moving average line

Buy

20-week cup-with-handle

Buy

3 weeks tight closes

Sell: climax top

35-week double bottom-with-handle

Add

Shakeout but never 8% below last buy point

9 weeks in-a-row up

Volume up

Buy

9-week cup-with-handle

Volume up

Price
340
300
260
220
190
160
140
120
100
80
70
60
50
40
34
30
26
22
19
16
14
12

Volume
130,000
50,000
16,000
6,000
2,000

Mar 1925 | Jun 1925 | Sep 1925 | Dec 1925 | Mar 1926 | Jun 1926 | Sep 1926 | Dec 1926 | Mar 1927 | Jun 1927 | Sep 1927 | Dec 1927 | Mar 1928 | Jun 1928 | Sep 1928 | Dec 1928 | Mar 1929 | Jun 1929 | Sep 1929 | Dec 1929

Du Pont de Nemours increased 1074% in 225 weeks.

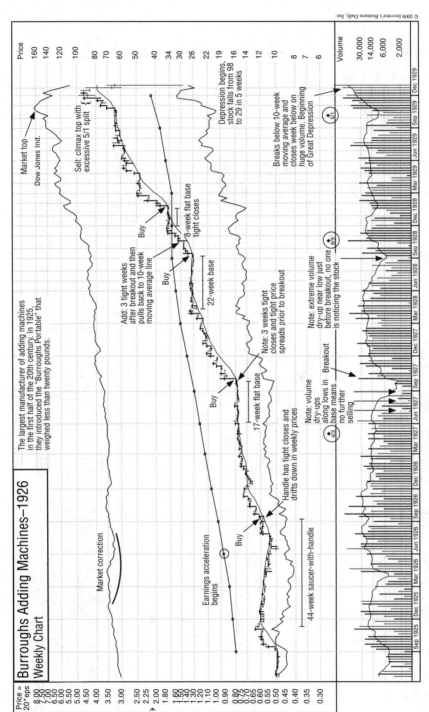

Burroughs Adding Machines increased 1992% in 168 weeks.

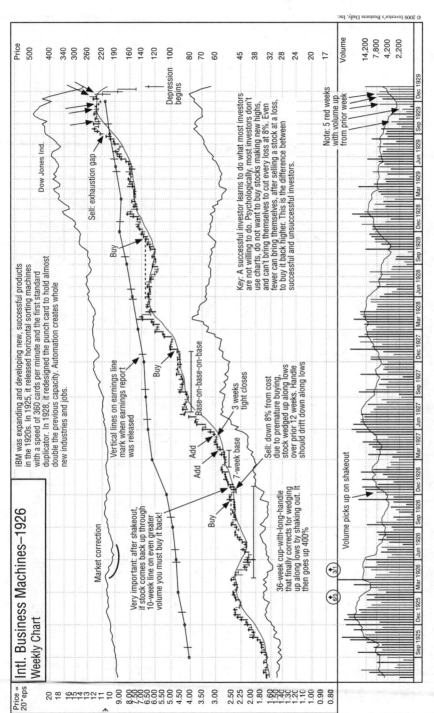

Intl. Business Machines–1926
Weekly Chart

Price =
20 eps

IBM was expanding and developing new, successful products
in the 1920s. In 1925, it released horizontal sorting machines
with a speed of 360 cards per minute and the first standard
duplicator. In 1928, it redesigned the punch card to hold almost
double the previous capacity. Automation creates whole
new industries and jobs.

Dow Jones Ind.

Sell: exhaustion gap

Market correction

Vertical lines on earnings line
mark when earnings report
was released

Very important: after shakeout,
if stock comes back up through
10-week line on even greater
volume you must buy it back!

Buy

Buy

Add   Base-on-base-on-base

Add

3 weeks
tight closes

7-week base

Buy

Sell: down 8% from cost
due to premature buying,
stock wedged up along lows
over prior 12 weeks. Handle
should drift down along lows

36-week cup-with-long-handle
that finally corrects for wedging
up along lows by shaking out. It
then goes up 400%

Depression
begins

Key: A successful investor learns to do what most investors
are not willing to do. Psychologically, most investors don't
use charts, do not want to buy stocks making new highs,
and can't bring themselves to cut every loss at 8%. Even
fewer can bring themselves, after selling a stock at a loss,
to buy it back higher. This is the difference between
successful and unsuccessful investors.

Volume picks up on shakeout

Note: 5 red weeks
with volume up
from prior week

Price
500

400
340
300
260
220
190
160
140
120
100

80
70
60

45
38
32
28
24
20
17

Volume
14,200
7,800
4,200
2,200

Price
20
18
16
15
14
13
12
11
10
9.00
8.00
7.00
6.50
6.00
5.50
5.00
4.50
4.00
3.50
3.00
2.50
2.25
2.00
1.80
1.60
1.50
1.40
1.30
1.20
1.10
1.00
0.90
0.80

Sep 1925 | Dec 1925 | Mar 1926 | Jun 1926 | Sep 1926 | Dec 1926 | Mar 1927 | Jun 1927 | Sep 1927 | Dec 1927 | Mar 1928 | Jun 1928 | Sep 1928 | Dec 1928 | Mar 1929 | Jun 1929 | Sep 1929 | Dec 1929

International Business Machines increased 400% in 161 weeks.

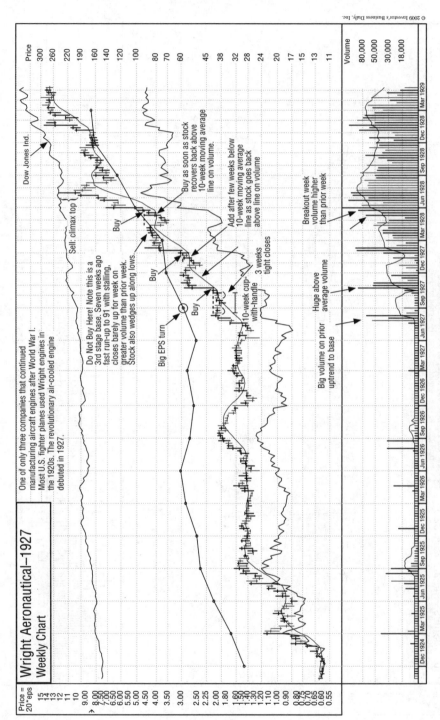

Wright Aeronautical—1927
Weekly Chart

One of only three companies that continued manufacturing aircraft engines after World War I. Most U.S. fighter planes used Wright engines in the 1920s. The revolutionary air-cooled engine debuted in 1927.

Dow Jones Ind.

Sell: climax top

Do Not Buy Here! Note this is a 3rd stage base. Seven weeks ago fast run-up to 91 with stalling, closes barely up for week on greater volume than prior week. Stock also wedges up along lows.

Buy

Big EPS turn

Buy

Buy

Buy as soon as stock recovers back above 10-week moving average line on volume.

Add after few weeks below 10-week moving average line as stock goes back above line on volume

10-week cup-with-handle

3 weeks tight closes

Breakout week volume higher than prior week

Big volume on prior uptrend to base

Huge above average volume

Price = 20*eps

Price

Wright Aeronautical increased 464% in 76 weeks.

Volume

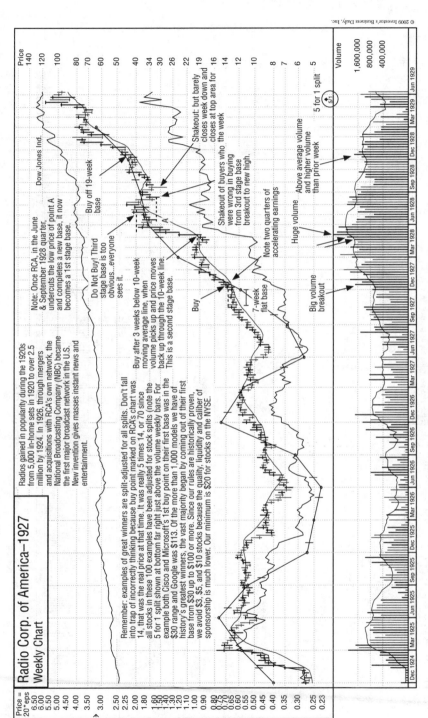

Radio Corporation of America increased 739% in 74 weeks.

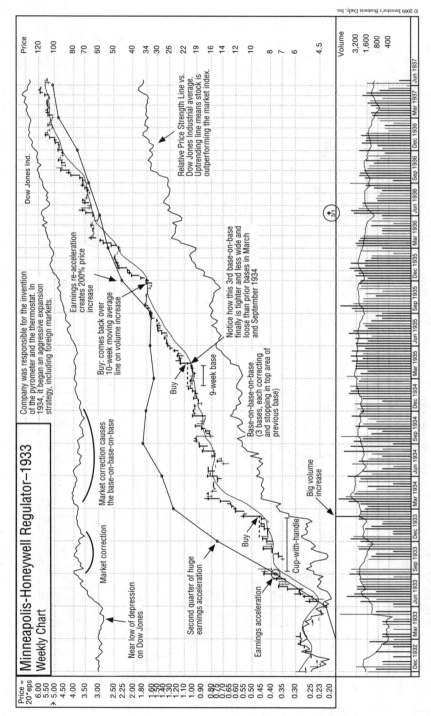

Minneapolis-Honeywell Regulator increased 987% in 170 weeks.

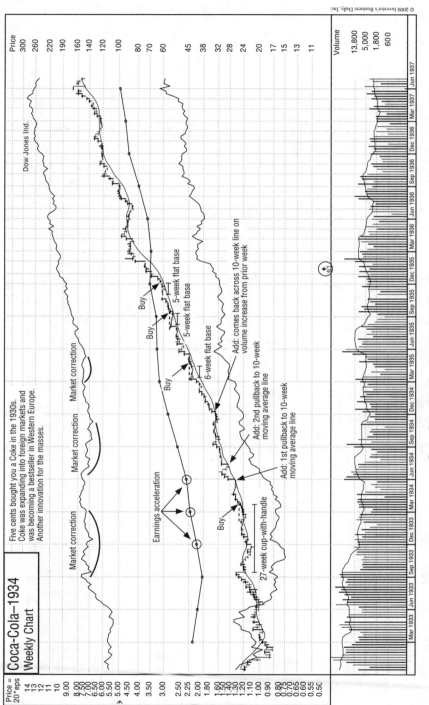

Coca-Cola—1934
Weekly Chart

Price =
20*eps

Five cents bought you a Coke in the 1930s.
Coke was expanding into foreign markets and
was becoming a bestseller in Western Europe.
Another innovation for the masses.

Dow Jones Ind.

Market correction

Market correction

Market correction

Market correction

Earnings acceleration

Buy

Buy

Buy

Buy

5-week flat base

5-week flat base

5-week flat base

6-week flat base

Add: comes back across 10-week line on
volume increase from prior week

Add: 2nd pullback to 10-week
moving average line

Add: 1st pullback to 10-week
moving average line

27-week cup-with-handle

Price
300
260
220
190
160
140
120
100
80
70
60
45
38
32
28
24
20
17
15
13
11

14
13
12
11
10
9.00
8.00
7.00
6.50
6.00
5.50
5.00
4.50
4.00
3.50
3.00
2.50
2.25
2.00
1.80
1.60
1.50
1.40
1.30
1.20
1.10
1.00
0.90
0.80
0.75
0.70
0.65
0.60
0.55
0.50

Volume
13,800
5,000
1,800
600

Mar 1933 | Jun 1933 | Sep 1933 | Dec 1933 | Mar 1934 | Jun 1934 | Sep 1934 | Dec 1934 | Mar 1935 | Jun 1935 | Sep 1935 | Dec 1935 | Mar 1936 | Jun 1936 | Sep 1936 | Dec 1936 | Mar 1937 | Jun 1937

Coca-Cola increased 565% in 165 weeks.

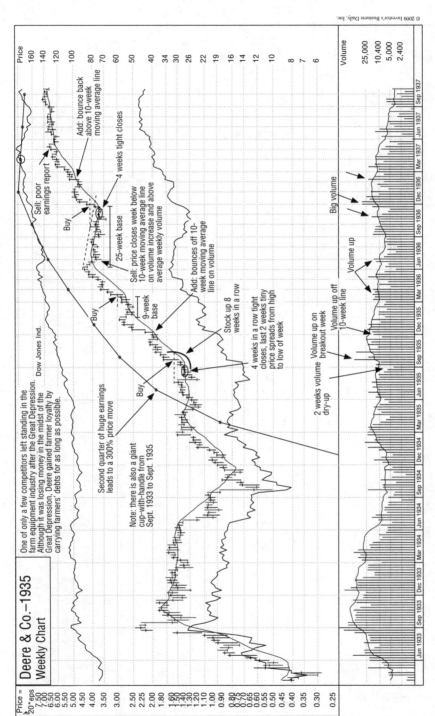

Deere & Co.–1935
Weekly Chart

Price = 20* eps

One of only a few competitors left standing in the farm equipment industry after the Great Depression. Although it was losing money in the midst of the Great Depression, Deere gained farmer loyalty by carrying farmers' debts for as long as possible.

Dow Jones Ind.

Second quarter of huge earnings leads to a 300% price move

Note: there is also a giant cup-with-handle from Sept. 1933 to Sept. 1935

Sell: poor earnings report

Add: bounce back above 10-week moving average line

4 weeks tight closes

Buy

25-week base

Sell: price closes week below 10-week moving average line on volume increase and above average weekly volume

9-week base

Buy

Add: bounces off 10-week moving average line on volume

Buy

Stock up 8 weeks in a row

4 weeks in a row tight closes, last 2 weeks tiny price spreads from high to low of week

2 weeks volume dry-up

Volume up on breakout week

Volume up off 10-week line

Volume up

Big volume

Volume

Deere & Co increased 307% in 104 weeks.

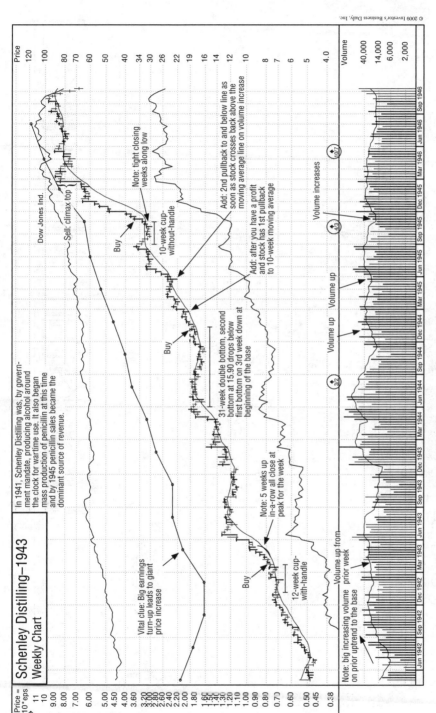

Schenley Distilling increased 1164% in 185 weeks.

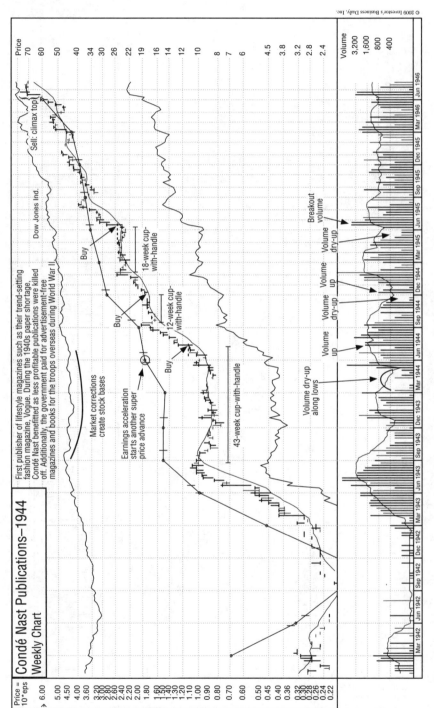

Condé Nast Publications—1944 Weekly Chart

Price = 10*eps

First publisher of lifestyle magazines such as their trend-setting fashion magazine, Vogue. During the 1940s paper shortage, Condé Nast benefitted as less profitable publications were killed off. Additionally, the government paid for advertisement-free magazines and books for the troops overseas during World War II.

Sell: climax top

Dow Jones Ind.

Buy

18-week cup-with-handle

Market corrections create stock bases

Earnings acceleration starts another super price advance

Buy

12-week cup-with-handle

Buy

43-week cup-with-handle

Volume dry-up along lows

Volume up

Volume dry-up

Volume up

Volume dry-up

Breakout volume

Condé Nast Publications increased 514% in 101 weeks.

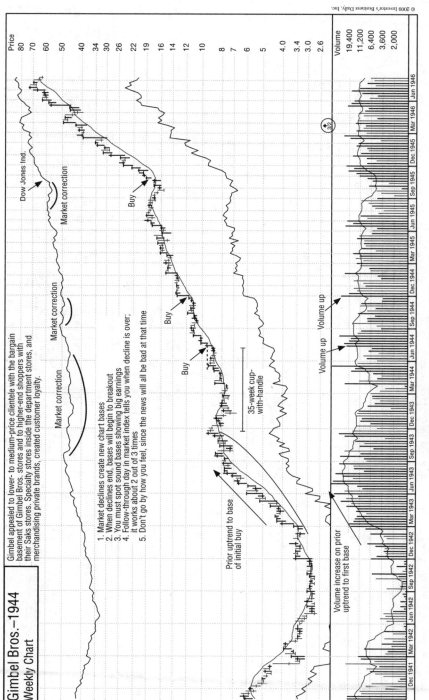

Gimbel Bros.—1944
Weekly Chart

Gimbel appealed to lower- to medium-price clientele with the bargain basement of Gimbel Bros. stores and to higher-end shoppers with their Saks stores. Specialty stores inside the department stores, and merchandising private brands, created customer loyalty.

1. Market declines create new chart bases
2. When declines end, bases will begin to breakout
3. You must spot sound bases showing big earnings
4. Follow-through day in market index tells you when decline is over; it works about 2 out of 3 times
5. Don't go by how you feel, since the news will all be bad at that time

Dow Jones Ind.

Market correction

Market correction

Market correction

Market correction

Buy

Buy

Buy

Buy

35-week cup-with-handle

Prior uptrend to base of initial buy

Volume increase on prior uptrend to first base

Volume up Volume up

Volume up

Price
80
70
60
50
40
34
30
26
22
19
16
14
12
10
8
7
6
5
4.0
3.4
3.0
2.6

Volume
19,400
11,200
6,400
3,600
2,000

© 2009 Investor's Business Daily, Inc.

Dec 1941 | Mar 1942 | Jun 1942 | Sep 1942 | Dec 1942 | Mar 1943 | Jun 1943 | Sep 1943 | Dec 1943 | Mar 1944 | Jun 1944 | Sep 1944 | Dec 1944 | Mar 1945 | Jun 1945 | Sep 1945 | Dec 1945 | Mar 1946 | Jun 1946

Gimbel Brothers increased 674% in 103 weeks.

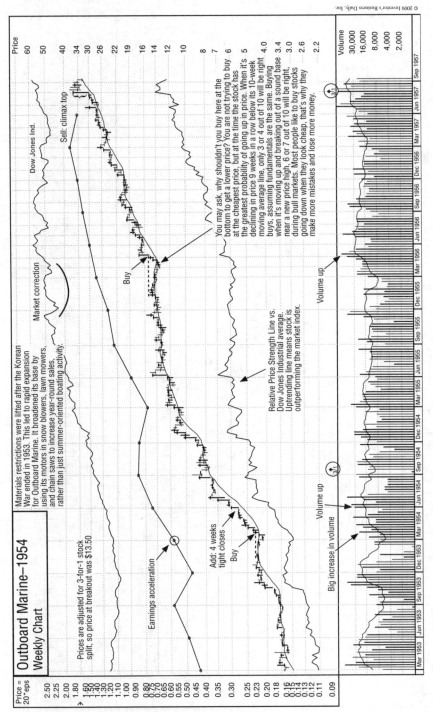

Outboard Marine—1954
Weekly Chart

Price = 20*eps

Materials restrictions were lifted after the Korean War ended in 1953. This led to rapid expansion for Outboard Marine. It broadened its base by using its motors in snow blowers, lawn mowers, and chain saws to increase year-round sales, rather than just summer-oriented boating activity.

Prices are adjusted for 3-for-1 stock split, so price at breakout was $13.50

Sell: climax top

Dow Jones Ind.

Market correction

Earnings acceleration

Buy

Add: 4 weeks tight closes

Buy

You may ask, why shouldn't you buy here at the bottom to get a lower price? You are not trying to buy at the cheapest price, but at the time the stock has the greatest probability of going up in price. When it's declining in price 9 weeks in a row below its 10-week moving average line, only 3 or 4 out of 10 will be right buys, assuming fundamentals are the same. Buying when it's moving up and breaking out of a sound base near a new price high, 6 or 7 out of 10 will be right, during bull markets. Most people like to buy stocks going down when they look cheap, that's why they make more mistakes and lose more money.

Relative Price Strength Line vs. Dow Jones Industrial average. Uptrending line means stock is outperforming the market index.

Volume up

Volume up

Big increase in volume

Outboard Marine increased 720% in 177 weeks.

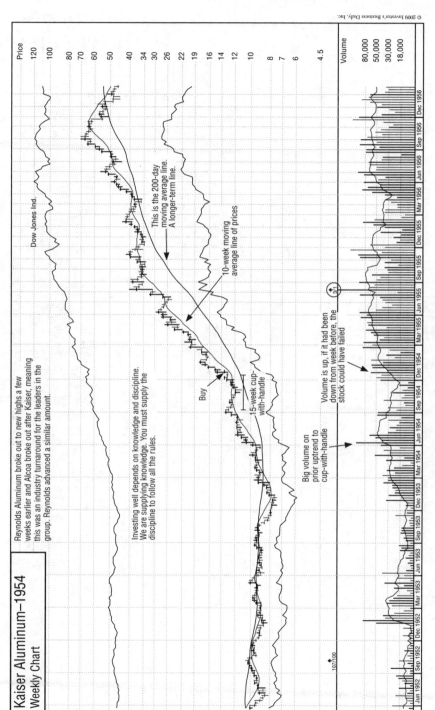

Kaiser Aluminum–1954
Weekly Chart

Reynolds Aluminum broke out to new highs a few weeks earlier and Alcoa broke out after Kaiser, meaning this was an industry turnaround for the leaders in the group. Reynolds advanced a similar amount.

Dow Jones Ind.

Investing well depends on knowledge and discipline. We are supplying knowledge. You must supply the discipline to follow all the rules.

This is the 200-day moving average line. A longer-term line.

10-week moving average line of prices

Buy

15-week cup-with-handle

Big volume on prior uptrend to cup-with-handle

Volume is up, if it had been down from week before, the stock could have failed

Price
120
100
80
70
60
50
40
34
30
26
22
19
16
14
12
10
8
7
6
4.5

Volume
80,000
50,000
30,000
18,000

Kaiser Aluminum increased 379% in 93 weeks.

Jun 1952 | Sep 1952 | Dec 1952 | Mar 1953 | Jun 1953 | Sep 1953 | Dec 1953 | Mar 1954 | Jun 1954 | Sep 1954 | Dec 1954 | Mar 1955 | Jun 1955 | Sep 1955 | Dec 1955 | Mar 1956 | Jun 1956 | Sep 1956 | Dec 1956

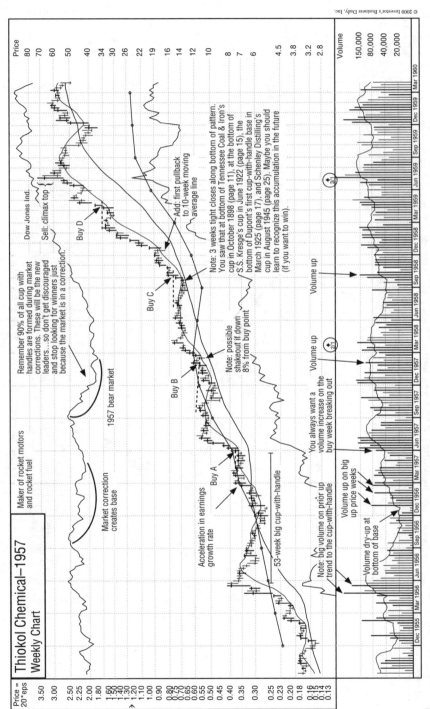

Thiokol Chemical increased 860% in 109 weeks.

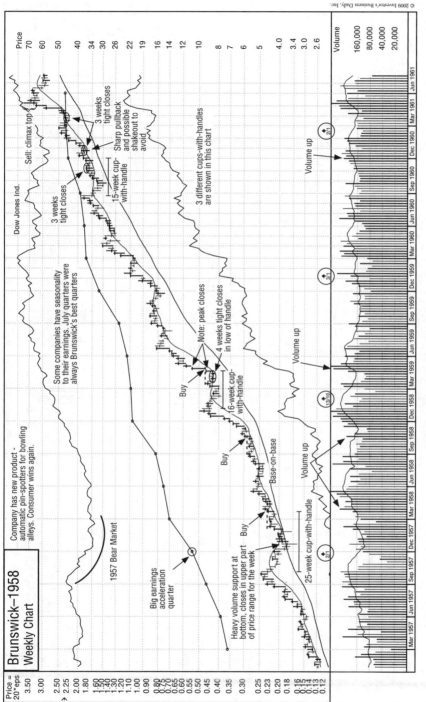

Brunswick increased 1500% in 162 weeks.

Price =
20*eps

**Brunswick–1958
Weekly Chart**

Company has new product -
automatic pin-spotters for bowling
alleys. Consumer wins again.

Dow Jones Ind.

Sell: climax top

3 weeks
tight closes

3 weeks
tight closes

Sharp pullback
and possible
shakeout to
avoid

15-week cup-
with-handle

Some companies have seasonality
to their earnings. July quarters were
always Brunswick's best quarters

3 different cups-with-handles
are shown in this chart

1957 Bear Market

Big earnings
acceleration
quarter

Note: peak closes

4 weeks tight closes
in low of handle

Buy

16-week cup-
with-handle

Buy

Base-on-base

Volume up

Heavy volume support at
bottom, closes in upper part
of price range for the week

Buy

25-week cup-with-handle

Volume up

Volume up

Volume up

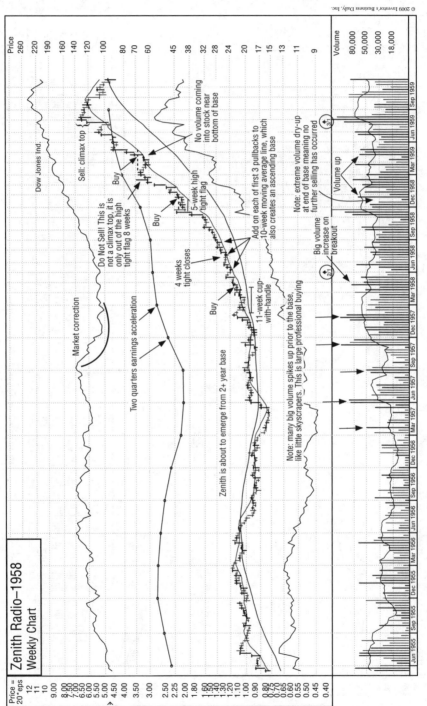

Zenith Radio—1958
Weekly Chart

Price = 20 * eps

Dow Jones Ind.

Market correction

Sell: climax top

Do Not Sell! This is not a climax top, it is only out of the high tight flag 8 weeks

Buy

Buy

5-week high tight flag

Two quarters earnings acceleration

4 weeks tight closes

Buy

11-week cup-with-handle

Zenith is about to emerge from 2+ year base

No volume coming into stock near bottom of base

Add on each of first 3 pullbacks to 10-week moving average line, which also creates an ascending base

Note: extreme volume dry-up at end of base meaning no further selling has occurred

Volume up

Big volume increase on breakout

Note: many big volume spikes up prior to the base, like little skyscrapers. This is large professional buying

Zenith Radio increased 493% in 66 weeks.

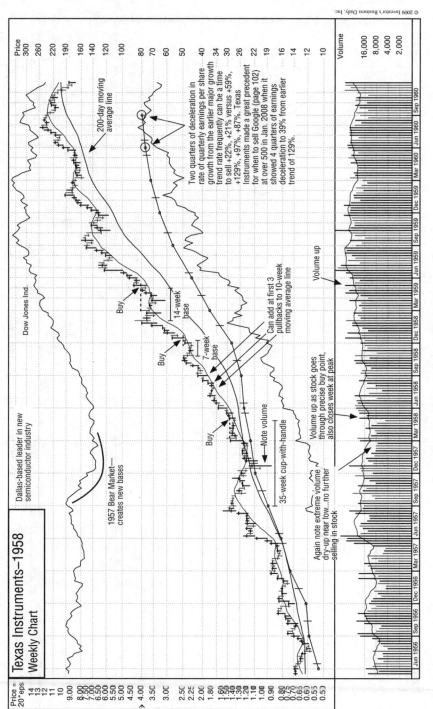

Texas Instruments increased 772% in 116 weeks.

Texas Instruments—1958
Weekly Chart

Dallas-based leader in new semiconductor industry

Dow Jones Ind.

200-day moving average line

1957 Bear Market—creates new bases

Buy

14-week base

7-week base

Buy

Buy

Note volume

Can add at first 3 pullbacks to 10-week moving average line

35-week cup-with-handle

Volume up

Volume up as stock goes through precise buy point, also closes week at peak

Again note extreme volume dry-up near low...no further selling in stock

Two quarters of deceleration in rate of quarterly earnings per share growth from the earlier major growth trend rate frequently can be a time to sell +22%, +21% versus +59%, +129%, +97%, +87%, Texas Instruments made a great precedent for when to sell Google (page 102) at over 500 in Jan. 2008 when it showed 4 quarters of earnings deceleration to 39% from earlier trend of 129%.

Volume

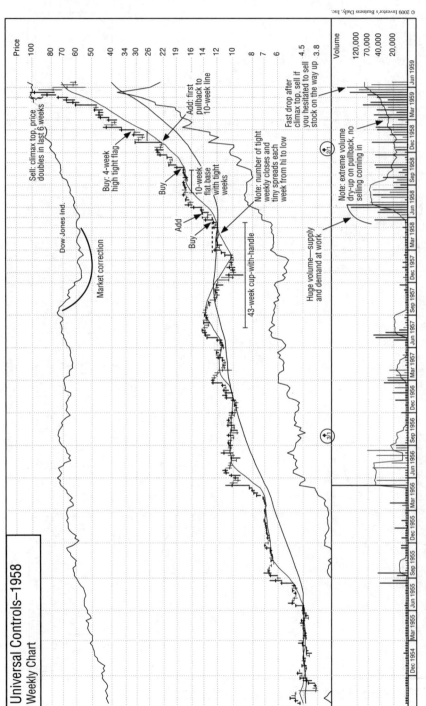

Universal Controls–1958
Weekly Chart

Dow Jones Ind.

Market correction

Sell: climax top, price doubles in last 6 weeks

Buy: 4-week high tight flag

Add: first pullback to 10-week line

Buy

Add

Buy

10-week flat base with tight weeks

Note: number of tight weekly closes and tiny spreads each week from hi to low

43-week cup-with-handle

Fast drop after climax top, sell if you hesitated to sell stock on the way up

Huge volume—supply and demand at work

Note: extreme volume dry-up on pullback, no selling coming in

Price
100
80
70
60
50
40
34
30
26
22
19
16
14
12
10
8
7
6
4.5
3.8

Volume
120,000
70,000
40,000
20,000

Dec 1954 Mar 1955 Jun 1955 Sep 1955 Dec 1955 Mar 1956 Jun 1956 Sep 1956 Dec 1956 Mar 1957 Jun 1957 Sep 1957 Dec 1957 Mar 1958 Jun 1958 Sep 1958 Dec 1958 Mar 1959 Jun 1959

Universal Controls increased 645% in 51 weeks.

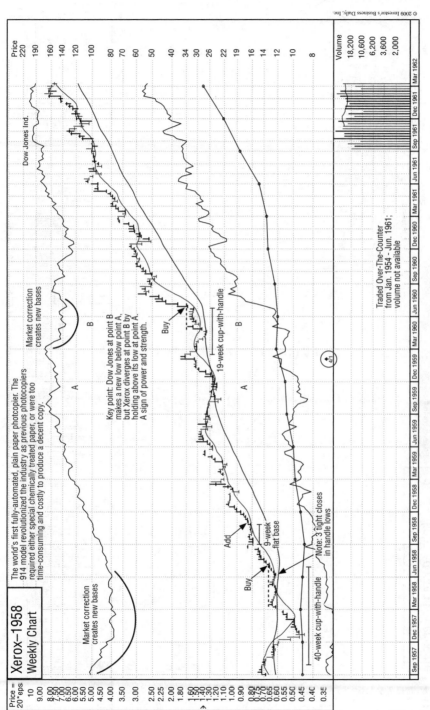

Xerox–1958
Weekly Chart

Price =
20*eps

The world's first fully-automated, plain paper photocopier. The 914 model revolutionized the industry as previous photocopiers required either special chemically treated paper, or were too time-consuming and costly to produce a decent copy.

Market correction creates new bases

Dow Jones Ind.

Market correction creates new bases

Key point: Dow Jones at point B makes a new low below point A, but Xerox diverges at point B by holding above its low at point A. A sign of power and strength.

Buy

19-week cup-with-handle

Add

9-week flat base

Buy

Note: 3 tight closes in handle lows

40-week cup-with-handle

Traded Over-The-Counter from Jan. 1954 - Jun. 1961; volume not available

Xerox increased 1201% in 188 weeks.

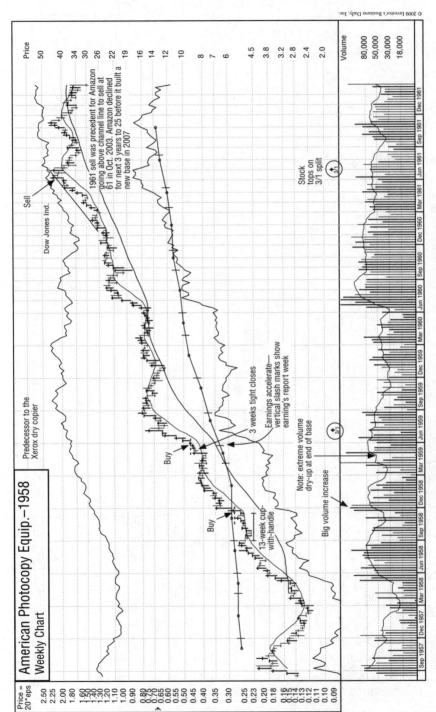

© 2009 Investor's Business Daily, Inc.

Price = 20*eps

American Photocopy Equip.–1958
Weekly Chart

Predecessor to the Xerox dry copier

Sell

Dow Jones Ind.

1961 sell was precedent for Amazon going above channel line to sell at 61 in Oct. 2003. Amazon declined for next 3 years to 25 before it built a new base in 2007

Buy

Earnings accelerate– vertical slash marks show earning's report week

3 weeks tight closes

Buy

13-week cup- with-handle

Note: extreme volume dry-up at end of base

Big volume increase

Stock tops on 3/1 split

Volume

American Photocopy Equipment increased 696% in 133 weeks

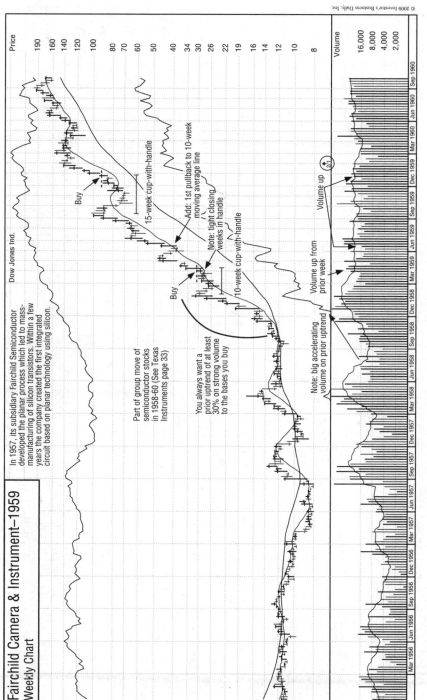

Fairchild Camera & Instrument—1959
Weekly Chart

In 1957, its subsidiary Fairchild Semiconductor developed the planar process which led to mass-manufacturing of silicon transistors. Within a few years the company created the first integrated circuit based on planar technology using silicon.

Dow Jones Ind.

Buy

15-week cup-with-handle

Add: 1st pullback to 10-week moving average line

Note: tight closing weeks in handle

Buy

10-week cup-with-handle

Part of group move of semiconductor stocks in 1958-60 (See Texas Instruments page 33)

You always want a prior uptrend of at least 30% on strong volume to the bases you buy

Note: big accelerating volume on prior uptrend

Volume up from prior week

Volume up

Price

190
160
140
120
100
80
70
60
50
40
34
30
26
22
19
16
14
12
10
8

Volume

16,000
8,000
4,000
2,000

Fairchild Camera & Instrument increased 582% in 73 weeks.

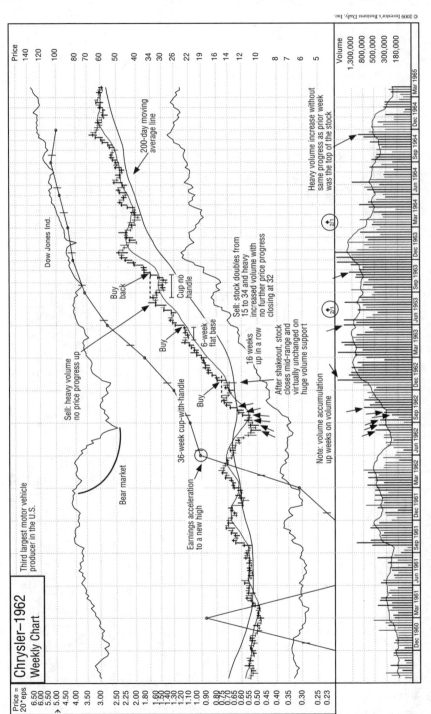

Chrysler—1962
Weekly Chart

Price = 20*eps

Third largest motor vehicle producer in the U.S.

Dow Jones Ind.

Sell: heavy volume no price progress up

Bear market

Earnings acceleration to a new high

36-week cup-with-handle

200-day moving average line

Buy back

Cup no handle

Buy

6-week flat base

Buy

16 weeks up in a row

Sell: stock doubles from 15 to 34 and heavy increased volume with no further price progress closing at 32

After shakeout, stock closes mid-range and virtually unchanged on huge volume support

Note: volume accumulation up weeks on volume

Heavy volume increase without same progress as prior week was the top of the stock

Chrysler increased 215% in 51 weeks.

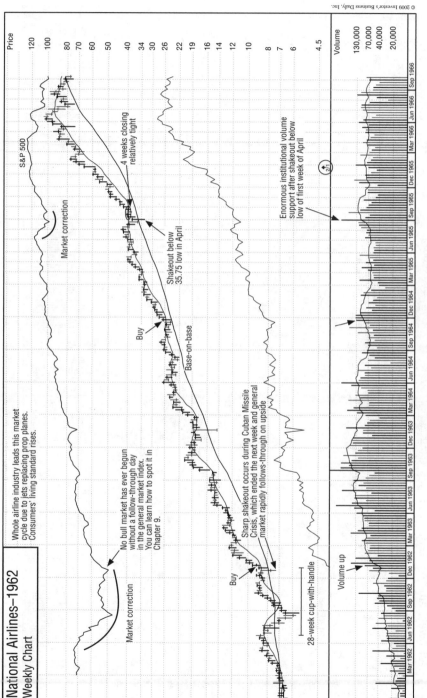

National Airlines—1962
Weekly Chart

Whole airline industry leads this market cycle due to jets replacing prop planes. Consumers' living standard rises.

S&P 500

Market correction

No bull market has ever begun without a follow-through day in the general market index. You can learn how to spot it in Chapter 9.

Market correction

4 weeks closing relatively tight

Buy

Shakeout below 35.75 low in April

Base-on-base

Sharp shakeout occurs during Cuban Missile Crisis, which ended the next week and general market rapidly follows-through on upside

Enormous institutional volume support after shakeout below low of first week of April

Buy

28-week cup-with-handle

Volume up

Price
120
100
80
70
60
50
40
34
30
26
22
19
16
14
12
10
8
7
6
4.5

Volume
130,000
70,000
40,000
20,000

Mar 1962 | Jun 1962 | Sep 1962 | Dec 1962 | Mar 1963 | Jun 1963 | Sep 1963 | Dec 1963 | Mar 1964 | Jun 1964 | Sep 1964 | Dec 1964 | Mar 1965 | Jun 1965 | Sep 1965 | Dec 1965 | Mar 1966 | Jun 1966 | Sep 1966

National Airlines increased 1004% in 179 weeks.

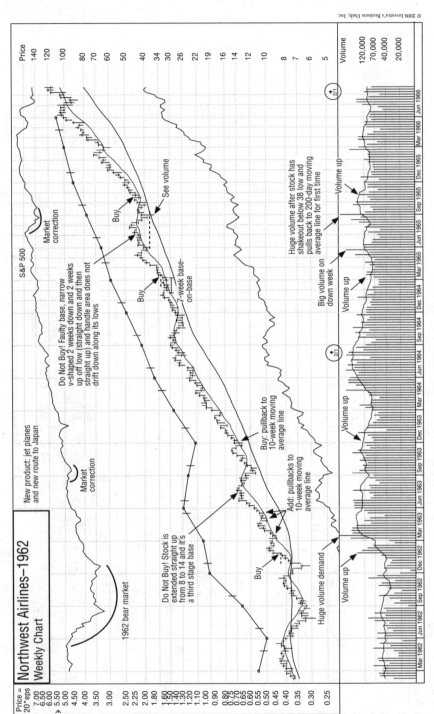

Price = 20*eps

Northwest Airlines–1962
Weekly Chart

New product: jet planes and new route to Japan

S&P 500

Market correction

Market correction

1962 bear market

Do Not Buy! Stock is extended straight up from 8 to 14 and it's a third stage base

Do Not Buy! Faulty base, narrow v-shaped 2 weeks down and 2 weeks up off low (straight up) and then straight down and handle area does not drift down along its lows

7-week base-on-base

See volume

Buy

Buy

Buy

Buy: pullback to 10-week moving average line

Add: pullbacks to 10-week moving average line

Huge volume demand

Huge volume after stock has shakeout below 38 low and pulls back to 200-day moving average line for first time

Big volume on down week

Volume up

Volume up

Volume up

Volume up

Volume up

Price

Volume

Northwest Airlines increased 1240% in 186 weeks.

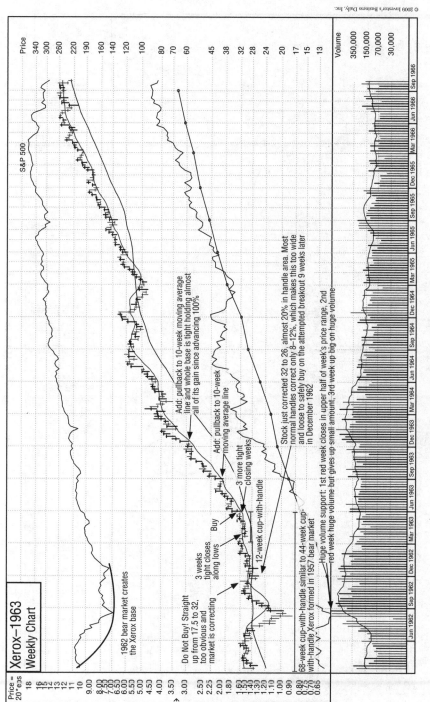

Xerox—1963 Weekly Chart

Price = 20¢ eps

S&P 500

1962 bear market creates the Xerox base

Do Not Buy! Straight up from 17.5 to 32, too obvious and market is correcting

3 weeks tight closes along lows

Buy

3 more tight closing weeks

12-week cup-with-handle

Add: pullback to 10-week moving average line and whole base is tight holding almost all of its gain since advancing 100%

Add: pullback to 10-week moving average line

Stock just corrected 32 to 26, almost 20% in handle area. Most normal handles correct only 8–12%, which makes this too wide and loose to safely buy on the attempted breakout 9 weeks later in December 1962

68-week cup-with-handle similar to 44-week cup-with-handle Xerox formed in 1957 bear market

Huge volume support: 1st red week closes in upper half of week's price range, 2nd red week huge volume but gives up small amount; 3rd week up big on big volume

Xerox increased 660% in 168 weeks.

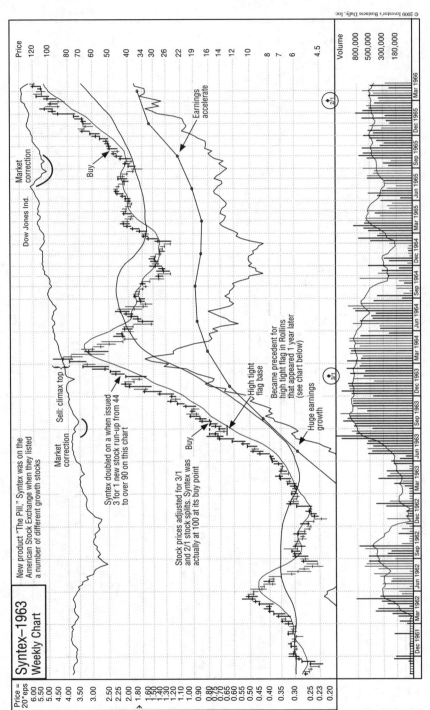

Syntex—1963
Weekly Chart

Price = 20* eps

New product "The Pill." Syntex was on the
American Stock Exchange when they listed
a number of different growth stocks

Market correction

Dow Jones Ind.

Sell: climax top

Market correction

Buy

Syntex doubled on a when issued
3 for 1 new stock run-up from 44
to over 90 on this chart

Stock prices adjusted for 3/1
and 2/1 stock splits. Syntex was
actually at 100 at its buy point

Buy

Earnings
accelerate

High tight
flag base

Became precedent for
high tight flag in Rollins
that appeared 1 year later.
(see chart below)

Huge earnings
growth

© 2009 Investor's Business Daily, Inc.

Syntex increased 451% in 25 weeks.

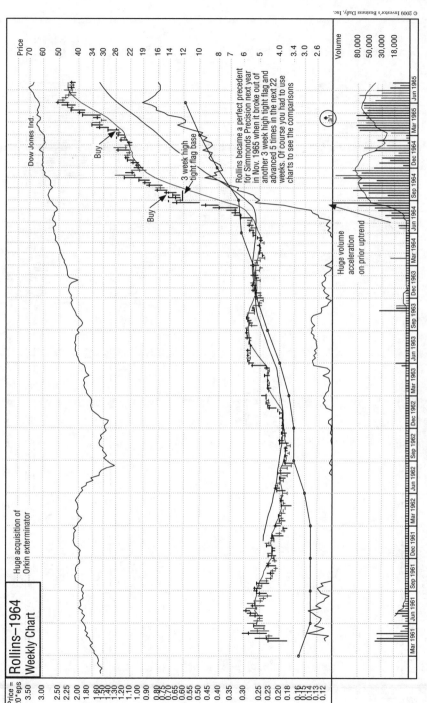

Rollins increased 254% in 36 weeks.

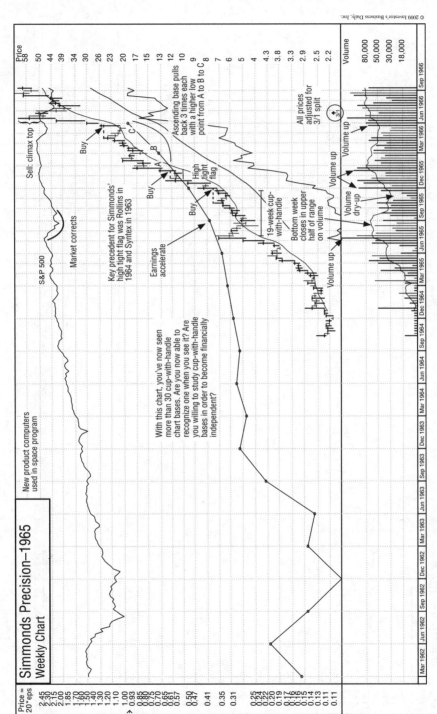

Simmonds Precision—1965
Weekly Chart

Price = 20× eps

New product computers used in space program

S&P 500

Market corrects

Sell: climax top

Buy

Key precedent for Simmonds' high tight flag was Rollins in 1964 and Syntex in 1963

Earnings accelerate

Buy

A · B

C

High tight flag

Buy

19-week cup-with-handle

Bottom week closes in upper half of range on volume

Ascending base pulls back 3 times each with a higher low point from A to B to C

All prices adjusted for 3/1 split

With this chart, you've now seen more than 30 cup-with-handle chart bases. Are you now able to recognize one when you see it? Are you willing to study cup-with-handle bases in order to become financially independent?

Volume up

Volume dry-up

Volume up

Volume up

Volume up

3/1

Simmonds Precision Products increased 672% in 38 weeks.

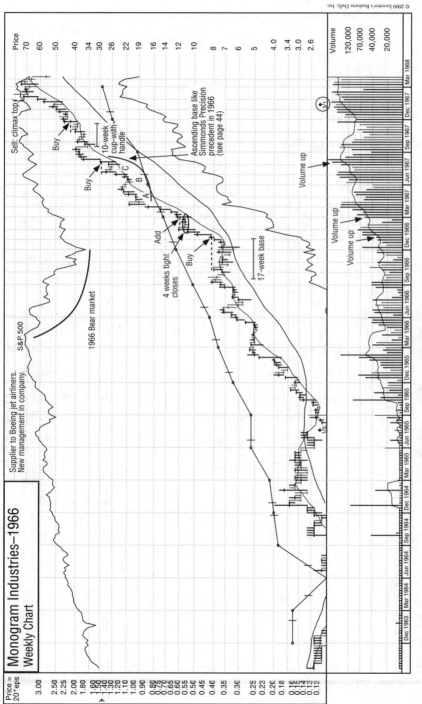

Monogram Industries–1966
Weekly Chart

Price =
20×eps

Supplier to Boeing jet airliners.
New management in company.

S&P 500

1966 Bear market

Sell: climax top

Buy

10-week
cup-with-
handle

Buy

C
B
A

Add

4 weeks tight
closes

Buy

17-week base

Ascending base like
Simmonds Precision
precedent in 1966
(see page 44)

Volume up

Volume up

Volume up

Volume up

Monogram Industries increased 891% in 57 weeks.

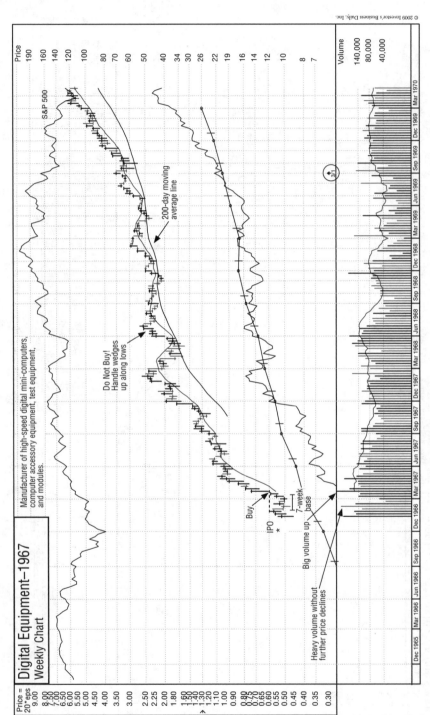

Digital Equipment–1967
Weekly Chart

Price =
20* eps

Manufacturer of high-speed digital mini-computers,
computer accessory equipment, test equipment,
and modules.

S&P 500

200-day moving
average line

Do Not Buy!
Handle wedges
up along lows

Buy

IPO
*

7-week
base

Big volume up

Heavy volume without
further price declines

Volume

Digital Equipment increased 743% in 156 weeks.

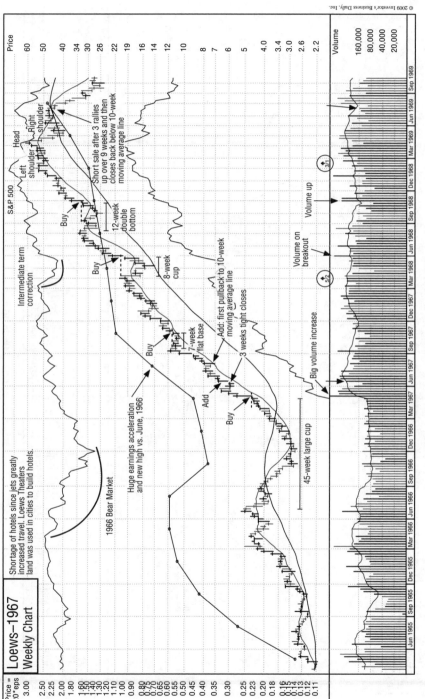

Loews–1967
Weekly Chart

Price =
20·eps

Shortage of hotels since jets greatly increased travel. Loews Theaters land was used in cities to build hotels.

Intermediate term correction

S&P 500

Left shoulder · Head · Right shoulder

Short sale after 3 rallies up over 9 weeks and then closes back below 10-week moving average line

12-week double bottom

8-week cup

Add: first pullback to 10-week moving average line

3 weeks tight closes

Buy

7-week flat base

Huge earnings acceleration and new high vs. June, 1966

1966 Bear Market

45-week large cup

Add

Buy

Big volume increase

Volume on breakout

Volume up

Volume

Loews increased 1025% in 101 weeks.

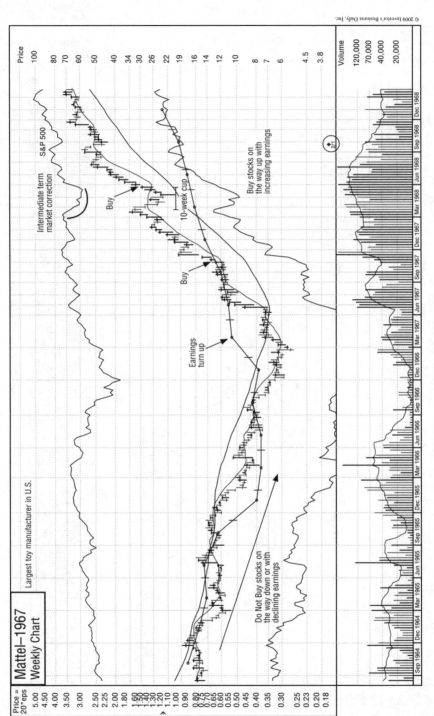

Mattel—1967
Weekly Chart

Price = 20* eps

Largest toy manufacturer in U.S.

Intermediate term market correction

S&P 500

Buy

10-week cup

Buy

Earnings turn up

Buy stocks on the way up with increasing earnings

Do Not Buy stocks on the way down or with declining earnings

Mattel increased 441% in 66 weeks.

© 2009 Investor's Business Daily, Inc.

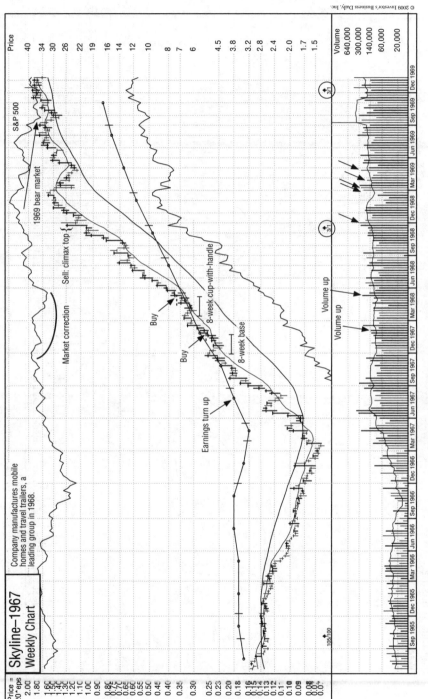

Skyline—1967
Weekly Chart

Company manufactures mobile homes and travel trailers, a leading group in 1968.

Price = 20*eps

S&P 500

1969 bear market

Market correction

Sell: climax top

Buy

Buy

Earnings turn up

8-week cup-with-handle

8-week base

Volume up

Volume up

Skyline increased 715% in 98 weeks.

© 2009 Investor's Business Daily, Inc.

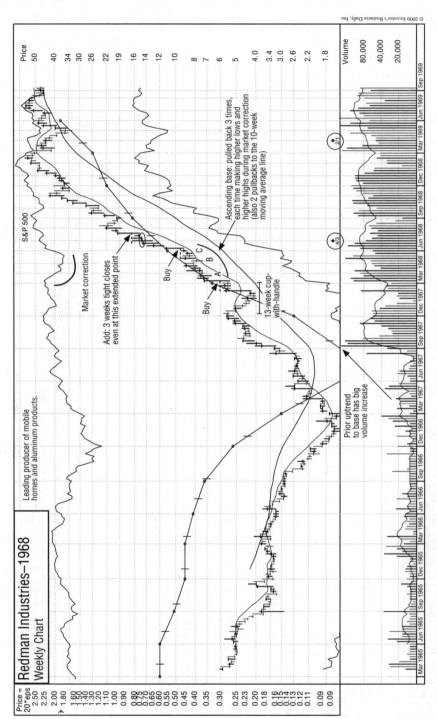

Price = 20*eps

Redman Industries–1968
Weekly Chart

Leading producer of mobile homes and aluminum products.

S&P 500

Market correction

Add: 3 weeks tight closes even at this extended point

Buy

Buy

A
B
C

Ascending base: pulled back 3 times; each time making higher lows and higher highs during market correction (also 2 pullbacks to the 10-week moving average line)

13-week cup-with-handle

Prior uptrend to base has big volume increase

Redman Industries increased 683% in 49 weeks.

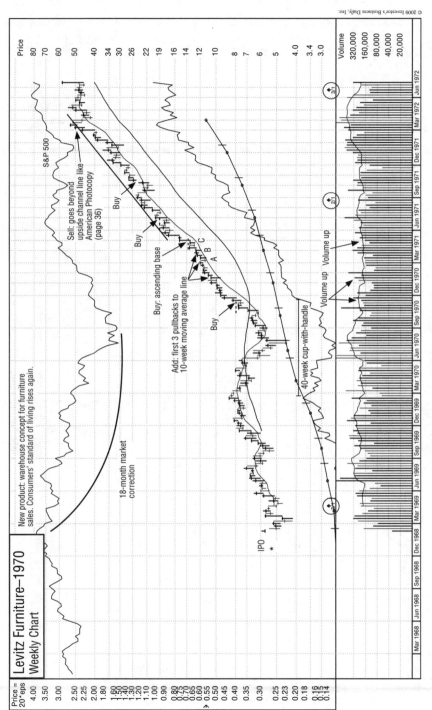

© 2009 Investor's Business Daily, Inc.

Levitz Furniture—1970
Weekly Chart

New product: warehouse concept for furniture sales. Consumers' standard of living rises again.

Price = 20*eps

S&P 500

Sell: goes beyond upside channel line like American Photocopy (page 36)

Buy

Buy

Buy: ascending base

Add: first 3 pullbacks to 10-week moving average line

A B C

Buy

40-week cup-with-handle

18-month market correction

IPO

Volume up   Volume up

Volume up   Volume up

Levitz Furniture increased 608% in 87 weeks.

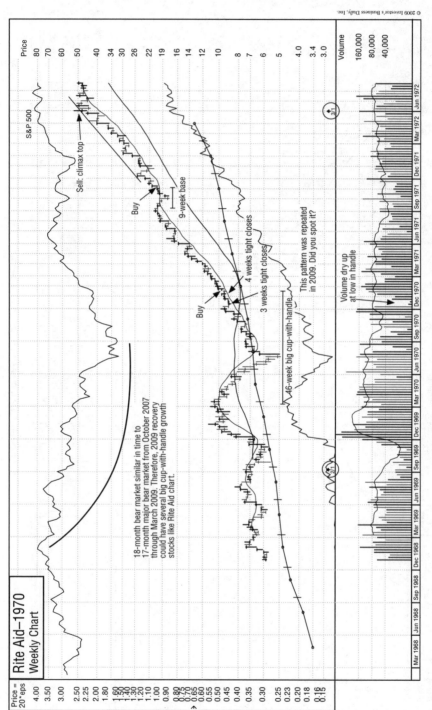

Rite Aid–1970
Weekly Chart

Price = 20*eps

Price

S&P 500

Sell: climax top

Buy

9-week base

4 weeks tight closes

Buy

3 weeks tight closes

46-week big cup-with-handle

This pattern was repeated in 2009. Did you spot it?

18-month bear market similar in time to 17-month major bear market from October 2007 through March 2009. Therefore, 2009 recovery could have several big cup-with-handle growth stocks like Rite Aid chart.

Volume

Volume dry up at low in handle

Rite Aid increased 421% in 71 weeks.

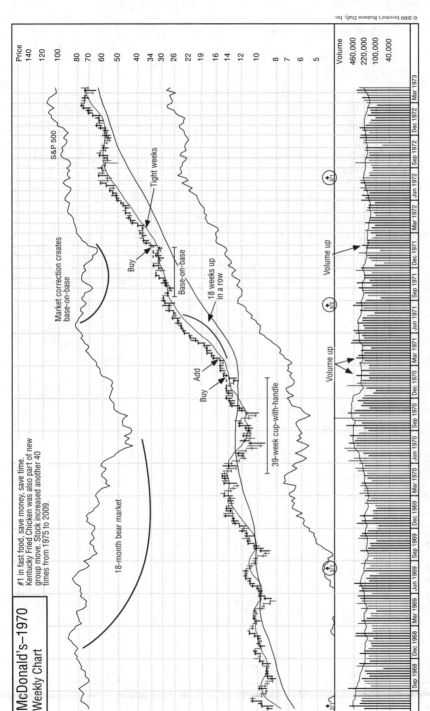

McDonald's–1970 Weekly Chart

#1 in fast food, save money, save time. Kentucky Fried Chicken was also part of new group move. Stock increased another 40 times from 1975 to 2009.

18-month bear market

Market correction creates base-on-base

S&P 500

Tight weeks

Buy

Base-on-base

18 weeks up in a row

Add

Buy

39-week cup-with-handle

Price
140
120
100
80
70
60
50
40
34
30
26
22
19
16
14
12
10
8
7
6
5

Volume
460,000
220,000
100,000
40,000

Volume up

Volume up

Sep 1968 Dec 1968 Mar 1969 Jun 1969 Sep 1969 Dec 1969 Mar 1970 Jun 1970 Sep 1970 Dec 1970 Mar 1971 Jun 1971 Sep 1971 Dec 1971 Mar 1972 Jun 1972 Sep 1972 Dec 1972 Mar 1973

McDonald's increased 422% in 108 weeks.

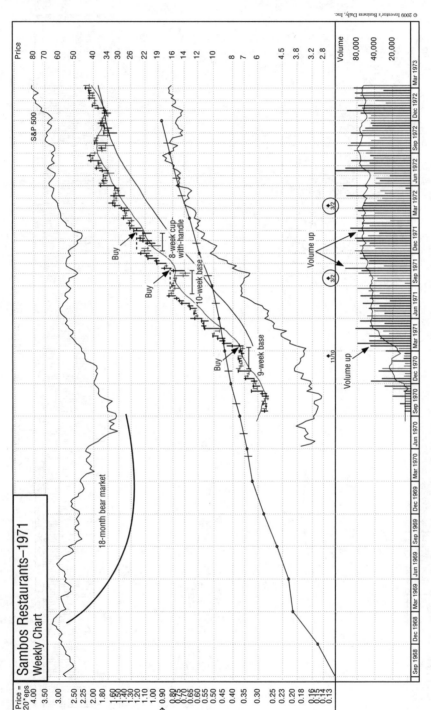

Sambos Restaurants–1971
Weekly Chart

Price = 20*eps

S&P 500

18-month bear market

8-week cup-with-handle

Buy

Buy

10-week base

Buy

9-week base

Volume up

Volume up

11/10

3/2

3/2

Volume

Sambos Restaurants increased 458% in 104 weeks.

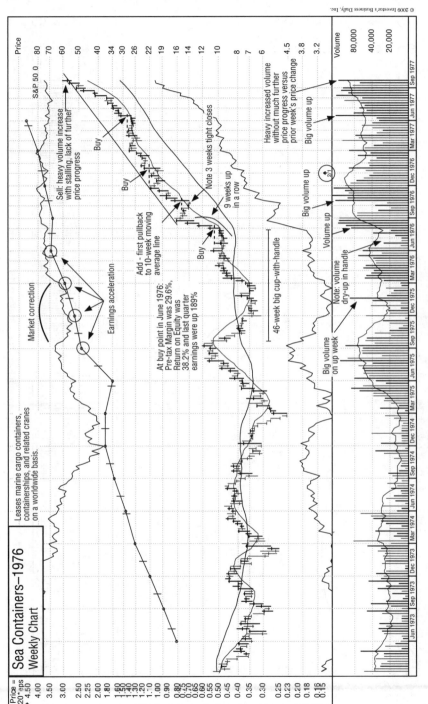

Sea Containers—1976
Weekly Chart

Leases marine cargo containers, containerships, and related cranes on a worldwide basis.

Market correction

Earnings acceleration

Sell: heavy volume increase with stalling, lack of further price progress

Buy

Add - first pullback to 10-week moving average line

At buy point in June 1976: Pre-tax Margin was 29.6%, Return on Equity was 38.2% and last quarter earnings were up 189%

Buy

Buy

Note 3 weeks tight closes

9 weeks up in a row

46-week big cup-with-handle

Heavy increased volume without much further price progress versus prior week's price change

Big volume up

Volume up

Big volume up

Big volume on up week

Note: volume dry-up in handle

Price = 20*eps

Sea Containers increased 448% in 59 weeks.

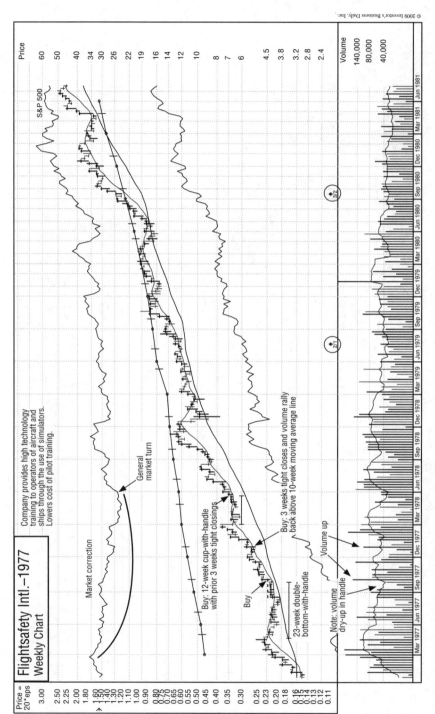

© 2009 Investor's Business Daily, Inc.

Flightsafety Intl.–1977
Weekly Chart

Price = 20*eps

Company provides high technology training to operators of aircraft and ships through the use of simulators. Lowers cost of pilot training.

Price — S&P 500

Market correction

General market turn

Buy: 12-week cup-with-handle with prior 3 weeks tight closings

Buy

23-week double-bottom-with-handle

Buy: 3 weeks tight closes and volume rally back above 10-week moving average line

Volume up

Note: volume dry-up in handle

Volume

Flightsafety International increased 958% in 195 weeks.

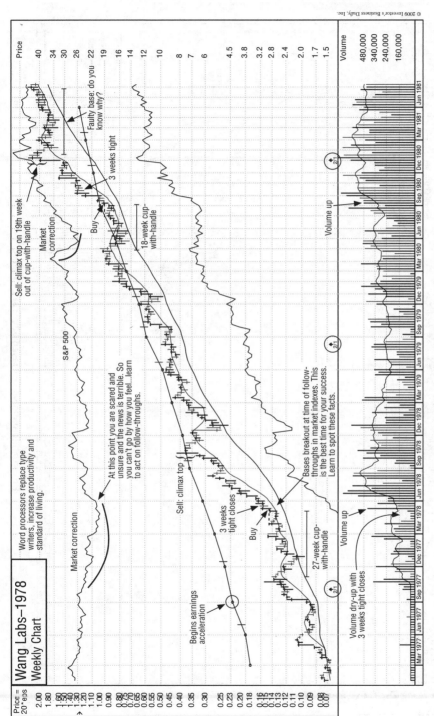

Price = 20* eps	Wang Labs—1978 Weekly Chart

Word processors replace type writers, increase productivity and standard of living.

Market correction

Begins earnings acceleration

At this point you are scared and unsure and the news is terrible. So you can't go by how you feel...learn to act on follow-throughs.

Market correction

Sell: climax top

3 weeks tight closes

Buy

27-week cup-with-handle

Bases breakout at time of follow-throughs in market indexes. This is the best time for your success. Learn to spot these facts.

S&P 500

Sell: climax top on 19th week out of cup-with-handle

Market correction

3 weeks tight

Buy

18-week cup-with-handle

Faulty base: do you know why?

Volume up

Volume up

Volume dry-up with 3 weeks tight closes

Price: 40, 34, 30, 26, 22, 19, 16, 14, 12, 10, 8, 7, 6, 4.5, 3.8, 3.2, 2.8, 2.4, 2.0, 1.7, 1.5

Price: 2.00, 1.80, 1.60, 1.50, 1.40, 1.30, 1.20, 1.10, 1.00, 0.90, 0.80, 0.70, 0.65, 0.60, 0.55, 0.50, 0.45, 0.40, 0.35, 0.30, 0.25, 0.23, 0.20, 0.18, 0.16, 0.15, 0.14, 0.13, 0.12, 0.11, 0.10, 0.09, 0.08, 0.07

Volume: 480,000, 340,000, 240,000, 160,000

Mar 1977, Jun 1977, Sep 1977, Dec 1977, Mar 1978, Jun 1978, Sep 1978, Dec 1978, Mar 1979, Jun 1979, Sep 1979, Dec 1979, Mar 1980, Jun 1980, Sep 1980, Dec 1980, Mar 1981, Jun 1981

Wang Laboratories increased 1348% in 139 weeks.

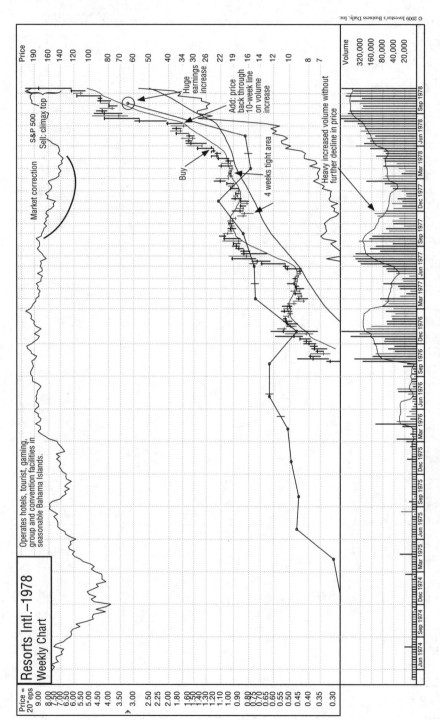

Price = 20*eps

Resorts Intl.–1978
Weekly Chart

Operates hotels, tourist, gaming, group and convention facilities in seasonable Bahama Islands.

Market correction

S&P 500

Sell: climax top

Buy

Huge earnings increase

Add: price back through 10-week line on volume increase

4 weeks tight area

Heavy increased volume without further decline in price

Resorts International increased 630% in 24 weeks.

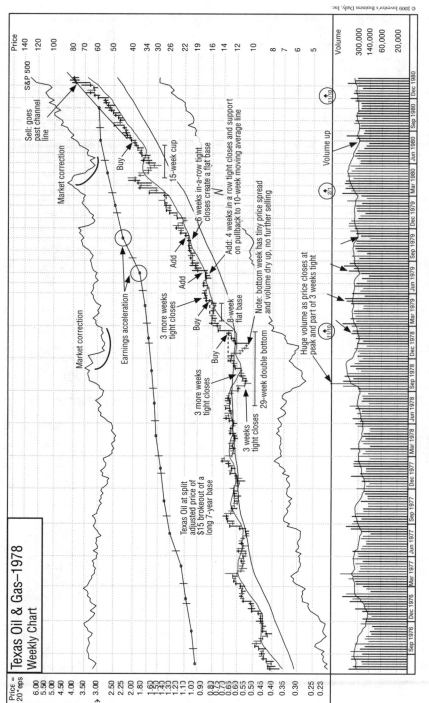

Texas Oil & Gas increased 529% in 101 weeks.

Texas Oil & Gas—1978
Weekly Chart

Price =
20*eps

Sell: goes
past channel
line

Market correction

Buy

Market correction

Earnings acceleration

15-week cup

6 weeks in-a-row tight
closes create a flat base

Add

3 more weeks
tight closes

Add

Buy

Add: 4 weeks in a row tight closes and support
on pullback to 10-week moving average line

8-week
flat base

Note: bottom week has tiny price spread
and volume dry up, no further selling

Buy

3 more weeks
tight closes

29-week double bottom

3 weeks
tight closes

Texas Oil at split
adjusted price of
$15 brokeout of a
long 7-year base

Huge volume as price closes at
peak and part of 3 weeks tight

Volume up

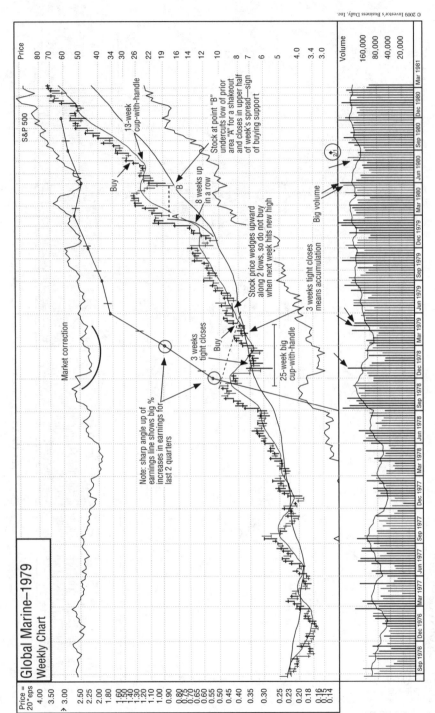

Global Marine—1979
Weekly Chart

Price = 20* eps

Note: sharp angle up of earnings line shows big % increases in earnings for last 2 quarters

Market correction

S&P 500

13-week cup-with-handle

Buy

8 weeks up in a row

Stock at point "B" undercuts low of prior area "A" for a shakeout and closes in upper half of week's spread—sign of buying support

Stock price wedges upward along 2 lows, so do not buy when next week hits new high

3 weeks tight closes

Buy

3 weeks tight closes means accumulation

25-week big cup-with-handle

Big volume

Volume

Global Marine increased 752% in 94 weeks.

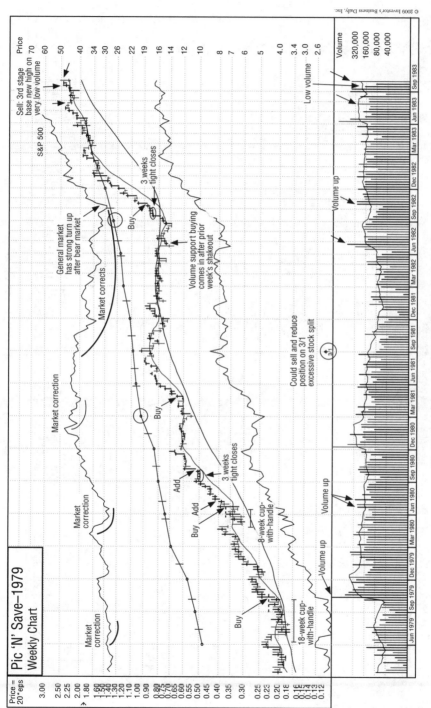

Pic 'N' Save—1979 Weekly Chart

Price = 20*eps

Price

Sell: 3rd stage base new high on very low volume

S&P 500

General market has strong turn up after bear market

Market corrects

3 weeks tight closes

Buy

Volume support buying comes in after prior week's shakeout

Market correction

Buy

Market correction

Add

Add

Buy

3 weeks tight closes

Could sell and reduce position on 3/1 excessive stock split

Market correction

8-week cup-with-handle

Buy

Volume up

18-week cup-with-handle

Volume up

Low volume

Volume up

Volume up

Volume

Pic 'N' Save increased 948% in 206 weeks.

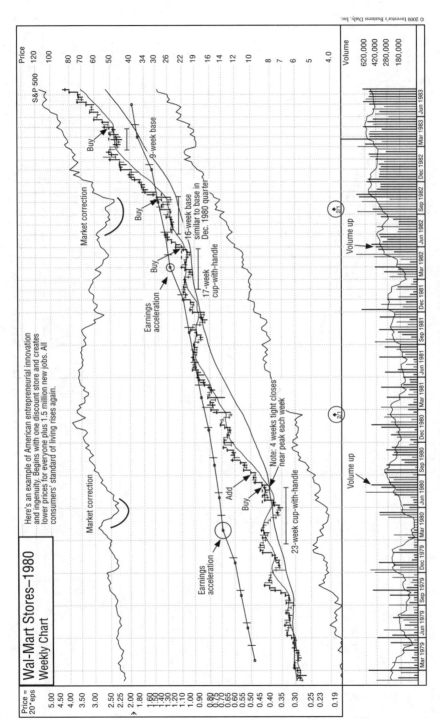

Wal-Mart Stores—1980
Weekly Chart

Price = 20* eps

Here's an example of American entrepreneurial innovation and ingenuity. Begins with one discount store and creates lower prices for everyone plus 1.5 million new jobs. All consumers' standard of living rises again.

Market correction

Market correction

Earnings acceleration

Add

Buy

23-week cup-with-handle

Note: 4 weeks tight closes near peak each week

Earnings acceleration

Buy

17-week cup-with-handle

16-week base similar to base in Dec. 1980 quarter

Buy

9-week base

Buy

S&P 500

Price

Volume up

Volume up

Volume

Wal-Mart Stores increased 882% in 158 weeks.

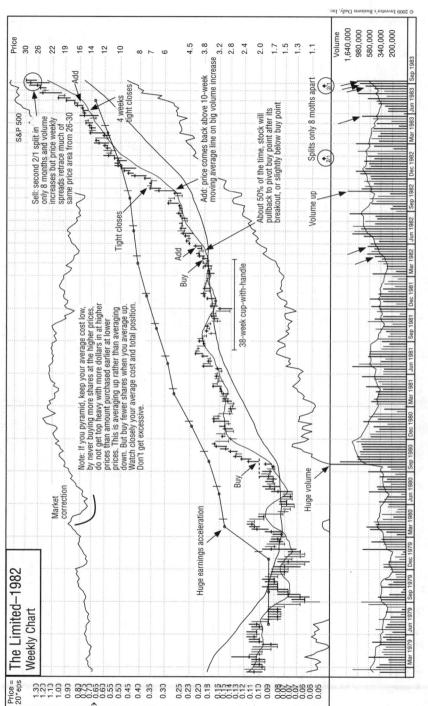

The Limited increased 673% in 71 weeks.

The Limited—1982 Weekly Chart

Price = 20*eps

© 2009 Investor's Business Daily, Inc.

S&P 500

Sell: second 2/1 split in only 8 months and volume increases but price weekly spreads retrace much of same price area from 26-30

Add

4 weeks tight closes

Tight closes

Add: price comes back above 10-week moving average line on big volume increase

Add

Buy

38-week cup-with-handle

About 50% of the time, stock will pullback to pivot buy point after its breakout, or slightly below buy point

Volume up

Splits only 8 months apart

Market correction

Note: If you pyramid, keep your average cost low, by never buying more shares at the higher prices, do not get top heavy with more dollars in at higher prices than amount purchased earlier at lower prices. This is averaging up rather than averaging down. But buy fewer shares when you average up. Watch closely your average cost and total position. Don't get excessive.

Huge earnings acceleration

Buy

Huge volume

Volume
1,640,000
980,000
580,000
340,000
200,000

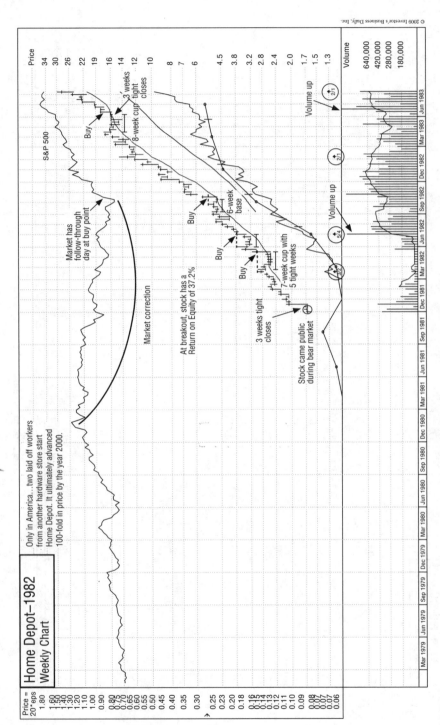

Home Depot increased 892% in 64 weeks.

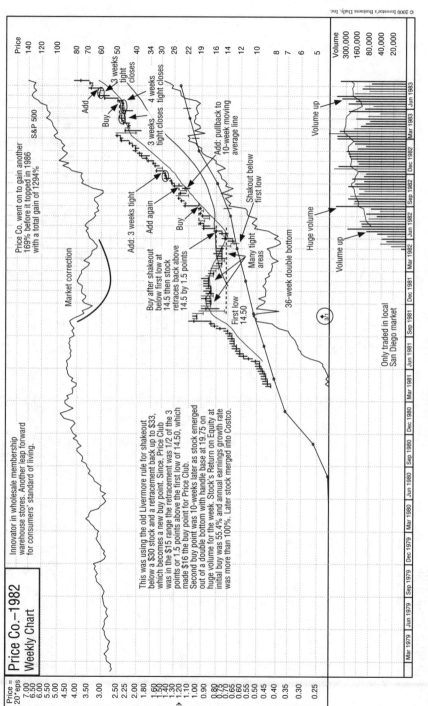

Price Company increased 417% in 60 weeks.

© 2009 Investor's Business Daily, Inc.

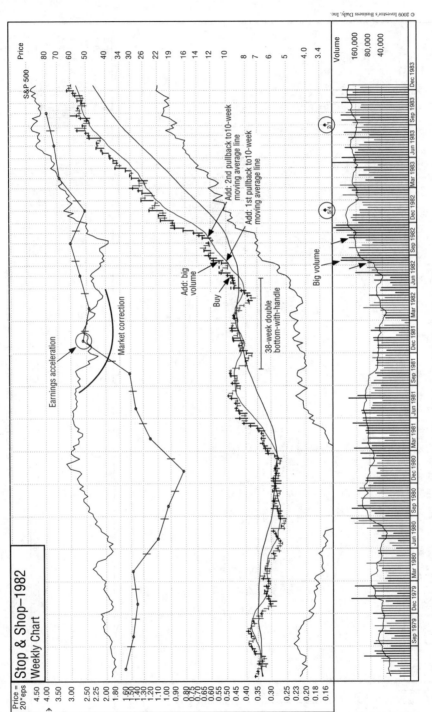

Stop & Shop—1982
Weekly Chart

Price =
20*eps

Price

S&P 500

Earnings acceleration

Market correction

Add: 2nd pullback to 10-week
moving average line

Add: 1st pullback to 10-week
moving average line

Add: big
volume

Buy

38-week double
bottom-with-handle

Big volume

Volume

Stop & Shop increased 536% in 74 weeks.

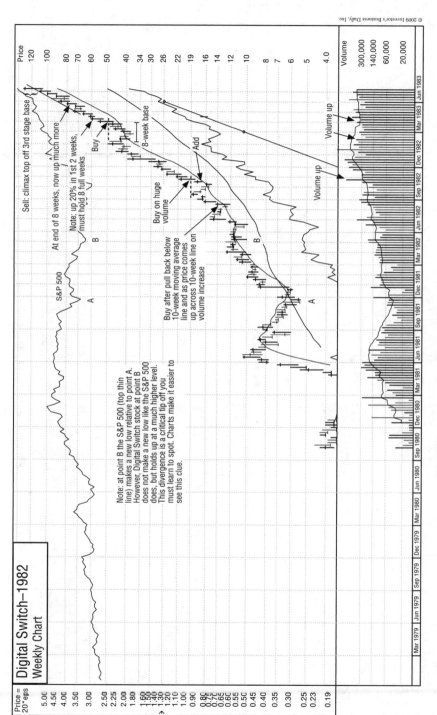

Price = 20*eps

Price
120
100
80
70
60
50
40
34
30
26
22
19
16
14
12
10
8
7
6
5
4.0

5.00	
4.50	
4.00	
3.50	
3.00	
2.50	
2.25	
2.00	
1.80	
1.60	
1.40	
1.30	
1.20	
1.10	
1.00	
0.90	
0.80	
0.70	
0.65	
0.60	
0.55	
0.50	
0.45	
0.40	
0.35	
0.30	
0.25	
0.23	
0.19	

Digital Switch—1982
Weekly Chart

Sell: climax top off 3rd stage base

At end of 8 weeks, now up much more

Note: up 20% in 1st 2 weeks, must hold 8 full weeks

Buy

S&P 500

8-week base

A

B

Add

Buy on huge volume

Buy after pull back below 10-week moving average line and as price comes up across 10-week line on volume increase

Note: at point B the S&P 500 (top thin line) makes a new low relative to point A. However, Digital Switch stock at point B does not make a new low like the S&P 500 does, but holds up at a much higher level. This divergence is a critical tip off you must learn to spot. Charts make it easier to see this clue.

B

A

Volume up

Volume up

Volume

Volume
300,000
140,000
60,000
20,000

Mar 1979 | Jun 1979 | Sep 1979 | Dec 1979 | Mar 1980 | Jun 1980 | Sep 1980 | Dec 1980 | Mar 1981 | Jun 1981 | Sep 1981 | Dec 1981 | Mar 1982 | Jun 1982 | Sep 1982 | Dec 1982 | Mar 1983 | Jun 1983

Digital Switch increased 843% in 46 weeks.

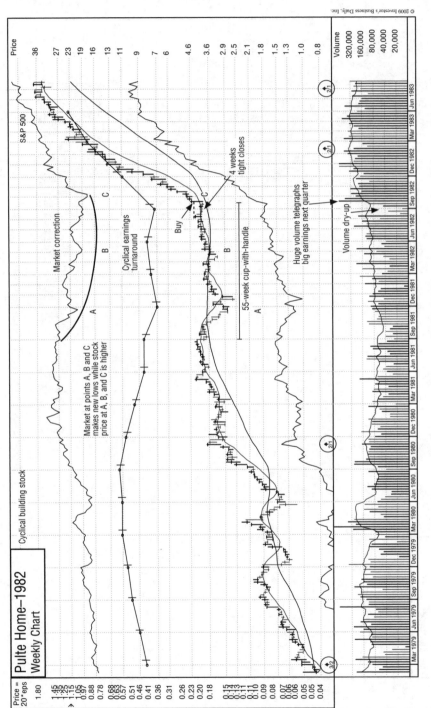

Pulte Home increased 733% in 47 weeks.

© 2009 Investor's Business Daily, Inc.

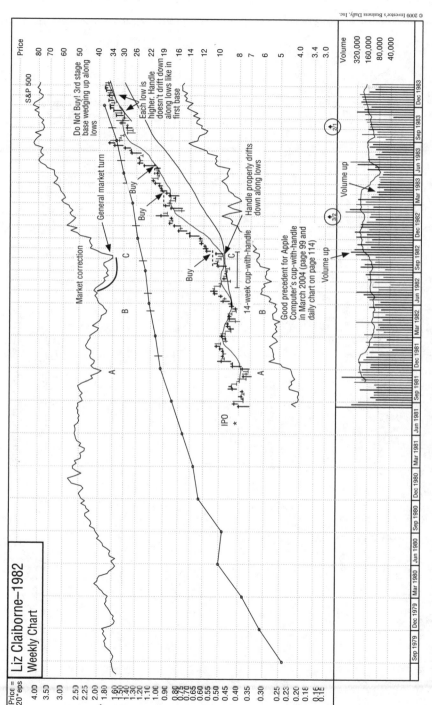

Liz Claiborne—1982
Weekly Chart

Price =
20*eps

S&P 500

Do Not Buy! 3rd stage
base wedging up along
lows

Each low is
higher. Handle
doesn't drift down
along lows like in
first base

General market turn

Market correction

Buy

Buy

Buy

Handle properly drifts
down along lows

Buy

14-week cup-with-handle

Good precedent for Apple
Computer's cup-with-handle
in March 2004 (page 99 and
daily chart on page 114)

IPO

Volume up

Volume up

Volume up

Liz Claiborne increased 211% in 43 weeks.

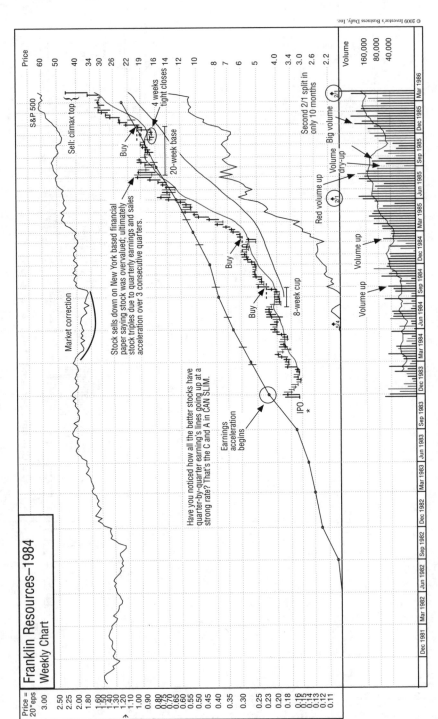

Franklin Resources increased 811% in 78 weeks.

Franklin Resources—1984
Weekly Chart

Price = 20*eps

S&P 500

Sell: climax top

Market correction

Stock sells down on New York based financial paper saying stock was overvalued; ultimately stock triples due to quarterly earnings and sales acceleration over 3 consecutive quarters.

4 weeks tight closes

Buy

20-week base

Have you noticed how all the better stocks have quarter-by-quarter earning's lines going up at a strong rate? That's the C and A in CAN SLIM.

Buy

8-week cup

Earnings acceleration begins

Buy

IPO
*

Second 2/1 split in only 10 months

Red volume up

Volume dry-up

Big volume

Volume up

Volume up

Volume up

Volume

© 2009 Investor's Business Daily, Inc.

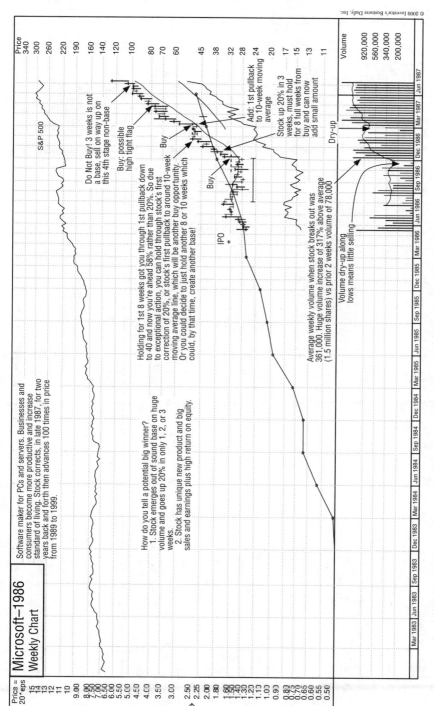

Microsoft—1986
Weekly Chart

Price = 20*eps

Software maker for PCs and servers. Businesses and consumers become more productive and increase standard of living. Stock corrects, in late 1987, for two years back and forth then advances 100 times in price from 1989 to 1999.

S&P 500

How do you tell a potential big winner?
1. Stock emerges out of sound base on huge volume and goes up 20% in only 1, 2, or 3 weeks.
2. Stock has unique new product and big sales and earnings plus high return on equity.

Do Not Buy! 3 weeks is not a base, sell on way up on this 4th stage non-base

Buy: possible high tight flag

Holding for 1st 8 weeks got you through 1st pullback down to 40 and now you're ahead 58% rather than 20%. So due to exceptional action, you can hold through stock's first correction of 20%, or stock's first pullback to around 10-week moving average line, which will be another buy opportunity. Or you could decide to just hold another 8 or 10 weeks which could, by that time, create another base!

Buy

Buy

IPO
*

Add: 1st pullback to 10-week moving average

Stock up 20% in 3 weeks, must hold for 8 full weeks from buy and can now add small amount

Average weekly volume when stock breaks out was 361,000. Huge volume increase of 317% above average (1.5 million shares) vs prior 2 weeks volume of 78,000

Dry-up

Volume dry-up along lows means little selling

© 2009 Investor's Business Daily, Inc.

Microsoft increased 272% in 30 weeks.

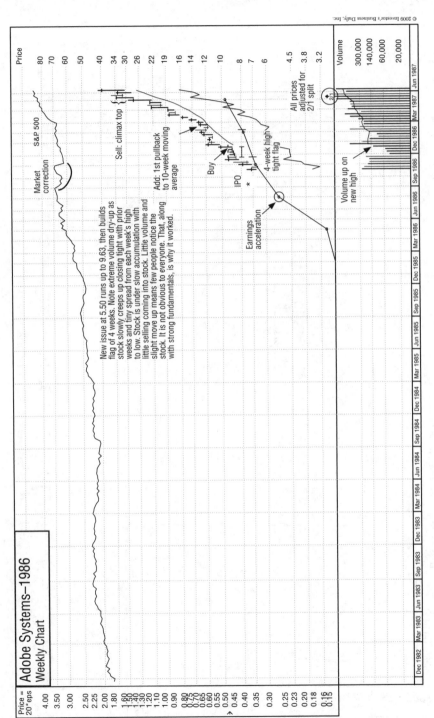

Adobe Systems increased 307% in 23 weeks.

Adobe Systems–1986
Weekly Chart

Price = 20*eps

New issue at 5.50 runs up to 9.63, then builds flag of 4 weeks. Note extreme volume dry-up as stock slowly creeps up closing tight with prior weeks and tiny spread from each week's high to low. Stock is under slow accumulation with little selling coming into stock. Little volume and slight move up means few people notice the stock. It is not obvious to everyone. That, along with strong fundamentals, is why it worked.

Market correction

S&P 500

Sell: climax top

Add: 1st pullback to 10-week moving average

Buy

IPO

Earnings acceleration

4-week high tight flag

All prices adjusted for 2/1 split

Volume up on new high

Volume

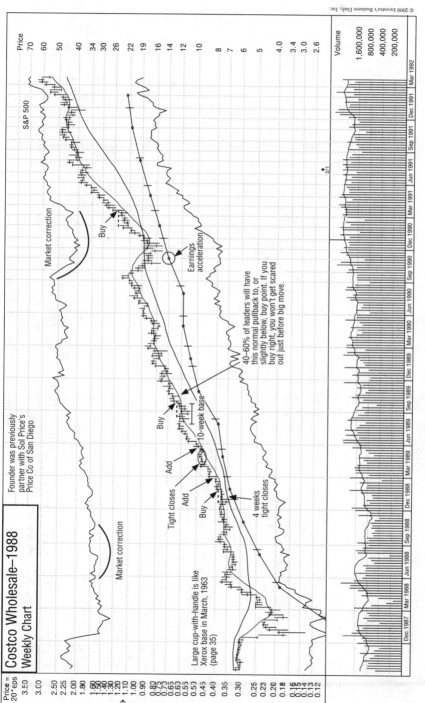

Costco Wholesale increased 712% in 163 weeks.

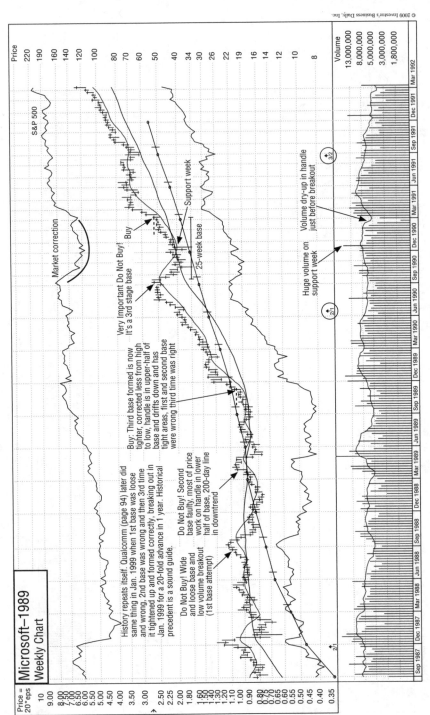

Microsoft increased 517% in 121 weeks.

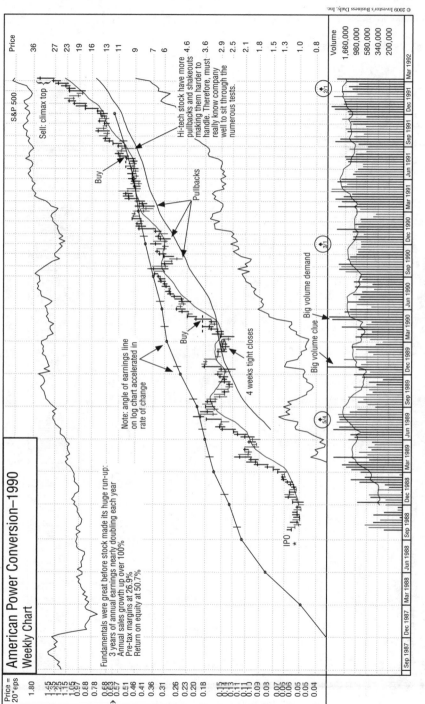

American Power Conversion—1990
Weekly Chart

Price = 20*eps

Fundamentals were great before stock made its huge run-up:
3 years of annual earnings nearly doubling each year
Annual sales growth up over 100%
Pre-tax margins at 26.9%
Return on equity at 50.7%

Note: angle of earnings line on log chart accelerated in rate of change

Sell: climax top

Buy

Pullbacks

Buy

4 weeks tight closes

IPO

Big volume demand

Big volume clue

Hi-tech stock have more pullbacks and shakeouts making them harder to handle. Therefore, must really know company well to sit through the numerous tests.

S&P 500

American Power Conversion increased 745% in 96 weeks.

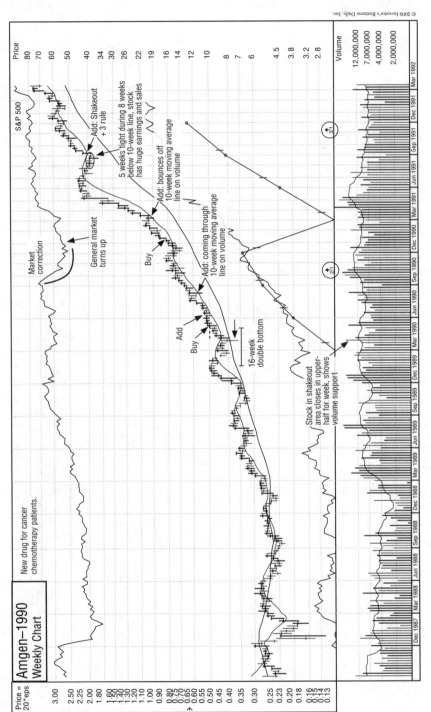

Amgen—1990
Weekly Chart

Price =
20*eps

New drug for cancer
chemotherapy patients.

S&P 500

Price

Market
correction

General market
turns up

Add: Shakeout
+ 3 rule

5 weeks tight during 8 weeks
below 10-week line, stock
has huge earnings and sales

Add: bounces off
10-week moving average
line on volume

Buy

Add: coming through
10-week moving average
line on volume

Add

Buy

16-week
double bottom

Stock in shakeout
area closes in upper-
half for week, shows
volume support

Volume

Amgen increased 681% in 96 weeks.

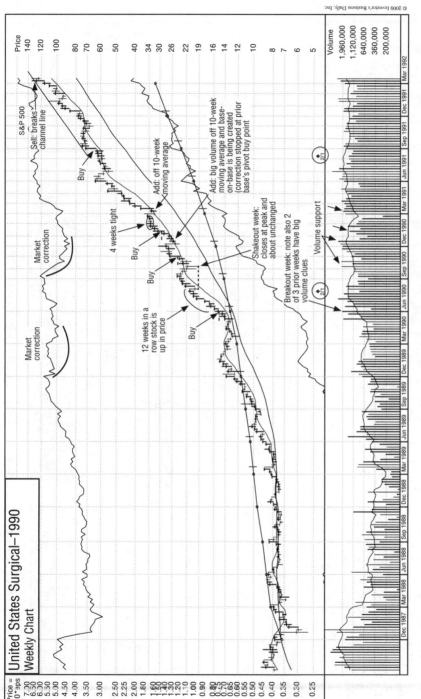

United States Surgical–1990
Weekly Chart

Price =
20¢ aps

Price
7.00
6.50
6.00
5.50
5.00
4.50
4.00
3.50
3.00
2.50
2.25
2.00
1.80
1.60
1.40
1.30
1.20
1.10
1.00
0.90
0.80
0.70
0.65
0.60
0.55
0.50
0.45
0.40
0.35
0.30
0.25

Price
140
120
100
80
70
60
50
40
34
30
26
22
19
16
14
12
10
8
7
6
5

S&P 500

Sell: breaks
channel line

Buy

Market
correction

Market
correction

4 weeks tight

Buy

Add: off 10-week
moving average

12 weeks in a
row stock is
up in price

Buy

Add: big volume off 10-week
moving average and base-
on-base is being created
(correction stopped at prior
base's pivot buy point

Shakeout week:
closes at peak and
about unchanged

Breakout week: note also 2
of 3 prior weeks have big
volume clues

Volume support

Volume
1,960,000
1,120,000
640,000
360,000
200,000

Dec 1987 Mar 1988 Jun 1988 Sep 1988 Dec 1988 Mar 1989 Jun 1989 Sep 1989 Dec 1989 Mar 1990 Jun 1990 Sep 1990 Dec 1990 Mar 1991 Jun 1991 Sep 1991 Dec 1991 Mar 1992

United States Surgical increased 786% in 93 weeks.

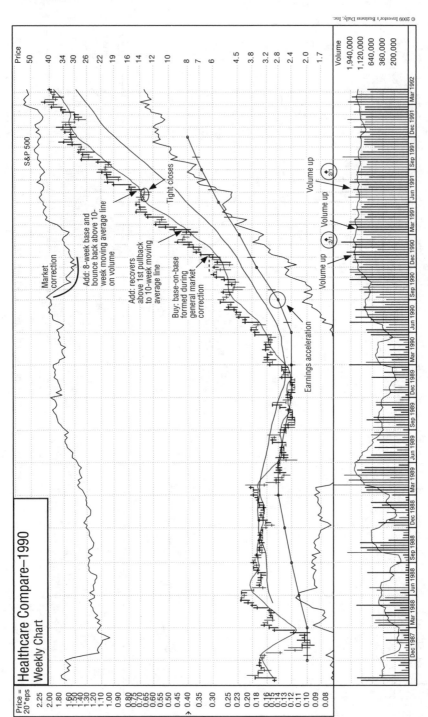

Healthcare Compare increased 540% in 61 weeks.

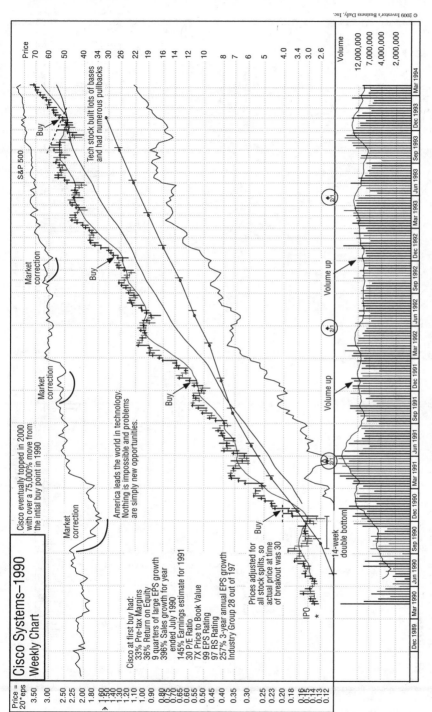

Cisco Systems increased 1602% in 169 weeks.

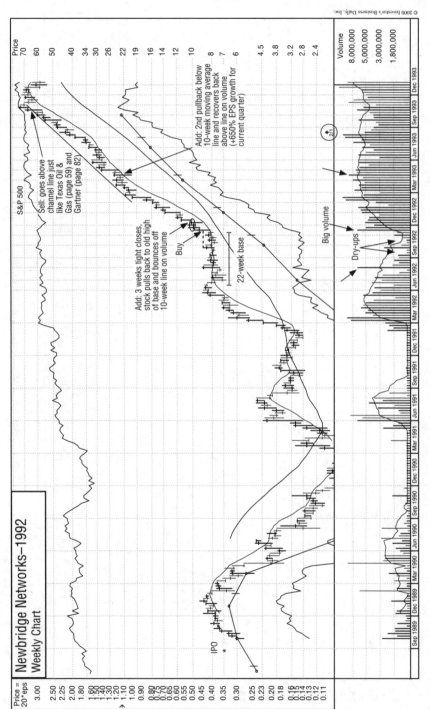

Newbridge Networks—1992
Weekly Chart

Price =
20*eps

S&P 500

Sell: goes above
channel line just
like Texas Oil &
Gas (page 59) and
Gartner (page 82)

Add: 2nd pullback below
10-week moving average
line and recovers back
above line on volume
(+650% EPS growth for
current quarter)

Add: 3 weeks tight closes,
stock pulls back to old high
of base and bounces off
10-week line on volume

Buy

22-week base

IPO
*

2:1

Big volume

Dry-ups

Volume
8,000,000
5,000,000
3,000,000
1,800,000

Price
70
60
50
40
34
30
26
22
19
16
14
12
10
8
7
6
4.5
3.8
3.2
2.8
2.4

3.00
2.50
2.25
2.00
1.80
1.60
1.50
1.40
1.30
1.20
1.10
1.00
0.90
0.80
0.75
0.70
0.65
0.60
0.55
0.50
0.45
0.40
0.35
0.30
0.25
0.23
0.20
0.18
0.16
0.15
0.14
0.13
0.12
0.11

Sep 1989 | Dec 1989 | Mar 1990 | Jun 1990 | Sep 1990 | Dec 1990 | Mar 1991 | Jun 1991 | Sep 1991 | Dec 1991 | Mar 1992 | Jun 1992 | Sep 1992 | Dec 1992 | Mar 1993 | Jun 1993 | Sep 1993 | Dec 1993

Newbridge Networks increased 699% in 49 weeks.

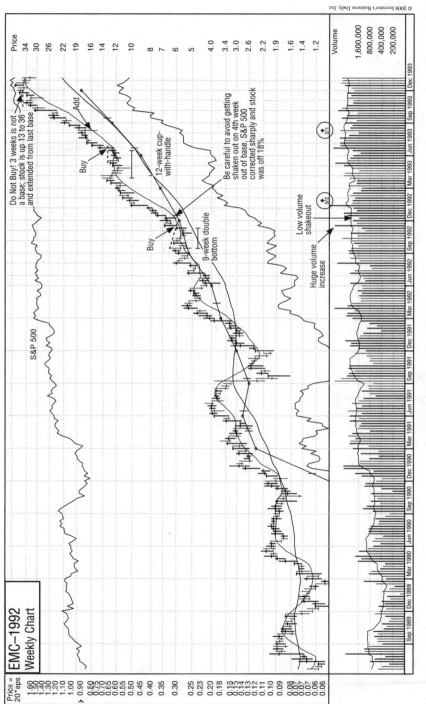

EMC–1992
Weekly Chart

Price =
20*eps

Do Not Buy! 3 weeks is not
a base; stock is up 13 to 36
and extended from last base

Add

Buy

S&P 500

12-week cup-
with-handle

Buy

9-week double
bottom

Be careful to avoid getting
shaken out on 4th week
out of base. S&P 500
corrected sharply and stock
was off 18%

Low volume
shakeout

Huge volume
increase

Price
34
30
26
22
19
16
14
12
10
8
7
6
5
4.0
3.4
3.0
2.6
2.2
1.9
1.6
1.4
1.2

Volume
1,600,000
800,000
400,000
200,000

1.90
1.40
1.30
1.20
1.10
1.00
0.90
0.80
0.75
0.70
0.65
0.60
0.55
0.50
0.45
0.40
0.35
0.30
0.25
0.23
0.20
0.18
0.16
0.14
0.13
0.12
0.11
0.10
0.09
0.09
0.08
0.07
0.06
0.06

Sep 1989 | Dec 1989 | Mar 1990 | Jun 1990 | Sep 1990 | Dec 1990 | Mar 1991 | Jun 1991 | Sep 1991 | Dec 1991 | Mar 1992 | Jun 1992 | Sep 1992 | Dec 1992 | Mar 1993 | Jun 1993 | Sep 1993 | Dec 1993

EMC increased 471% in 56 weeks.

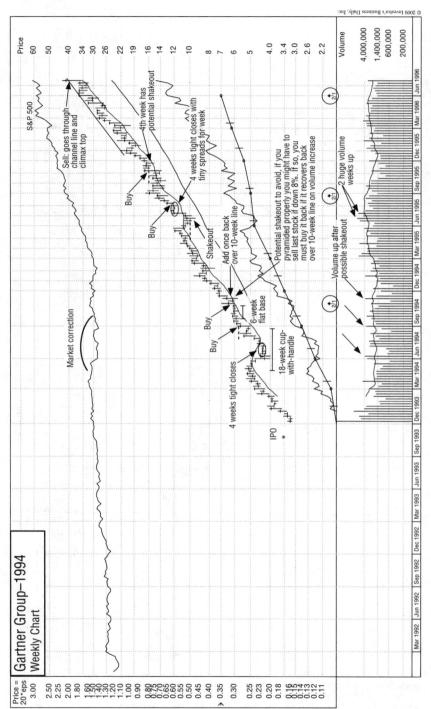

Gartner Group increased 667% in 98 weeks.

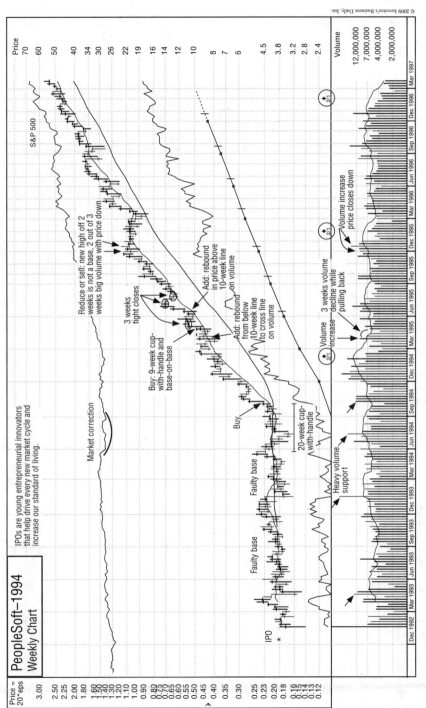

PeopleSoft—1994
Weekly Chart

Price = 20*eps

IPOs are young entrepreneurial innovators that help drive every new market cycle and increase our standard of living.

Market correction

S&P 500

Reduce or sell: new high off 2 weeks is not a base, 2 out of 3 weeks big volume with price down

3 weeks tight closes

Add: rebound in price above 10-week line on volume

Buy: 9-week cup-with-handle and base-on-base

Add: rebound from below 10-week line to cross line on volume

Buy

20-week cup-with-handle

Faulty base

Faulty base

IPO

Heavy volume support

Volume increase price closes down

Volume increase 3 weeks volume decline while pulling back

Volume

PeopleSoft increased 1145% in 129 weeks.

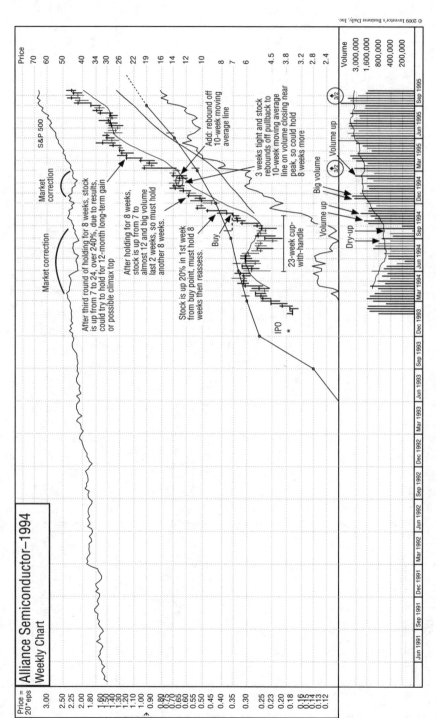

Alliance Semiconductor–1994
Weekly Chart

Price = 20*eps

Price

S&P 500

Market correction

Market correction

After third round of holding for 8 weeks, stock is up from 7 to 24, over 240%, due to results, could try to hold for 12-month long-term gain or possible climax top

After holding for 8 weeks, stock is up from 7 to almost 12 and big volume last 2 weeks, so must hold another 8 weeks.

Stock is up 20% in 1st week from buy point, must hold 8 weeks then reassess.

Add: rebound off 10-week moving average line

3 weeks tight and stock rebounds off pullback to 10-week moving average line on volume closing near peak, so could hold 8 weeks more

Buy

23-week cup-with-handle

IPO
*

Big volume

Volume up

Dry-up

Volume up

Volume

Alliance Semiconductor increased 539% in 47 weeks.

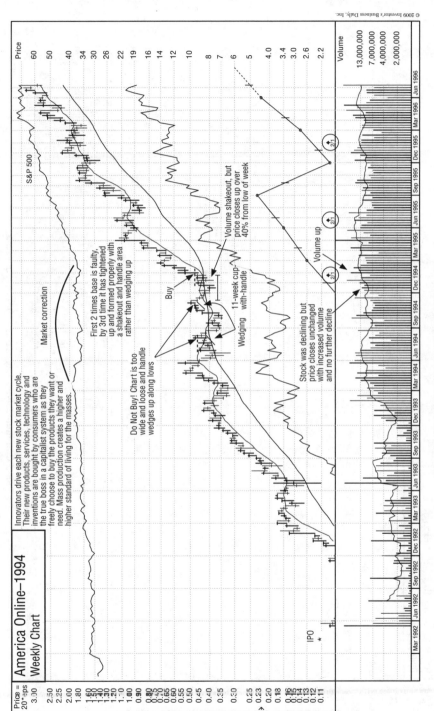

America Online—1994
Weekly Chart

Price = 20 x eps

Innovators drive each new stock market cycle. Their new products, services, technology and inventions are bought by consumers who are the true boss in a capitalist system as they freely choose to buy the products they want or need. Mass production creates a higher and higher standard of living for the masses.

Market correction

S&P 500

First 2 times base is faulty, by 3rd time it has tightened up and formed properly with a shakeout and handle area rather than wedging up

Do Not Buy! Chart is too wide and loose and handle wedges up along lows

Buy

Wedging

11-week cup-with-handle

Volume shakeout, but price closes up over 40% from low of week

Stock was declining but price closes unchanged with increased volume and no further decline

Volume up.

IPO

Volume

America Online increased 570% in 75 weeks.

© 2009 Investor's Business Daily, Inc.

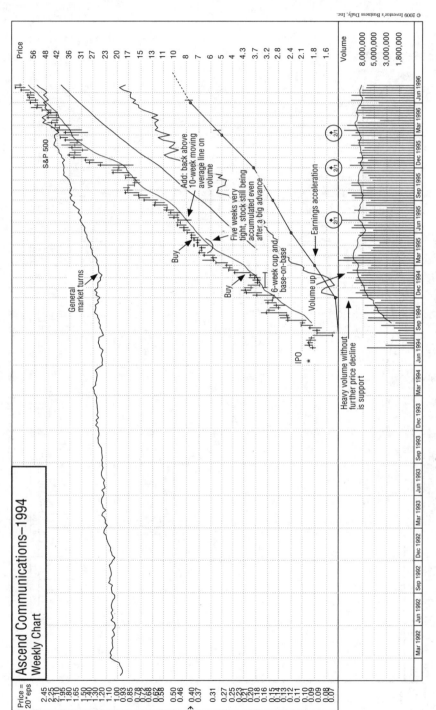

Ascend Communications increased 1384% in 75 weeks.

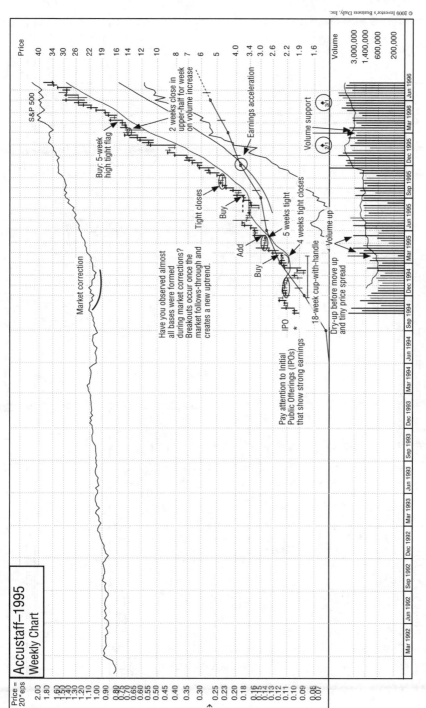

Accustaff—1995
Weekly Chart

Price =
20*eps

Price

40
34
30
26
22
19
16
14
12
10

8
7
6

5

4.0
3.4
3.0

2.6

2.2
1.9

1.6

S&P 500

Market correction

Have you observed almost
all bases were formed
during market corrections?
Breakouts occur once the
market follows-through and
creates a new uptrend.

Pay attention to Initial
Public Offerings (IPOs)
that show strong earnings

Buy: 5-week
high tight flag

2 weeks close in
upper-half for week
on volume increase

Earnings acceleration

Tight closes

Buy

Add

Buy

5 weeks tight

4 weeks tight closes

Volume support

IPO

*

18-week cup-with-handle

Dry-up before move up
and tiny price spread

Volume up

Volume

3,000,000
1,400,000
600,000

200,000

Accustaff increased 1359% in 68 weeks.

2.00
1.80
1.60
1.50
1.40
1.30
1.20
1.10
1.00
0.90
0.80
0.75
0.70
0.65
0.60
0.55
0.50
0.45
0.40
0.35
0.30
0.25
0.23
0.20
0.18
0.15
0.14
0.13
0.12
0.11
0.10
0.09
0.08
0.07

Mar 1992 | Jun 1992 | Sep 1992 | Dec 1992 | Mar 1993 | Jun 1993 | Sep 1993 | Dec 1993 | Mar 1994 | Jun 1994 | Sep 1994 | Dec 1994 | Mar 1995 | Jun 1995 | Sep 1995 | Dec 1995 | Mar 1996 | Jun 1996

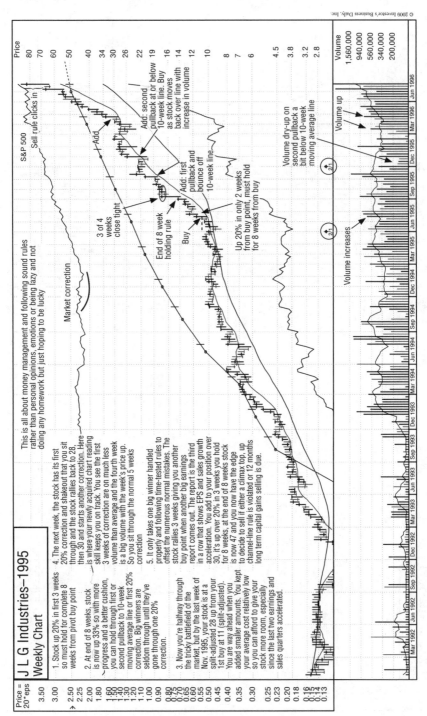

J L G Industries increased 670% in 53 weeks.

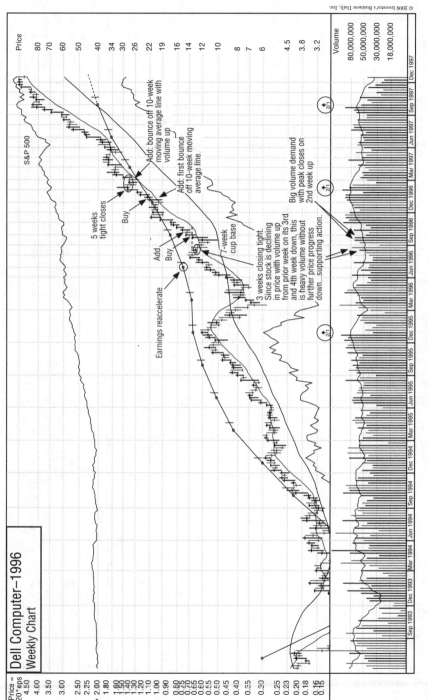

Dell Computer–1996
Weekly Chart

Price =
20*eps

S&P 500

Earnings reaccelerate

Buy

Add

Buy

5 weeks
tight closes

Add: first bounce
off 10-week moving
average line

Add: bounce off 10-week
moving average line with
volume up

7-week
cup base

3 weeks closing tight.
Since stock is declining
in price with volume up
from prior week on its 3rd
and 4th week down, this
is heavy volume without
further price progress
down...supporting action.

Big volume demand
with peak closes on
2nd week up

Volume

Dell Computer increased 587% in 61 weeks.

Price
80
70
60
50
40
34
30
26
22
19
16
14
12
10
8
7
6
4.5
3.8
3.2

80,000,000
50,000,000
30,000,000
18,000,000

4.50
4.00
3.50
3.00
2.50
2.25
2.00
1.80
1.60
1.50
1.40
1.30
1.20
1.10
1.00
0.90
0.80
0.70
0.65
0.60
0.55
0.50
0.45
0.40
0.35
0.30
0.25
0.23
0.20
0.18
0.16
0.15

Sep 1993 | Dec 1993 | Mar 1994 | Jun 1994 | Sep 1994 | Dec 1994 | Mar 1995 | Jun 1995 | Sep 1995 | Dec 1995 | Mar 1996 | Jun 1996 | Sep 1996 | Dec 1996 | Mar 1997 | Jun 1997 | Sep 1997 | Dec 1997

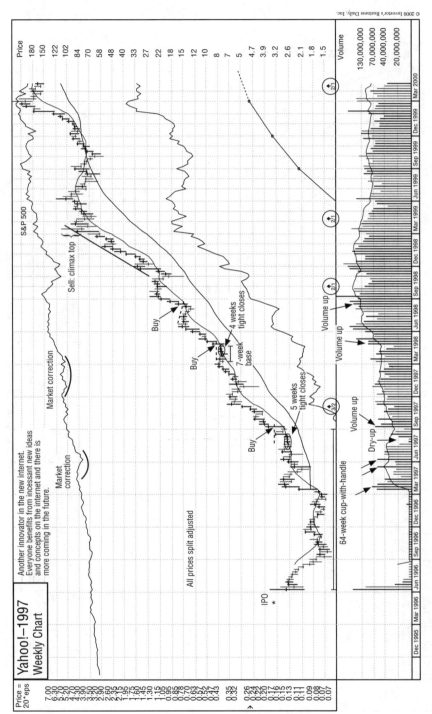

Yahoo!–1997
Weekly Chart

Price = 20 × eps

S&P 500

Another innovator in the new internet. Everyone benefits from incessant new ideas and concepts on the internet and there is more coming in the future.

Market correction

Market correction

Sell: climax top

All prices split adjusted

Buy

Buy

4 weeks tight closes

7-week base

5 weeks tight closes

Buy

64-week cup-with-handle

IPO

Volume up

Volume up

Volume up

Volume up

Dry-up

Price
180
150
122
102
84
70
58
48
40
33
27
22
18
15
12
10
8
7
5
4.7
3.9
3.2
2.6
2.1
1.8
1.5

7.00
6.30
5.20
4.70
3.90
3.30
3.00
2.60
2.35
2.15
1.95
1.75
1.60
1.45
1.30
1.15
0.95
0.78
0.70
0.63
0.52
0.47
0.43
0.35
0.26
0.24
0.22
0.20
0.16
0.15
0.13
0.11
0.09
0.08
0.07

Volume
130,000,000
70,000,000
40,000,000
20,000,000

Dec 1995 | Mar 1996 | Jun 1996 | Sep 1996 | Dec 1996 | Mar 1997 | Jun 1997 | Sep 1997 | Dec 1997 | Mar 1998 | Jun 1998 | Sep 1998 | Dec 1998 | Mar 1999 | Jun 1999 | Sep 1999 | Dec 1999 | Mar 2000

Yahoo! Increased 6723% in 130 weeks.

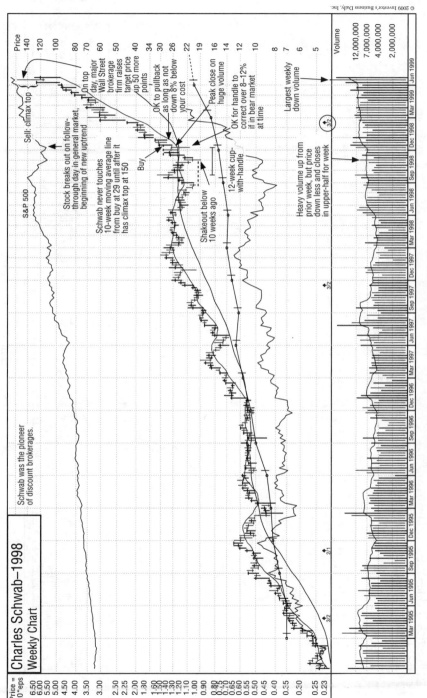

Charles Schwab increased 409% in 26 weeks.

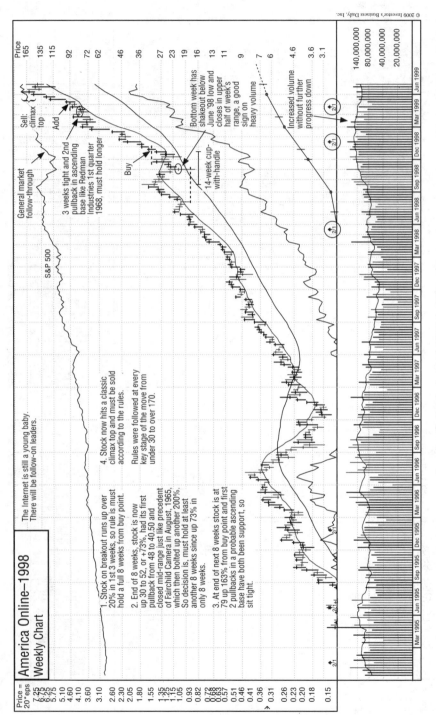

America Online–1998
Weekly Chart

Price = 20*eps

The Internet is still a young baby. There will be follow-on leaders.

General market follow-through

S&P 500

Sell: climax top

Add

3 weeks tight and 2nd pullback in ascending base like Redman Industries 1st quarter 1968; must hold longer

Buy

Bottom week has shakeout below June '98 low and closes in upper half of week's range, a good sign on heavy volume

14-week cup-with-handle

Increased volume without further progress down

1. Stock on breakout runs up over 20% in 1st 3 weeks, so rule is must hold a full 8 weeks from buy point.

2. End of 8 weeks, stock is now up 30 to 52, or +73%, had its first pullback from 48 to 40.50 and closed mid-range just like precedent of Fairchild Camera in August, 1965, which then bolted up another 200%. So decision is, must hold at least another 8 weeks since up 73% in only 8 weeks.

3. At end of next 8 weeks stock is at 79 up 163% from buy point and first 2 pullbacks in a probable ascending base have both been support, so sit tight.

4. Stock now hits a classic climax top and must be sold according to the rules.

Rules were followed at every key stage of the move from under 30 to over 170.

America Online increased 451% in 23 weeks.

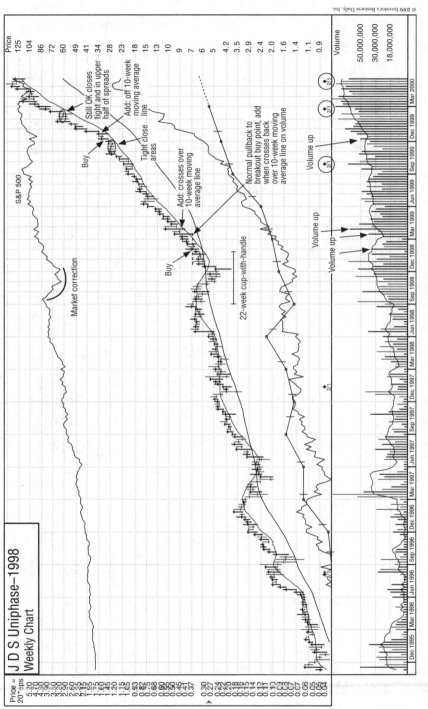

© 2009 Investor's Business Daily, Inc.

J D S Uniphase—1998
Weekly Chart

Price

Price	EPS
125	
104	
86	
72	
60	
49	
41	
34	
28	
23	
18	
15	
13	
10	
9	
7	
6	
5	
4.2	
3.5	
2.9	
2.4	
2.0	
1.6	
1.4	
1.1	
0.9	

Still OK closes
tight and in upper
half of spreads

Add: off 10-week
moving average
line

Buy

Tight close
areas

Add: crosses over
10-week moving
average line

Buy

22-week cup-with-handle

Normal pullback to
breakout buy point, add
when crosses back
over 10-week moving
average line on volume

Volume up

Volume up

Volume up

S&P 500

Market correction

Volume

50,000,000

30,000,000

18,000,000

J D S Uniphase increased 1946% in 66 weeks.

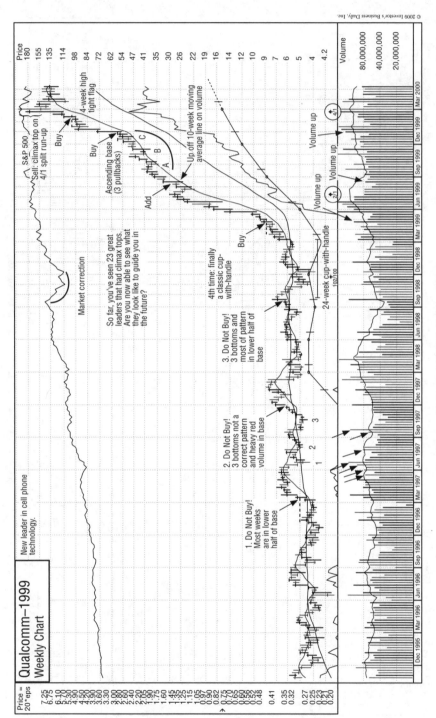

Qualcomm—1999
Weekly Chart

New leader in cell phone technology.

Price = 20*eps

S&P 500
Sell: climax top on 4/1 split run-up
Buy
4-week high tight flag
Buy
Ascending base (3 pullbacks)
Add
C
B
A
Up off 10-week moving average line on volume

Market correction

So far, you've seen 23 great leaders that had climax tops. Are you now able to see what they look like to guide you in the future?

4th time: finally a classic cup-with-handle
Buy
102/100
24-week cup-with-handle

3. Do Not Buy! 3 bottoms and most of pattern in lower half of base

2. Do Not Buy! 3 bottoms not a correct pattern and heavy red volume in base

1. Do Not Buy! Most weeks are in lower half of base

1
2
3

Volume up
Volume up
4/1
2/1
Volume up

Volume

Qualcomm increased 2091% in 45 weeks.

© 2009 Investor's Business Daily, Inc.

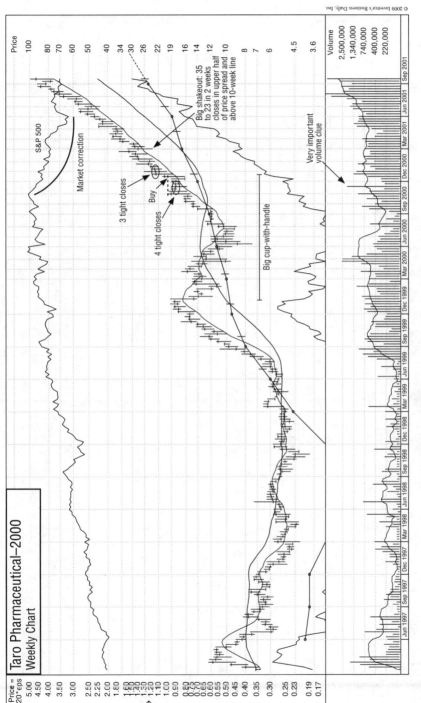

Taro Pharmaceutical–2000
Weekly Chart

Price =
20*eps

S&P 500

Market correction

3 tight closes

Buy

4 tight closes

Big cup-with-handle

Big shakeout: 35
to 23 in 2 weeks
closes in upper half
of price spread and
above 10-week line

Very important
volume clue

Taro Pharmaceuticals increased 382% in 39 weeks.

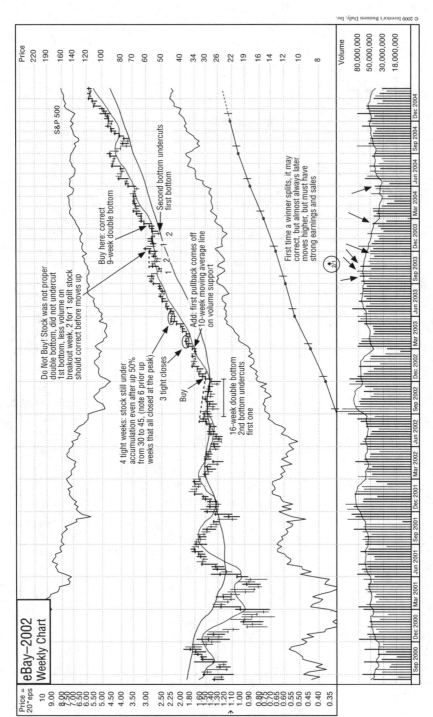

eBay–2002
Weekly Chart

Price = 20*eps

Do Not Buy! Stock was not proper double bottom, did not undercut 1st bottom, less volume on breakout week, 2 for 1 split stock should correct before moves up

Buy here: correct 9-week double bottom

Second bottom undercuts first bottom

4 tight weeks: stock still under accumulation even after up 50% from 30 to 45, (note 6 prior up weeks that all closed at the peak)

3 tight closes

Buy

Add: first pullback comes off 10-week moving average line on volume support

16-week double bottom 2nd bottom undercuts first one

First time a winner splits, it may correct, but almost always later moves higher, but must have strong earnings and sales

S&P 500

eBay increased 282% in 115 weeks.

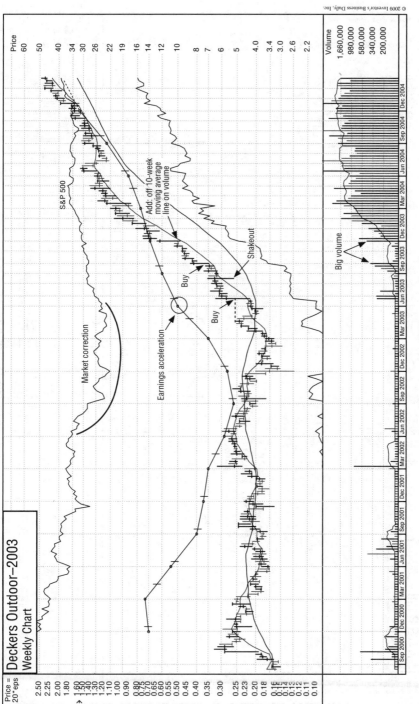

Deckers Outdoor increased 766% in 88 weeks.

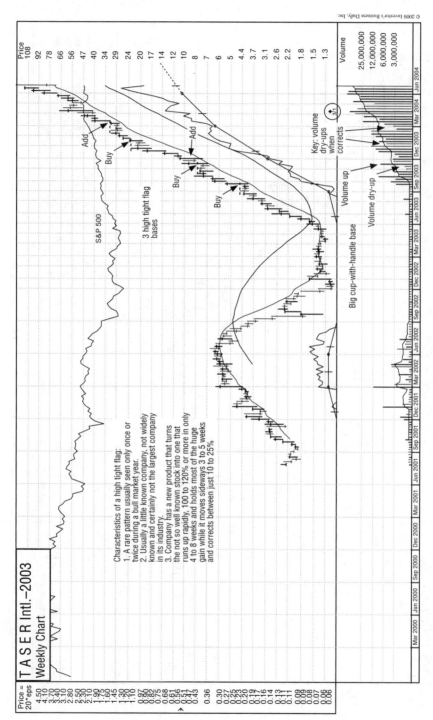

Price =
20*eps

Price
108
92
78
66
56
47
40
34
29
24
20
17
14
12
10
8
7
6
5
4.4
3.7
3.1
2.6
2.2
1.8
1.5
1.3

Volume
25,000,000
12,000,000
6,000,000
3,000,000

T A S E R Intl.–2003
Weekly Chart

S&P 500

Add

Buy

3 high tight flag
bases

Add

Buy

Buy

Characteristics of a high tight flag:
1. A rare pattern usually seen only once or
twice during a bull market year.
2. Usually a little known company, not widely
known and certainly not the largest company
in its industry.
3. Company has a new product that turns
the not so well known stock into one that
runs up rapidly, 100 to 120% or more in only
4 to 8 weeks and holds most of the huge
gain while it moves sideways 3 to 5 weeks
and corrects between just 10 to 25%

Big cup-with-handle base

Volume up

Volume dry-up

Key: volume
dry-ups
when
corrects

Mar 2000 | Jun 2000 | Sep 2000 | Dec 2000 | Mar 2001 | Jun 2001 | Sep 2001 | Dec 2001 | Mar 2002 | Jun 2002 | Sep 2002 | Dec 2002 | Mar 2003 | Jun 2003 | Sep 2003 | Dec 2003 | Mar 2004 | Jun 2004

T A S E R International increased 2228% in 39 weeks.

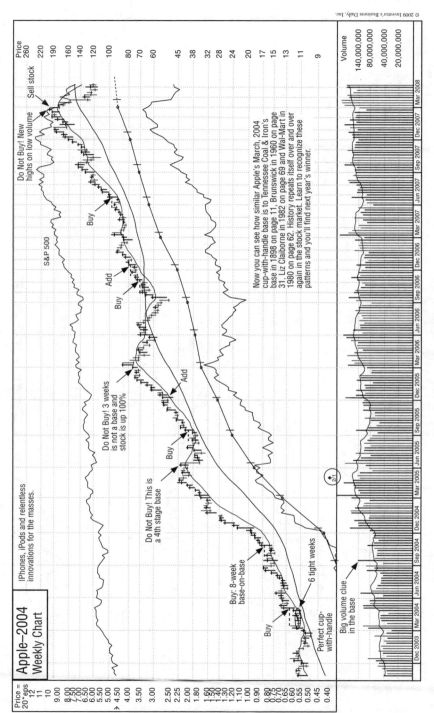

Apple increased 1418% in 199 weeks.

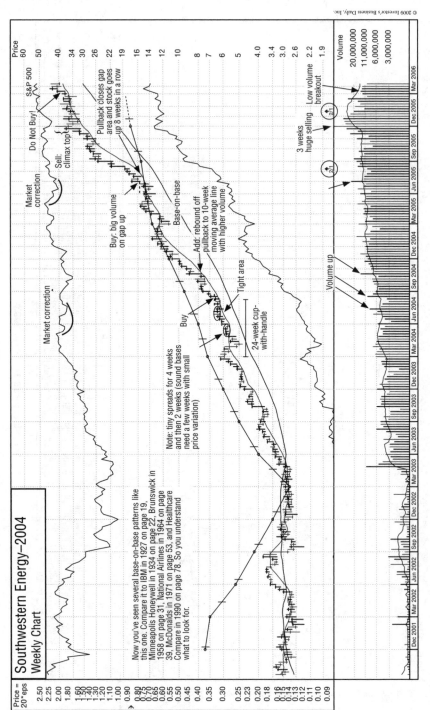

Southwestern Energy–2004
Weekly Chart

Now you've seen several base-on-base patterns like this one. Compare it to IBM in 1927 on page 19, Minneapolis Honeywell in 1934 on page 22, Brunswick in 1958 on page 31, National Airlines in 1964 on page 39, McDonalds in 1971 on page 53, and Healthcare Compare in 1990 on page 78. So you understand what to look for.

Market correction

Market correction

Do Not Buy!

S&P 500

Sell: climax top

Pullback closes gap area and stock goes up 8 weeks in a row

Buy: big volume on gap up

Base-on-base

Add: rebound off pullback to 10-week moving average line with higher volume

Tight area

Buy

24-week cup-with-handle

Note: tiny spreads for 4 weeks and then 2 weeks (sound bases need a few weeks with small price variation)

3 weeks huge selling

Low volume breakout

Volume up

Price = 20*eps

Price	Price
2.50	60
2.25	50
2.00	40
1.80	34
1.60	30
1.50	26
1.40	22
1.30	19
1.20	16
1.10	14
1.00	12
0.90	10
0.80	8
0.70	7
0.65	6
0.60	5
0.55	
0.50	
0.45	4.0
0.40	3.4
0.35	3.0
0.30	2.6
0.25	2.2
0.23	1.9
0.20	
0.18	
0.16	
0.15	
0.14	
0.13	
0.12	
0.11	
0.10	
0.09	

Volume
20,000,000
11,000,000
6,000,000
3,000,000

Dec 2001 · Mar 2002 · Jun 2002 · Sep 2002 · Dec 2002 · Mar 2003 · Jun 2003 · Sep 2003 · Dec 2003 · Mar 2004 · Jun 2004 · Sep 2004 · Dec 2004 · Mar 2005 · Jun 2005 · Sep 2005 · Dec 2005 · Mar 2006

Southwestern Energy increased 556% in 83 weeks.

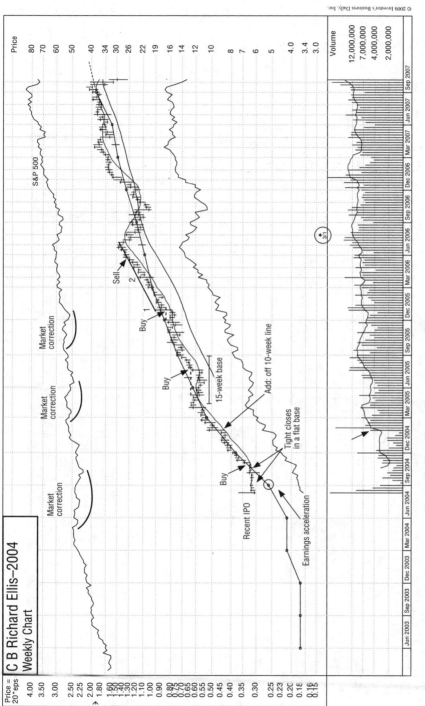

C B Richard Ellis Group increased 538% in 149 weeks.

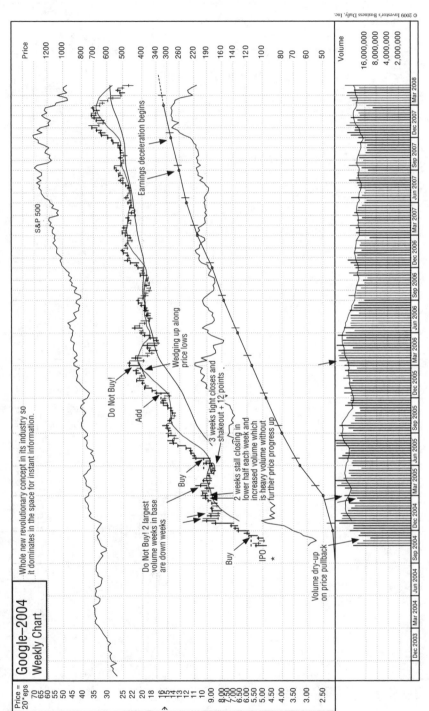

Google—2004 Weekly Chart

Whole new revolutionary concept in its industry so it dominates in the space for instant information.

Price = 20*eps

S&P 500

Earnings deceleration begins

Do Not Buy!

Add

Wedging up along price lows

3 weeks tight closes and shakeout + 12 points

Buy

Do Not Buy 2 largest volume weeks in base are down weeks

2 weeks stall closing in lower half each week and increased volume which is heavy volume without further price progress up

Buy

IPO

Volume dry-up on price pullback

Volume

Google increased 536% in 164 weeks.

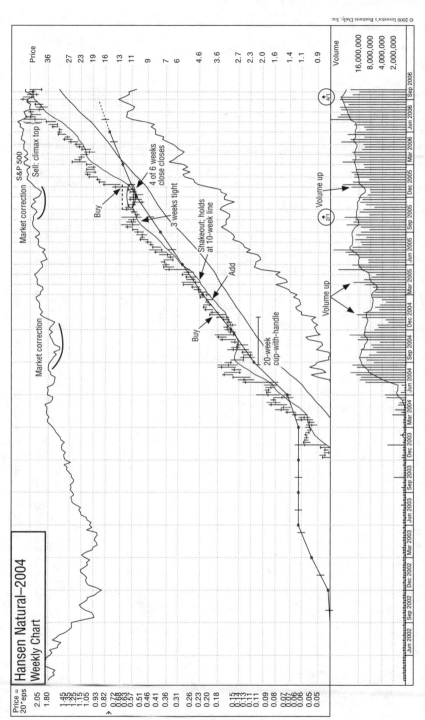

Hansen Natural increased 1219% in 86 weeks.

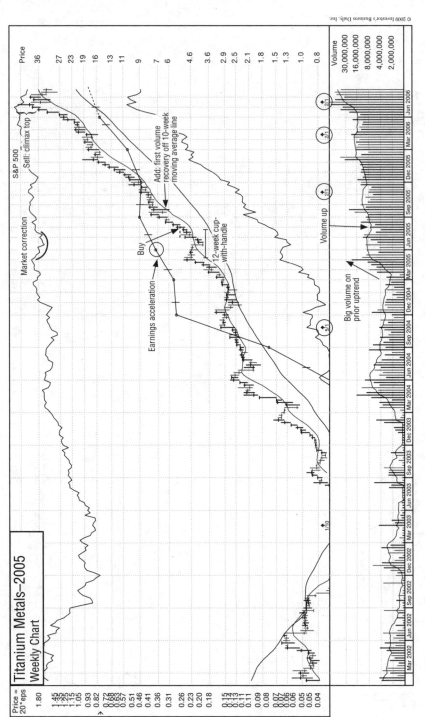

Titanium Metals–2005
Weekly Chart

Price =
20*eps

Titanium Metals increased 764% in 49 weeks.

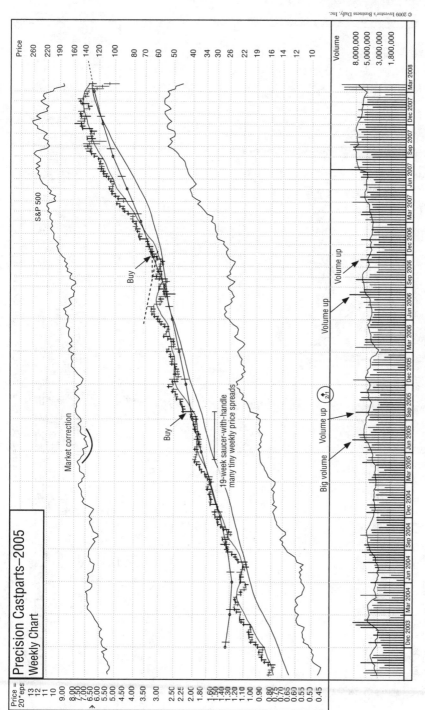

Precision Castparts–2005
Weekly Chart

Price =
20*eps

S&P 500

Market correction

Buy

Buy

19-week saucer-with-handle
many tiny weekly price spreads

Big volume   Volume up

Volume up

Volume up

Price

Volume

Precision Castparts increased 259% in 115 weeks.

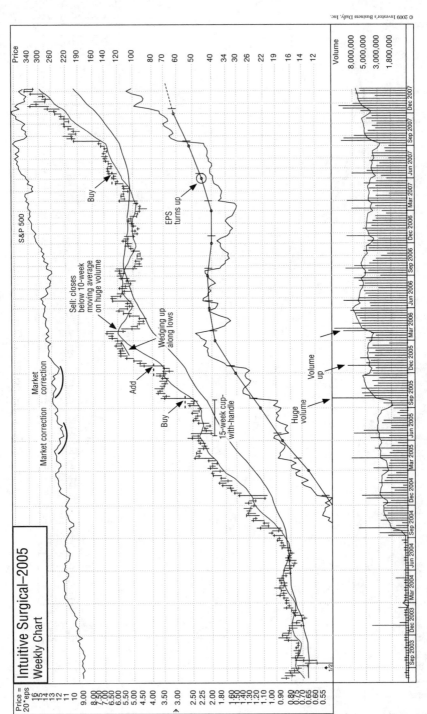

Intuitive Surgical increased 418% in 123 weeks.

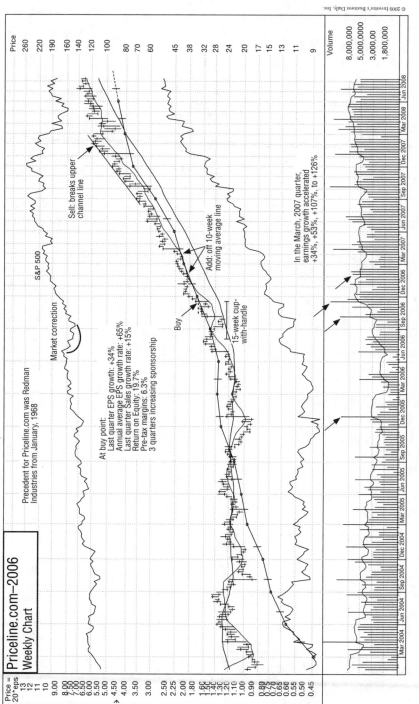

Priceline.com—2006
Weekly Chart

Price = 20 * eps

Precedent for Priceline.com was Redman
Industries from January, 1968

S&P 500

Market correction

Sell: breaks upper
channel line

At buy point:
Last quarter EPS growth: +34%
Annual average EPS growth rate: +65%
Last quarter Sales growth rate: +15%
Return on Equity: 19.7%
Pre-tax margins: 6.3%
3 quarters increasing sponsorship

Buy

Add: off 10-week
moving average line

15-week cup-
with-handle

In the March, 2007 quarter,
earnings growth accelerated
+34%, +53%, +107%, to +126%

Priceline.com increased 320% in 85 weeks.

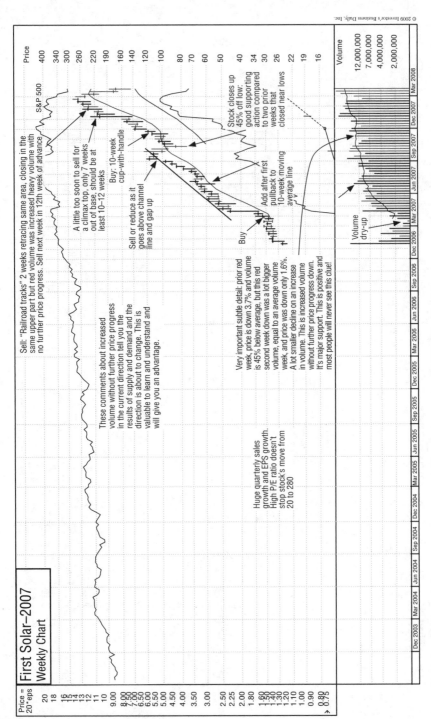

First Solar–2007
Weekly Chart

Price = 20*eps

Sell: "Railroad tracks" 2 weeks retracing same area, closing in the same upper part but red volume was increased heavy volume with no further price progress. Sell next week in 12th week of advance

A little too soon to sell for a climax top, only 7 weeks out of base, should be at least 10–12 weeks

Buy: 10-week cup-with-handle

Sell or reduce as it goes above channel line and gap up

Stock closes up 45% off low: good supporting action compared to two prior weeks that closed near lows

Add after first pullback to 10-week moving average line

Buy

These comments about increased volume without further price progress in the current direction tell you the results of supply and demand and the direction is about to change. This is valuable to learn and understand and will give you an advantage.

Very important subtle detail: prior red week, price is down 3.7% and volume is 45% below average, but this red second week down was a lot bigger volume, equal to an average volume week, and price was down only 1.6%. A lot smaller decline on an increase in volume. This is increased volume without further price progress down. It's major support. This is positive and most people will never see this clue!

Huge quarterly sales growth and EPS growth. High P/E ratio doesn't stop stock's move from 20 to 280

Volume dry-up

First Solar increased 807% in 47 weeks.

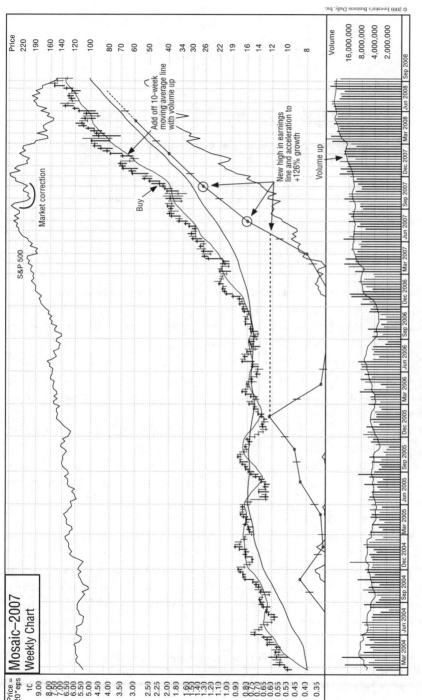

Mosaic increased 265% in 40 weeks.

How to Read Charts Like a Pro and Improve Your Selection and Timing

In the world of medicine, X-rays, MRIs, and brain scans are "pictures" that doctors study to help them diagnose what's going on in the human body. EKGs and ultrasound waves are recorded on paper or shown on TV-like monitors to illustrate what's happening to the human heart.

Similarly, maps are plotted and set to scale to help people understand exactly where they are and how to get to where they want to go. And seismic data are traced on charts to help geologists study which structures or patterns seem most likely to contain oil.

In almost every field, there are tools available to help people evaluate current conditions correctly and receive accurate information. The same is true in investing. Economic indicators are plotted on graphs to assist in their interpretation. A stock's price and volume history are recorded on charts to help investors determine whether the stock is strong, healthy, and under accumulation or whether it's weak and behaving abnormally.

Would you allow a doctor to open you up and perform heart surgery if he had not utilized the critical necessary tools? Of course not. That would be just plain irresponsible. However, many investors do exactly that when they buy and sell stocks without first consulting stock charts. Just as doctors would be irresponsible not to use X-rays, CAT scans, and EKGs on their patients, investors are just plain foolish if they don't learn to interpret the price and volume patterns found on stock charts. If nothing else, charts can tell you when a stock is not acting right and should be sold.

Individual investors can lose a lot of money if they don't know how to recognize when a stock tops and starts into a significant correction or if they have been depending on someone else who also doesn't know this.

Chart Reading Basics

A chart records the factual price performance of a stock. Price changes are the result of daily supply and demand in the largest auction marketplace in the world. Investors who train themselves to decode price movements on charts have an enormous advantage over those who either refuse to learn, just don't know any better, or are a bit lazy.

Would you fly in a plane without instruments or take a long cross-country trip in your car without a road map? Charts are your investment road map. In fact, the distinguished economists Milton and Rose Friedman devoted the first 28 pages of their excellent book *Free to Choose* to the power of market facts and the unique ability of prices to provide important and accurate information to decision makers.

Chart patterns, or "bases," are simply areas of price correction and consolidation after an earlier price advance. Most of them (80% to 90%) are created and formed as a result of corrections in the general market. The skill you need to learn in order to analyze these bases is how to diagnose whether the price and volume movements are normal or abnormal. Do they signal strength or weakness?

Major advances occur off strong, recognizable price patterns (discussed later in this chapter). Failures can always be traced to bases that are faulty or too obvious to the typical investor.

Fortunes are made every year by those who take the time to learn to interpret charts properly. Professionals who don't make use of charts are confessing their ignorance of highly valuable measurement and timing mechanisms. To further emphasize this point: I have seen many high-level investment professionals ultimately lose their jobs as a result of weak performance.

When this happens, their poor records are often a direct result of not knowing very much about market action and chart reading. Universities that teach finance or investment courses and dismiss charts as irrelevant or unimportant are demonstrating their complete lack of knowledge and understanding of how the market really works and how the best professionals operate.

As an individual investor, you too need to study and benefit from stock charts. It's not enough to buy a stock simply because it has good fundamental characteristics, like strong earnings and sales. In fact, no *Investor's Business Daily*® reader should ever buy a stock based solely on IBD's proprietary *SmartSelect*® Ratings. A stock's chart must always be checked to determine whether the stock is in a proper position to buy, or whether it is the stock of a sound, leading company but is too far extended in price above a solid basing area and thus should temporarily be avoided.

As the number of investors in the market has increased over recent years, simple price and volume charts have become more readily available. (*Investor's Business Daily* subscribers have free access to 10,000 daily and weekly charts on the Web at Investors.com.) Chart books and online chart services can help you follow hundreds and even thousands of stocks in a highly organized, time-saving way. Some are more advanced than others, offering both fundamental and technical data in addition to price and volume movement. Subscribe to one of the better chart services, and you'll have at your fingertips valuable information that is not easily available elsewhere.

History Repeats Itself: Learn to Use Historical Precedents

As mentioned in the introduction, and as shown on the annotated charts of history's best winners in Chapter 1, our system for selecting winning stocks is based on how the market actually operates, not on my or anyone else's personal opinions or academic theories. We analyzed the greatest winning stocks of the past and discovered they all had seven common characteristics, which can be summarized in the two easy-to-remember words CAN SLIM. We also discovered there were a number of successful price patterns and consolidation structures that repeated themselves over and over again. In the stock market, history repeats itself. This is because human nature doesn't change. Neither does the law of supply and demand. Price patterns of the great stocks of the past can clearly serve as models for your future selections. There are several price patterns you'll want to look for when you're analyzing a stock for purchase. I'll also go over some signals to watch out for that indicate that a price pattern may be faulty and unsound.

The Most Common Chart Pattern: "Cup with Handle"

One of the most important price patterns looks like a cup with a handle when the outline of the cup is viewed from the side. Cup patterns can last from 7 weeks to as long as 65 weeks, but most of them last for three to six months. The usual correction from the absolute peak (the top of the cup) to the low point (the bottom of the cup) of this price pattern varies from around the 12% to 15% range to upwards of 33%. A strong price pattern of any type should always have a clear and definite price uptrend prior to the beginning of its base pattern. You should look for at least a 30% increase in price in the prior uptrend, together with improving relative strength and a very substantial increase in trading volume at some points in the prior uptrend.

In most, but not all, cases, the bottom part of the cup should be rounded and give the appearance of a "U" rather than a very narrow "V." This char-

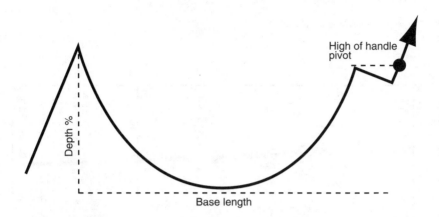

acteristic allows the stock time to proceed through a needed natural correction, with two or three final little weak spells around the lows of the cup. The "U" area is important because it scares out or wears out the remaining weak holders and takes other speculators' attention away from the stock. A more solid foundation of strong owners who are much less apt to sell during the next advance is thereby established. The accompanying chart from Daily Graphs Online® shows the daily price and volume movements for Apple Computer in February 2004.

It's normal for growth stocks to create cup patterns during intermediate declines in the general market and to correct 1½ to 2½ times the market averages. Your best choices are generally stocks with base patterns that deteriorate the least during an intermediate market decline. Whether you're in a bull market or a bear market, stock downturns that exceed 2½ times the market averages are usually too wide and loose and must be regarded with suspicion. Dozens of former high-tech leaders, such as JDS Uniphase, formed wide, loose, and deep cup patterns in the second and third quarters of 2000. These were almost all faulty, failure-prone patterns signaling that the stocks should have been avoided when they attempted to break out to new highs.

A few volatile leaders can plunge 40% or 50% in a bull market. Chart patterns correcting more than this during bull markets have a higher failure rate if they try to make new highs and resume their advance. The reason? A downswing of over 50% from a peak to a low means a stock must increase more than 100% from its low to get back to its high. Historical research shows stocks that make new price highs after such huge moves tend to fail 5% to 15% beyond their breakout prices. Stocks that come straight off the bottom into new highs off cups can be more risky because they had no pullbacks. Deep 50% to 75% cup-with-handle bases worked in 2009 since they were made by a 58% drop in the S&P 500.

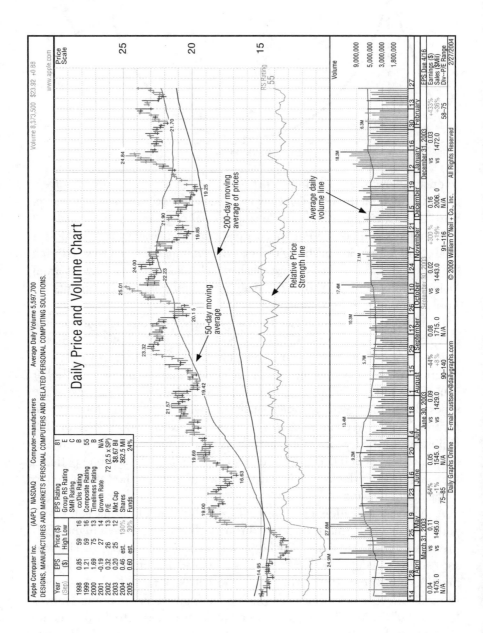

Daily Price and Volume Chart

Sea Containers was a glowing exception. It descended about 50% during an intermediate decline in the 1975 bull market. It then formed a perfectly shaped cup-with-handle price structure and proceeded to increase 554% in

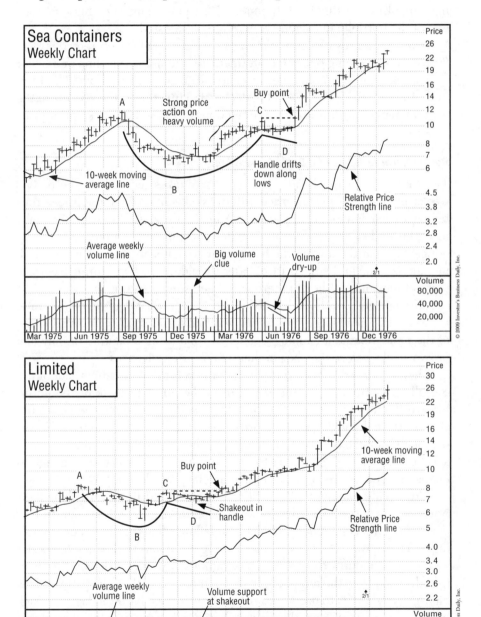

the next 101 weeks. This stock, with its 54% earnings growth rate and its latest quarterly results up 192%, was one of several classic cup-with-handle stocks that I presented to Fidelity Research & Management in Boston during a monthly meeting in early June 1975. Upon seeing such big numbers, one of the portfolio managers was instantly interested.

As you can see by this example, some patterns that have corrected 50% to 60% or more coming out of an intermediate bull market decline or a major bear market can succeed. (See the charts for Sea Containers and The Limited.) In most cases, the percent of decline is a function of the severity of the general market decline and the tremendous extent of the stock's prior price run-up.

Basic Characteristics of a Cup's Handle Area

The formation of the handle area generally takes more than one or two weeks and has a downward price drift or "shakeout" (where the price drops below a prior low point in the handle made a few weeks earlier), usually near the end of its down-drifting price movement. Volume may dry up noticeably near the lows in the handle's price pullback phase. During a bull market, volume in the majority of cases should not pick up during a correction in the handle, although there have been some exceptions.

Although cups without handles have a somewhat higher failure rate, many stocks can advance successfully without forming a handle. Also, some of the more volatile technology names in 1999 formed handles of only one or two weeks before they began their major price advances.

When handles do occur, they almost always form in the upper half of the overall base structure, as measured from the absolute peak of the entire base to the absolute low of the cup. The handle should also be above the stock's 10-week moving average price line. Handles that form in the lower half of an overall base or completely below the stock's 10-week line are weak and failure-prone. Demand up to that point has not been strong enough to enable the stock to recover more than half its prior decline.

Additionally, handles that consistently wedge up (drift upward along their price lows or just go straight sideways along their lows rather than drifting down) have a much higher probability of failing when they break out to new highs. This upward-wedging behavior along low points in the handle doesn't let the stock undergo the needed shakeout or sharp price pullback after having advanced from the low of the base into the upper half of the pattern. This high-risk trait tends to occur in third- or fourth-stage bases, in laggard stock bases, or in very active market leaders that become too widely followed and therefore too obvious. You should beware of wedging handles.

A price drop in a proper handle should be contained within 8% to 12% of its peak during bull markets unless the stock forms a very large cup, as in the rather unusual case of Sea Containers in 1975. Downturns in handles that exceed this percentage during bull markets look wide and erratic and in most cases are improper and risky. However, if you're in the last shake-out area of a bear market bottom, the unusual general market weakness will cause some handle areas to quickly decline around 20% to 30%, but the price pattern can still be sound if the general market then follows through on the upside, creating a new major uptrend. (See Chapter 9, "M = Market Direction: How You Can Determine It.")

Constructive Patterns Have Tight Price Areas

There should also be at least some tight areas in the price patterns of stocks under accumulation. On a weekly chart, tightness is defined as small price variations from high to low for the week, with several consecutive weeks' prices closing unchanged or remarkably near the previous week's close. If the base pattern has a wide spread between the week's high and low points every week, it's been constantly in the market's eye and frequently will not succeed when it breaks out. However, amateur chartists typically will not notice the difference, and the stock can run up 5% to 15%, drawing in less-discriminating traders, before it breaks badly and fails.

Find Pivot Points and Watch "Volume Percent Change"

When a stock forms a proper cup-with-handle chart pattern and then charges through an upside buy point, which Jesse Livermore referred to as the "pivot point" or "line of least resistance," the day's volume should increase at least 40% to 50% above normal. During major breakouts, it's not uncommon for new market leaders to show volume spikes 200%, 500%, or 1,000% greater than the average daily volume. In almost all cases, it's professional institutional buying that causes the big, above-average volume increases in the better-priced, better-quality growth-oriented stocks at pivot breakouts. A full 95% of the general public is usually afraid to buy at such points because it's scary and it seems risky and rather absurd to buy stocks at their highest prices.

Your objective isn't to buy at the cheapest price or near the low, but to begin buying at exactly the right time, when your chances for success are greatest. This means that you have to learn to wait for a stock to move up and trade at your buy point before you make an initial commitment. If you work and cannot watch the market constantly, small quote devices or quotes available on cell phones and Web sites will help you stay on top of potential breakout points.

The winning individual investor waits to buy at these precise pivot points. This is where the real move generally starts and all the exciting action begins. If you try to buy before this point, you may be premature. In many cases the stock will never get to its breakout point, but rather will stall or actually decrease in price. You want a stock to prove its strength to you before you invest in it. Also, if you buy at more than 5% to 10% past the precise buy point, you are buying late and will more than likely get caught in the next price correction. Your automatic 8% loss-cutting rule (see Chapter 10, "When You Must Sell and Cut Every Loss . . . Without Exception") will then force you to sell because the stock was extended in price and didn't have enough room to go through a perfectly normal sharp but minor correction. So don't get into the bad habit of chasing stocks up too high.

Pivot buy points in correct chart base patterns are not typically based on a stock's old high price. Most of them occur at 5% to 10% below the prior peak. The peak price in the handle area is what determines most buy points, and this is almost always somewhat below the base's actual high. This is very important to remember. If you wait for an actual new high price, you will often buy too late. Sometimes you can get a slight head start by drawing a downtrend line from the overall pattern's absolute peak downward across the peak where the stock begins building the handle. Then begin your purchase when the trend line is broken on the upside a few weeks later. However, you have to be right in your chart and stock analysis to get away with this.

Look for Volume Dry-Ups Near the Lows of a Price Pattern

Nearly all proper bases will show a dramatic drying up of volume for one or two weeks along the very low of the base pattern and in the low area or few last weeks of the handle. This means that all of the selling has been exhausted and there is very little stock coming into the marketplace. Healthy stocks that are under accumulation almost always show this symptom. The combination of tightness in prices (daily or weekly price closes being very near each other) and dried-up volume at key points is generally quite constructive.

Big Volume Clues Are Valuable

Another clue that is valuable to the trained chart specialist is the occurrence of big daily and weekly volume spikes. Microsoft is an example of an outstanding stock that flashed heavy accumulation just before a huge run-up.

Weeks of advancing prices on heavy volume, followed in other weeks by extreme volume dry-ups, are also a very constructive sign. If you use a Daily

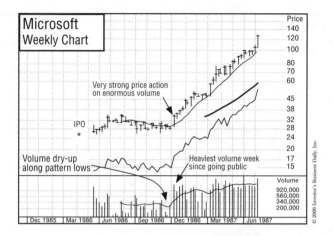

Graphs Online chart service in conjunction with the weekly graphs, you'll be able to see unusual trading activity that sometimes happens on only one day. The day Microsoft broke out at its 31½ buy point, its volume was 545% above average, signaling really important institutional buying. It then had a 13-year bull run from a split-adjusted 10 cents to $53.98. How's that for a big percentage move?

Volume is a remarkable subject that is worthy of careful study. It can help you recognize whether a stock is under accumulation (institutional buying) or distribution (institutional selling). Once you acquire this skill, you won't have to rely on the personal opinions of analysts and supposed experts. Big volume at certain key points is indispensable.

Volume is your best measure of supply and demand and institutional sponsorship—two vital ingredients in successful stock analysis. Learn how to use charts to time your purchases correctly. Making buys at the wrong time or, worse, buying stocks that are not under accumulation or that have unsound, faulty price patterns is simply too costly.

The next time you consider buying a stock, check its weekly volume. It's usually a constructive sign when the number of weeks that the stock closes up in price on above-average weekly volume outnumbers the number of weeks that it closes down in price on above-average volume while still in its chart base.

A Few Normal-Size Cups with Handles

Texas Instruments, Apple, General Cable, and Precision Castparts were all similar-size patterns in length and depth. Can you recognize the similarity between Apple and Precision Castparts? As you learn to do this with greater skill, you will in the future be able to spot many cups with handles just like these past winners.

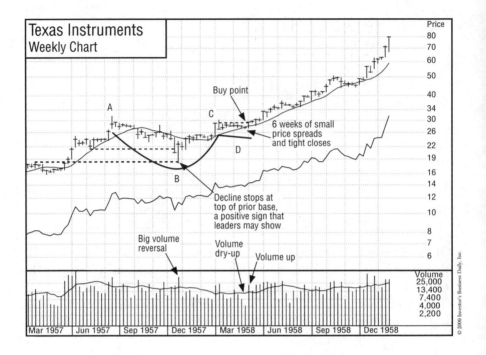

Texas Instruments
Weekly Chart

Buy point

6 weeks of small
price spreads
and tight closes

Decline stops at
top of prior base,
a positive sign that
leaders may show

Big volume
reversal

Volume
dry-up

Volume up

© 2009 Investor's Business Daily, Inc.

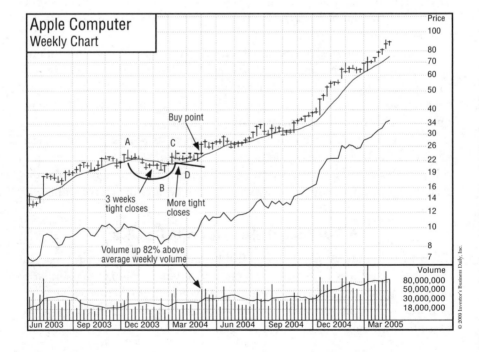

Apple Computer
Weekly Chart

Buy point

3 weeks
tight closes

More tight
closes

Volume up 82% above
average weekly volume

© 2009 Investor's Business Daily, Inc.

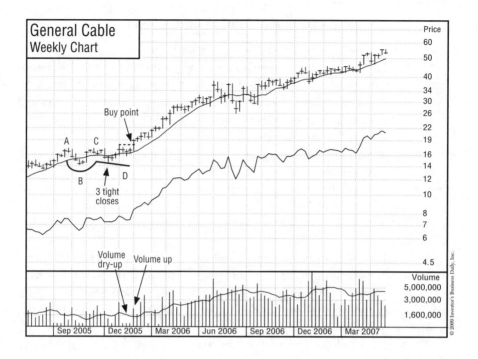

General Cable
Weekly Chart

Price
60
50
40
34
30
26
22
19
16
14
12
10
8
7
6
4.5

Buy point

A   C

B   D

3 tight
closes

Volume
dry-up   Volume up

Volume
5,000,000
3,000,000
1,600,000

Sep 2005 Dec 2005 Mar 2006 Jun 2006 Sep 2006 Dec 2006 Mar 2007

© 2009 Investor's Business Daily, Inc.

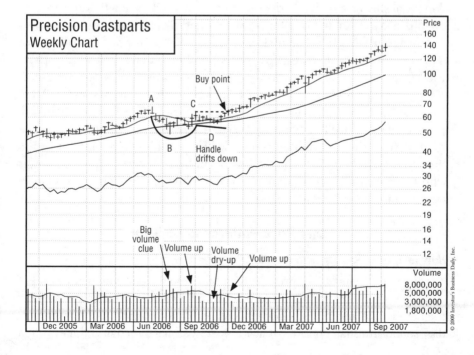

Precision Castparts
Weekly Chart

Price
160
140
120
100
80
70
60
50
40
34
30
26
22
19
16
14
12

Buy point

A

C

B   D

Handle
drifts down

Big
volume
clue   Volume up   Volume
dry-up   Volume up

Volume
8,000,000
5,000,000
3,000,000
1,800,000

Dec 2005 Mar 2006 Jun 2006 Sep 2006 Dec 2006 Mar 2007 Jun 2007 Sep 2007

© 2009 Investor's Business Daily, Inc.

The Value of Market Corrections

Since 80% to 90% of price patterns are created during market corrections, you should never get discouraged and give up on the stock market's potential during intermediate-term sell-offs or short or prolonged bear markets. America always comes back because of its inventors and entrepreneurs and the total freedom and unlimited opportunity that do not exist in communist or dictator-controlled countries.

Bear markets can last as little as three, six, or nine months or as long as two or, in very rare cases, three years. If you follow the sell rules in this book carefully, you will sell and nail down most of your profits, cut short any losses, raise significant cash, and move off margin (borrowed money) in the early stages of each new bear market (see the success stories at the end of the book).

In fact, *Investor's Business Daily* conducted four surveys in late 2008 that indicated that about 60% of IBD subscribers used our rules to sell and raise cash in December 2007 or June 2008 and thereby preserved most of their capital prior to the more serious decline in late 2008 that resulted from the subprime loan debacle.

Even if you sell out completely and move to cash, you never want to throw in the towel on stock investing because bear markets create new bases in new stocks, some of which could be the next cycle's 1,000% winners. You don't foolishly give up while the greatest opportunities of a lifetime are setting up and may sooner or later be just around the corner.

A bear market is the time to do a postanalysis of your prior decisions. Plot on daily or weekly charts exactly where you bought and sold all the stocks you traded in the past year. Study your decisions and write out some new rules that will let you avoid the mistakes you made in the past cycle. Then study several of the biggest winners that you missed or mishandled. Develop some rules to make sure that you buy the real leaders and handle them right in the next bull market cycle. They will be there, and this is the time to be watching for them as they begin to form bases. The question is whether *you* will be there with a carefully thought-through game plan to totally capitalize on them.

Other Price Patterns to Look For

How to Spot a "Saucer-with-Handle" Price Pattern

A "saucer with handle" is a price pattern similar to the cup with handle except that the saucer part tends to stretch out over a longer period of time, making the pattern shallower. (If the names "cup with handle" and "saucer with handle" sound unusual, consider that for years you have recognized and called

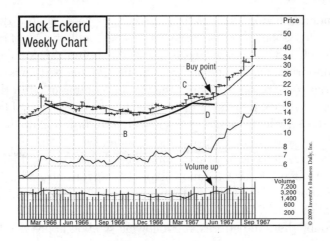

certain constellations of stars the "Big Dipper" and the "Little Dipper.") Jack Eckerd in April 1967 was an example of the saucer-with-handle base.

Recognizing a "Double-Bottom" Price Pattern

A "double-bottom" price pattern looks like the letter "W." This pattern also doesn't occur quite as often as the cup with handle, but it still occurs frequently. It is usually important that the second bottom of the W match the price level (low) of the first bottom or, as in almost all cases, clearly undercut it by one or two points, thereby creating a shakeout of weaker investors. Fail-

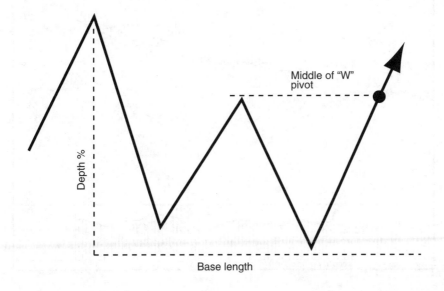

ure to undercut may create a faulty, more failure-prone "almost" double bottom. Double bottoms may also have handles, although this is not essential.

The depth and horizontal length of a double bottom are similar to those of the cup formation. The pivot buy point in a double bottom is located on the top right side of the W, where the stock is coming up after the second leg down. The pivot point should be equal in price to the top of the middle peak of the W, which should stop somewhere a little below the pattern's peak price. If the double bottom has a handle, then the peak price of the handle determines the pivot buy point. See the accompanying charts for Dome Petroleum, Price Co., and Cisco Systems for outstanding examples of double-bottom price patterns found during 1977, 1982, and 1990. Some later examples are EMC, NVR, and eBay.

For double-bottom patterns, the following symbols apply: A = beginning of base; B = bottom of first leg; C = middle of W that sets the buy point; D = bottom of second leg. If the double-bottom pattern has a handle, then E = top of the handle (sets the price of the buy point that occurs several weeks later) and F = bottom of the handle.

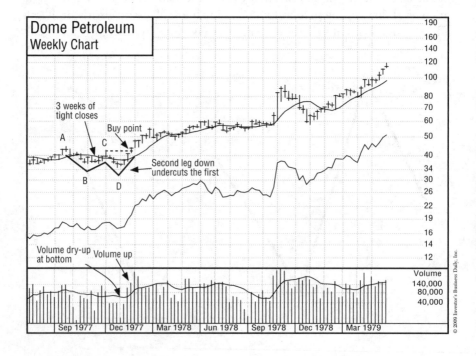

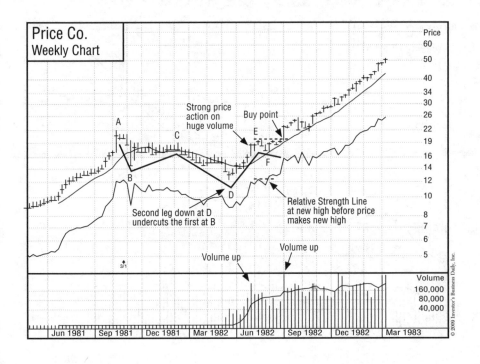

Price Co.
Weekly Chart

Strong price action on huge volume

Buy point

Second leg down at D undercuts the first at B

Relative Strength Line at new high before price makes new high

Volume up

Volume up

Price
60
50
40
34
30
26
22
19
16
14
12
10
8
7
6
5

Volume
160,000
80,000
40,000

Jun 1981 | Sep 1981 | Dec 1981 | Mar 1982 | Jun 1982 | Sep 1982 | Dec 1982 | Mar 1983

© 2009 Investor's Business Daily, Inc.

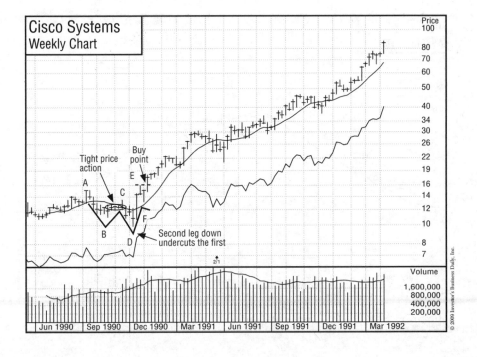

Cisco Systems
Weekly Chart

Tight price action

Buy point

Second leg down undercuts the first

Price
100
80
70
60
50
40
34
30
26
22
19
16
14
12
10
8
7

Volume
1,600,000
800,000
400,000
200,000

Jun 1990 | Sep 1990 | Dec 1990 | Mar 1991 | Jun 1991 | Sep 1991 | Dec 1991 | Mar 1992

© 2009 Investor's Business Daily, Inc.

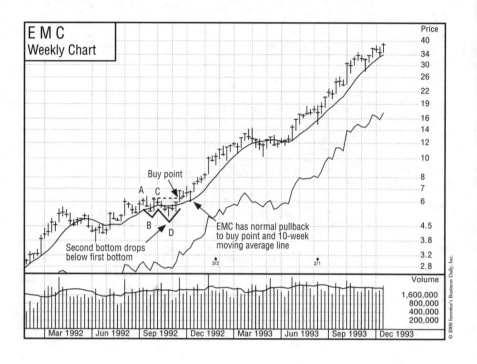

EMC
Weekly Chart

Buy point

A C

B

D

Second bottom drops
below first bottom

EMC has normal pullback
to buy point and 10-week
moving average line

Price
40
34
30
26
22
19
16
14
12
10
8
7
6
4.5
3.8
3.2
2.8

Volume
1,600,000
800,000
400,000
200,000

Mar 1992 | Jun 1992 | Sep 1992 | Dec 1992 | Mar 1993 | Jun 1993 | Sep 1993 | Dec 1993

© 2009 Investor's Business Daily, Inc.

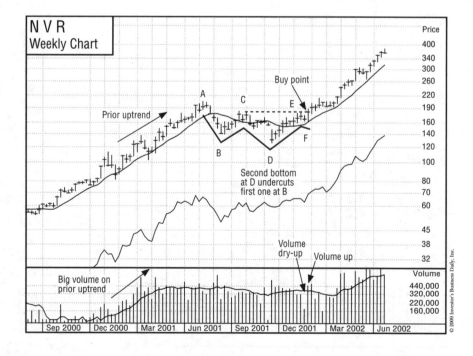

NVR
Weekly Chart

Prior uptrend

A

B

C

D

E

F

Buy point

Second bottom
at D undercuts
first one at B

Volume
dry-up

Volume up

Big volume on
prior uptrend

Price
400
340
300
260
220
190
160
140
120
100
80
70
60
45
38
32

Volume
440,000
320,000
220,000
160,000

Sep 2000 | Dec 2000 | Mar 2001 | Jun 2001 | Sep 2001 | Dec 2001 | Mar 2002 | Jun 2002

© 2009 Investor's Business Daily, Inc.

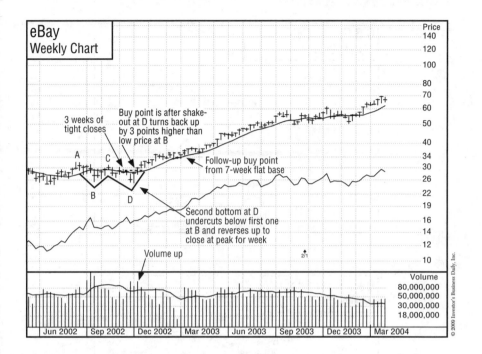

eBay
Weekly Chart

3 weeks of tight closes

Buy point is after shake-out at D turns back up by 3 points higher than low price at B

A

C

Follow-up buy point from 7-week flat base

B

D

Second bottom at D undercuts below first one at B and reverses up to close at peak for week

Volume up

Volume

© 2009 Investor's Business Daily, Inc.

Jun 2002 | Sep 2002 | Dec 2002 | Mar 2003 | Jun 2003 | Sep 2003 | Dec 2003 | Mar 2004

Definition of a "Flat-Base" Price Structure

A flat base is another rewarding price structure. It is usually a second-stage base that occurs after a stock has advanced 20% or more off a cup with handle, saucer with handle, or double bottom. The flat base moves straight sideways in a fairly tight price range for at least five or six weeks, and it does not correct more than 10% to 15%. Standard Oil of Ohio in May 1979, Smith-Kline in March 1978, and Dollar General in 1982 are good examples of flat

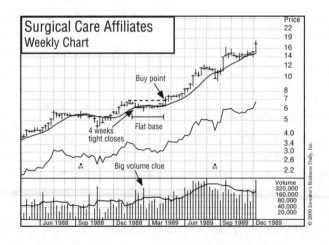

Surgical Care Affiliates
Weekly Chart

Buy point

4 weeks tight closes

Flat base

Big volume clue

Volume

© 2009 Investor's Business Daily, Inc.

Jun 1988 | Sep 1988 | Dec 1988 | Mar 1989 | Jun 1989 | Sep 1989 | Dec 1989

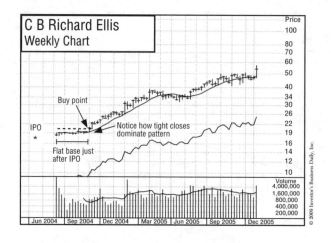

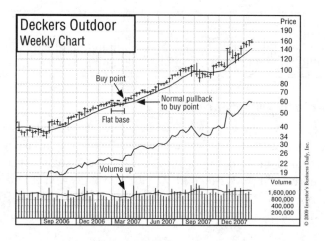

bases. Pep Boys in March 1981 formed a longer flat base. If you miss a stock's initial breakout from a cup with handle, you should keep your eye on it. In time it may form a flat base and give you a second opportunity to get on board. Here are a few more recent examples: Surgical Care Affiliates, CB Richard Ellis, and Deckers Outdoor.

Here's a New Base We've Dubbed a Square Box

After moving up from a cup with handle or double bottom, this formation typically lasts four to seven weeks; doesn't correct too much, usually 10% to 15%; and has a square, boxy look. I've noted this over recent years, but finally we've studied, measured, and classified it. Here are some examples: Lorillard, Korvette, Texas Instruments, Home Depot, Dell, and Taro. The dashed line shows the buy point.

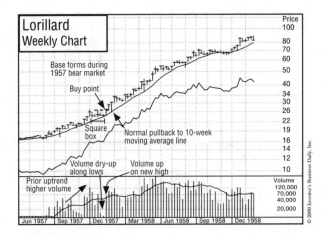

Lorillard
Weekly Chart

Base forms during 1957 bear market

Buy point

Square box

Normal pullback to 10-week moving average line

Volume dry-up along lows

Volume up on new high

Prior uptrend higher volume

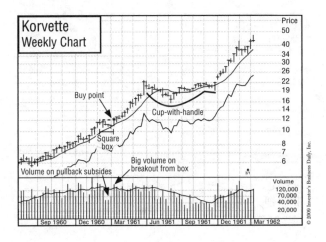

Korvette
Weekly Chart

Buy point

Cup-with-handle

Square box

Volume on pullback subsides

Big volume on breakout from box

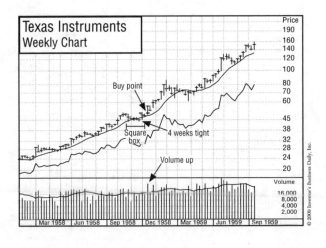

Texas Instruments
Weekly Chart

Buy point

Square box

4 weeks tight

Volume up

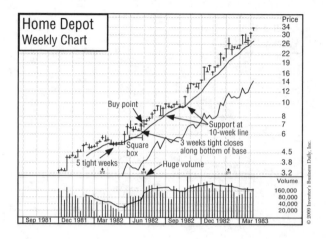

Home Depot
Weekly Chart

Buy point

Support at
10-week line

Square
box

3 weeks tight closes
along bottom of base

5 tight weeks

Huge volume

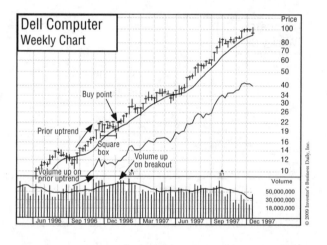

Dell Computer
Weekly Chart

Buy point

Prior uptrend

Square
box

Volume up
on breakout

Volume up on
prior uptrend

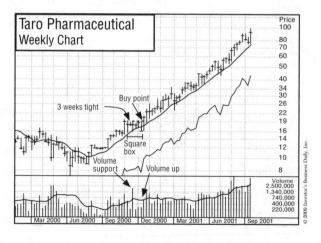

Taro Pharmaceutical
Weekly Chart

3 weeks tight

Buy point

Square
box

Volume
support

Volume up

High, Tight Flags Are Rare

A "high, tight flag" price pattern is rare, occurring in no more than a few stocks during a bull market. It begins with the stock moving generally 100% to 120% in a very short period of time (four to eight weeks). It then corrects sideways no more than 10% to 25%, usually in three, four, or five weeks.

This is the strongest of patterns, but it's also very risky and difficult to interpret correctly. Many stocks can skyrocket 200% or more off this formation. (See the charts for Bethlehem Steel, May 1915; American Chain & Cable, October 1935; E. L. Bruce, June 1958; Zenith, October 1958; Universal Controls, November 1958; Certain-teed, January 1961; Syntex, July 1963; Rollins, July 1964; Simmonds Precision, November 1965; Accustaff, January 1995; Emulex, October 1999; JDS Uniphase, October 1999; Qualcomm, December 1999; Taser International, November 2003; and Google, September 2004. Each earlier pattern serves as a precedent for each later pattern, so study them carefully.

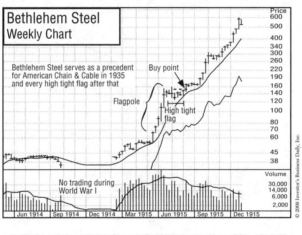

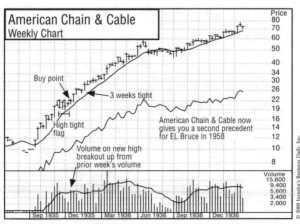

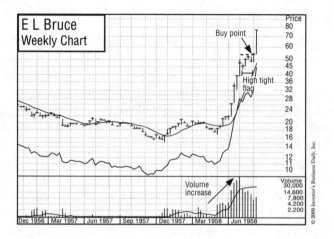

E L Bruce
Weekly Chart

Buy point

High tight flag

Volume increase

Price
80
70
60
50
45
40
36
32
28
24
20
18
16
14
12
11
10

Volume
30,000
14,600
7,800
4,200
2,200

Dec 1956 | Mar 1957 | Jun 1957 | Sep 1957 | Dec 1957 | Mar 1958 | Jun 1958

© 2009 Investor's Business Daily, Inc.

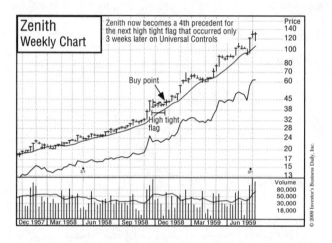

Zenith
Weekly Chart

Zenith now becomes a 4th precedent for the next high tight flag that occurred only 3 weeks later on Universal Controls

Buy point

High tight flag

Price
140
120
100
80
70
60
45
38
32
28
24
20
17
15
13

Volume
80,000
50,000
30,000
18,000

Dec 1957 | Mar 1958 | Jun 1958 | Sep 1958 | Dec 1958 | Mar 1959 | Jun 1959

© 2009 Investor's Business Daily, Inc.

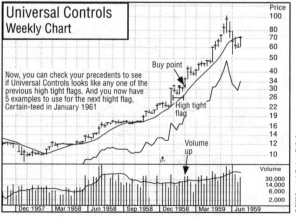

Universal Controls
Weekly Chart

Now, you can check your precedents to see if Universal Controls looks like any one of the previous high tight flags. And you now have 5 examples to use for the next hight flag, Certain-teed in January 1961

Buy point

High tight flag

Volume up

Price
100
80
70
60
50
40
34
30
26
22
19
16
14
12
10

Volume
30,000
14,000
6,000
2,000

Dec 1957 | Mar 1958 | Jun 1958 | Sep 1958 | Dec 1958 | Mar 1959 | Jun 1959

© 2009 Investor's Business Daily, Inc.

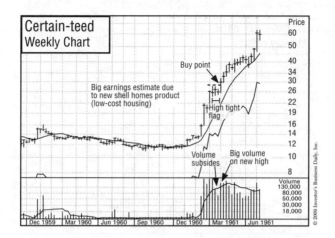

Certain-teed
Weekly Chart

Price
60
50
40
34
30
26
22
19
16
14
12
10
8

Buy point

Big earnings estimate due
to new shell homes product
(low-cost housing)

High tight
flag

Volume
subsides

Big volume
on new high

Volume
130,000
80,000
50,000
30,000
18,000

Dec 1959 | Mar 1960 | Jun 1960 | Sep 1960 | Dec 1960 | Mar 1961 | Jun 1961

© 2009 Investor's Business Daily, Inc.

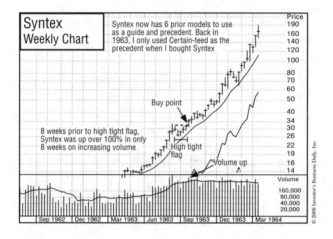

Syntex
Weekly Chart

Syntex now has 6 prior models to use
as a guide and precedent. Back in
1963, I only used Certain-teed as the
precedent when I bought Syntex

Price
190
160
140
120
100
80
70
60
50
40
34
30
26
22
19
16
14

Buy point

8 weeks prior to high tight flag,
Syntex was up over 100% in only
8 weeks on increasing volume

High tight
flag

Volume up

Volume
160,000
80,000
40,000
20,000

Sep 1962 | Dec 1962 | Mar 1963 | Jun 1963 | Sep 1963 | Dec 1963 | Mar 1964

© 2009 Investor's Business Daily, Inc.

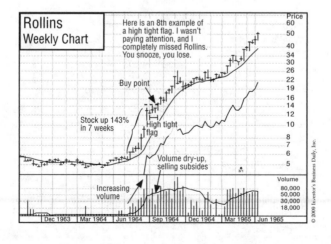

Rollins
Weekly Chart

Here is an 8th example of
a high tight flag. I wasn't
paying attention, and I
completely missed Rollins.
You snooze, you lose.

Price
60
50
40
34
30
26
22
19
16
14
12
10
8
7
6
5

Buy point

Stock up 143%
in 7 weeks

High tight
flag

Volume dry-up,
selling subsides

Increasing
volume

Volume
80,000
50,000
30,000
18,000

Dec 1963 | Mar 1964 | Jun 1964 | Sep 1964 | Dec 1964 | Mar 1965 | Jun 1965

© 2009 Investor's Business Daily, Inc.

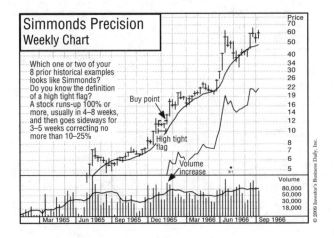

Simmonds Precision
Weekly Chart

Which one or two of your
8 prior historical examples
looks like Simmonds?
Do you know the definition
of a high tight flag?
A stock runs-up 100% or
more, usually in 4–8 weeks,
and then goes sideways for
3–5 weeks correcting no
more than 10–25%

Buy point

High tight
flag

Volume
increase

© 2009 Investor's Business Daily, Inc.

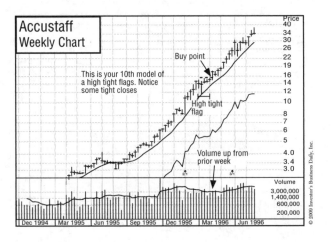

Accustaff
Weekly Chart

This is your 10th model of
a high tight flags. Notice
some tight closes

Buy point

High tight
flag

Volume up from
prior week

© 2009 Investor's Business Daily, Inc.

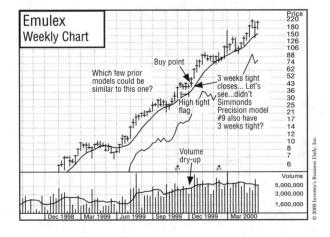

Emulex
Weekly Chart

Which few prior
models could be
similar to this one?

Buy point

High tight
flag

3 weeks tight
closes... Let's
see...didn't
Simmonds
Precision model
#9 also have
3 weeks tight?

Volume
dry-up

© 2009 Investor's Business Daily, Inc.

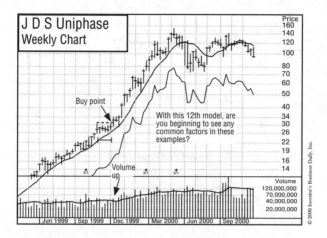

J D S Uniphase
Weekly Chart

Buy point

With this 12th model, are you beginning to see any common factors in these examples?

Volume up

Price
160
140
120
100
80
70
60
50
40
34
30
26
22
19
16
14

Volume
120,000,000
70,000,000
40,000,000
20,000,000

Jun 1999 | Sep 1999 | Dec 1999 | Mar 2000 | Jun 2000 | Sep 2000

© 2009 Investor's Business Daily, Inc.

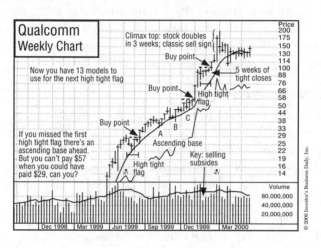

Qualcomm
Weekly Chart

Climax top: stock doubles in 3 weeks; classic sell sign

Buy point

5 weeks of tight closes

Now you have 13 models to use for the next high tight flag

Buy point

High tight flag

Buy point

A
B
C

Ascending base

If you missed the first high tight flag there's an ascending base ahead. But you can't pay $57 when you could have paid $29, can you?

High tight flag

Key: selling subsides

Price
200
175
150
130
114
100
88
76
66
58
50
44
38
33
29
25
22
19
16
14

Volume
80,000,000
40,000,000
20,000,000

Dec 1998 | Mar 1999 | Jun 1999 | Sep 1999 | Dec 1999 | Mar 2000

© 2009 Investor's Business Daily, Inc.

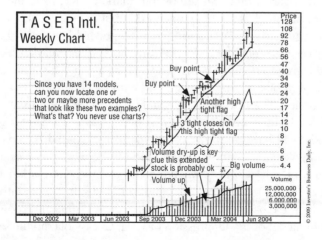

T A S E R Intl.
Weekly Chart

Buy point

Buy point

Since you have 14 models, can you now locate one or two or maybe more precedents that look like these two examples? What's that? You never use charts?

Another high tight flag

3 tight closes on this high tight flag

Volume dry-up is key clue this extended stock is probably ok

Big volume

Volume up

Price
128
108
92
78
66
56
47
40
34
29
24
20
17
14
12
10
8
7
6
5
4.4

Volume
25,000,000
12,000,000
6,000,000
3,000,000

Dec 2002 | Mar 2003 | Jun 2003 | Sep 2003 | Dec 2003 | Mar 2004 | Jun 2004

© 2009 Investor's Business Daily, Inc.

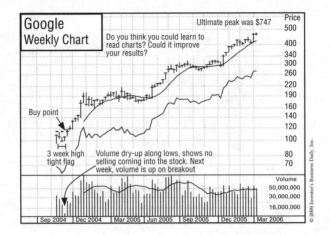

The E. L. Bruce pattern in the second quarter of 1958, at around $50, provided a perfect chart pattern precedent for the Certain-teed advance that occurred in 1961. Certain-teed, in turn, became the chart model that I used to buy my first super winner, Syntex, in July 1963.

What Is a Base on Top of a Base?

During the latter stages of a bear market, a seemingly negative condition flags what may be aggressive new leadership in the new bull phase. I call this unusual case a "base on top of a base."

What happens is that a powerful stock breaks out of its base and advances, but is unable to increase a normal 20% to 30% because the general market begins another leg down. The stock therefore pulls back in price and builds a second back-and-forth price consolidation area just on top of its previous base while the general market averages keep making new lows.

When the bearish phase in the overall market ends, as it always does at some point, this stock is apt to be one of the first to emerge at a new high en route to a huge gain. It's like a spring that is being held down by the pressure of a heavy object. Once the object (in this case, a bear market) is removed, the spring is free to do what it wanted to do all along. This is another example of why it's foolhardy to get upset and emotional with the market or lose your confidence. The next big race could be just a few months away.

Two of our institutional services firm's best ideas in 1978—M/A-Com and Boeing—showed base-on-top-of-a-base patterns. One advanced 180%, the other 950%. Ascend Communications and Oracle were other examples of a base on top of a base. After breaking out at the bear market bottom of December 1994, Ascend bolted almost 1,500% in 17 months. Oracle repeated the same base-on-base pattern in October 1999 and zoomed nearly 300%. Coming out of the Depression in 1934, Coca-Cola did the same thing.

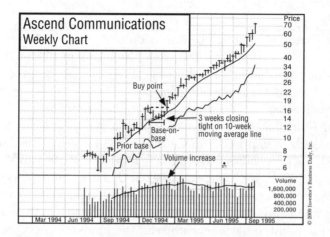

Ascend Communications
Weekly Chart

Buy point

3 weeks closing tight on 10-week moving average line

Base-on-base

Prior base

Volume increase

Price
70
60
50
40
34
30
26
22
19
16
14
12
10
8
7
6

Volume
1,600,000
800,000
400,000
200,000

Mar 1994 | Jun 1994 | Sep 1994 | Dec 1994 | Mar 1995 | Jun 1995 | Sep 1995

© 2009 Investor's Business Daily, Inc.

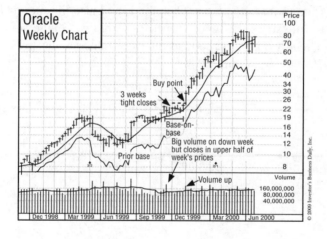

Oracle
Weekly Chart

Buy point

3 weeks tight closes

Base-on-base

Big volume on down week but closes in upper half of week's prices

Prior base

Volume up

Price
100
80
70
60
50
40
34
30
26
22
19
16
14
12
10
8

Volume
160,000,000
80,000,000
40,000,000

Dec 1998 | Mar 1999 | Jun 1999 | Sep 1999 | Dec 1999 | Mar 2000 | Jun 2000

© 2009 Investor's Business Daily, Inc.

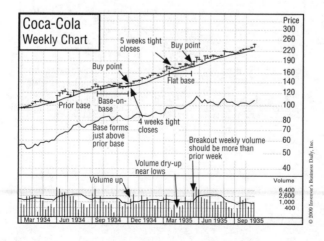

Coca-Cola
Weekly Chart

5 weeks tight closes

Buy point

Buy point

Flat base

Base-on-base

Prior base

Base forms just above prior base

4 weeks tight closes

Breakout weekly volume should be more than prior week

Volume dry-up near lows

Volume up

Price
300
260
220
190
160
140
120
100
80
70
60
50
40

Volume
6,400
2,600
1,000
400

Mar 1934 | Jun 1934 | Sep 1934 | Dec 1934 | Mar 1935 | Jun 1935 | Sep 1935

© 2009 Investor's Business Daily, Inc.

Ascending Bases

Ascending bases, like flat bases, occur midway along a move up after a stock has run up off an earlier base. They have three 10% to 20% pullbacks with each low in price during the sell-off being higher than the preceding one, which is why I call them ascending bases.

Each pullback occurs due to the general market declining at the time.

Boeing formed a 13-week ascending base in the second quarter of 1954 and then doubled in price. Redman Industries, a builder of mobile homes, had an 11-week ascending base in the first quarter of 1968 and proceeded to increase 500% in just 37 weeks. America Online created the same type of base in the first quarter of 1999 and resumed what turned out to be a 500% run-up from the breakout of a 14-week cup with handle in October 1998.

So you see, history does repeat itself. The more historical patterns you learn to recognize, the more money you should be able to make in future markets. (See chart examples in Chapter 1, and also Simmonds Precision, Monogram Industries, Redman Industries, America Online, and Titanium Metals.) The buy point is as soon as the stock makes a new price high after the third 10% to 20% pullback.

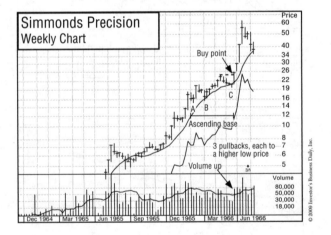

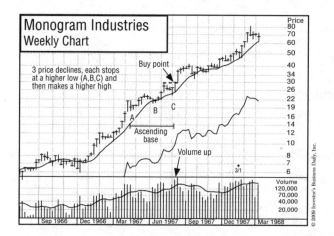

Monogram Industries
Weekly Chart

3 price declines, each stops at a higher low (A,B,C) and then makes a higher high

Buy point

A B C

Ascending base

Volume up

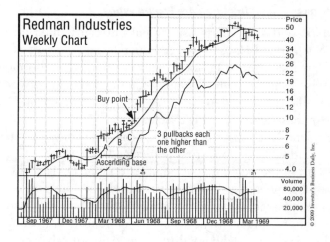

Redman Industries
Weekly Chart

Buy point

A B C

Ascending base

3 pullbacks each one higher than the other

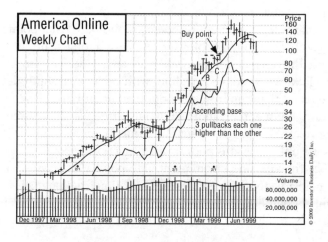

America Online
Weekly Chart

Buy point

A B C

Ascending base

3 pullbacks each one higher than the other

© 2009 Investor's Business Daily, Inc.

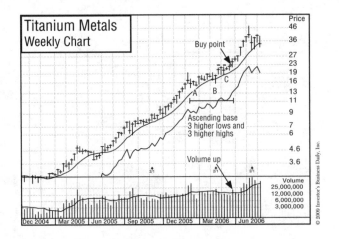

Titanium Metals
Weekly Chart

Buy point

C

A B

Ascending base
3 higher lows and
3 higher highs

Volume up

Price
46
36
27
23
19
16
13
11
9
7
6
4.6
3.6

Volume
25,000,000
12,000,000
6,000,000
3,000,000

Dec 2004 | Mar 2005 | Jun 2005 | Sep 2005 | Dec 2005 | Mar 2006 | Jun 2006

© 2009 Investor's Business Daily, Inc.

Wide-and-Loose Price Structures Are Failure Prone

Wide-and-loose-looking charts usually fail but can tighten up later. New England Nuclear and Houston Oil & Minerals are two cases of stocks that tightened up following wide, loose, and erratic price movements. I cite them because I missed both of them at the time. It's always wise to review big winners that you missed to find out why you didn't recognize them when they were exactly right and ready to soar.

New England Nuclear formed a wide, loose, and faulty price pattern that looked like a double bottom from points A, B, C, D, and E. It declined about 40% from the beginning at point A to point D. That was excessive, and it took too much time—almost six months—to hit bottom. Note the additional clue provided by the declining trend of its relative strength line (RS) throughout the faulty pattern. Buying at point E was wrong. The handle was also too short and did not drift down to create a shakeout. It wedged up along its low points.

New England Nuclear then formed a second base from points E to F to G. But if you tried to buy at point G, you were wrong again. It was premature because the price pattern was still wide and loose. The move from point E to point F was a prolonged decline, with relative strength deteriorating badly. The rise straight up from the bottom at point F to the bogus breakout point G was too fast and erratic, taking only three months. Three months of improving relative strength versus the prior 17 months of decline weren't enough to turn the previous poor trend into a positive one.

The stock then declined from point G to point H to form what appeared to be a handle area for the possible cup formation from points E to F to G. If you bought at point I on the breakout attempt, the stock failed again. Reason: the handle was too loose; it declined 20%. However, after failing that time,

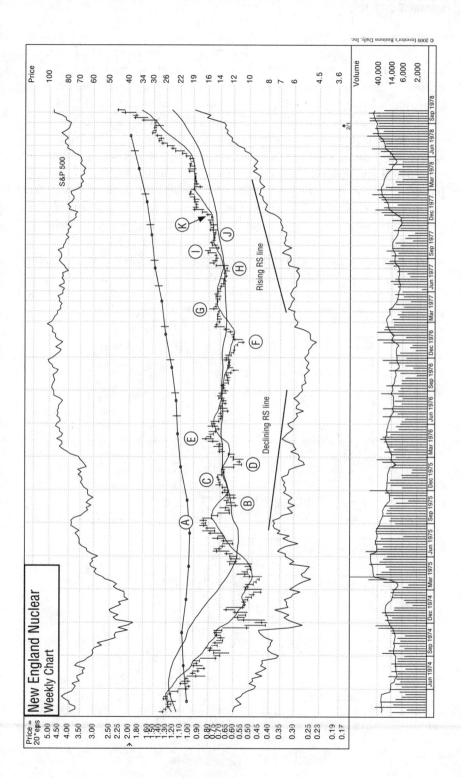

New England Nuclear
Weekly Chart

S&P 500

Rising RS line

Declining RS line

(A) (B) (C) (D) (E) (F) (G) (H) (I) (J) (K)

Price = 20*eps
5.00
4.50
4.00
3.50
3.00
2.50
2.25
2.00
1.80
1.60
1.50
1.40
1.30
1.20
1.10
1.00
0.90
0.80
0.70
0.65
0.60
0.55
0.50
0.45
0.40
0.35
0.30
0.25
0.23
0.19
0.17

Price
100
80
70
60
50
40
34
30
26
22
19
16
14
12
10
8
7
6
4.5
3.6

Volume
40,000
14,000
6,000
2,000

Jun 1974 | Sep 1974 | Dec 1974 | Mar 1975 | Jun 1975 | Sep 1975 | Dec 1975 | Mar 1976 | Jun 1976 | Sep 1976 | Dec 1976 | Mar 1977 | Jun 1977 | Sep 1977 | Dec 1977 | Mar 1978 | Jun 1978 | Sep 1978 the stock at last tightened up its price structure from points I to J to K, and 15 weeks later, at point K, it broke out of a tight, sound base and nearly tripled in price afterwards. Note the stock's strong uptrend and materially improved relative strength line for 11 months from point K back to point F.

So, there really is a right time and a wrong time to buy a stock, but understanding the difference requires some study. There's no such thing as being an overnight success in the stock market, and success has nothing to do with listening to tips from other people or being lucky. You have to study and prepare yourself so that you can become successful on your own with your investing. So make yourself more knowledgeable. It isn't easy at first, but it can be very rewarding. Anyone can learn to do it. You can do it. Believe in your ability to learn. Unlearn past assumptions that didn't work.

Here are some faulty wide-and-loose patterns that faked people into buying during the prolonged bear market that began in March 2000: Veritas

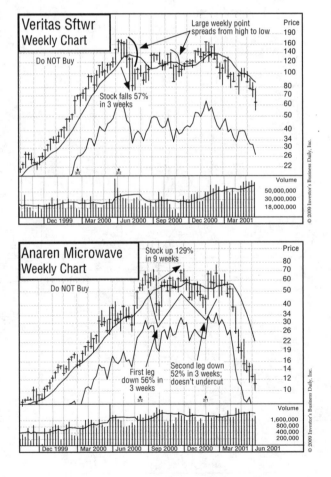

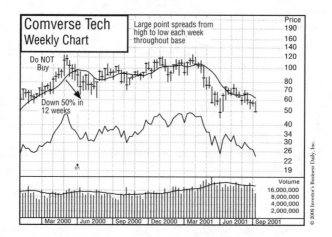

Software on October 20, 2000; Anaren Microwave on December 28, 2000; and Comverse Technology on January 24, 2001.

The aforementioned Houston Oil & Minerals is an even more dramatic example of the handle correction from point F to point G being a wide-and-loose pattern that later tightened up into a constructive price formation (see the accompanying chart). A to B to C was extremely wide, loose, and erratic (the percent decline was too great). B to C was straight up from the bottom without any pullback in price. Points C and D were false attempts to break out of a faulty price pattern, and so was point H, which tried to break out of a wide-and-loose cup with handle. Afterward, a tight nine-week base formed from points H to I to J. (Note the extreme volume dry-up along the December 1975 lows.)

An alert stockbroker in Hartford, Connecticut, called this structure to my attention. However, I'd been so conditioned by the two prior years of poor price patterns and less-than-desirable earnings that my mind was slow to change when the stock suddenly altered its behavior in only nine weeks. I was probably also intimidated by the tremendous price increase that had occurred in Houston Oil in the earlier 1973 bull market. This proves that opinions and feelings are frequently wrong, but markets rarely are.

It also points out a very important principle: it takes time for all of us to change opinions that we have built up over a substantial period. In this instance, even the current quarterly earnings turning up 357% after three down quarters didn't change my incorrect bearish view of the stock to a bullish one. The right buy point was in January 1976.

In August 1994, PeopleSoft repeated the New England Nuclear and Houston Oil patterns. It failed in its breakout attempt from a wide, loose, wedging-upward pattern in September 1993. It then failed a second time in its breakout attempt in March 1994, when its handle area formed in the lower

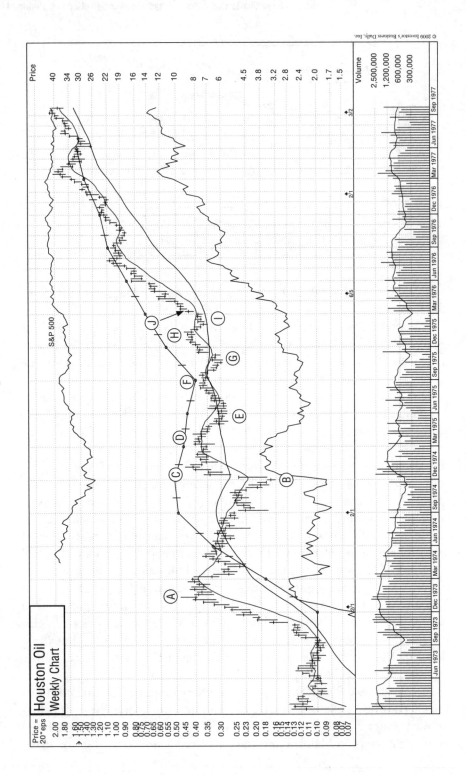

Houston Oil
Weekly Chart

S&P 500

© 2009 Investor's Business Daily, Inc.

144

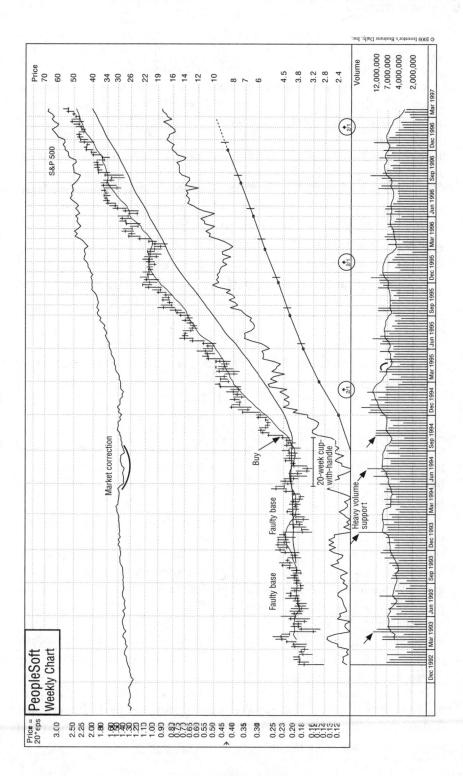

PeopleSoft
Weekly Chart

Price =
20*eps

S&P 500

Market correction

Buy

Faulty base

Faulty base

20-week cup-
with-handle

Heavy volume
support

Price
70
60
50
40
34
30
26
22
19
16
14
12
10
8
7
6
4.5
3.8
3.2
2.8
2.4

3.00
2.50
2.25
2.00
1.80
1.60
1.50
1.40
1.30
1.20
1.10
1.00
0.90
0.82
0.75
0.70
0.65
0.60
0.55
0.50
0.45
0.40
0.35
0.30
0.25
0.23
0.20
0.18
0.16
0.15
0.14
0.13
0.12

Volume
12,000,000
7,000,000
4,000,000
2,000,000

Dec 1992 Mar 1993 Jun 1993 Sep 1993 Dec 1993 Mar 1994 Jun 1994 Sep 1994 Dec 1994 Mar 1995 Jun 1995 Sep 1995 Dec 1995 Mar 1996 Jun 1996 Sep 1996 Dec 1996 Mar 1997

145

half of its cup-with-handle pattern. Finally, when the chart pattern and the general market were right, PeopleSoft skyrocketed starting in August 1994.

In the first week of January 1999, San Diego–based Qualcomm followed PeopleSoft's three-phased precedent. In October 1997, Qualcomm charged into new-high ground straight up from a loose, faulty base with too much of its base in its lower half. It then built a second faulty base, broke out of a handle in the lower part, and failed. The third base was the charm: a properly formed cup with handle that worked in the first week in January 1999. Qualcomm went straight through the roof from a split-adjusted $7.50 to $200 in only one year. Maybe you should spend more time studying historical precedents. What do you think? If you had invested $7,500 in Qualcomm, a year later it would have been worth $200,000.

Detecting Faulty Price Patterns and Base Structures

Unfortunately, no original or thorough research on price pattern analysis has been done in the last 78 years. In 1930, Richard Schabacker, a financial editor of *Forbes*, wrote a book, *Stock Market Theory and Practice*. In it he discussed many patterns, including triangles, coils, and pennants. Our detailed model building and investigations of price structure over the years have shown these patterns to be unreliable and risky. They probably worked in the latter part of the "Roaring '20s," when most stocks ran up in a wild, climactic frenzy. Something similar happened in 1999 and the first quarter of 2000, when many loose, faulty patterns at first seemed to work, but then failed. These periods were just like the Dutch tulip bulb craze of the seventeenth century, during which rampant speculation caused varieties of tulip bulbs to skyrocket to astronomical prices and then crash.

Our studies show that, with the exception of high, tight flags, which are extremely rare and hard to interpret, flat bases of five or six weeks, and the square box of four to seven weeks, the most reliable base patterns must have a minimum of seven to eight weeks of price consolidation. Most coils, triangles, and pennants are simply weak foundations without sufficient time or price correction to become proper bases. One-, two-, and three-week bases are risky. In almost all cases, they should be avoided.

In 1948, John McGee and Robert D. Edwards wrote *Technical Analysis of Stock Trends*, a book that discusses many of the same faulty patterns presented in Schabacker's earlier work.

In 1962, William Jiler wrote an easy-to-read book, *How Charts Can Help You in the Stock Market*, that explains many of the correct principles behind technical analysis. However, it too seems to have continued the display and discussion of certain failure-prone patterns of the pre-Depression era.

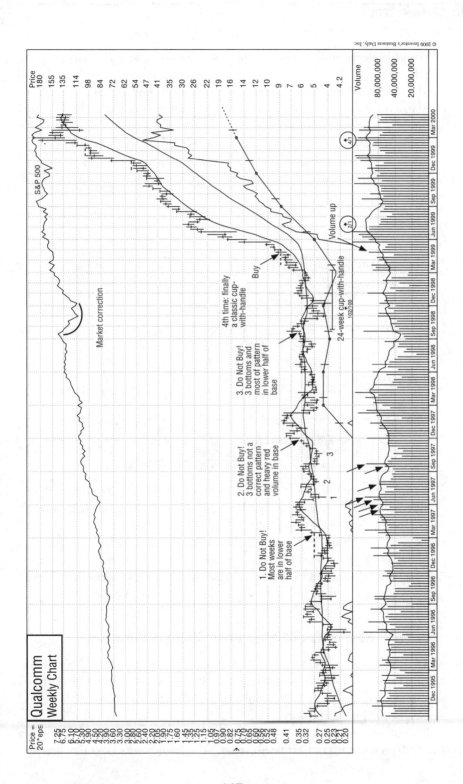

Qualcomm
Weekly Chart

Price = 20* eps

S&P 500

Market correction

1. Do Not Buy!
Most weeks
are in lower
half of base

2. Do Not Buy!
3 bottoms not a
correct pattern
and heavy red
volume in base

3. Do Not Buy!
3 bottoms and
most of pattern
in lower half of
base

4th time: finally
a classic cup-
with-handle

Buy

102/100

24-week cup-with-handle

Volume up

Volume

80,000,000
40,000,000
20,000,000

Triple bottoms and head-and-shoulders bottoms are patterns that are widely mentioned in several books on technical analysis. We have found these to be weaker patterns as well. A head-and-shoulders bottom may succeed in a few instances, but it has no strong prior uptrend, which is essential for most powerful market leaders.

When it comes to signifying a top in a stock, however, head-and-shoulders top patterns are among the most reliable. Be careful: if you have only a little knowledge of charts, you can misinterpret what is a correct head-and-shoulders top. Many pros don't interpret the pattern properly. The right (second) shoulder must be slightly below the left shoulder (see the chart for Alexander & Alexander).

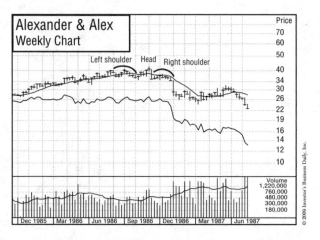

A triple bottom is a looser, weaker, and less-attractive base pattern than a double bottom. The reason is that the stock corrects and falls back sharply to its absolute low three times rather than twice, as with a double bottom, or once, as in the strong cup with handle. As mentioned earlier, a cup with a wedging handle is also usually a faulty, failure-prone pattern, as you can see in the Global Crossing Ltd. chart example. A competent chart reader would have avoided or sold Global Crossing, which later went bankrupt.

How to Use Relative Price Strength Correctly

Many fundamental securities analysts think that technical analysis means buying those stocks with the strongest relative price strength. Others think that technical research refers only to the buying of "high-momentum" stocks. Both views are incorrect.

It's not enough to just buy stocks that show the highest relative price strength on some list of best performers. You should buy stocks that are per-

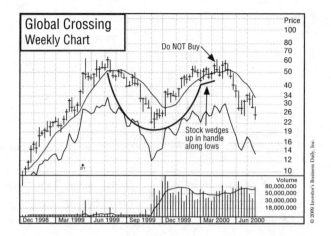

forming better than the general market just as they are beginning to emerge from sound base-building periods. The time to sell is when the stock has advanced rapidly, is extended materially from its base, and is showing extremely high relative price strength. To recognize the difference, you have to use daily or weekly charts.

What Is Overhead Supply?

A critically important concept to learn in analyzing price movements is the principle of overhead supply. Overhead supply is when there are significant areas of price resistance in a stock as it moves up after experiencing a downtrend.

These areas of resistance represent prior purchases of a stock and serve to limit and frustrate its upward movement because the investors who made these purchases are motivated to sell when the price returns to their entry point. (See the chart for At Home.) For example, if a stock advances from $25 to $40, then declines back to $30, most of the people who bought it in the upper $30s and at $40 will have a loss in the stock unless they were quick to sell and cut their loss (which most people don't do). If the stock later climbs back to the high $30s or $40 area, the investors who had losses can now get out and break even.

These are the holders who promised themselves: "If I can just get out even, I will sell." Human nature doesn't change. So it's normal for a number of these people to sell when they see a chance to get their money back after having been down a large amount.

Good chartists know how to recognize the price zones that represent heavy areas of overhead supply. They will never make the fatal mistake of

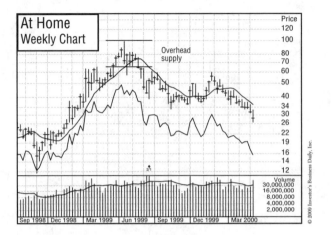

buying a stock that has a large amount of recent overhead supply. This is a serious mistake that many analysts who are concerned solely with fundamentals sometimes make.

A stock that's able to fight its way through its overhead supply, however, may be safer to buy, even though the price is a little higher. It has proved to have sufficient demand to absorb the supply and move past its level of resistance. Supply areas more than two years old create less resistance. Of course, a stock that has just broken out into new high ground for the first time has no overhead supply to contend with, which adds to its appeal.

Excellent Opportunities in Unfamiliar, Newer Stocks

Alert investors should have a way of keeping track of all new stock issues that have emerged over the last 10 to 15 years. This is important because some of these newer and younger companies will be among the most stunning performers of the next year or two. Most of these issues trade on the Nasdaq market.

Some new issues move up a small amount and then retreat to new price lows during a bear market, making a poor initial impression. But when the next bull market begins, a few of these forgotten newcomers will sneak back up unnoticed, form base patterns, and suddenly take off and double or triple in price if they have earnings and sales that are good and improving.

Most investors miss these outstanding price moves because they occur in new names that are largely unknown to most people. A charting service can help you spot these unfamiliar, newer companies, but make sure that your service follows a large number of stocks (not just one or two thousand).

Successful, young growth stocks tend to enjoy their fastest earnings growth between their fifth and tenth years in business, so keep an eye on them during their early growth periods.

To summarize, dramatically improve your stock selection and overall portfolio performance by learning to read and use charts. They provide a gold mine of information. It will take some time and study on your part to become good at this, but it's an invaluable skill you can learn. You may have to re-read this chapter several times in the first year or two if you really want to be good at chart reading. The big secret is for you to combine skillful chart reading with stocks that have outstanding earnings and sales growth, plus superior returns on equity or pre-tax profit margins. You need both fundamentals and chart reading, not just one or the other.

● **A Loud Warning to the Wise about Bear Markets!!!**

Let me offer one last bit of judicious guidance. If you are new to the stock market or the historically tested and proven strategies outlined in this book, or, more importantly, if you are reading this book for the first time near the beginning or middle of a bear market, do not expect the presumed buy patterns to work. Most of them will definitely be defective. *You absolutely do not buy breakouts during a bear market.* Most of them will fail.

The price patterns will be too deep, wide, and loose in appearance compared to earlier patterns. They will be third- and fourth-stage bases; have wedging or loose, sloppy handles; have handles in the lower half of the base; or show narrow "V" formations moving straight up from the bottom of a base into new highs, without any handle forming. Some patterns may show laggard stocks with declining relative strength lines and price patterns with too much adverse volume activity or every week's price spread wide.

It isn't that bases, breakouts, or the method isn't working anymore; it's that the timing and the stocks are simply all wrong. The price and volume patterns are phony, faulty, and unsound. The general market is turning negative. It is selling time. Be patient, keep studying, and be 100% prepared. Later, at the least expected time, when all the news is terrible, winter will ultimately pass and a great new bull market will suddenly spring to life. The practical techniques and proven disciplines discussed here should work for you for many, many future economic cycles. So get prepared and do your homework. Create your own buy and sell rules that you will constantly use.

C = Current Big or Accelerating Quarterly Earnings and Sales per Share

Dell Computer, Cisco Systems, America Online—why, among the thousands of stocks that trade each day, did these three perform so well during the 1990s, posting gains of 1,780%, 1,467%, and 557%, respectively?

Or for that matter, what about Google, which started trading at $85 a share in August 2004 and didn't stop climbing until it peaked at over $700 in 2007? Or Apple, which had emerged from a perfect cup-with-handle pattern six months earlier at a split-adjusted $12 a share and reached $202 in 45 months?

What key traits, among the hundreds that can move stocks up and down, did these companies all have in common?

These are not idle questions. The answers unlock the secret to true success in the stock market. Our study of all the stock market superstars from the last century and a quarter found that they did indeed share common characteristics.

None of these characteristics, however, stood out as boldly as the large percentage earnings per share increase each big winner reported in the latest quarter or two before its major price advance. For example:

- Dell's earnings per share surged 74% and 108% in the two quarters prior to its price increase from November 1996.

- Cisco posted earnings gains of 150% and 155% in the two quarters ending October 1990, prior to its giant run-up over the next three years.

- America Online's earnings were up 900% and 283% before its six-month burst from October 1998.

- Google showed earnings gains of 112% and 123% in the two quarters before it made its spectacular debut as a public company.

- Apple's earnings were up 350% in the quarter before it took off, and its next quarter was up another 300%.

But this isn't just a recent phenomenon. Explosive earnings have accompanied big stock moves throughout the stock market's great history in America. Studebaker's earnings were up 296% before it sped from $45 to $190 in eight months in 1914, and Cuban American Sugar's earnings soared 1,175% in 1916, the same year its stock climbed from $35 to $230.

In the summer of 1919, Stutz Motor Car was showing an earnings gain of 70% before the prestigious manufacturer of high-performance sports cars—you remember the Bearcat, don't you?—raced from $75 to $385 in just 40 weeks.

Earnings at U.S. Cast Iron Pipe rose from $1.51 a share at the end of 1922 to $21.92 at the end of 1923, an increase of 1,352%. In late 1923, the stock traded at $30; by early 1925, it went for $250.

And in March of 1926, du Pont de Nemours showed earnings up 259% before its stock took off from $41 that July and got to $230 before the 1929 break.

In fact, if you look down a list of the market's biggest winners year-in and year-out, you'll instantly see the relationship between booming profits and booming stocks.

And you'll see why our studies have concluded that

The stocks you select should show a major percentage increase in current quarterly earnings per share (the most recently reported quarter) when compared to the prior year's same quarter.

Buy Stocks Showing "Huge Current Earnings Increases"

In our models of the 600 best-performing stocks from 1952 to 2001, three out of four showed earnings increases averaging more than 70% in the latest publicly reported quarter *before* they began their major advances. Those that *did not* show solid current quarterly earnings increases did so in *the very next quarter*, with an average earnings increase of 90%!

Priceline.com was showing earnings up "only" 34% in the June quarter of 2006, when its stock began a move from $30 to $140. But its earnings accelerated, rising 53%, 107%, and 126%, in the quarters that followed.

From 1910 to 1950, most of the very best performers showed quarterly earnings gains ranging from 40% to 400% before their big price moves.

So, if the best stocks had profit increases of this magnitude before they advanced rapidly in price, why should you settle for anything less? You may find that only 1% or 2% of stocks listed on Nasdaq or the New York Stock Exchange show earnings gains of this size. But remember: you're looking for stocks that are exceptional, not lackluster. Don't worry; they're out there.

As with any search, however, there can be traps and pitfalls along the way, and you need to know how to avoid them.

The earnings per share (EPS) number you want to focus on is calculated by dividing a company's total after-tax profits by the number of common shares outstanding. This percentage change in EPS is the single most important element in stock selection today. The greater the percentage increase, the better.

And yet during the Internet boom of the wild late 1990s, some people bought stocks based on nothing more than big stories of profits and riches to come, as most Internet and dot-com companies had shown only deficits to date. Given that companies such as AOL and Yahoo! were actually showing earnings, risking your hard-earned money in other, unproven stocks was simply not necessary.

AOL and Yahoo! were the real leaders at that time. When the inevitable market correction (downturn) hit, lower-grade, more speculative companies with no earnings rapidly suffered the largest declines. You don't need that added risk.

I am continually amazed at how some professional money managers, let alone individual investors, buy common stocks when the current reported quarter's earnings are flat (no change) or down. There is absolutely no good reason for a stock to go anywhere in a big, sustainable way if its current earnings are poor.

Even profit gains of 5% to 10% are insufficient to fuel a major price movement in a stock. Besides, a company showing an increase of as little as 8% or 10% is more likely to suddenly report lower or slower earnings the next quarter.

Unlike some institutional investors such as mutual funds, banks, and insurance companies, which have billions under management and which may be restricted by the size of their funds, individual investors have the luxury of investing in only the very best stocks in each bull cycle. While some companies with no earnings (like Amazon.com and Priceline.com) had big moves in their stocks in 1998–1999, most investors in that time period would have been better off buying stocks like America Online and Charles Schwab, both of which had strong earnings.

Following the CAN SLIM strategy's emphasis on earnings ensures that an investor will always be led to the strongest stocks in any market cycle, regardless of any temporary, highly speculative "bubbles" or euphoria. Of course, you never buy on earnings growth alone. Several other factors, which we'll cover in the chapters that follow, are also essential. It's just that EPS percentage increase is the *most* important.

Watch Out for Misleading Earnings Reports

Have you ever read a corporation's quarterly earnings report that went like this:

> We had a terrible first three months. Prospects for our company are turning down because of inefficiencies at the home office. Our competition just came out with a better product, which will adversely affect our sales. Furthermore, we are losing our shirt on the new Midwestern operation, which was a real blunder on management's part.

No way! Here's what you see instead:

> Greatshakes Corporation reports record sales of $7.2 million versus $6 million (+20%) for the quarter ended March 31.

If you're a Greatshakes stockholder, this sounds like wonderful news. You certainly aren't going to be disappointed. After all, you believe that this is a fine company (if you didn't, you wouldn't have invested in it in the first place), and the report confirms your thinking.

But is this "record-breaking" sales announcement a good report? Let's suppose the company also had record earnings of $2.10 per share, up 5% from the $2.00 per share reported for the same quarter a year ago. Is it even better now? The question you have to ask is, why were sales up 20% but earnings ahead only 5%? What does this say about the company's profit margins?

Most investors are impressed with what they read, and companies love to put their best foot forward in their press releases and TV appearances. However, even though this company's sales grew 20% to an all-time high, it didn't mean much for the company's profits. The key question for the winning investor must always be:

**How much are the current quarter's earnings per share up
(in percentage terms) from the same quarter the year before?**

Let's say your company discloses that sales climbed 10% and net income advanced 12%. Sound good? Not necessarily. You shouldn't be concerned with the company's total net income. You don't own the whole organization; you own shares in it. Over the last 12 months, the company might have issued additional shares or "diluted" the common stock in other ways. So while net income may be up 12%, earnings per share—your main focus as an investor—may have edged up only 5% or 6%.

You must be able to see through slanted presentations. Don't let the use of words like *sales* and *net income* divert your attention from the truly vital facts like current quarterly earnings. To further clarify this point:

> **You should always compare a company's earnings per share to the same quarter a year earlier, not to the prior quarter, to avoid any distortion resulting from seasonality. In other words, you don't compare the December quarter's earnings per share to the prior September quarter's earnings per share. Rather, compare the December quarter to the December quarter of the previous year for a more accurate evaluation.**

Omit a Company's One-Time Extraordinary Gains

The winning investor should avoid the trap of being influenced by nonrecurring profits. For example, if a computer maker reports earnings for the last quarter that include nonrecurring profits from activities such as the sale of real estate, this portion of earnings should be subtracted from the report. Such earnings represent a one-time event, not the true, ongoing profitability of corporate operations. Ignore the earnings that result from such events.

Is it possible that the earnings of New York's Citigroup bank may have been propped up at times during the 1990s by nonrecurring sales of commercial real estate prior to the bank's later leveraged involvement in the subprime disaster?

Set a Minimum Level for Current Earnings Increases

Whether you're a new or an experienced investor, I would advise against buying any stock that doesn't show earnings per share up at least 18% or 20% in the most recent quarter versus the same quarter the year before. In our study of the greatest winning companies, we found that they all had this in common *prior* to their big price moves. Many successful investors use 25% or 30% as their minimum earnings parameter.

To be even safer, insist that both of the last two quarters show significant earnings gains. During bull markets (major market uptrends), I prefer to concentrate on stocks that show powerful earnings gains of 40% to 500% or more. You have thousands of stocks to choose from. Why not buy the very best merchandise available?

To further sharpen your stock selection process, look ahead to the next quarter or two and check the earnings that were reported for those same quarters the previous year. See if the company will be coming up against unusually large or small earnings achieved a year ago. When the unusual year-earlier results are not caused by seasonal factors, this step may help you anticipate a strong or poor earnings report in the coming months.

Also, be sure to check consensus earnings estimates (projections that combine the earnings estimates of a large group of analysts) for the next several quarters—and for the next year or two—to make sure the company is projected to be on a positive track. Some earnings estimate services even show an estimated annual earnings growth rate for the next five years for many companies.

Many individuals and even some institutional investors buy stocks whose earnings were down in the most recently reported quarter because they like the company and think that its stock price is "cheap." Usually they accept the story that earnings will rebound strongly in the near future. In some cases this may be true, but in many cases it isn't. Again, the point is that you have the choice of investing in thousands of companies, many of which are actually showing strong operating results. You don't have to accept promises of earnings that may never occur.

Requiring that current quarterly earnings be up a hefty amount is just another smart way for the intelligent investor to reduce the risk of mistakes in stock selection. But you must also understand in the late stage of a bull market, some or even many leaders that have had long runs can top out even though their current earnings are up 100%. This usually fools investors and analysts alike. It pays to know your market history.

Avoid Big Older Companies with Maintainer Management

In fact, many older American corporations have mediocre management that continually produces second-rate earnings results. I call these people the "entrenched maintainers" or "caretaker management." You want to avoid these companies until someone has the courage to change the top executives. Not coincidentally, they are generally the companies that strain to pump up their current earnings a still-dull 8% or 10%. True growth companies with outstanding new products or improved management do not have to inflate their current results.

Look for Accelerating Quarterly Earnings Growth

Our analysis of the most successful stocks also showed that, in almost every case, earnings growth *accelerated* sometime in the 10 quarters before a towering price move began. In other words, it's not just increased earnings and the size of the increase that cause a big move. It's also that the increase represents an improvement from the company's prior rate of earnings growth. If a company's earnings have been up 15% a year and suddenly begin spurting 40% to 50% or more—what Wall Street usually calls "earnings surprises"—this usually creates the conditions for important stock price improvement.

Other valuable ways to track a stock's earnings include determining how many times in recent months analysts have raised their estimates for the company plus the percentage by which several previous quarterly earnings reports have actually beaten their consensus estimates.

Insist on Sales Growth as Well as Earnings Growth

Strong and improving quarterly earnings should always be supported by sales growth of at least 25% for the latest quarter, or at least an acceleration in the rate of sales percentage improvement over the last three quarters. Certain superior newer issues (initial public offerings) may show sales growth averaging 100% or more in each of the prior 8, 10, or 12 quarters. Check all these stocks out.

Take particular note if the growth of *both* sales and earnings has accelerated for the last three quarters. You don't want to get impatient and sell your stock if it shows this type of acceleration. Stick to your position.

Some professional investors bought Waste Management at $50 in early 1998 because earnings had jumped three quarters in a row from 24% to 75% and 268%. But sales were up only 5%. Several months later, the stock collapsed to $15 a share.

This demonstrates that companies can inflate earnings for a few quarters by reducing costs or spending less on advertising, research and development, and other constructive activities. To be sustainable, however, earnings growth must be supported by higher sales. Such was not the case with Waste Management.

It will also improve your batting average if the latest quarter's after-tax profit margins for your stock selections are at or near a new high and among the very best in the company's industry. Yes, you have to do a little homework if you want to really improve your results. No pain, no gain.

Two Quarters of Major Earnings Deceleration Can Be Trouble for Your Stock

Just as it's important to recognize when quarterly earnings growth is accelerating, it's also important to know when earnings begin to *decelerate*, or slow down significantly. If a company that has been growing at a quarterly rate of 50% suddenly reports earnings gains of only 15%, that might spell trouble, and you may want to avoid that company.

Even the best organizations can have a slow quarter every once in a while. So before turning negative on a company's earnings, I prefer to see two consecutive quarters of *material* slowdown. This usually means a decline of two-thirds or greater from the previous rate—a slowdown from 100% earnings growth to 30%, for example, or from 50% to 15%.

Consult Log-Scale Weekly Graphs

Understanding the principle of earnings acceleration or deceleration is essential.

Securities analysts who recommend stocks because of the absolute level of earnings expected for the following year could be looking at the wrong set of numbers. The fact that a stock earned $5 per share and expects to report $6 the next year (a "favorable" 20% increase) could be misleading unless you know the previous trend in the percentage rate of earnings change. What if earnings were previously up 60%? This partially explains why so few investors make significant money following the buy and sell recommendations of securities analysts.

Logarithmic-scale graphs are of great value in analyzing stocks because they can clearly show acceleration or deceleration in the percentage rate of quarterly earnings increases. One inch anywhere on the price or earnings scale represents the same percentage change. This is not true of arithmetically scaled charts.

On arithmetically scaled charts, a 100% price move from $10 to $20 shows the same space change as a 50% increase from $20 to $30. But a log-scale graph shows a 100% increase as twice as large as the 50% increase. Weekly charts in Daily Graphs Online are properly logarithmic.

As a do-it-yourself investor, you can take the latest quarterly earnings per share along with the prior three quarters' EPS, and plot them on a logarithmic-scale graph to get a clear picture of earnings acceleration or deceleration. For the best companies, plotting the most recent 12-month earnings each quarter should put the earnings per share point close to or already at new highs.

Check Other Stocks in the Group

For additional validation, check the earnings of other companies in your stock's industry group. If you can't find at least one other impressive stock displaying strong earnings in the group, chances are you may have selected the wrong investment.

Where to Find Current Quarterly Earnings Reports

Quarterly corporate earnings statements used to be published in the business sections of most local newspapers and financial publications every day. But most newspapers have downsized their business sections these days, dropping data right and left. As a result, they no longer adequately cover the critical facts investors need to know.

This is not true of *Investor's Business Daily*. IBD not only continues to provide detailed earnings coverage, but goes a step further and separates all new earnings reports into companies with "up" earnings and those reporting "down" results, so you can easily see who produced excellent gains and who didn't.

Chart services such as Daily Graphs® and Daily Graphs Online also show earnings reported during the week as well as the most recent earnings figures for every stock they chart. Once you locate the percentage change in earnings per share when compared to the same year-ago quarter, also compare the percentage change in EPS on a quarter-by-quarter basis. Looking at the March quarter and then at the June, September, and December quarters will tell you if a company's earnings growth is accelerating or decelerating.

You now have the first crucial rule for improving your stock selection:

Current quarterly earnings per share should be up a major percentage—25% to 50% at a minimum—over the same quarter the previous year. The best companies can show earnings up 100% to 500% or more!

A mediocre 10% or 12% isn't enough. When you're picking winning stocks, it's the bottom line that counts.

A = Annual Earnings Increases: Look for Big Growth

Any company can report a good earnings quarter every once in a while. And as we've seen, strong current quarterly earnings are critical to picking most of the market's biggest winners. But they're not enough.

To make sure the latest results aren't just a flash in the pan, and the company you're looking at is of high quality, you must insist on more proof. The way to do that is by reviewing the company's *annual* earnings growth rate.

Look for annual earnings per share that have increased in each of the last three years. You normally don't want the second year's earnings to be down, even if the results in the following year rebound to the highest level yet. It's the combination of strong earnings in the last several quarters plus a record of solid growth in recent years that creates a superb stock, or at least one with a higher probability of success during an uptrending general market.

Select Stocks with 25% to 50% and Higher Annual Earnings Growth Rates

The annual rate of earnings growth for the companies you pick should be 25%, 50%, or even 100% or more. Between 1980 and 2000, the median annual growth rate of all outstanding stocks in our study at their early emerging stage was 36%. Three out of four big winners showed at least some positive annual growth over the three years, and in some cases the five years, preceding the stocks' big run-ups.

A typical earnings-per-share progression for the five years preceding the stock's move might be something like $0.70, $1.15, $1.85, $2.65, and $4.00.

In a few cases, you might accept one down year in five as long as the following year's earnings move back to new high ground.

It's possible a company could earn $4.00 a share one year, $5.00 the next, $6.00 the next, and then $3.00 a share. If the next annual earnings statement was, say, $4.00 per share versus the prior year's $3.00, this would not be a good report despite the 33% increase over the prior year. The only reason it might seem positive is that the previous year's earnings ($3.00 a share) were so depressed that any improvement would look good. The point is, profits are recovering slowly and are still well below the company's peak annual earnings of $6.00 a share.

The consensus among analysts on what earnings will be for the next year should also be up—the more, the better. But remember: estimates are personal opinions, and opinions may be wrong (too high or too low). Actual reported earnings are facts.

Look for a Big Return on Equity

You should also be aware of two other measurements of profitability and growth: return on equity and cash flow per share.

Return on equity, or ROE, is calculated by dividing net income by shareholders' equity. This shows how efficiently a company uses its money, thereby helping to separate well-managed firms from those that are poorly managed. Our studies show that nearly all the greatest growth stocks of the past 50 years had ROEs of at least 17%. (The really superior growth situations will sport 25% to 50% ROEs.)

To determine cash flow, add back the amount of depreciation the company shows to reflect the amount of cash that is being generated internally. Some growth stocks can also show annual cash flow per share that is at least 20% greater than actual earnings per share.

Check the Stability of a Company's Three-Year Earnings Record

Through our research, we've determined another factor that has proved important in selecting growth stocks: the stability and consistency of annual earnings growth over the past three years. Our stability measurement, which is expressed on a scale of 1 to 99, is calculated differently from most statistics. The lower the figure, the more stable the past earnings record. The figures are calculated by plotting quarterly earnings for the past three or five years and fitting a trend line around the plotted points to determine the degree of deviation from the basic growth trend.

Growth stocks with steady earnings tend to have a stability figure below 20 or 25. Companies with stability ratings over 30 are more cyclical and a little less dependable in terms of their growth. All other things being equal, you may want to look for stocks showing a greater degree of sustainability, consistency, and stability in past earnings growth. Some companies that are growing 25% per year could have a stability rating of 1, 2, or 3. When the quarterly earnings for several years are plotted on a log-scale chart, the earnings line should be nearly straight, consistently moving up. In most cases there will be some acceleration in the rate of increase in recent quarters.

Ctrip.com	Nov. 13, 2009
EPS Growth Rate	46%
Earnings Stability	8
P/E Ratio	47 (2.0 x SP)
5-Year P/E Range	13–66
Return on Equity	35%
Cash Flow	$1.34

© William O'Neil + Co., Inc.

Sample earnings stability

Earnings stability numbers are customarily shown right after a company's annual growth rate, but most analysts and investment services don't bother to make the calculation. We show them in many of our institutional products as well as in Daily Graphs and Daily Graphs Online, which are designed for individual investors.

If you restrict your stock selections to ventures with proven growth records, you will avoid the hundreds of investments with erratic histories or cyclical recoveries in profits. A few such stocks could "top out" as they approach the peaks of their prior earnings cycle.

What Is a Normal Stock Market Cycle?

History demonstrates most bull (up) markets last two to four years and are followed by a recession or a bear (down) market. Then another bull market starts.

In the beginning phase of a new bull market, growth stocks are usually the first to lead and make new price highs. These are companies whose profits have grown quarter to quarter, but whose stocks have been held back by the poor general market conditions. The combination of a general market decline and a stock's continued profit growth will have compressed the price/earnings (P/E) ratio to a point where it is attractive to institutional investors, for whom P/Es are important.

Cyclical stocks in basic industries such as steel, chemicals, paper, rubber, autos, and machinery usually lag in the new bull market's early phase.

Young growth stocks will typically dominate for at least two bull market cycles. Then the emphasis may change to cyclicals, turnarounds, or other newly improved sectors for a short period.

While three out of four big market winners in the past were growth stocks, one in four was a cyclical or turnaround situation. In 1982, Chrysler and Ford were two such spirited turnaround plays. Cyclical and turnaround opportunities led in the market waves of 1953–1955, 1963–1965, and 1974–1975. Cyclicals including paper, aluminum, autos, chemicals, and plastics returned to the fore in 1987, and home-building stocks, which are also cyclical, have led in other periods. Examples of turnaround situations include IBM in 1994 and Apple in 2003.

Yet even when cyclical stocks are in favor, some pretty dramatic young growth issues are also available. Cyclical stocks in the United States are often those in older, less-efficient industries. Some of these companies weren't competitive until the demand for steel, copper, chemicals, and oil surged as a result of the rapid buildup of basic industries in China. That's why cyclicals were resurrected aggressively after the 2000 bear market ended in 2003.

They are still cyclical stocks, however, and they may not represent America's true future. In addition, large, old-line companies in America frequently have the added disadvantage of size: they are simply too large to be able to innovate and continually renew themselves so that they can compete with nimble foreign rivals and with America's young new entrepreneurs.

Rallies in cyclical stocks may tend to be more short-lived and prone to falter at the first hint of a recession or an earnings slowdown. Should you decide to buy a turnaround stock, look for annual earnings growth of at least 5% to 10% and two straight quarters of sharp earnings recovery that lift results for the latest 12 months into or very near new high ground. Check the 12-month earnings line on a stock chart; the sharper the angle of the earnings upswing, the better.

If the profit upswing is so dramatic that it reaches a new high, one quarter of earnings turnaround will sometimes suffice. Cleveland Cliffs, a supplier of iron ore pellets to the steel industry (and now known as Cliffs Natural Resources), came from a deficit position to dramatically accelerate quarterly earnings in 2004 by 64% and then by 241%. With that impetus, the stock rapidly advanced 170% in the next eight months.

How to Weed Out the Losers in a Group

Insisting on three years of earnings growth will help you quickly weed out 80% of the stocks in any industry group. Growth rates for most stocks in most groups are lackluster or nonexistent—unlike, for example,

- Xerox, which was growing at a 32% annual rate before its shares soared 700% from March 1963 to June 1966
- Wal-Mart Stores, which consistently created an annual growth rate of 43% before rocketing 11,200% from 1977 to 1990
- Cisco Systems, whose earnings were exploding at a 257% rate in October 1990, and Microsoft, which was growing at a 99% clip in October 1986, before their enormous advances
- Priceline.com, which from 2004 to 2006 more than doubled its earnings from 96 cents a share to $2.03, before it tripled in price in the next five quarters
- Google, which had already expanded its earnings from 55 cents a share in 2002 to $2.51 a share in 2004 before its stock climbed from $200 to $700 by 2007

Keep in mind that an annual growth record doesn't necessarily make a company a solid growth stock. In fact, some so-called growth stocks report substantially slower growth than they did in earlier market periods. Many growth leaders in one cycle do not repeat in the next cycle.

The stock of a company that has an outstanding three-year growth record of 30% but whose earnings growth has slowed to 10% or 15% in the last several quarters acts like a fully mature growth stock. Older and larger organizations are usually characterized by slower growth, and many of them should be avoided. America is continually led and driven by new innovative entrepreneurial companies. They, and not our government, create our new industries.

Insist on Both Annual and Current Quarterly Earnings Being Excellent

A standout stock needs both a sound growth record in recent years and a strong current earnings record in the last several quarters. It's the powerful combination of these two critical factors, rather than one or the other, that creates a super stock, or at least one that has a higher chance for true success.

The fastest way to find a company with strong and accelerating current earnings and solid three-year growth is by checking the proprietary Earnings per Share (EPS) Rating provided for every stock listed in *Investor's Business Daily's* research stock tables.

The EPS Rating measures a company's two most recent quarters of earnings growth against the same quarters the year before and examines its growth rate over the last three years. The results are then compared with those of all other publicly traded companies and rated on a scale from 1 to 99, with 99 being best. An EPS Rating of 99 means a company

has outperformed 99% of all other companies in terms of both annual and recent quarterly earnings performance.

If the stock is newly issued and the company doesn't have a three-year earnings record, look for big earnings increases and even bigger sales growth over the last five or six quarters. One or two quarters of profitability are often not enough and indicate a less-proven stock that might fall apart somewhere down the line.

Are Price/Earnings Ratios Really Important?

If you're like most investors, you've probably learned the most important thing you need to know about a stock is its P/E ratio. Well, prepare yourself for a bubble-bursting surprise.

For years, analysts have used P/E ratios as their basic measurement tool in deciding whether a stock is undervalued (has a low P/E) and should be bought, or is overvalued (has a high P/E) and should be sold. But our ongoing analysis of the most successful stocks from 1880 to the present shows that, contrary to most investors' beliefs, P/E ratios were not a relevant factor in price movement and have very little to do with whether a stock should be bought or sold.

Much more crucial, we found, was the percentage increase in earnings per share. To say that a security is "undervalued" because it's selling at a low P/E or because it's in the low end of its historical P/E range can be nonsense. **Primary consideration should be given to whether the rate of change in earnings is substantially increasing or decreasing.**

From 1953 through 1985, the average P/E ratio for the best-performing stocks at their early emerging stage was 20. (The average P/E of the Dow Jones Industrials over the same period was 15.) As they advanced, the biggest winners expanded their P/Es by 125%, to about 45. From 1990 to 1995, the real leaders began with an average P/E of 36 and expanded into the 80s. But these were just the averages. Beginning P/Es for most big winners ranged from 25 to 50, and the P/E expansions varied from 60 to 115. In the market euphoria of the late 1990s, these valuations increased to even greater levels. Value buyers missed almost all of these tremendous investments.

Why You Missed Some Fabulous Stocks!

These findings strongly suggest that if you weren't willing to buy growth stocks at 25 to 50 times earnings, or even much more, you automatically eliminated most of the best investments available! You missed Microsoft, Cisco Systems, Home Depot, America Online, and many, many others during their periods of greatest market performance.

Our studies suggest P/E ratios are an end effect of accelerating earnings that, in turn, attract big institutional buyers, resulting in strong price performance. P/Es are not a cause of excellent performance. High P/Es, for example, were found to occur because of bull markets. Low P/Es, with the exception of those on cyclical stocks, generally occurred because of bear markets.

In a roaring bull market, don't overlook a stock just because its P/E seems too high. It could be the next great winner. And never buy a stock just because the P/E ratio makes it look like a bargain. There are usually good reasons why the P/E is low, and there's no golden rule that prevents a stock that sells at 8 or 10 times earnings from going even lower and selling at 4 or 5 times earnings.

Many years ago, when I first began to study the market, I bought Northrop at 4 times earnings and watched in disbelief as the stock declined to a P/E ratio of 2.

How Price/Earnings Ratios Are Misused

Many Wall Street analysts put a stock on their "buy" list because it's selling at the low end of its historical P/E range. They'll also recommend a stock when the price starts to drop, thereby lowering the P/E and making it seem like an even bigger bargain.

In 1998, Gillette and Coca-Cola looked like great buys because they had sold off several points and their P/Es looked more attractive. In actuality, the earnings at both companies were showing a material deceleration that justified a lower valuation. A great deal of P/E analysis is based on personal opinions and theories that have been handed down through the years by analysts, academicians, and others, whose track records when it comes to making money in the market are both questionable and undocumented. In 2008, some Wall Street analysts recommended buying Bank of America all the way down. There are no safe, sure things in the market. That's why you need avoid or sell rules as well as buy rules.

Reliance on P/E ratios often ignores more basic trends. The general market, for example, may have topped, in which case all stocks are headed lower. To say a company is undervalued because at one time it was selling at 22 times earnings and it can now be bought for 15 is ridiculous and somewhat naive.

One way I *do* sometimes use P/E ratios is to estimate the potential price objective for a growth stock over the next 6 to 18 months based on its estimated future earnings. I may take the earnings estimate for the next two years and multiply it by the stock's P/E ratio at the initial chart base buy point, then multiply the result by 100% or slightly more. This is the degree of P/E expansion possible on average if a growth stock has a major price move. This tells me what a growth stock could potentially sell for during bull market conditions. However, there are some bull markets and certain growth stocks that may have little or no P/E expansion.

For example, if Charles Schwab's stock breaks out of its first base at $43.75 per share (as it did in late 1998) and its P/E ratio at the beginning buy point is 40, multiply 40 by 130% to see that the P/E ratio could possibly expand to 92 if the stock has a huge price move. Next, multiply the potential P/E ratio of 92 by the consensus earnings estimate two years out of $1.45 per share. This tells you what a possible price objective for your growth stock might be.

The Wrong Way to Analyze Companies in an Industry

Another faulty use of P/E ratios, by amateurs and professionals alike, is to evaluate the stocks in an industry and conclude the one selling at the cheapest P/E is always undervalued and therefore the most attractive purchase. The reality is, the lowest P/E usually belongs to the company with the most ghastly earnings record.

The simple truth is that at any given time, stocks usually sell near their current value. The stock that sells at 20 times earnings is at that level for one set of reasons, and the stock that trades at 15 times earnings is at that level for another set of reasons. A stock selling at, say, 7 times earnings does so because its overall record is more deficient than that of a stock with a higher P/E ratio. Also, keep in mind that cyclical stocks normally have lower P/Es, and that, even in good periods, they do not show the P/E expansion that occurs in growth stocks.

You can't buy a Mercedes for the price of a Chevrolet, and you can't buy oceanfront property for the same price you'd pay for land a couple of miles inland. Everything sells for about what it's worth at the time based on the law of supply and demand.

The increased value of great paintings was brought about almost singlehandedly many years ago by a fine-arts dealer named Joseph Duveen. He would travel to Europe and buy one-of-a-kind paintings by Rembrandt and others, paying more than the market price. He would then bring them back to the United States and sell them to Henry Ford and other industrialists of that era for substantially more than he had paid. In other words, Lord Duveen bought the one-of-a-kind masterpieces high and sold them much higher.

The point is, anyone can buy a mediocre piece of art for a low price, but the very best costs more. The very best stocks, like the very best art, usually command a higher price.

If a company's price and P/E ratio change in the near future, it's because conditions, events, psychology, and earnings have continued to improve or started to deteriorate. Eventually, a stock's P/E will reach a peak, but this normally occurs when the general market averages are topping out and starting a significant decline. It could also be a signal the company's rate of earnings growth is about to weaken.

It's true, high-P/E stocks will be more volatile, particularly if they're in the high-tech area. The price of a high-P/E stock can also temporarily get ahead of itself, but the same can be said for lower-P/E stocks.

Examples of High P/Es That Were Great Bargains

In situations where small but captivating growth companies have revolutionary new products, what seems like a high P/E ratio can actually be low. For instance,

- Xerox, which introduced the first dry copier in 1959, sold for 100 times earnings in 1960—*before* it advanced 3,300% in price (from a split-adjusted $5 to $170).

- Syntex, the first company to submit a patent for a birth control pill, sold for 45 times earnings in July 1963—before it advanced 400%.

- Genentech, a pioneer in the use of genetic information to develop new wonder drugs and the first biotech company to go public, was initially priced at 200 times earnings in November 1985. In five months, the new stock bolted 300%.

- America Online, whose software gave millions access to the revolutionary new world of the Internet, sold for over 100 times earnings in November 1994 before climbing 14,900% to its peak in December 1999.

- Google's P/E was in the 50s and 60s from $115 a share in September 2004 until it hit $475 a share in early January 2006.

The fact is, investors with a bias against what they consider to be high P/Es will miss out on some of the greatest opportunities of this or any other time. During bull markets, in particular, such a bias could literally cost you a fortune.

Don't Sell High-P/E Stocks Short

In June 1962, when the stock market was at rock bottom, a big Beverly Hills investor barged into the office of a broker friend of mine and shouted that, at 50 times earnings, Xerox was drastically overpriced. He proceeded to sell

2,000 shares short at $88 (borrowing stock from his broker to sell in hopes the stock would decline and he could later buy it back cheaper, making money on the difference in price). Sure enough, the stock took off at once and ultimately reached a price of $1,300 (before adjusting for splits) with a P/E ratio that topped 80.

So much for opinions about P/Es being too high! Investors' personal opinions are usually wrong; the market is almost always right. So stop fighting and arguing with the market.

You now possess a powerful secret to materially improve your stock selection and timing. Buy stocks with proven records of significant sales and earnings growth in each of the last three years plus strong recent quarterly improvements and a high return on equity. Get the best chart service you can find; learn to spot sound chart patterns and combine your new charting skill with the stocks with great earnings, sales, and return on equity. Don't accept anything less . . . if you want better results.

N = Newer Companies, New Products, New Management, New Highs Off Properly Formed Chart Bases

It takes something new to produce a startling advance in the price of a stock. It can be an important new product or service that sells rapidly and causes earnings to accelerate faster than previous rates of increase. Or it can be a change of management that brings new vigor, new ideas, or at least a new broom to sweep everything clean. New industry conditions—such as supply shortages, price increases, or the introduction of revolutionary technologies—can also have a positive effect on most stocks in an industry group.

In our study of the greatest stock market winners, which now spans the period from 1880 through 2008, we discovered that more than 95% of successful stocks with stunning growth in American industry fell into at least one of these categories. In the late 1800s, there was the new railroad industry connecting every part of our country, electricity, the telephone, and George Eastman's camera. Edison created the phonograph, the motion picture camera, and the lightbulb. Next came the auto, the airplane, and then the radio. The refrigerator replaced the icebox. Television, the computer, jet planes, the personal computer, fax machines, the Internet, cell phones . . . America's relentless inventors and entrepreneurs never quit. They built and created America's amazing growth record with their new products and new companies. These, in turn, created millions and millions of new jobs and a higher standard of living for the vast majority of Americans. In spite of bumps in the road, most Americans are unquestionably far better off than they or their parents were 25 or 40 years ago.

New Products That Created Super Successes

The way a company can achieve enormous success, thereby enjoying large gains in its stock price, is by introducing dramatic new products into the marketplace. I'm not talking about a new formula for dish soap. I'm talking about products that revolutionize the way we live. Here are just a few of the thousands of entrepreneurial companies that drove America and, during their time in the sun, created millions of jobs and a higher standard of living in the United States than in other areas of the world:

1. Northern Pacific was chartered as the first transcontinental railroad. Around 1900, its stock rocketed more than 4,000% in just 197 weeks.

2. General Motors began as the Buick Motor Company. In 1913–1914, GM stock increased 1,368%.

3. RCA, by 1926, had captured the market for commercial radio. Then, from June 1927, when the stock traded at $50, it advanced on a presplit basis to $575 before the market collapsed in 1929.

4. After World War II, Rexall's new Tupperware division helped push the company's stock to $50 a share in 1958, from $16.

5. Thiokol came out with new rocket fuels for missiles in 1957–1959, propelling its shares from $48 to the equivalent of $355.

6. Syntex marketed the oral contraceptive pill in 1963. In six months, the stock soared from $100 to $550.

7. McDonald's, with low-priced fast-food franchising, snowballed from 1967 to 1971 to create a 1,100% profit for stockholders.

8. Levitz Furniture's stock soared 660% in 1970–1971 on the popularity of the company's giant warehouse discount-furniture centers.

9. Houston Oil & Gas, with a major new oil field, ran up 968% in 61 weeks in 1972–1973 and picked up another 367% in 1976.

10. Computervision's stock advanced 1,235% in 1978–1980 with the introduction of its new CAD-CAM factory-automation equipment.

11. Wang Labs' Class B shares grew 1,350% in 1978–1980 on the development of its new word-processing office machines.

12. Price Company's stock shot up more than 15 times in 1982–1986 with the opening of a southern California chain of innovative wholesale warehouse membership stores.

13. Amgen developed two successful new biotech drugs, Epogen and Neupogen, and the stock raced ahead from $60 in 1990 to the equivalent of $460 in early 1992.

14. Cisco Systems, yet another California company, created routers and networking equipment that enabled companies to link up geographically dispersed local area computer networks. The stock rose nearly 2,000% from November 1990 to March 1994. In 10 years—1990 to 2000—it soared an unbelievable 75,000%.

15. International Game Technology surged 1,600% in 1991–1993 with new microprocessor-based gaming products.

16. Microsoft stock was carried up almost 1,800% from March 1993 to the end of 1999 as its innovative Windows software products dominated the personal computer market.

17. PeopleSoft, the number one maker of personnel software, achieved a 20-fold increase in the 3½ years starting in August 1994.

18. Dell Computer, the leader and innovator in build-to-order, direct PC sales, advanced 1,780% from November 1996 to January 1999.

19. EMC, with superior computer memory devices, capitalized on the ever-increasing need for network storage and raced up 478% in the 15 months starting in January 1998.

20. AOL and Yahoo!, the two top Internet leaders providing consumers with the new "portals" needed to access the wealth of services and information on the Internet, both produced 500% gains from the fall of 1998 to their peaks in 1999.

21. Oracle's database and e-business applications software drove its stock from $20 to $90 in only 29 weeks, starting in 1999.

22. Charles Schwab, the number one online discount broker, racked up a 414% gain in just six months starting in late 1998, a period that saw a shift to online trading.

23. Hansen Natural's "Monster" energy drinks were a hit with the workout crowd, and Hansen Natural's stock bolted 1,219% in only 86 weeks beginning in late 2004.

24. Google gave the world instant information via the Internet, and its stock advanced 536% from its initial offering in 2004.

25. Apple and the new iPod music player created a sensation that carried the company's stock up 1,580% from a classic cup-with-handle base price pattern that was easy to spot on February 27, 2004—if you used charts.

And if you missed that last golden opportunity, you had four more classic base pattern chances to buy Apple: on August 27, 2004; July 15, 2005; September 1, 2006; and April 27, 2007—plus four more after March 2009.

In the years ahead, hundreds and thousands of new creative leaders just like these will continue to surface and be available for you to purchase. People from all over the world come to America to capitalize on its freedom and opportunity. That's one secret of our success that many countries do not have. So don't ever get discouraged and give up on the lifetime opportunity that the stock market will provide. If you study, save, prepare, and educate yourself, you too will be able to recognize many of the future big winners as they appear. You can do it, if you have the necessary drive and determination. It doesn't make any difference who you are or where you came from or your current position in life. It's all up to you. Do you want to get ahead?

The Stock Market's "Great Paradox"

There is another fascinating phenomenon we found in the early stage of all winning stocks. We call it the "Great Paradox." Before I tell you what it is, I want you to look at the accompanying graphs of three typical stocks.

Which one looks like the best buy to you, A, B, or C? Which would you avoid? We'll give you the answer at the end of this chapter.

The staggering majority of individual investors, whether new or experienced, take delightful comfort in buying stocks that are down substantially from their peaks, thinking that they're getting a bargain. Among the hundreds of thousands of individual investors attending my investment lectures in the 1970s, 1980s, 1990s, and 2000s, many said that they do not buy stocks that are making new highs in price.

This bias is not limited to individual investors, however. I have provided extensive historical precedent research for more than 600 major institutional investors, and I have found that a number of them are also "bottom buyers." They, too, feel it's safer to buy stocks that look like bargains because they're either down a lot in price or actually selling near their lows.

Our study of the greatest stock market winners proved that the old adage "buy low, sell high" was completely wrong. In fact, our study proved the exact opposite. The hard-to-believe Great Paradox in the stock market is

What seems too high in price and risky to the majority usually goes higher eventually, and what seems low and cheap usually goes lower.

Are you finding this "high-altitude paradox" a little difficult to act upon? Let me cite another study we conducted. In this one, we analyzed two groups of stocks—those that made new highs and those that made new lows—over many bull market periods. The results were conclusive: stocks on the new-high list tended to go higher in price, while those on the new-low list tended to go lower.

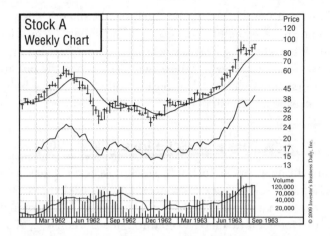

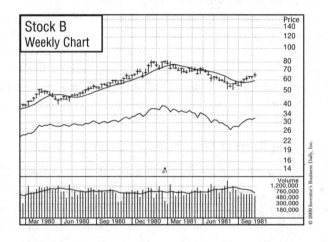

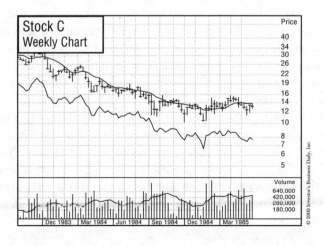

Based on our research, a stock on *Investor's Business Daily's* "new price low" list tends to be a pretty poor prospect and should be avoided. In fact, decisive investors should sell such stocks long before they ever get near the new-low list. A stock making the new-high list—especially one making the list for the first time while trading on big volume during a bull market— might be a prospect with big potential.

How Does a Stock Go from $50 to $100?

If you can't bring yourself to buy a stock at a level it has never before achieved, ask yourself: What does a stock that has traded between $40 and $50 a share over many months, and is now selling at $50, have to do to double in price? Doesn't it first have to go through $51, then $52, $53, $54, $55, and so on—all new price highs—before it can reach $100?

As a smart investor, your job is to buy when a stock looks too high to the majority of conventional investors and sell after it moves substantially higher and finally begins to look attractive to some of those same investors. If you had bought Cisco in November of 1990 at the highest price it had ever sold for, when it had just made a new high and looked scary, you would have enjoyed a nearly 75,000% increase from that point forward to its peak in the year 2000.

The Correct Time to Begin Buying a Stock

Just because a stock is making a new price high doesn't necessarily mean that this is the right time to buy. Using stock charts is an important piece of the stock selection process. A stock's historical price movement should be reviewed carefully, and you should look for stocks that are making new price highs as they break out of proper, correct bases. (Refer back to Chapter 2 for more detail on reading charts and identifying chart patterns.) The 100 great full-page examples in Chapter 1 should have given you a real head start.

These correctly created breakouts are the points at which most really big price advances begin and the possibility of a significant price move is the greatest. A sound consolidation, or base-building, period could last from seven or eight weeks up to 15 months.

As noted in Chapter 2, the perfect time to buy is during a bull market just as a stock is starting to break out of its price base. (See the America Online chart on page 178.) If the stock is more than 5% or 10% above the exact buy point off the base, it should be avoided. Buying it at this level greatly increases the chance of getting shaken out in the next normal correction or sharp pullback in price. You can't just buy the best stocks any old time. There's a right time, and then there are all the other times.

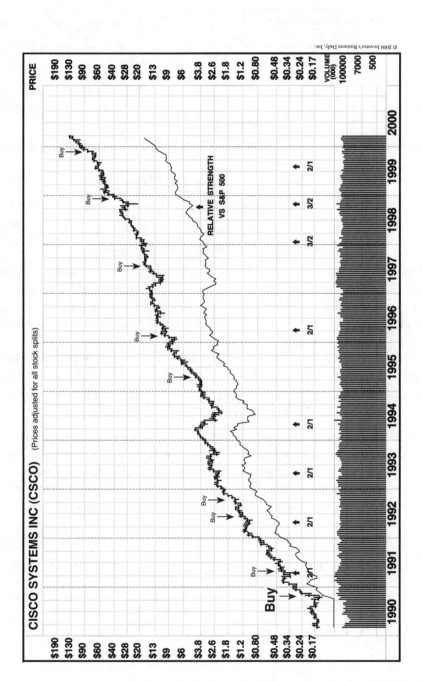

CISCO SYSTEMS INC (CSCO) (Prices adjusted for all stock splits)

177

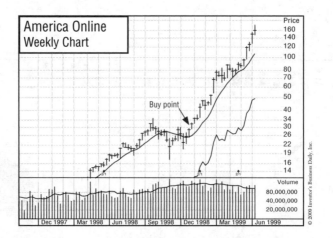

Answers to the Market's Great Paradox

Now that you know the Great Paradox, would you still pick the same stock you did earlier in the chapter? The right one to buy was Stock A, Syntex Corp., which is shown on the next page. The arrow pointing to July 1963's weekly price movements indicates the buy point. This arrow coincides with the price and volume activity at the end of the Stock A chart, adjusted for a 3-for-1 split. Syntex enjoyed a major price advance from its July 1963 buy point. In contrast, Stocks B (Halliburton) and C (Comdata Network) both declined, as you can see from the charts given on the next page. (The arrows indicate where the corresponding charts shown earlier left off.)

> **Search for companies that have developed important new products or services, or that have benefited from new management or materially improved industry conditions. Then buy their stocks when they are emerging from sound, correctly analyzed price consolidation patterns and are close to, or actually making, new price highs on increased volume.**

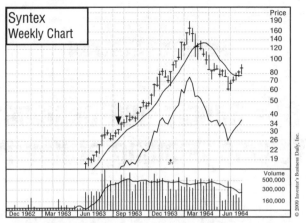

Stock A: 482% increase in 6 months from buy arrow.

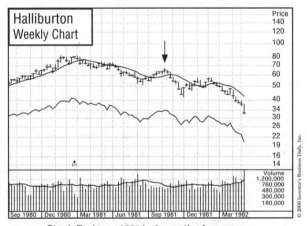

Stock B: down 42% in 6 months from arrow.

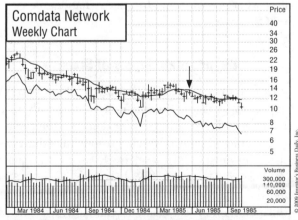

Stock C: down 21% in 5 months from arrow.

S = Supply and Demand:
Big Volume Demand at Key Points

The price of almost everything in your daily life is determined by the law of supply and demand. What you pay for your lettuce, tomatoes, eggs, and beef depends on how much of each is available and how many people want these items. Even in former Communist countries, where the difference between haves and have-nots was theoretically nonexistent, supply and demand held sway. There, state-owned goods were always in short supply and were often available only to the privileged class or on the black market to those who could pay the exorbitant prices.

This basic principle of supply and demand also applies to the stock market, where it is more important than the opinions of all the analysts on Wall Street, no matter what schools they attended, what degrees they earned, or how high their IQs.

Big or Small Supply of Stock

It's hard to budge the price of a stock that has 5 billion shares outstanding because the supply is so large. Producing a rousing rally in these shares would require a huge volume of buying, or demand. On the other hand, it takes only a reasonable amount of buying to push up the price of a stock with 50 million shares outstanding, a relatively smaller supply.

So if you're choosing between two stocks to buy, one with 5 billion shares outstanding and the other with 50 million, the smaller one will usually be the better performer, if other factors are equal. However, since smaller-capitalization stocks are less liquid, they can come down as fast as they go up, sometimes even faster. In other words, with greater opportunity comes significant additional risk. But there are definite ways of minimizing your risk, which will be discussed in Chapters 10 and 11.

The total number of shares outstanding in a company's capital structure represents the potential amount of stock available. But market professionals also look at the "floating supply"—the number of shares that are available for possible purchase after subtracting stock that is closely held. Companies in which top management owns a large percentage of the stock (at least 1% to 3% in a large company, and more in small companies) generally are better prospects because the managers have a vested interest in the stock.

There's another fundamental reason, besides supply and demand, why companies with a large number of shares outstanding frequently produce slower results: the companies themselves may be much older and growing at a slower rate. They are simply too big and sluggish.

In the 1990s, however, bigger-capitalization stocks outperformed small-cap issues for several years. This was in part related to the size problem experienced by the mutual fund community. It suddenly found itself awash in new cash as more and more people bought funds. As a result, larger funds were forced to buy more bigger-cap stocks. This need to put their new money to work made it appear that they favored bigger-cap issues. But this was contrary to the normal supply/demand effect, which favors smaller-cap stocks with fewer shares available to meet increases in institutional investor demand.

Big-cap stocks do have some advantages: greater liquidity, generally less downside volatility, better quality, and in some cases less risk. And the immense buying power that large funds have these days can make top-notch big stocks advance nearly as fast as shares of smaller companies.

Pick Entrepreneurial Management Rather than Caretakers

Big companies may seem to have a great deal of power and influence, but size often begets a lack of imagination and productive efficiency. Large companies are often run by older and more conservative "caretaker managements" that are less willing to innovate, take risks, and move quickly and wisely to keep up with rapidly changing times. In most cases, top managers of large companies don't own a lot of their company's stock. This is a serious deficiency that should be corrected. To the savvy investor, it suggests that the company's management and employees don't have a personal interest in seeing the company succeed. In some cases, large companies also have multiple layers of management that separate senior executives from what's going on at the customer level. And for companies competing in a capitalist economy, the ultimate boss is the customer.

Communication of information continues to change at an ever-faster rate. A company that has a hot new product today will find its sales slipping within two or three years if it doesn't continue to bring relevant, superior new products to market. Most new products, services, and inventions come from young, hungry, and innovative small- and medium-sized companies with entrepreneurial management. Not coincidentally, these smaller public and nonpublic companies grow faster and create somewhere between 80% and 90% of the new jobs in the United States. Many of them are in the service or technology and information industries. This is possibly where the great future growth of America lies. Microsoft, Cisco Systems, and Oracle are just a few examples of dynamic small-cap innovators of the 1980s and 1990s that continually grew and eventually became big-cap stocks.

If a mammoth older company creates an important new product, it may not help the stock materially because the product will probably account for only a small percentage of the company's total sales and earnings. The product is simply a small drop in a bucket that's now just too big.

Excessive Stock Splits May Hurt

From time to time, companies make the mistake of splitting their stocks excessively. This is sometimes done on advice from Wall Street investment bankers. In my opinion, it's usually better for a company to split its shares 2-for-1 or 3-for-2 than to split them 3-for-1 or 5-for-1. (When a stock splits 2-for-1, you get two shares for each share you previously held, but the new shares sell for half the price.) Oversized splits create a substantially larger supply and may put a company in the more lethargic, big-cap status sooner.

Incidentally, a stock will usually end up moving higher after its first split in a new bull market. But before it moves up, it will go through a correction for a period of weeks.

It may be unwise for a company whose stock has gone up in price for a year or two to declare an extravagant split near the end of a bull market or in the early stage of a bear market. Yet this is exactly what many corporations do.

Generally speaking, these companies feel that lowering the share price of their stock will attract more buyers. This may be the case with some smaller buyers, but it also may produce the opposite result—more sellers—especially if it's the second split within a year or two. Knowledgeable pros and a few shrewd individual traders will probably use the excitement generated by the oversized split as an opportunity to sell and take their profits. In addition, large holders who are thinking of selling might figure it will be easier to unload their 100,000 shares before a 3-for-1 split than to sell 300,000 shares afterward. And smart short sellers pick on stocks that are heavily owned by institutions and are starting to falter after huge price run-ups.

A stock will often reach a price top around the second or third time it splits. Our study of the biggest winners found that only 18% of them had splits in the year preceding their great price advances. Qualcomm topped in December 1999, just after its 4-for-1 stock split.

Look for Companies Buying Their Own Stock in the Open Market

In most but not all cases, it's usually a good sign when a company, especially a small- to medium-sized growth company that meets the CAN SLIM criteria, buys its own stock in the open market consistently over a period of time. (A 10% buyback would be considered big.) This reduces the number of shares and usually implies that the company expects improved sales and earnings in the future.

As a result of the buyback, the company's net income will be divided by a smaller number of shares, thereby increasing earnings per share. And as already noted, the percentage increase in earnings per share is one of the principal driving forces behind outstanding stocks.

From the mid-1970s to the early 1980s, Tandy, Teledyne, and Metromedia successfully repurchased their own stock, and all three achieved higher EPS growth and spectacular stock gains. Charles Tandy once told me that when the market went into a correction, and his stock was down, he would go to the bank and borrow money to buy back his stock, then repay the loans after the market recovered. Of course, this was also when his company was reporting steady growth in earnings.

Tandy's (split-adjusted) stock increased from $2.75 to $60 in 1983, Metromedia's soared from $30 in 1971 to $560 in 1977, and Teledyne zoomed from $8 in 1971 to $190 in 1984. Teledyne used eight separate buybacks to shrink its capitalization from 88 million shares to 15 million and increase its earnings from $0.61 a share to nearly $20.

In 1989 and 1990, International Game Technology announced that it was buying back 20% of its stock. By September 1993, IGT had advanced more than 20 times. Another big winner, home builder NVR Inc., had large buybacks in 2001. All these were growth companies. I'm not sure that company buybacks when earnings are not growing are all that sound.

A Low Corporate Debt-to-Equity Ratio Is Generally Better

After you've found a stock with a reasonable number of shares, check the percentage of the company's total capitalization represented by long-term debt or bonds. Usually, the lower the debt ratio, the safer and better the company. The earnings per share of companies with high debt-to-equity ratios could be clobbered in difficult periods when interest rates are high or during more severe recessions. These highly leveraged companies are generally of lower quality and carry substantially higher risk.

The use of extreme leverage of up to 40-to-1 or 50-to-1 was common among banks, brokers, mortgage lenders, and quasi-government agencies like Fannie Mae and Freddie Mac starting in 1995 and continuing until 2007. These institutions were strongly encouraged by the federal government's actions to invest large amounts of money in subprime loans to lower-income buyers, which ultimately led to the financial and credit crisis in 2008.

Rule 1 for all competent investors and homeowners is never ever borrow more than you can pay back. Excessive debt hurts all people, companies, and governments.

A corporation that's been reducing its debt as a percentage of equity over the last two or three years is worth considering. If nothing else, interest costs will be sharply reduced, helping to generate higher earnings per share.

Another thing to watch for is the presence of convertible bonds in the capital structure; earnings could be diluted if and when the bonds are converted into shares of common stock.

Evaluating Supply and Demand

The best way to measure a stock's supply and demand is by watching its daily trading volume. This is uniquely important. It's why *Investor's Business Daily*'s stock tables show both a stock's trading volume each day and the percentage volume is above or below the stock's average daily volume in the last three months. These facts, plus a proprietary rating of the amount of recent accumulation or distribution in the stock, are key information available in no other daily publication, including the *Wall Street Journal*.

When a stock pulls back in price, you typically want to see volume dry up at some point, indicating there is no further selling pressure. When the stock rallies in price, in most situations you want to see volume rise, which usually represents buying by institutions, not the public.

When a stock breaks out of a price consolidation area (see Chapter 2 on chart reading of price patterns of winning stocks), trading volume should jump 40% or 50% above normal. In many cases, it will be 100% or more that day, indicating solid buying and likely further price increases. Using daily, weekly, and monthly charts helps you analyze and interpret a stock's price and volume action.

You should analyze a stock's base pattern week by week, beginning with the first week a stock closes down in a new base and continuing each week until the current week, where you think it may break out of the base. You judge how much price progress up or down the stock made each week and whether it was on increased or decreased volume from the prior week. You also note where the stock closed within the price spread of each week's high and low. You do both a week-by-week check and evaluate the pattern's overall shape to see if it is sound and under accumulation or if it has too many defects.

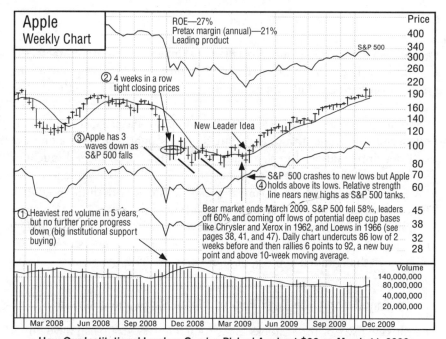

How Our Institutional Leaders Service Picked Apple at $92 on March 11, 2009

Any size capitalization can be bought using the CAN SLIM system. But small-cap stocks will be a lot more volatile. From time to time, the market shifts emphasis from small to large caps. Companies buying back their stock in the open market and showing stock ownership by management are preferred.

L = Leader or Laggard: Which Is Your Stock?

People tend to buy stocks that make them feel either good or comfortable. But in a bull market populated by dynamic leaders that just keep surprising on the upside, these sentimental favorites often turn out to be the dullest laggards.

Suppose you want to own a stock in the computer industry. If you buy the best performer in the group, and your timing is right, you have a crack at real price appreciation. But if you buy a stock that hasn't moved much, or that has even fallen to a price that makes it seem like a bargain and therefore safer, chances are that you've picked a stock with little potential. There's a reason, after all, that it's at the bottom of the pile.

Don't just dabble in stocks, buying what you like for whatever reason. Dig in, do some detective work, and find out what makes some stocks go up much more than others. You can do it, if you work at it.

Buy Among the Best Two or Three Stocks in a Group

The top one, two, or three stocks in a strong industry group can have unbelievable growth, while others in the pack may hardly stir.

The great computer stocks in the bull market of 1979 and 1980—Wang Labs, Prime Computer, Datapoint, Rolm, and Tandy—had five-, six-, and sevenfold advances before they topped and retreated. But the sentimental favorite, grand old IBM, just sat there, and giants Burroughs, NCR, and Sperry Rand were just as lifeless. In the bull market of 1981–1983, however, IBM sprang to life and produced excellent results.

In the retail sector, Home Depot advanced 10 times from 1988 to 1992, while the laggards in the home-improvement niche, Waban and Hechinger, dramatically underperformed.

You should buy the really great companies—those that lead their industries and are number one in their particular fields. All of my best big winners—Syntex in 1963, Pic 'N' Save from 1976 to 1983, Price Co. from 1982 to 1985, Franklin Resources from 1985 to 1986, Genentech from 1986 to 1987, Amgen from 1990 to 1991, America Online from 1998 to 1999, Charles Schwab from 1998 to 1999, Sun Microsystems from 1998 to 1999, Qualcomm in 1999, eBay from 2002 to 2004, Google from 2004 to 2007, and Apple from 2004 to 2007—were the number one companies in their industry space at the time I purchased them.

By number one, I don't mean the largest company or the one with the most recognized brand name. I mean the one with the best quarterly and annual earnings growth, the highest return on equity, the widest profit margins, the strongest sales growth, and the most dynamic stock-price action. This type of company will also have a unique and superior product or service and be gaining market share from its older, less-innovative competitors.

Avoid Sympathy Stocks, Buy New Innovative Leaders

Our studies show that very little in the stock market is really new; history just keeps repeating itself.

When I first bought stock in Syntex, the developer of the birth-control pill, in July 1963 off a high, tight flag pattern (and it then rapidly shot up 400%), most people wouldn't touch it. The stock had just made a new price high at $100 on the American Stock Exchange, and its price plus its P/E ratio, 45, made it seem too high and scary. No brokerage firms had research reports on it then, and the only mutual fund that owned it—a Value Line fund—had sold it the prior quarter when it began moving up. Instead, several Wall Street investment firms later recommended G. D. Searle as a "sympathy play." Searle had a product similar to Syntex's, and its stock looked much cheaper because it hadn't gone up as much. But its stock failed to produce the same results. Syntex was the leader; Searle the laggard.

A sympathy play is a stock in the same industry group that is bought in the hope that the luster of the real leader will rub off on it. But the profits of such companies usually pale in comparison. The stocks will eventually try to move up "in sympathy" with the leader, but they never do as well.

In 1970, Levitz Furniture, the leader in the then-new warehouse business, became an electrifying market winner. Wickes Corp. copied Levitz, and many people bought its shares because they were "cheaper," but Wickes never performed and ultimately got into financial trouble. Levitz, meanwhile, appreciated 900% before it finally topped.

As steel industry pioneer Andrew Carnegie said in his autobiography: "The first man gets the oyster; the second, the shell." Each new business cycle in America is driven by new innovators, inventors, and entrepreneurs.

If our government really wants to create jobs and not welfare packages, the most powerful way would be to provide strong tax incentives for the first two or three years to people who want to start new, small entrepreneurial businesses. Our data show that in the last 25 years, small businesses in America were responsible for creating 80% to 90% of all new jobs. This is a significantly higher percentage than that shown in government data, where new jobs are not accounted for in a realistic, comprehensive manner.

For example, the Small Business Administration defines a small business as one with fewer than 500 people. Yes, when Sam Walton started Wal-Mart and Bill Gates started Microsoft, each company had maybe 30 or 40 people. A year later they had maybe 75, the next year 120, then 200, then 320, then 501. From that point on, they were no longer considered to be small companies. But over the next 10 or 15 years, one of them created more than a million jobs and the other 500,000 jobs. Those jobs were all created by a dynamic entrepreneur who started a brand-new company, and they should be recognized and counted as such.

We have a huge database on all public companies. In the past 25 years, big business created no net new jobs. When a big business buys another company, thereby instantly padding its payrolls, it doesn't create *new* jobs. In fact, it usually consolidates and lays off people in duplicative positions. Many such companies also downsize over time. Our inefficient, bureaucratic government needs to start counting all jobs created by new or small businesses during their first 15 or 20 years in business.

How to Separate the Leaders from the Laggards: Using Relative Price Strength

If you own a portfolio of stocks, you must learn to sell the worst performers first and keep the best a little longer. In other words, always sell your mistakes while the loss is still small, and watch your better selections to see if they progress into your big winners. Human nature being what it is, most people do it backwards: they hold their losers and sell their winners, a formula that always leads to bigger losses.

How do you tell which stock is better and which is worse? The fastest and easiest way is by checking its Relative Price Strength (RS) Rating in *Investor's Business Daily*.

The proprietary RS Rating measures the price performance of a given stock against the rest of the market for the past 52 weeks. Every stock in the market is assigned a rating from 1 to 99, with 99 being best. An RS Rating of 99 means that the stock has outperformed 99% of all other companies in terms of price performance. A RS of 50 means that half of all other stocks have done better and half have done worse.

If your stock's RS Rating is below 70, it is lagging the better-performing stocks in the overall market. That doesn't mean that it can't go up in price. It just means that if by some chance it does go up, it'll probably go up less.

From the early 1950s through 2008, the average RS Rating of the best-performing stocks *before* their major run-ups was 87. In other words, the best stocks were already doing better than nearly 9 out of 10 others when they were starting out on their most explosive advance yet. So the rule for those who are determined to be big winners in the stock market is: look for the genuine leaders and avoid laggards and sympathy plays. Don't buy stocks with Relative Strength Ratings in the 40s, 50s, or 60s.

The Relative Price Strength Rating is shown each day for all stocks listed in *Investor's Business Daily's* stock tables. You can't find this information in any other daily business or local newspaper. Updated RS Ratings are also shown on the Daily Graphs Online charting service.

A stock's relative strength can also be plotted on a chart. If the RS line has been sinking for seven months or more, or if the line has an abnormally sharp decline for four months or more, the stock's price behavior is highly questionable, and it should probably be sold.

Pick 80s and 90s That Are in Sound and Proper Base Patterns

If you want to upgrade your stock selection so that you're zeroing in on the leaders, restrict your purchases to companies showing RS Ratings of 80 or higher. There's no point in buying a stock that's straggling behind. Yet that's exactly what many investors do—including some who work at America's largest investment firms.

I don't like to buy stocks with Relative Price Strength Ratings less than 80. In fact, the really big moneymakers generally have RS Ratings of 90 or higher just before they break out of their first or second base structure. The RS Rating of a potential winning stock should be in the same league as a pitcher's fastball. The average big-league fastball is clocked at 86 miles per hour, and the best pitchers throw "heat" in the 90s.

When you buy a stock, make absolutely sure that it's coming out of a sound base or price consolidation area. Also make sure that you buy it at its exact buy, or pivot, point. As mentioned before, avoid buying stocks that are extended more than 5% or 10% above the precise initial buy point. This will keep you from chasing stocks that race up in price too rapidly and makes it less likely that you will be shaken out during sharp market sell-offs.

The unwillingness of investors to set and follow minimum standards for stock selection reminds me of doctors years ago who were ignorant of the need to sterilize their instruments before each operation. They kept killing off patients until surgeons finally and begrudgingly accepted studies by researchers Louis Pasteur and Joseph Lister. Ignorance rarely pays off in any walk of life, and it's no different in the stock market.

Finding New Leaders during Market Corrections

Corrections, or price declines, in the general market can help you recognize new leaders—if you know what to look for. The more desirable growth stocks normally correct 1½ to 2½ times the general market averages. In other words, if the overall market comes down 10%, the better growth stocks will correct 15% to 25%. However, in a correction during a bull, or upward-trending, market, the growth stocks that decline the least (percentagewise) are usually your best selections. Those that drop the most are normally the weakest.

Say the general market average suffers an intermediate-term correction of 10%, and three of your successful growth stocks come off 15%, 25%, and 35%. The two that are off only 15% or 25% are likely to be your best investments after they recover. A stock that slides 35% to 40% in a general market decline of 10% could be flashing a warning signal. In most cases, you should heed it.

Once a general market decline is definitely over, the first stocks that bounce back to new price highs are almost always your authentic leaders. These chart breakouts continue week by week for about 13 weeks. The best ones usually come out in the first three or four weeks. This is the ideal period to buy stocks . . . you absolutely don't want to miss it. Be sure to read the chapter on general market direction carefully to learn how you determine it.

Pros Make Many Mistakes Too

Many professional investment managers make the serious mistake of buying stocks that have just suffered unusually large price drops. Our studies indicate that this is a surefire way to get yourself in trouble.

In June 1972, an otherwise capable institutional investor in Maryland bought Levitz Furniture after its first abnormal price break—a one-week drop from $60 to around $40. The stock rallied for a few weeks, then rolled over and broke to $18.

In October 1978, several institutional investors bought Memorex, a leading supplier of computer peripheral equipment, when it had its first unusual price break and looked to be a real value. It later plunged.

In September 1981, certain money managers in New York bought Dome Petroleum on a break from $16 to $12. To them, it seemed cheap, and a favorable story about the stock was going around Wall Street. Months later, Dome sold for $1.

Institutional buyers snapped up Lucent Technologies, a Wall Street darling after it was spun off from AT&T in the mid-1990s, after it broke from $78 to $50. Later that year, it collapsed to $5.

Also in 2000, many people bought Cisco Systems when it dropped to $50 from its early-year high of $82. The maker of computer networking equipment had been a huge winner in the 1990s, when it soared 75,000%, so it looked cheap at $50. It went to $8 and never got back to $50. In 2008, eight years after those buyers saw value at $50, Cisco was selling for only $17. To do well in the stock market, you've got to stop doing what got you into trouble in the past and create new and far better rules and methods to guide you in the future.

Suppose Joe Investor missed buying Crocs, the footwear company, at a split-adjusted $15 as it came out of the perfect cup-with-handle pattern in September 2006. Suppose he also missed the next cup pattern in April 2007 at 28. Then the stock roars up to $75 by October, with earnings up 100% every quarter. A month later, however, the stock drops to 47, and Joe sees his chance to get into this big winner that he missed all the way up and that's now at a cheaper price. But the stock just keeps falling, and by January 2009 it's trading at $1. Buying stocks on the way down is dangerous. You can get wiped out. So stop this risky bad habit.

How about buying a blue chip, a top-flight bank that's a leader in its industry—Bank of America? In December 2006, it was $55 a share, but you could have gotten it cheaper a year later at $40. Another year later, however, it had plunged to $6. But you're still a long-term investor, getting your 4-cent dividend.

This is why I say don't buy a supposed good stock on the way down and why we recommend cutting all losses at 7% or 8%. Any stock can do anything. You must have rules to protect your hard-earned money. We all make mistakes. You must learn to correct yours without vacillating.

None of the pros or individual investors who owned or bought Cisco, Crocs, or BofA when they were falling recognized the difference between normal price declines and highly abnormal big-volume corrections that can signal potential disaster. But the real problem was they relied on stories they'd heard and a method of fundamental analysis that equates lower P/E ratios with "value." They didn't heed the market action that could have told them what was really going on.

Those who listen and learn the difference between normal and abnormal action are said to have a "good feel for the market." Those who ignore what the market says usually pay a heavy price. Anyone who buys stocks on the way down in price because they look cheap will learn the hard way this is how you can lose a lot of money.

Look for Abnormal Strength on a Weak Market Day

In the spring of 1967, I remember walking through a broker's office in New York on a day when the Dow Jones Industrial Average was down more than 12 points. That was a lot in those days, when the Dow was around 800 compared with 8,000 in 2008. When I looked up at the electronic ticker tape moving across the wall and showing prices, I saw that Control Data—a pioneer in supercomputers—was trading at $62, up 3½ points on heavy volume. I bought the stock at once. I knew Control Data well, and this was highly abnormal strength in the face of a weak overall market. The stock later ran up to $150.

In April 1981, just as the 1981 bear market was getting under way, MCI Communications, a telecommunications stock trading in the over-the-counter market, broke out of a price base at $15. It advanced to the equivalent of $90 in 21 months. This was another great example of highly abnormal strength during a weak market.

Lorillard, the tobacco company, did the same thing in the 1957 bear market, Software Toolworks soared in the down market of early 1990, wireless telecom firm Qualcomm made big progress even during the difficult midyear market of 1999, and Taro Pharmaceutical late in 2000 bucked the bear market that had begun that spring. Also in 2000, home builder NVR took off at $50 and rode steadily lower interest rates up to $360 by March 2003. The new bull market in 2003 uncovered many leaders, including Apple, Google, Research in Motion, Potash, and several Chinese stocks.

So don't forget: **It seldom pays to invest in laggard stocks, even if they look tantalizingly cheap. Look for, and confine your purchases to, market leaders. Get out of your laggard losers if you're down 8% below the price you paid so that you won't risk getting badly hurt.**

I = Institutional Sponsorship

It takes big demand to push up prices, and by far the biggest source of demand for stocks is institutional investors, such as mutual funds, pension funds, hedge funds, insurance companies, large investment counselors, bank trust departments, and state, charitable, and educational institutions. These large investors account for the lion's share of each day's market activity.

What Is Institutional Sponsorship?

Institutional sponsorship refers to the shares of any stock owned by such institutions. For measurement purposes, I have never considered brokerage research reports or analyst recommendations as institutional sponsorship, although a few may exert short-term influence on some securities for a few days. Investment advisory services and market newsletters also aren't considered to be institutional or professional sponsorship by this definition because they lack the concentrated or sustained buying or selling power of institutional investors.

A winning stock doesn't need a huge number of institutional owners, but it should have several at a minimum. Twenty might be a reasonable minimum number in a few rare cases involving small or newer companies, although most stocks have many, many more. If a stock has no professional sponsorship, chances are that its performance will be more run-of-the-mill, as this means that at least some of the more than 10,000 institutional investors have looked at the stock and passed over it. Even if they're wrong, it still takes large buying volume to stimulate an important price increase.

Look for Both Quality and Increasing Numbers of Buyers

Diligent investors dig down yet another level. They want to know not only how *many* institutional sponsors a stock has, but whether that number has steadily increased in recent quarters, and, more important, whether the most recent quarter showed a materially larger increase in the number of owners. They also want to know *who* those sponsors are, as shown by services reporting this information. They look for stocks that are held by at least one or two of the more savvy portfolio managers who have the best performance records. This is referred to as analyzing the *quality* of sponsorship.

In analyzing the recorded quality of a stock's institutional sponsorship, the latest 12 months plus the last three years of the investment performance of mutual fund sponsors are usually most relevant. A quick and easy way to get this information is by checking a mutual fund's 36-Month Performance Rating in *Investor's Business Daily*. An A+ rating indicates that a fund is in the top 5% in terms of performance. Funds with ratings of B+ or higher are considered the better performers. Keep in mind that the rating of a good growth stock mutual fund may be a little lower during a bear market, when most growth stocks will definitely correct.

Results may change significantly, however, if key portfolio managers leave one money-management firm and go to another. The leaders in the ratings of top institutional mutual funds generally rotate and change slowly as the years go by.

Several financial services publish fund holdings and the investment performance records of various institutions. For example, you can learn the top 25 holdings of each fund plus other data at Morningstar.com. In the past, mutual funds tended to be more aggressive in the market. More recently, new "entrepreneurial-type" investment-counseling firms have cropped up to manage public and institutional money.

Buy Companies That Show Increasing Sponsorship

As mentioned earlier, it's less crucial to know how *many* institutions own a stock than to know *which* of the limited number of better-performing institutions own a stock or have bought it recently. It's also key to know whether the total number of sponsors is increasing or decreasing. The main thing to look for is the recent quarterly trend. It's always best to buy stocks showing strong earnings and sales and an increasing number of institutional owners over several recent quarters.

Note New Stock Positions
Bought in the Last Quarter

A significant new position taken by an institutional investor in the most recently reported period is generally more relevant than existing positions that have been held for some time. When a fund establishes a new position, chances are that it will continue to add to that position and be less likely to sell it in the near future. Reports on such activities are available about six weeks after the end of a fund's three- or six-month period. They are helpful to those who can identify the wiser picks and who understand correct timing and proper analysis of daily and weekly charts.

Many investors feel that disclosures of a fund's new commitments are published too long after the fact to be of any real value. But these individual opinions typically aren't correct.

Institutional trades also tend to show up on some ticker tapes as transactions of from 1,000 to 100,000 shares or more. Institutional buying and selling can account for up to 70% of the activity in the stocks of most leading companies. This is the sustained force behind most major price moves. About half of the institutional buying that shows up on the New York Stock Exchange ticker tape may be in humdrum stocks. Much of it may also be wrong. But out of the other half, you may have several truly phenomenal selections.

Your task, then, is to separate intelligent, highly informed institutional buying from poor, faulty buying. This is hard at first, but it will get easier as you learn to apply and follow the proven rules, guidelines, and principles presented in this book.

To get a better sense for what works in the market, it's important to study the investment strategies of a well-managed mutual fund. When reviewing the tables in *Investor's Business Daily*, look for growth funds with A, A-, or B+ ratings during bull markets and then call to obtain a prospectus. From the prospectus, you'll learn the investment philosophy and techniques used by the individual funds as well as the type and caliber of stocks they've purchased. For example:

- Fidelity's Contrafund, managed by Will Danoff, has been the best-performing large, multibillion-dollar fund for a number of years. He scours the country and international equities to get in early on every new concept or story in a stock.

- American Century Heritage fund uses computers to find stocks with accelerating percentage increases in recent sales and earnings.

- Ken Heebner's CGM Focus and CGM Mutual have both had superior results for many years. His Focus fund concentrates on 20 to 100 stocks at one time. This makes it more volatile, but Ken likes to make big sector bets that in most cases have worked very well for him.

- Jeff Vinik was a top-flight manager at Fidelity who left and started what is regarded as one of the country's best-performing hedge funds.
- Janus 20, headquartered in Denver, runs a concentrated portfolio of fewer than 30 growth stocks.

Some funds buy on new highs; others buy around lows and may sell on new highs. New fund leaders can emerge over time.

Is Your Stock "Overowned" by Institutions?

It's possible for a stock to have too much institutional sponsorship. *Overowned* is a term we coined in 1969 to describe stocks in which institutional ownership has become excessive. The danger is that excessive sponsorship might translate into large potential selling if something goes wrong at the company or if a bear market begins.

Janus Funds alone owned more than 250 million shares of Nokia and 100 million shares of America Online, which contributed to an adverse supply/demand imbalance in 2000 and 2001. WorldCom (in 1999) and JDS Uniphase and Cisco Systems (in 2000 and 2001) were other examples of overowned stocks.

Thus, the "Favorite 50" and other widely owned institutional stocks can be poor, risky prospects. By the time a company's strong performance is so obvious that almost all institutions own the stock, it's probably too late to climb aboard. The heart is already out of the watermelon.

Look how many institutions thought Citigroup should be a core holding in the late 1990s and 2000s. At one point during the 2008 bank subprime loan and credit crisis, the stock of this leading New York City bank got down to $3.00 and later $1.00. Only two years earlier it was $57. This is why, since its first edition, *How to Make Money in Stocks* has always had two detailed chapters on the subject of when to sell your stock. Most investors have no rules or plan for when to sell. That is a serious mistake. So get realistic.

Another case was American International Group. In 2008, AIG had more than 3,600 institutional owners when it tanked to 50 cents from the over $100 it had sold for in 2000. The government-sponsored Fannie Mae collapsed to less than a dollar during the same financial fiasco.

America Online in the summer of 2001 and Cisco Systems in the summer of 2000 were also overowned by more than a thousand institutions. This potential heavy supply can adversely affect a stock during bear market periods. Many funds will pile into certain leaders on the way up and pile out on the way down.

An Unassailable Institutional Growth Stock Tops

Some stocks may seem invincible, but the old saying is true: what goes up must eventually come down. No company is forever immune to management problems, economic slowdowns, and changes in market direction. Savvy investors know that in the stock market, there are few "sacred cows." And there are certainly no guarantees.

In June 1974, few people could believe it when William O'Neil + Co. put Xerox on its institutional avoid or sell list at $115. Until then, Xerox had been one of the most amazingly successful and widely held institutional stocks, but our data indicated that it had topped and was headed down. It was also overowned. Institutional investors went on to make Xerox their most widely purchased stock for that year. But when the stock tumbled in price, it showed the true condition of the company at that time.

That episode called attention to our institutional services firm and got us our first major insurance company account in New York City. The firm had been buying Xerox in the $80s on the way down until we persuaded it that it should be selling instead.

We also received a lot of resistance in 1998 when we put Gillette, another sacred cow, on our avoid list near $60 before it tanked. Enron was removed from our new ideas list on November 29, 2000, at $72.91, and we stopped following it. (Six months later it was $45, and six months after that it was below $5 and headed for bankruptcy.)

A list of some of the technology stocks that were removed from our New Stock Market Ideas (NSMI) institutional service potential new ideas list in 2000, when most analysts were incorrectly calling them buys, appears on page 198. The lesson: don't be swayed by a stock's broad-based popularity or an analyst advising investors to buy stocks on the way down in price.

Institutional Sponsorship Means Market Liquidity

Another benefit to you as an individual investor is that institutional sponsorship provides buying support when you want to sell your investment. If there's no sponsorship, and you try to sell your stock in a poor market, you may have problems finding someone to buy it. Daily marketability is one of the big advantages of owning high-quality stocks in the United States. (Real estate is far less liquid, and sales commissions and fees are much higher.) Good institutional sponsorship provides continuous liquidity for you. In a poor real estate market, there is no guarantee that you can find a willing buyer when you want to sell. It could take you six months to a year, and you could sell for a much lower price than you expected.

Stocks Removed from NSMI Buys in 2000

Symbol	Name	Date Removed	Price Removed	Low Price as of 10/30/01	Percent Decline as of 10/30/01*
AMAT	Applied Materials	5/11/2000	$80.56	$26.59	67%
CSCO	Cisco Systems	8/1/2000	$63.50	$11.04	83%
CNXT	Conexant Systems	3/3/2000	$84.75	$6.57	92%
DELL	Dell Computer Corp	5/9/2000	$46.31	$16.01	65%
EMC	E M C Corp	12/15/2000	$74.63	$10.01	87%
EXDS	Exodus Communications	3/30/2000	$69.25	$0.14	100%
INTC	Intel Corp	9/15/2000	$58.00	$18.96	67%
JDSU	J D S Uniphase	10/10/2000	$90.50	$5.12	94%
MOT	Motorola	3/30/2000	$51.67	$10.50	80%
NXTL	Nextel Communications	4/12/2000	$55.41	$6.87	88%
NT	Nortel Networks	10/2/2000	$59.56	$4.76	92%
PMCS	P M C Sierra Inc	8/1/2000	$186.25	$9.37	95%
QLGC	Qlogic Corp	3/14/2000	$167.88	$17.21	90%
SEBL	Siebel Systems Inc	12/15/2000	$76.88	$12.24	84%
SUNW	Sun Microsystems	11/9/2000	$49.32	$7.52	85%
VIGN	Vignette Corp	3/15/2000	$88.33	$3.08	97%
YHOO	Yahoo!	3/30/2000	$175.25	$8.02	95%

*Percentages have been rounded to the nearest whole number.

In summary: **buy only those stocks that have at least a few institutional sponsors with better-than-average recent performance records and that have added institutional owners in recent quarters.** If I find that a stock has a large number of sponsors, but that none of the sponsors is on my list of the 10 or so excellent-performing funds, in the majority of cases I will pass over the stock. Institutional sponsorship is one more important tool to use as you analyze a stock for purchase. From your list of most savvy funds, check to see what were the two or three stocks each one put the most dollars into in the most recent quarter. You might get one or two names to research. Just make sure these prospects pass the critical CAN SLIM rules and the chart is in the right position to buy before you act.

M = Market Direction: How You Can Determine It

You can be right on every one of the factors in the last six chapters, but if you're wrong about the direction of the general market, and that direction is down, three out of four of your stocks will plummet along with the market averages, and you will lose money big time, as many people did in 2000 and again in 2008. Therefore, in your analytical tool kit, you absolutely must have a proven, reliable method to accurately determine whether you're in a bull (uptrending) market or a bear (downtrending) market. Very few investors or stockbrokers have such an essential tool. Many investors depend on someone else to help them with their investments. Do these other advisors or helpers have a sound set of rules to determine when the general market is starting to get into trouble?

That's not enough, however. If you're in a bull market, you need to know whether it's in the early stage or a later stage. And more importantly, you need to know what the market is doing right now. Is it weak and acting badly, or is it merely going through a normal intermediate decline (typically 8% to 12%)? Is it doing just what it should be, considering the basic current conditions in the country, or is it acting abnormally strong or weak? To answer these and other vital questions, you'll want to learn to analyze the overall market correctly, and to do that, you must start at the most logical point.

The market direction method we discovered and developed many years ago is such a key element in successful investing you'll want to reread this chapter several times until you understand and can apply it on a day-to-day basis for the rest of your investment life. If you learn to do this well, you should never in the future find your investment portfolio down 30% to 50% or more in a bad bear market.

The best way for you to determine the direction of the market is to look carefully at, follow, interpret, and understand the daily charts of the three or four major general market averages and what their price and volume changes are doing on a day-to-day basis. This might sound intimidating at first, but with patience and practice, you'll soon be analyzing the market like a true pro. This is the most important lesson you can learn if you want to stop losing and start winning. Are you ready to get smarter? Are your future peace of mind and financial independence worth some extra effort and determination on your part?

Don't ever let anyone tell you that you can't time the market. This is a giant myth passed on mainly by Wall Street, the media, and those who have never been able to do it, so they think it's impossible. We've heard from thousands of readers of this chapter and *Investor's Business Daily's The Big Picture* column who have learned how to do it. They took the time to read the rules and do their homework so that they were prepared and knew exactly what facts to look for. As a result, they had the foresight and understanding to sell stocks and raise cash in March 2000 and from November 2007 to January 2008 and June 2008, protecting much of the gains they made during 1998 and 1999 and in the strong five-year Bush bull market in stocks that lasted from March 2003 to June 2008.

The erroneous belief that you can't time the market—that it's simply impossible, that no one can do it—evolved more than 40 years ago after a few mutual fund managers tried it unsuccessfully. They had to both sell at exactly the right time and then get back into the market at exactly the right time. But because of their asset size problems, and because they had no system, it took a number of weeks for them to believe the turn and finally reenter the market. They relied on their personal judgments and feelings to determine when the market finally hit bottom and turned up for real. At the bottom, the news is all negative. So these managers, being human, hesitated to act. Their funds therefore lost some relative performance during the fast turnarounds that frequently happen at market bottoms.

For this reason, and despite the fact that twice in the 1950s, Jack Dreyfus successfully raised cash in his Dreyfus Fund at the start of a bear market, top management at most mutual funds imposed rigid rules on money managers that required them to remain fully invested (95% to 100% of assets). This possibly fits well with the sound concept that mutual funds are truly long-term investments. Also, because funds are typically widely diversified (owning a hundred or more stocks spread among many industries), in time they will always recover when the market recovers. So owning them for 15 or 20 years has always been extremely rewarding in the past and should continue to be in the future. However, you, as an individual investor owning 5, 10, or 20 stocks, don't have a large size handicap. Some of your stocks can drop substantially and maybe never come back or take years to do so. Learning when it's wise to raise cash is very important for you . . . so study and learn how to successfully use this technique to your advantage.

What Is the General Market?

The *general market* is a term referring to the most commonly used market indexes. These broad indexes tell you the approximate strength or weakness in each day's overall trading activity and can be one of your earliest indications of emerging trends. They include

- *The Standard & Poor's (S&P) 500*. Consisting of 500 companies, this index is a broader, more modern representation of market action than the Dow.
- *The Nasdaq Composite*. This has been a somewhat more volatile and relevant index in recent years. The Nasdaq is home to many of the market's younger, more innovative, and faster-growing companies that trade via the Nasdaq network of market makers. It's a little more weighted toward the technology sector.
- *The Dow Jones Industrial Average (DJIA)*. This index consists of 30 widely traded big-cap stocks. It used to focus primarily on large, cyclical, industrial issues, but it has broadened a little in recent years to include companies such as Coca-Cola and Home Depot. It's a simple but rather out-of-date average to study because it's dominated by large, established, old-line companies that grow more slowly than today's more entrepreneurial concerns. It can also be easily manipulated over short time periods because it's limited to only 30 stocks.
- *The NYSE Composite*. This is a market-value-weighted index of all stocks listed on the New York Stock Exchange.

All these key indexes are shown in *Investor's Business Daily* in large, easy-to-analyze charts that also feature a moving average and an Accumulation/Distribution Rating (ACC/DIS RTG®) for each index. The Accumulation/Distribution Rating tells you if the index has been getting buying support recently or is undergoing significant selling. I always try to check these indexes every day because a key change can occur over just a few weeks, and you don't want to be asleep at the switch and not see it. IBD's "The Big Picture" column also evaluates these indexes daily to materially help you in deciphering the market's current condition and direction.

Why Is Skilled, Careful Market Observation So Important?

A Harvard professor once asked his students to do a special report on fish. His scholars went to the library, read books about fish, and then wrote their expositions. But after turning in their papers, the students were shocked when the professor tore them up and threw them in the wastebasket.

When they asked him what was wrong with the reports, the professor said, "If you want to learn anything about fish, sit in front of a fishbowl and look at fish." He made his students sit and watch fish for hours. Then they rewrote their assignment solely on their observations of the objects themselves.

Being a student of the market is like being a student in this professor's class: if you want to learn about the market, you must observe and study the major indexes carefully. In doing so, you'll come to recognize when the daily market averages are changing at key turning points—such as major market tops and bottoms—and learn to capitalize on this with real knowledge and confidence.

There's an important lesson here. To be highly accurate in any pursuit, you must observe and analyze the objects themselves carefully. If you want to know about tigers, you need to watch tigers—not the weather, not the vegetation, and not the other animals on the mountain.

Years ago, when Lou Brock set his mind to breaking baseball's stolen base record, he had all the big-league pitchers photographed with high-speed film from the seats behind first base. Then he studied the film to learn what part of each pitcher's body moved first when he threw to first base. The pitcher was the object that Brock was trying to beat, so it was the pitchers themselves that he studied in great detail.

In the 2003 Super Bowl, the Tampa Bay Buccaneers were able to inter-cept five Oakland Raider passes by first studying and then concentrating on the eye movements and body language of Oakland's quarterback. They "read" where he was going to throw.

Christopher Columbus didn't accept the conventional wisdom about the earth being flat because he himself had observed ships at sea disappearing over the horizon in a way that told him otherwise. The government uses wiretaps, spy planes, unmanned drones, and satellite photos to observe and analyze objects that could threaten our security. That's how we discovered Soviet missiles in Cuba.

It's the same with the stock market. To know which way it's going, you must observe and analyze the major general market indexes daily. Don't ever, ever ask anyone: "What do you think the market's going to do?" Learn to accurately read what the market is actually doing each day as it is doing it.

Recognizing when the market has hit a top or has bottomed out is fre-quently 50% of the whole complicated investment ball game. It's also the *key* investing skill virtually all investors, whether amateur or professional, seem to lack. In fact, Wall Street analysts completely missed calling the market top in 2000, particularly the tops in every one of the high-technology leaders. They didn't do much better in 2008.

We conducted four surveys of IBD subscribers in 2008 and also received hundreds of letters from subscribers that led us to believe that 60% of IBD readers sold stock and raised cash in either December 2007 or June 2008 with the help of "The Big Picture" column and by applying and acting on our rule about five or six distribution days over any four- or five-week period. They preserved their capital and avoided the brunt of the dramatic and costly market collapse in the fall of 2008 that resulted from excessive problems in the market for subprime mortgage real estate loans (which had been sponsored and strongly encouraged by the government). You may have seen some of our subscribers' comments in IBD at the top of a page space titled "You Can Do It Too." You'll learn exactly how to apply IBD's general market distribution rules later in this chapter.

The Stages of a Stock Market Cycle

The winning investor should understand how a normal business cycle unfolds and over what period of time. The investor should pay particular attention to recent cycles. There's no guarantee that just because cycles lasted three or four years in the past, they'll last that long in the future.

Bull and bear markets don't end easily. It usually takes two or three tricky pullbacks up or down to fake out or shake out the few remaining speculators. After everyone who can be run in or run out has thrown in the towel, there isn't anyone left to take action in the same market direction. Then the market will finally turn and begin a whole new trend. Most of this is crowd psychology constantly at work.

Bear markets usually end while business is still in a downtrend. The reason is that stocks are anticipating, or "discounting," all economic, political, and worldwide events many months in advance. The stock market is a *leading* economic indicator, not a *coincident* or *lagging* indicator, in our government's series of key economic indicators. The market is exceptionally perceptive, taking all events and basic conditions into account. It will react to what is taking place and what it can mean for the nation. The market is not controlled by Wall Street. Its action is determined by lots of investors all across the country and thousands of large institutions and is a consensus conclusion on whether it likes or doesn't like what it foresees—such as what our government is doing or about to do and what the consequences could be.

Similarly, bull markets usually top out and turn down before a recession sets in. For this reason, looking at economic indicators is a poor way to determine when to buy or sell stocks and is not recommended. Yet, some investment firms do this very thing.

The predictions of many economists also leave a lot to be desired. A few of our nation's presidents have had to learn this lesson the hard way. In early 1983, for example, just as the economy was in its first few months of recovery, the head of President Reagan's Council of Economic Advisers was concerned that the capital goods sector was not very strong. This was the first hint that this advisor might not be as sound as he should be. Had he understood historical trends, he would have seen that capital goods demand has never been strong in the early stage of a recovery. This was especially true in the first quarter of 1983, when U.S. plants were operating at a low percentage of capacity.

You should check earlier cycles to learn the sequence of industry-group moves at various stages of the market cycle. If you do, you'll see that railroad equipment, machinery, and other capital goods industries are late movers in a business or stock market cycle. This knowledge can help you get a fix on where you are now. When these groups start running up, you know you're near the end. In early 2000, computer companies supplying Internet capital goods and infrastructure were the last-stage movers, along with telecommunications equipment suppliers.

Dedicated students of the market who want to learn more about cycles and the longer-term history of U.S. economic growth may want to write to Securities Research Company, 27 Wareham Street, #401, Boston, MA 02118, and purchase one of the company's long-term wall charts. Also, in 2008, Daily Graphs, Inc., created a 1900 to 2008 stock market wall chart that shows major market and economic events.

Some charts of market averages also include major news events over the last 12 months. These can be very valuable, especially if you keep and review back copies. You then have a history of both the market averages and the events that have influenced their direction. It helps to know, for example, how the market has reacted to new faces in the White House, rumors of war, controls on wages and prices, changes in discount rates, or just loss of confidence and "panics" in general. The accompanying chart of the S&P 500 Index shows several past cycles with the bear markets shaded.

You Should Study the General Market Indexes Each Day

In bear markets, stocks usually open strong and close weak. In bull markets, they tend to open weak and close strong. The general market averages need to be checked every day, since reverses in trends can begin on any

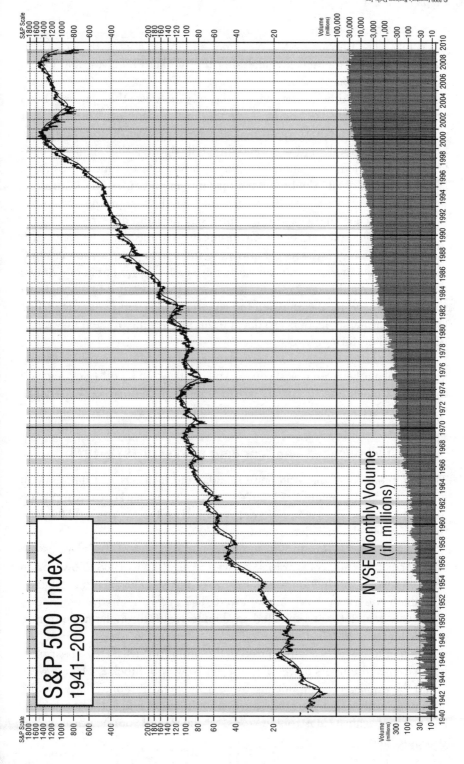

S&P Scale
1800
1600
1400
1200
1000
800

600

400

200
180
160
140
120
100

80

60

40

20

S&P 500 Index
1941–2009

NYSE Monthly Volume
(in millions)

Volume
(millions)
100,000
30,000
10,000
3,000
1,000
300
100
30
10

given few days. Relying on these primary indexes is a more direct, practical, and effective method for analyzing the market's behavior and determining its direction.

Don't rely on other, subsidiary indicators because they haven't been proven to be effective at timing. Listening to the many market newsletter writers, technical analysts, or strategists who pore over 30 to 50 different technical or economic indicators and then tell you what they think the market should be doing is generally a very costly waste of time. Investment newsletters can create doubt and confusion in an investor's mind. Interestingly enough, history shows that the market tends to go up just when the news is all bad and these experts are most skeptical and uncertain.

When the general market tops, you must sell to raise at least some cash and to get off margin (the use of borrowed money) to protect your account. As an individual investor, you can easily raise cash and get out in one or two days, and you can likewise reenter later when the market is finally right. If you don't sell and raise cash when the general market tops, your diversified list of former market leaders can decline sharply. Several of them may never recover to their former levels.

Your best bet is to learn to interpret daily price and volume charts of the key general market averages. If you do, you can't get too far off-track, and you won't need much else. It doesn't pay to argue with the market. Experience teaches that second-guessing the market can be a very expensive mistake.

The Prolonged Two-Year Bear Market of 1973–1974

The combination of the Watergate scandal and hearings and the 1974 oil embargo by OPEC made 1973–1974 the worst stock market catastrophe up to that time since the 1929–1933 depression. The Dow corrected 50%, but the average stock plummeted more than 70%.

This was a big lesson for stockholders and was almost as severe as the 90% correction the average stock showed from 1929 to 1933. However, in 1933, industrial production was only 56% of the 1929 level, and more than 13 million Americans were unemployed. The peak unemployment rate in the 1930s was 25%. It remained in double digits throughout the entire decade and was 20% in 1939.

The markets were so demoralized in the prolonged 1973–1974 bear market that most members on the floor of the New York Stock Exchange were afraid the exchange might not survive as a viable institution. This is why it's absolutely critical that you study the market averages and learn how to protect yourself against catastrophic losses, for the sake of your health as well as your portfolio.

A 33% Drop Requires a 50% Rise to Break Even

The critical importance of knowing the change in direction of the general market cannot be overemphasized. If you have a 33% loss in a stock portfolio, you need a 50% gain just to get back to breakeven. If, for example, you let a $10,000 portfolio drop to $6,666 (a 33% decline), it has to rise $3,333 (or 50%) just to get you back where you started. In the 2007–2009 bear market, the S&P 500 fell 58%, meaning that a 140% rebound will be needed for the index to fully recover. And how easy is it for you to make 140%? Maybe it's time for you to learn what you're doing, adopt new selling rules and methods, and stop doing the things that create 50% losses.

You positively must always act to preserve as much as possible of the profit you've built up during a bull market rather than ride your investments back down through difficult bear market periods. To do this, you must learn historically proven stock and general market selling rules. (See Chapters 10 and 11 for more on selling rules.)

The Myths about "Long-Term Investing" and Being Fully Invested

Many investors like to think of, or at least describe, themselves as "long-term investors." Their strategy is to stay fully invested through thick and thin. Most institutions do the same thing. But such an inflexible approach can have tragic results, particularly for individual investors. Individuals and institutions alike may get away with standing pat through relatively mild (25% or less) bear markets, but many bear markets are not mild. Some, such as 1973–1974, 2000–2002, and 2007–2008, are downright devastating.

The challenge always comes at the beginning, when you start to sense an impending bear market. In most cases, you cannot project how bad economic conditions might become or how long those bad conditions could linger. The war in Vietnam, inflation, and a tight money supply helped turn the 1969–1970 correction into a two-year decline of 36.9%. Before that, bear markets averaged only nine months and took the averages down 26%.

Most stocks fall during a bear market, but not all of them recover. If you hold on during even a modest bear correction, you can get stuck with damaged merchandise that may never see its former highs. You definitely must learn to sell and raise at least some cash when the overall environment changes and your stocks are not working.

Buy-and-hold investors fell in love with Coca-Cola during the 1980s and 1990s. The soft-drink giant chugged higher year after year, rising and falling with the market. But it stopped working in 1998, as did Gillette, another favorite of long-term holders. When the market slipped into its mild bear correction that summer, Coke followed along. Two years later—after some of the market's most exciting gains in decades—Coke was still stuck in a downtrend. In some instances, stocks of this kind may come back. But this much is certain: Coke investors missed huge advances in 1998 and 1999 in names such as America Online and Qualcomm.

The buy-and-hold strategy was also disastrous to anyone who held technology stocks from 2000 through 2002. Many highfliers lost 75% to 90% of their value, and some may never return to their prior highs. Take a look now at Time Warner, Corning, Yahoo!, Intel, JDS Uniphase, and EMC, former market leaders in 1998–2000.

Protecting Yourself from Market Downturns

Napoleon once wrote that never hesitating in battle gave him an advantage over his opponents, and for many years he was undefeated. In the battlefield that is the stock market, there are the quick and there are the dead!

After you see the first several definite indications of a market top, don't wait around. Sell quickly before real weakness develops. When market indexes peak and begin major downside reversals, you should act immediately by putting 25% or more of your portfolio in cash, selling your stocks at market prices. The use of limit orders (buying or selling at a specific price, rather than buying or selling at market prices using market orders) is not recommended. Focus on your ability to get into or out of a stock when you need to. Quibbling over an eighth- or quarter-point (or their decimal equivalents) could make you miss an opportunity to buy or sell a stock.

Lightning-fast action is even more critical if your stock account is on margin. If your portfolio is fully margined, with half of the money in your stocks borrowed from your broker, a 20% decline in the price of your stocks will cause you to lose 40% of your money. A 50% decline in your stocks could wipe you out! Never, ever try to ride through a bear market on margin.

In the final analysis, there are really only two things you can do when a new bear market begins: sell and retreat or go short. When you retreat, you should stay out until the bear market is over. This usually means five or six months or more. In the prolonged, problem-ridden 1969–1970 and 1973–1974 periods, however, it meant up to two years. The bear market that began in March 2000 during the last year of the Clinton administration lasted longer and was far more severe than normal. Nine out of ten investors lost a lot of money, particularly in high-tech stocks. It was the end of a period of many excesses during the late 1990s, a decade when America got careless and let down its guard. It was the "anything goes" period, with stocks running wild.

Selling short can be profitable, but be forewarned: it's a very difficult and highly specialized skill that should be attempted only during bear markets. Few people make money at it. Short selling is discussed in more detail in Chapter 12.

Using Stop-Loss Orders

If you use stop-loss orders or mentally record a selling price and act upon it, a market that is starting to top out will mechanically force you, robotlike, out of many of your stocks. A stop-loss order instructs the specialist in the stock on the exchange floor that once the stock has dropped to your specified price, the order becomes a market order, and the stock will be sold out on the next transaction.

It's usually better not to enter stop-loss orders. In doing so, you and other similarly minded investors are showing your hand to market makers, and at times they might drop the stock to shake out stop-loss orders. Instead, watch your stocks closely and know ahead of time the exact price at which you will immediately sell to cut a loss. However, some people travel a lot and aren't able to watch their stocks closely, and others have a hard time making sell decisions and getting out when they are losing. In such cases, stop-loss orders help compensate for distance and indecisiveness.

If you use a stop-loss order, remember to cancel it if you change your mind and sell a stock before the order is executed. Otherwise, you could later accidentally sell a stock that you no longer own. Such errors can be costly.

How You Can Learn to Identify Stock Market Tops

To detect a market top, keep a close eye on the daily S&P 500, NYSE Composite, Dow 30, and Nasdaq Composite as they work their way higher. On one of the days in the uptrend, volume for the market as a whole will increase from the day before, but the index itself will show stalling action (a significantly smaller price increase for the day compared with the prior day's much larger price increase). I call this "heavy volume without further price progress up." The average doesn't have to close down for the day, but in most instances it will, making the distribution (selling) much easier to see, as professional investors liquidate stock. The spread from the average's daily high to its daily low may in some cases be a little wider than on previous days.

Normal liquidation near the market peak will usually occur on three to six specific days over a period of four or five weeks. In other words, the market comes under distribution while it's advancing! This is one reason so few people know how to recognize distribution. After four or five days of definite distribution over any span of four or five weeks, the general market will almost always turn down.

Four days of distribution, if correctly spotted over a two- or three-week period, are sometimes enough to turn a previously advancing market into a decline. Sometimes distribution can be spread over six weeks if the market attempts at some point to rally back to new highs. If you are asleep or unaware and you miss the topping signals given off by the S&P 500, the NYSE Composite, the Nasdaq, or the Dow (which is easy to do, since they sometimes occur on only a few days), you could be wrong about the market direction and therefore wrong on almost everything you do.

One of the biggest problems is the time it takes to reverse investors' positive personal opinions and views. If you always sell and cut your losses 7% or 8% below your buy points, you may automatically be forced to sell at least one or two stocks as a correction in the general market starts to develop. This should get you into a questioning, defensive frame of mind sooner. Following this one simple but powerful rule of ours saved a lot of people big money in 2000's devastating decline in technology leaders and in the 2008 subprime loan bear market.

It takes only one of the indexes to give you a valid repeated signal of too much distribution. You don't normally need to see several of the major indexes showing four, five, or six distribution days. Also, if one of the indexes is down for the day on volume larger than the prior day's volume, it should decline more than 0.2% for this to be counted as a distribution day.

After the Initial Decline Off the Top, Track Each Rally Attempt on the Way Down

After the required number of days of increased volume distribution around the top and the first decline resulting from this, there will be either a poor rally in the market averages, followed by a rally failure, or a positive and powerful follow-through day up on price and volume. You should learn in detail exactly what signals to look for and remain unbiased about the market. Let the day-by-day averages tell you what the market has been doing and is doing. (See "How You Can Spot Stock Market Bottoms" later in this chapter for a further discussion of market rallies.)

Three Signs the First Rally Attempt May Fail

After the market does top out, it typically will rally feebly and then fail. After the first day's rebound, for instance, the second day will open strongly but suddenly turn down near the end of the session. The abrupt failure of the market to follow through on its first recovery attempt should probably be met with further selling on your part.

You'll know that the initial bounce back is feeble if (1) the index advances in price on the third, fourth, or fifth rally day, but on volume that is lower than that of the day before, (2) the average makes little net upward price progress compared with its progress the day before, or (3) the market average recovers less than half of the initial drop from its former absolute intraday high. When you see these weak rallies and failures, further selling is advisable.

How CAN SLIM and IBD Red-Flagged the March 2000 Nasdaq Top

In October 1999, the market took off on a furious advance. Fears of a Y2K meltdown on January 1, 2000, had faded. Companies were announcing strong profits for the third quarter just ended. Both leading tech stocks and speculative Internet and biotechnology issues racked up huge gains in just five months. But cracks started to appear in early March 2000.

On March 7, the Nasdaq closed lower on higher volume, the first time it had done so in more than six weeks. That's unusual action during a roaring bull market, but one day of distribution isn't significant on its own. Still, it was the first yellow flag and was worth watching carefully.

Three days later, the Nasdaq bolted up more than 85 points to a new high in the morning. But it reversed in the afternoon and finished the day up only 2 points on heavy volume that was 13% above average. This was the second warning sign. That churning action (a lot of trading but no real price progress—a clear sign of distribution) was all the more important because leading stocks started showing their own symptoms of hitting climax tops— action that will be discussed in Chapter 11. Just two days later, on March 14, the market closed down 4% on a large volume increase. This was the third major warning signal of distribution and one where you should have been taking some selling action.

The index managed to put together a suspect rally from March 16 to 24, then stalled again for a fourth distribution day. It soon ran out of steam and rolled over on heavier volume two days later for a fifth distribution day and a final, definite confirmation of the March 10 top. The market itself was telling you to sell, raise cash, and get out of your stocks. All you had to do was read it right and react, instead of listening to your or other people's opinions. Other people are too frequently wrong and are probably clueless about recognizing or understanding distribution days.

During the next two weeks, the Nasdaq, along with the S&P 500 and the Dow, suffered repeated bouts of distribution as the indexes sold off on heavier volume than on the prior day. Astute CAN SLIM investors who had read, studied, and prepared themselves by knowing exactly what to watch for had long since taken their profits.

Study our chart examples of this and other market tops. History repeats itself when it comes to the stock market; you'll see this type of action again and again in the future. So get with it.

Spotting the 2007 Top in the Market

As mentioned earlier, several surveys showed that approximately 60% of IBD subscribers sold stock in 2008 before the rapid stock market break occurred. IBD's "The Big Picture" column clearly pointed out in its special Market Pulse box when the market indexes had five distribution days and the outlook had switched to "Market in correction," and then the column suggested that it was time to raise cash. I'm sure most of those people had read and studied this chapter, including our description of how we retreated from the market in March 2000. They were finally able to use and apply IBD's general market rules to preserve their gains and not have to undergo the severe declines that can occur when you have no protective rules or methods. And hopefully, those who didn't follow the rules will be able to better apply them in the future.

Not much happens by accident in the market. It takes effort on your part to learn what you must know in order to spot each market top. Here's what Apple CEO Steve Jobs said about effort: "The things I've done in my life have required a lot of years of work before they took off." Annotated market topping charts for the period from the 1976 top to the 2007 top start on page 214. Study them . . . if you want to survive and win.

Historical Tops for Further Study

Historically, intermediate-term distribution tops (those that are usually followed by 8% to 12% declines in the general market averages) occur as they did during the first week of August 1954. First, there was increased New York Stock Exchange volume without further upward price progress on the Dow Jones Industrials. That was followed the next day by heavy volume without further price progress up and with a wide price spread from high to low on the Dow. Another such top occurred in the first week of July 1955. It was characterized by a price climax with a wide price spread from the day's low to its high, followed the next day by increased volume with the Dow closing down in price, and then, three days later, increased NYSE volume with the Dow again closing down.

Other bear market and intermediate-term tops for study include

September 1955	June 1966	August 1987
November 1955	May 1967	October 1987
April 1956	September 1967	October 1989
August 1956	December 1967	January 1990
January 1957	December 1968	July 1990
July 1957	May 1969	June 1992
November 1958	April 1971	February 1994
January 1959	September 1971	September 1994
May 1959	January 1973	May 1996
June 1959	October 1973	March 1997
July 1959	July 1975	October 1997
January 1960	September 1976	July 1998
June 1960	September 1978	August 1999
April 1961	September 1979	January 2000
May 1961	February 1980	April 2000
September 1961	November 1980	September 2000
November 1961	April 1981	February 2001
December 1961	June 1981	May 2001
March 1962	December 1981	December 2001
June 1963	May 1982	January 2004
October 1963	January 1984	April 2006
May 1965	July 1986	November 2007
February 1966	September 1986	June 2008
April 1966	April 1987	

If you study the following daily market average graphs of several tops closely and understand how they came about, you'll come to recognize the same indications as you observe future market environments. Each numbered day on these charts is a distribution day.

Follow the Leaders for Clues to a Market Top

The second most important indicator of a primary change in market direction, after the daily averages, is the way leading stocks act. After the market has advanced for a couple of years, you can be fairly sure that it's headed for trouble if most of the individual stock leaders start acting abnormally.

One example of abnormal activity can be seen when leading stocks break out of third- or fourth-stage chart base formations on the way up. Most of these base structures will be faulty, with price fluctuations appearing much

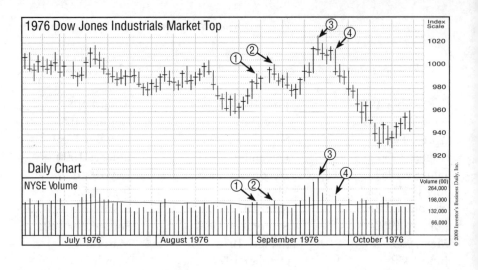

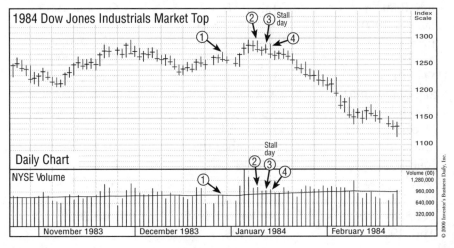

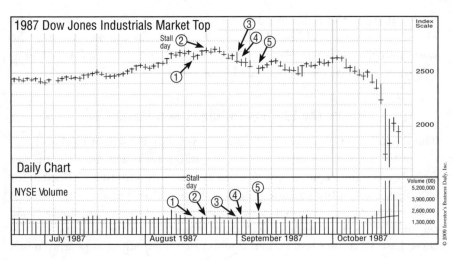

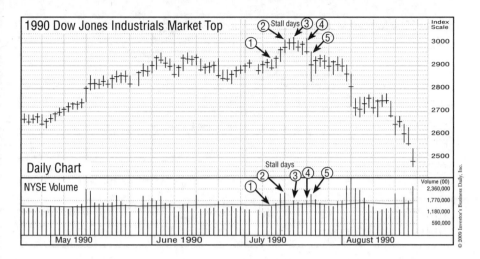

1990 Dow Jones Industrials Market Top

② Stall days ③ ④
①
⑤

Index Scale
3000
2900
2800
2700
2600
2500

Daily Chart

Stall days
②
①
③ ④ ⑤

NYSE Volume

Volume (00)
2,360,000
1,770,000
1,180,000
590,000

May 1990   June 1990   July 1990   August 1990

© 2009 Investor's Business Daily, Inc.

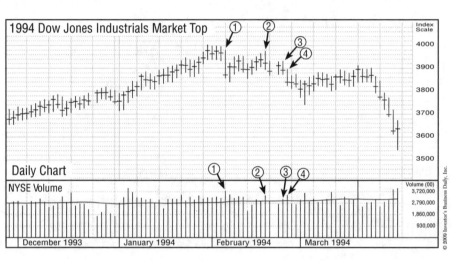

1994 Dow Jones Industrials Market Top

①   ②
③
④

Index Scale
4000
3900
3800
3700
3600
3500

Daily Chart

①   ②   ③   ④

NYSE Volume

Volume (00)
3,720,000
2,790,000
1,860,000
930,000

December 1993   January 1994   February 1994   March 1994

© 2009 Investor's Business Daily, Inc.

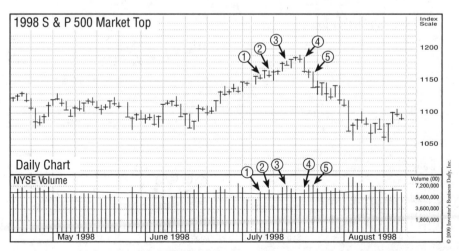

1998 S & P 500 Market Top

③
②   ④
①   ⑤

Index Scale
1200
1150
1100
1050

Daily Chart

① ② ③   ④ ⑤

NYSE Volume

Volume (00)
7,200,000
5,400,000
3,600,000
1,800,000

May 1998   June 1998   July 1998   August 1998

© 2009 Investor's Business Daily, Inc.

215

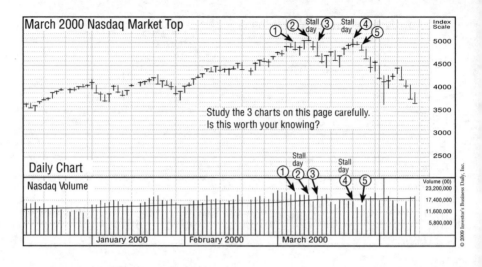

March 2000 Nasdaq Market Top

Study the 3 charts on this page carefully. Is this worth your knowing?

Daily Chart

Nasdaq Volume

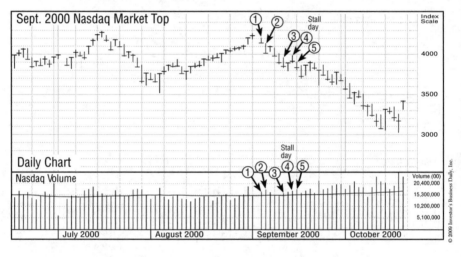

Sept. 2000 Nasdaq Market Top

Daily Chart

Nasdaq Volume

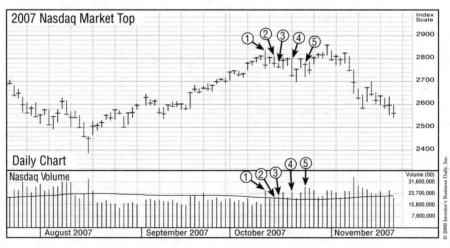

2007 Nasdaq Market Top

Daily Chart

Nasdaq Volume

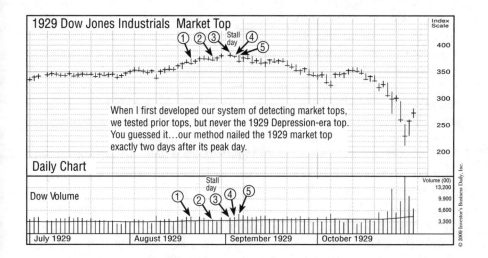

1929 Dow Jones Industrials Market Top

When I first developed our system of detecting market tops, we tested prior tops, but never the 1929 Depression-era top. You guessed it…our method nailed the 1929 market top exactly two days after its peak day.

Daily Chart

Dow Volume

July 1929 | August 1929 | September 1929 | October 1929

© 2009 Investor's Business Daily, Inc.

wider and looser. A faulty base (wide, loose, and erratic) can best be recognized and analyzed by studying charts of a stock's daily or weekly price and volume history.

Another sign of abnormal activity is the "climax" top. Here, a leading stock will run up more rapidly for two or three weeks in a row, after having advanced for many months. (See Chapter 11 on selling.)

A few leaders will have their first abnormal price break off the top on heavy volume but then be unable to rally more than a small amount from the lows of their correction. Still others will show a serious loss of upward momentum in their most recent quarterly earnings reports.

Shifts in market direction can also be detected by reviewing the last four or five stock purchases in your own portfolio. If you haven't made a dime on any of them, you could be picking up signs of a new downtrend.

Investors who use charts and understand market action know and understand that very few leading stocks are attractive around market tops. There simply aren't any stocks coming out of sound, properly formed chart bases. The best merchandise has been bought, played, and well picked over.

Most bases will be wide and loose—a big sign of real danger that you must learn to understand and obey. All that's left to show strength at this stage are laggard stocks. The sight of sluggish or low-priced, lower-quality laggards strengthening is a signal to the wise market operator the up market may be near its end. Even turkeys can try to fly in a windstorm.

During the early phase of a bear market, certain leading stocks will seem to be bucking the trend by holding up in price, creating the impression of strength, but what you're seeing is just a postponement of the inevitable. When they raid the house, they usually get everyone, and eventually all the leaders will succumb to the selling. This is exactly what happened in the 2000 bear market. Cisco and other high-tech leaders all eventually collapsed in spite of the many analysts who incorrectly said that they should be bought.

That's also what happened at the top of the Nasdaq in June and July of 2008. The steels, fertilizers, and oils that had led the 2003–2007 bull market all rolled over and finally broke down after they appeared to be bucking the overall market top that actually began with at least five distribution days in October of 2007. U.S. Steel tanked even though its next two quarterly earnings reports were up over 100%. Potash topped when its current quarter was up 181% and its next quarter was up 220%. This fooled most analysts, who were focused on the big earnings that had been reported or were expected. They had not studied all past historical tops and didn't realize that many past leaders had topped when earnings were up 100%. Why did these stocks finally cave in? They were in a bear market that had begun eight months earlier, in late 2007.

Market tops, whether intermediate (8% to 12% declines) or primary bull market peaks, sometimes occur five, six, or seven months after the last major buy point in leading stocks and in the averages. Thus, top reversals (when the market closes at the bottom of its trading range after making a new high that day) are usually late signals—the last straw before a cave-in. In most cases, distribution, or selling, has been going on for days or even weeks in individual market leaders. Use of individual stock selling rules, which we'll discuss in Chapters 10 and 11, should already have led you to sell one or two of your holdings on the way up, just before the market peak.

Other Bear Market Warnings

If the original market leaders begin to falter, and lower-priced, lower-quality, more-speculative stocks begin to move up, watch out! When the old dogs begin to bark, the market is on its last feeble leg. Laggards can't lead the market higher. Among the telltale signs are the poor-quality stocks that start to dominate the most-active list on market "up" days. This is simply a matter of weak leadership trying to command the market. If the best ones can't lead, the worst certainly aren't going to do so for very long.

Many top reversals have occurred between the third and the ninth day of a rally after the averages moved into new high ground off short chart bases (meaning that the time span from the start to the end of the pattern was really too short). It's important to note that the conditions under which the tops occurred were all about the same.

At other times, a topping market will recover for a couple of months and get back nearly to its old high or even above it before breaking down in earnest. This occurred in December 1976, January 1981, and January 1984. There's an important psychological reason for this: the majority of people in the market can't be exactly right at exactly the right time. In 1994, the Nasdaq didn't top until weeks after the Dow did. A similar thing happened in early 2000.

The majority of people in the stock market, including both professional and individual investors, will be fooled first. It's all about human psychology and emotions. If you were smart enough to sell or sell short in January 1981, the powerful rebound in February and March probably forced you to cover your short sales at a loss or buy some stocks back during the strong rally. It was an example of how treacherous the market really can be at turning points.

Don't Jump Back In Too Early

I didn't have much problem recognizing and acting upon the early signs of the many bear markets from 1962 through 2008. But a few times I made the mistake of buying back too early. When you make a mistake in the stock market, the only sound thing to do is to correct it. Don't fight it. Pride and ego never pay off; neither does vacillation when losses start to show up.

The typical bear market (and some aren't typical) usually has three separate phases, or legs, of decline interrupted by a couple of rallies that last just long enough to convince investors to begin buying. In 1969 and 1974, a few of these phony, drawn-out rallies lasted up to 15 weeks. Most don't last that long.

Many institutional investors love to "bottom fish." They'll start buying stocks off a supposed bottom and help make the rally convincing enough to draw you in. You're better off staying on the sidelines in cash until a new bull market really starts.

How You Can Spot Stock Market Bottoms

Once you've recognized a bear market and have scaled back your stock holdings, the big question is how long you should remain on the sidelines. If you plunge back into the market too soon, the apparent rally may fade, and you'll lose money. But if you hesitate at the brink of the eventual roaring recovery, opportunities will pass you by. Again, the daily general market averages provide the best answer by far. Markets are always more reliable than most investors' emotions or personal opinions.

At some point in every correction—whether that correction is mild or severe—the stock market will always attempt to rally. Don't jump back in right away. Wait for the market itself to confirm the new uptrend.

A rally attempt begins when a major market average closes higher after a decline that happened either earlier in the day or during the previous session. For example, the Dow plummets 3% in the morning but then recovers later in the day and closes higher. Or the Dow closes down 2% and then rebounds the next day. We typically call the session in which the Dow finally closes higher the first day of the attempted rally, although there have been some exceptions. For example, the first day of the early October market bottom in 1998 was actually down on heavy volume, but it closed in the upper half of that day's price range. Sit tight and be patient. The first few days of improvement can't tell you whether the rally will succeed.

Starting on the fourth day of the attempted rally, look for one of the major averages to "follow through" with a booming gain on heavier volume than the day before. This tells you the rally is far more likely to be real. The most powerful follow-throughs usually occur on the fourth to seventh days of the rally. The 1998 bottom just mentioned followed through on the sixth day of the attempted rally. The market was up 2.1%. A follow-through day should give the feeling of an explosive rally that is strong, decisive, and conclusive—not begrudging and on the fence or barely up 1½%. The market's volume for the day should in most cases be above its average daily volume, in addition to always being higher than the prior day's trading.

Occasionally, but rarely, a follow-through occurs as early as the third day of the rally. In such a case, the first, second, and third days must all be very powerful, with a major average up 1½% to 2% or more each session in heavy volume.

I used to consider 1% to be the percentage increase for a valid follow-through day. However, in recent years, as institutional investors have learned of our system, we've moved the requirement up a significant amount for the Nasdaq and the Dow. By doing this, we are trying to minimize the possibility that professionals will manipulate a few of the 30 stocks in the Dow Jones average to create false or faulty follow-through days.

There will be cases in which confirmed rallies fail. A few large institutional investors, armed with their immense buying power, can run up the averages on a particular day and create the impression of a follow-through. Unless the smart buyers are getting back on board, however, the rally will implode— sometimes crashing on heavy volume within the next several days.

However, just because the market corrects the day after a follow-through doesn't mean the follow-through was false. When a bear market bottoms, it frequently pulls back and settles above or near the lows made during the previous few weeks. It is more constructive when these pullbacks or "tests" hold at least a little above the absolute intraday lows made recently in the market averages.

A follow-through signal doesn't mean you should rush out and buy with abandon. It just gives you the go-ahead to begin buying high-quality stocks with strong sales and earnings as they break out of sound price bases, and it is a vital second confirmation the attempted rally is succeeding.

Remember, no new bull market has ever started without a strong price and volume follow-through confirmation. It pays to wait and listen to the market and act on what it tells you. The following graphs are examples of seven bottoms in the stock market between 1974 and 2003.

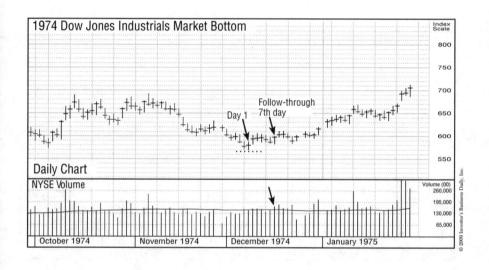

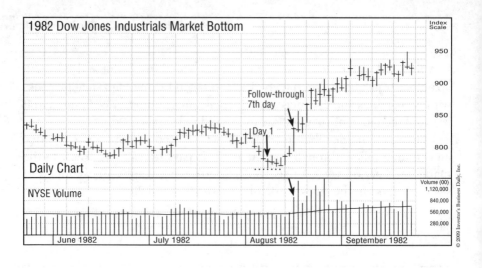

1982 Dow Jones Industrials Market Bottom

Index Scale

950

900

Follow-through
7th day

850

Day 1

800

Daily Chart

NYSE Volume

Volume (00)
1,120,000
840,000
560,000
280,000

June 1982 | July 1982 | August 1982 | September 1982

© 2009 Investor's Business Daily, Inc.

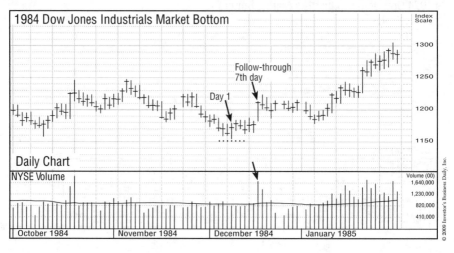

1984 Dow Jones Industrials Market Bottom

Index Scale

1300

1250

Follow-through
7th day

Day 1

1200

1150

Daily Chart

NYSE Volume

Volume (00)
1,640,000
1,230,000
820,000
410,000

October 1984 | November 1984 | December 1984 | January 1985

© 2009 Investor's Business Daily, Inc.

1990 Dow Jones Industrials Market Bottom

Index Scale

3000

2800

Follow-through
5th day

Day 1

2600

2400

Daily Chart

NYSE Volume

Volume (00)
2,360,000
1,770,000
1,180,000
590,000

September 1990 | October 1990 | November 1990 | December 1990

© 2009 Investor's Business Daily, Inc.

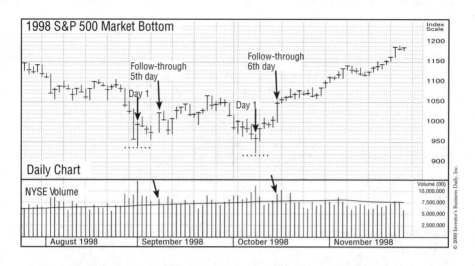

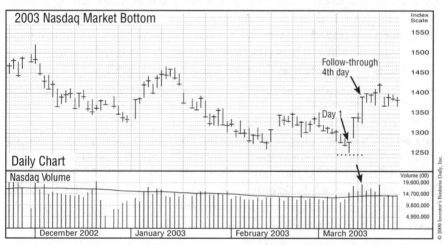

The Big Money Is Made in the First Two Years

The really big money is usually made in the first one or two years of a normal new bull market cycle. It is during this period that you must always recognize, and fully capitalize upon, the golden opportunities presented.

The rest of the "up" cycle usually consists of back-and-forth movement in the market averages, followed by a bear market. The year 1965 was one of the few exceptions, but that strong market in the third year of a new cycle was caused by the beginning of the Vietnam War.

In the first or second year of a new bull market, there should be a few intermediate-term declines in the market averages. These usually last a couple of months, with the market indexes dropping by from 8% to an occasional 12% or 15%. After several sharp downward adjustments of this nature, and after at least two years of a bull market have passed, heavy volume without further upside progress in the daily market averages could indicate the early beginning of the next bear market.

Since the market is governed by supply and demand, you can interpret a chart of the general market averages about the same way you read the chart of an individual stock. The Dow Jones Industrial Average and the S&P 500 are usually displayed in the better publications. *Investor's Business Daily* displays the Nasdaq Composite, the New York Stock Exchange Composite, and the S&P 500, with large-size daily price and volume charts stacked one on top of the other for ease of comparing the three. These charts should show the high, low, and close of the market averages day by day for at least six months, together with the daily NYSE and Nasdaq volume in millions of shares traded.

Incidentally, when I began in the market about 50 years ago, an average day on the New York Stock Exchange was 3.5 million shares. Today, 1.5 billion shares are traded on average each day—an incredible 150-fold increase that clearly demonstrates beyond any question the amazing growth and success of our free enterprise, capitalist system. Its unparalleled freedom and opportunity have consistently attracted millions of ambitious people from all around the world who have materially increased our productivity and inventiveness. It has led to an unprecedented increase in our standard of living, so that the vast majority of Americans and all areas of our population are better off than they were before. There are always problems that need to be recognized and solved. But our system is the most successful in the world, and it offers remarkable opportunities to grow and advance to those who are willing to work, train, and educate themselves. The 100 charts in Chapter 1 are only a small sample of big past investment opportunities.

Normal bear markets show three legs of price movement down, but there's no rule saying you can't have four or even five down legs. You have to evaluate overall conditions and events in the country objectively and let the market averages tell their own story. And you have to understand what that story is.

Additional Ways to Identify Key Market Turning Points

Look for Divergence of Key Averages

Several averages should be checked at market turning points to see if there are significant divergences, meaning that they are moving in different directions (one up and one down) or that one index is advancing or declining at a much greater rate than another.

For example, if the Dow is up 100 and the S&P 500 is up only the equivalent of 20 on the Dow for the day (the S&P 500 being a broader index), it would indicate the rally is not as broad and strong as it appears. To compare the change in the S&P 500 to that in the Dow, divide the S&P 500 into the Dow average and then multiply by the change in the S&P 500.

For example, if the Dow closed at 9,000 and the S&P 500 finished at 900, the 9,000 Dow would be 10 times the S&P 500. Therefore, if the Dow, on a particular day, is up 100 points and the S&P 500 is up 5 points, you can multiply the 5 by 10 and find that the S&P 500 was up only the equivalent of 50 points on the Dow.

The Dow's new high in January 1984 was accompanied by a divergence in the indexes: the broader-based, more significant S&P 500 did not hit a new high. This is the reason most professionals plot the key indexes together—to make it easier to spot nonconfirmations at key turning points. Institutional investors periodically run up the 30-stock Dow while they liquidate the broader Nasdaq or a list of technology stocks under cover of the Dow run-up. It's like a big poker game, with players hiding their hands, bluffing, and faking.

Certain Psychological Market Indicators Might at Times Help

Now that trading in *put* and *call* options is the get-rich-quick scheme for many speculators, you can plot and analyze the ratio of calls to puts for another valuable insight into crowd temperament. Options traders buy calls, which are options to buy common stock, or puts, which are options to sell common stock. A call buyer hopes prices will rise; a buyer of put options wishes prices to fall.

If the volume of call options in a given period of time is greater than the volume of put options, a logical assumption is that option speculators as a group are expecting higher prices and are bullish on the market. If the volume of put options is greater than that of calls, speculators hold a bearish attitude. When option players buy more puts than calls, the put-to-call ratio index rises a little above 1.0. Such a reading coincided with general market bottoms in 1990, 1996, 1998, and April and September 2001, but you can't always expect this to occur. These are contrary indicators.

The *percentage of investment advisors who are bearish* is an interesting measure of investor sentiment. When bear markets are near the bottom, the great majority of advisory letters will usually be bearish. Near market tops, most will be bullish. The majority is usually wrong when it's most important to be right. However, you cannot blindly assume that because 65% of investment advisors were bearish the last time the general market hit bottom, a major market decline will be over the next time the investment advisors' index reaches the same point.

The *short-interest ratio* is the amount of short selling on the New York Stock Exchange, expressed as a percentage of total NYSE volume. This ratio can reflect the degree of bearishness shown by speculators in the market. Along bear market bottoms, you will usually see two or three major peaks showing sharply increased short selling. There's no rule governing how high the index should go, but studying past market bottoms can give you an idea of what the ratio looked like at key market junctures.

An index that is sometimes used to measure the degree of speculative activity is the *Nasdaq volume as a percentage of NYSE volume*. This measure provided a helpful tip-off of impending trouble during the summer of 1983, when Nasdaq volume increased significantly relative to the Big Board's (NYSE). When a trend persists and accelerates, indicating wild, rampant speculation, you're close to a general market correction. The volume of Nasdaq trading has grown larger than that on the NYSE in recent years because so many new entrepreneurial companies are listed on the Nasdaq, so this index must be viewed differently now.

Interpret the Overrated Advance-Decline Line

Some technical analysts religiously follow advance-decline (A-D) data. These technicians take the number of stocks advancing each day versus the number that are declining, and then plot that ratio on a graph. Advance-decline lines are far from precise because they frequently veer sharply lower long before a bull market finally tops. In other words, the market keeps advancing toward higher ground, but it is being led by fewer but better stocks.

The advance-decline line is simply not as accurate as the key general market indexes because analyzing the market's direction is not a simple total numbers game. Not all stocks are created equal; it's better to know where the real leadership is and how it's acting than to know how many more mediocre stocks are advancing and declining.

The NYSE A-D line peaked in April 1998 and trended lower during the new bull market that broke out six months later in October. The A-D line continued to fall from October 1999 to March 2000, missing one of the market's most powerful rallies in decades.

An advance-decline line can sometimes be helpful when a clear-cut bear market attempts a short-term rally. If the A-D line lags the market averages and can't rally, it's giving an internal indication that, despite the strength of the rally in the Dow or S&P, the broader market remains frail. In such instances, the rally usually fizzles. In other words, it takes more than just a few leaders to make a new bull market.

At best, the advance-decline line is a secondary indicator of limited value. If you hear commentators or TV market strategists extolling its virtues bullishly or bearishly, they probably haven't done their homework. No secondary measurements can be as accurate as the major market indexes, so you don't want to get confused and overemphasize the vast array of other technical measures that most people use, usually with lack-luster or damaging results.

Watch Federal Reserve Board Rate Changes

Among fundamental general market indicators, changes in the Federal Reserve Board's discount rate (the interest rate the FRB charges member banks for loans), the fed funds rate (the interest rate banks with fund reserves charge for loans to banks without fund reserves), and occasionally stock margin levels are valuable indicators to watch.

As a rule, interest rates provide the best confirmation of basic economic conditions, and changes in the discount rate and the fed funds rate are by far the most reliable. In the past, three successive significant hikes in Fed interest rates have generally marked the beginning of bear markets and impending recessions.

Bear markets have usually, but not always, ended when the rate was finally lowered. On the downside, the discount rate increase to 6% in September 1987, just after Alan Greenspan became chairman, led to the severe market break that October.

Money market indicators mirror general economic activity. At times I have followed selected government and Federal Reserve Board measurements, including 10 indicators of the supply and demand for money and indicators of interest-rate levels. History proves that the direction of the general market, and also that of several industry groups, is often affected by changes in interest rates because the level of interest rates is usually tied to tight or easy Fed monetary policy.

For the investor, the simplest and most relevant monetary indicators to follow and understand are the changes in the discount rate and fed funds rate.

With the advent of program trading and various hedging devices, some funds now hedge portions of their portfolio in an attempt to provide some downside protection during risky markets. The degree to which these hedges are successful again depends greatly on skill and timing, but one possible effect for some managers may be to lessen the pressure to dump portfolio securities on the market.

Most funds operate with a policy of being widely diversified and fully or nearly fully invested at all times. This is because most fund managers, given the great size of today's funds (billions of dollars), have difficulty getting out of the market and into cash at the right time and, most importantly, then getting back into the market fast enough to participate in the initial power-

S&P 500 Index and Federal Reserve Board Discount Rate

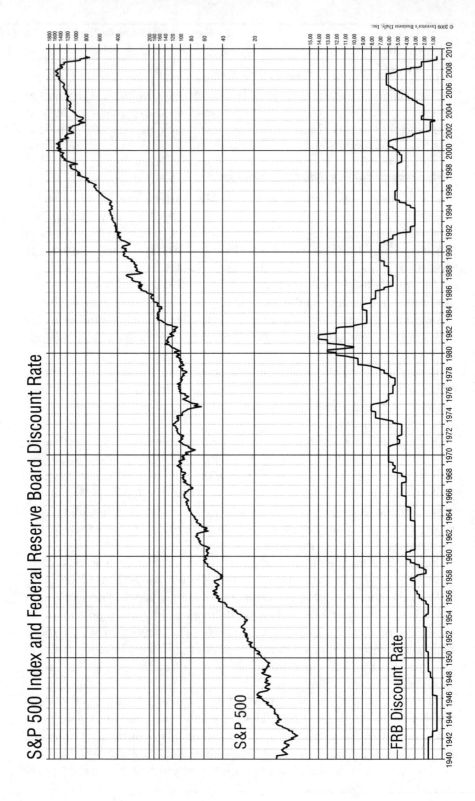

S&P 500

FRB Discount Rate

ful rebound off the ultimate bottom. So they may try to shift their emphasis to big-cap, semidefensive groups.

The Fed Crushes the 1981 Economy. The bear market and the costly, protracted recession that began in 1981, for example, came about solely because the Fed increased the discount rate in rapid succession on September 26, November 17, and December 5 of 1980. Its fourth increase, on May 8, 1981, thrust the discount rate to an all-time high of 14%. That finished off the U.S. economy, our basic industries, and the stock market for the time being.

Fed rate changes, however, should not be your primary market indicator because the stock market itself is always your best barometer. Our analysis of market cycles turned up three key market turns that the discount rate did not help predict.

Independent Fed actions are typically very constructive, as the Fed tries to counteract overheated excesses or sharp contractions in our economy. However, its actions and results clearly demonstrate how much our overall federal government, not our stock markets reacting to all events, can and does at times significantly influence our economic future, for good or bad.

The 2008 Financial Collapse. The subprime mortgage meltdown and financial credit crisis that led to the 2008 market collapse can be easily traced to moves in 1995 by the then-current administration to substantially beef up the Community Reinvestment Act (CRA) of 1977. These actions mandated banks to make more higher-risk loans in lower-income areas than they would otherwise have made. Failure to comply meant stiff penalties, lawsuits, and limits on getting approvals for mergers and branch expansion.

Our government, in effect, encouraged and coerced major banks to lower their long-proven safe-lending standards. Most of the more than $1 trillion of new subprime CRA loans had adjustable rates. Many such loans eventually came to require no documentation of the borrower's income and in some cases little or no down payment.

In addition, for the first time, new regulatory rules not only allowed but encouraged lenders to bundle the new, riskier subprime loans with prime loans and sell these assumed government-sponsored loan packages to other institutions and countries that thought they were buying safe AAA bonds. The first of these bundled loans hit the investment market in 1997. That action allowed loan originators and big banks to make profits faster and eliminate future risk and responsibility for many of those lower-quality loans. It let the banks turn around and make even more CRA-type loans, then sell them off in packages again, with little future risk or responsibility.

The unintended result was a gigantic government-sponsored and aggressively promoted pyramiding device, with Fannie Mae and Freddie Mac providing the implied government backing by buying, at government's direction, vast quantities of far more subprimes; this led to their facing bankruptcy and needing enormous government bailouts. Freddie and Fannie's management also received huge bonuses and were donors to certain members of Congress, who repeatedly defended the highly leveraged, extremely risky lending against any sound reforms.

Bottom line: it was a Big Government program that started with absolutely good, worthy social intentions, but with little judgment and absolutely zero foresight that over time resulted in severe damage and enormous unintended consequences that affected almost everything and everyone, including, sadly, the very lower-income people this rather inept government operation was supposed to be helping. It put our whole financial system in jeopardy. Big Wall Street firms got involved after the rescinding of the Glass-Steagall Act in 1998, and both political parties, Congress, and the public all played key parts in creating the great government financial fiasco.

The 1962 Stock Market Break. Another notable stock market break occurred in 1962. In the spring, nothing was wrong with the economy, but the market got skittish after the government announced an investigation of the stock market and then got on the steel companies for raising prices. IBM dropped 50%. That fall, after the Cuban missile showdown with the Russians, a new bull market sprang to life. All of this happened with no change in the discount rate.

There have also been situations in which the discount rate was lowered six months after the market bottom was reached. In such cases, you would be late getting into the game if you waited for the discount rate to drop. In a few instances, after Fed rate cuts occurred, the markets continued lower or whipsawed for several months. This also occurred dramatically in 2000 and 2001.

The Hourly Market Index and Volume Changes

At key turning points, an active market operator can watch the market indexes and volume changes hour by hour and compare them to volume in the same hour of the day before.

A good time to watch hourly volume figures is during the first attempted rally following the initial decline off the market peak. You should be able to see if volume is dull or dries up on the rally. You can also see if the rally starts to fade late in the day, with volume picking up as it does, a sign that the rally is weak and will probably fail.

Hourly volume data also come in handy when the market averages reach an important prior low point and start breaking that "support" area. (A support area is a previous price level below which investors hope that an index will not fall.) What you want to know is whether selling picks up dramatically or by just a small amount as the market collapses into new low ground. If selling picks up dramatically, it represents significant downward pressure on the market.

After the market has undercut previous lows for a few days, but on only slightly higher volume, look for either a volume dry-up day or one or two days of increased volume without the general market index going lower. If you see this, you may be in a "shakeout" area (when the market pressures many traders to sell, often at a loss), ready for an upturn after scaring out weak holders.

Overbought and Oversold: Two Risky Words

The short-term overbought/oversold indicator has an avid following among some individual technicians and investors. It's a 10-day moving average of advances and declines in the market. But be careful. At the start of a new bull market, the overbought/oversold index can become substantially "overbought." This should *not* be taken as a sign to sell stocks.

A big problem with indexes that move counter to the trend is that you always have the question of how bad things can get before everything finally turns. Many amateurs follow and believe in overbought/oversold indicators.

Something similar can happen in the early stage or first leg of a major bear market, when the index can become unusually oversold. This is really telling you that a bear market may be imminent. The market was "oversold" all the way down during the brutal market implosion of 2000.

I once hired a well-respected professional who relied on such technical indicators. During the 1969 market break, at the very point when everything told me the market was getting into serious trouble, and I was aggressively trying to get several portfolio managers to liquidate stocks and raise large amounts of cash, he was telling them that it was too late to sell because his overbought/oversold indicator said that the market was already very oversold. You guessed it: the market then split wide open.

Needless to say, I rarely pay attention to overbought/oversold indicators. What you learn from years of experience is usually more important than the opinions and theories of experts using their many different favorite indicators.

Other General Market Indicators

Upside/downside volume is a short-term index that relates trading volume in stocks that close up in price for the day to trading volume in stocks that close down. This index, plotted as a 10-week moving average, may show divergence at some intermediate turning points in the market. For example, after a 10% to 12% dip, the general market averages may continue to penetrate into new low ground for a week or two. Yet the upside/downside volume may suddenly shift and show steadily increasing upside volume, with downside volume easing. This switch usually signals an intermediate-term upturn in the market. But you'll pick up the same signals if you watch the changes in the daily Dow, Nasdaq, or S&P 500 and the market volume.

Some services measure the *percentage of new money flowing into corporate pension funds* that is invested in common stocks and the percentage that is invested in cash equivalents or bonds. This opens another window into institutional investor psychology. However, majority—or crowd—thinking is seldom right, even when it's done by professionals. Every year or two, Wall Street seems to be of one mind, with everyone following each other like a herd of cattle. Either they all pile in or they all pile out.

An *index of "defensive" stocks*—more stable and supposedly safer issues, such as utilities, tobaccos, foods, and soaps—may often show strength after a couple of years of bull market conditions. This may indicate the "smart money" is slipping into defensive positions and that a weaker general market lies ahead. But this doesn't always work. None of these secondary market indicators is anywhere near as reliable as the key general market indexes.

Another indicator that is helpful at times in evaluating the stage of a market cycle is the *percentage of stocks in defensive or laggard categories that are making new price highs.* In pre-1983 cycles, some technicians rationalized their lack of concern with market weakness by citing the number of stocks that were still making new highs. But analysis of new-high lists shows that a large percentage of preferred or defensive stocks signals possible bear market conditions. Superficial knowledge can hurt you in the stock market.

To summarize this complex but vitally important chapter: learn to interpret the daily price and volume changes of the general market indexes and the action of individual market leaders. Once you know how to do this correctly, you can stop listening to all the costly, uninformed, personal market opinions of amateurs and professionals alike. As you can see, **the key to staying on top of the stock market is not predicting or knowing what the market is going to do. It's knowing and understanding what the market has actually done in the past few weeks and what it is currently doing now.** We don't want to give personal opinions or predictions; we carefully observe market supply and demand as it changes day by day.

One of the great values of this system of interpreting the price and volume changes in the market averages is not just the ability to better recognize market top and bottom areas but also the ability to track each rally attempt when the market is on its way down. In most instances, waiting for powerful follow-through days keeps you from being drawn prematurely into rally attempts that ultimately end in failure. In other words, you have rules that will continue to keep you from getting sucked into phony rallies. This is how we were able to stay out of the market and in money market funds for most of 2000 through 2002, preserve the majority of the gains we had made in 1998 and 1999, and help those who read and followed our many basic rules. There is a fortune for you in this paragraph.

Part I Review: How to Remember and Use What You've Read So Far

It isn't enough just to read. You need to remember and apply *all* of what you've read. The CAN SLIM system will help you remember what you've read so far. Each letter in the CAN SLIM system stands for one of the seven basic fundamentals of selecting outstanding stocks. Most successful stocks have these seven common characteristics at emerging growth stages, so they are worth committing to memory. Repeat the formula until you can recall and use it easily. Keep it with you when you invest.

C = Current Quarterly Earnings per Share. Quarterly earnings per share must be up at least 18% or 20%, but preferably up 40% to 100% or 200% or more—the higher, the better. They should also be accelerating at some point in recent quarters. Quarterly sales should also be accelerating or up 25% or more.

A = Annual Earnings Increases. There must be significant (25% or more) growth in each of the last three years and a return on equity of 17% or more (with 25% to 50% preferred). If return on equity is too low, pretax profit margin must be strong.

N = New Products, New Management, New Highs. Look for new products or services, new management, or significant new changes in industry conditions. And most important, buy stocks as they emerge from sound, properly formed chart bases and begin to make new highs in price.

S = Supply and Demand—Shares Outstanding plus Big Volume Demand. Any size capitalization is acceptable in today's new economy as long as a company fits all the other CAN SLIM rules. Look for big volume increases when a stock begins to move out of its basing area.

L = Leader or Laggard. Buy market leaders and avoid laggards. Buy the number one company in its field or space. Most leaders will have Relative Price Strength Ratings of 80 to 90 or higher and composite ratings of 90 or more in bull markets.

I = Institutional Sponsorship. Buy stocks with increasing sponsorship and at least one or two mutual fund owners with top-notch recent performance records. Also look for companies with management ownership.

M = Market Direction. Learn to determine the overall market direction by accurately interpreting the daily market indexes' price and volume movements and the action of individual market leaders. This can determine whether you win big or lose. You need to stay in gear with the market. It doesn't pay to be out of phase with the market.

Is CAN SLIM Momentum Investing?

I'm not even sure what "momentum investing" is. Some analysts and reporters who don't understand anything about how we invest have given that name to what we talk about and do. They say it's "buying the stocks that have gone up the most in price" and that have the strongest relative price strength. No one in their right mind invests that way. What we do is identify companies with strong fundamentals—large sales and earnings increases resulting from unique new products or services—and then buy their stocks when they emerge from properly formed price consolidation periods and before they run up dramatically in price during bull markets.

When bear markets are beginning, we want people to protect themselves and nail down their gains by knowing when to sell and start raising cash. We are not investment advisors. We do not write and disseminate any research reports. We do not call or visit companies. We do not make markets in stocks, deal in derivatives, do underwritings, or arrange mergers. We don't manage any public or institutional money.

We are historians, studying and discovering how stocks and markets actually work and teaching and training people everywhere who want to make money investing intelligently and realistically. These are ordinary people from all walks of life, including professionals. We do not give them fish. We teach them how to fish for their whole future so that they too can capitalize on the American Dream.

Experts, Education, and Egos

On Wall Street, wise men can be drawn into booby traps just as easily as fools. From what I've seen over many years, the length and quality of one's education and the level of one's IQ have very little to do with making money investing in the market. The more intelligent people are—particularly men—the more they think they really know what they're doing, and the more they may have to learn the hard way how little they really know about outsmarting the markets.

We've all now witnessed firsthand the severe damage that supposedly bright, intelligent, and highly educated people in New York and Washington, D.C., caused this country in 2008. U.S. senators, heads of congressional committees, political types working for government-sponsored entities such as Fannie Mae and Freddie Mac, plus heads of top New York–based brokerage firms, lending banks, and mortgage brokers all thought they knew what they were doing, with many of them using absurd leverage of 50 to 1, and even higher, to invest in subprime real estate loans.

They created sophisticated derivatives and insurance to justify such incredible risks. No one group was solely to blame, since both Democrats and Republicans were involved. However, it all began as a well-intended government program that top politicians accelerated in 1995, 1997, and 1998, when Glass-Steagall was rescinded, and things kept escalating out of control. Politicians accept no blame, just blame others.

So maybe it's time for you to take more control of your investing and make up your mind that you're going to learn how to save and invest your hard-earned money more safely and wisely than Washington and Wall Street have done since the late 1990s. If you really want to do it, you certainly can. Anyone can.

The few people I've known over the years who've been unquestionably successful investing in America were decisive individuals without huge egos. The market has a simple way of whittling all excessive pride and overblown egos down to size. After all, the whole idea is to be completely objective and recognize what the marketplace is telling you, rather than trying to prove that what you said or did yesterday or six weeks ago was right. The fastest way to take a bath in the stock market is to try to prove that you are right and the market is wrong. Humility and common sense provide essential balance.

Sometimes, listening to quoted and accepted experts can get you into trouble. In the spring and summer of 1982, a well-known expert insisted that government borrowing was going to crowd out the private sector and that interest rates and inflation would soar back to new highs. Things turned out exactly the opposite: inflation broke and interest rates came crashing down. Another expert's bear market call in the summer of 1996 came only one day before the market bottom.

Week after week during the 2000 bear market, one expert after another kept saying on CNBC that it was time to buy high-tech stocks—only to watch the techs continue to plummet further. Many high-profile analysts and strategists kept telling investors to capitalize on these once-in-a-lifetime "buying opportunities" on the way down! Buying on the way down can be a very dangerous pastime.

Conventional wisdom or consensus thinking in the market is seldom right. I never pay any attention to the parade of experts voicing their personal opinions on the market in print or on TV. It creates entirely too much confusion and can cost you a great deal of money. In 2000, some strategists were telling people to buy the dips (short-term declines in price) because the cash position of mutual funds had increased greatly and all this money was sitting on the sidelines waiting to be invested. To prove this wrong, all anyone had to do was look at the General Markets & Sectors page in *Investor's Business Daily*. It showed that while mutual fund cash positions had indeed risen, they were still significantly below their historical highs and even below their historical averages.

On the flip side, market bottoms are often accompanied by overwhelming negativity from the "experts." For example, in March 2009 investors had just faced a financial crisis, 17-month bear market, and the president warning of the possibility of another Great Depression. Most people, understandably, were afraid to jump back into the market despite the follow-through day on March 12 (see chart below).

You can't go by how you *feel* in the market. The only thing that works well is to let the market indexes tell you when it's time to enter and exit. Never fight the market—it's bigger than you are.

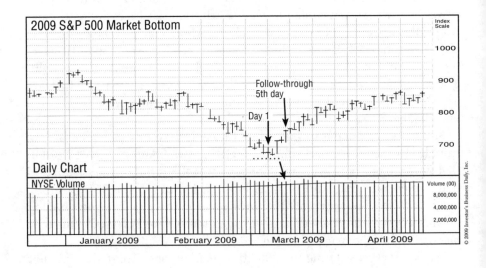

Be Smart
from
the Start

When You Must Sell and Cut Every Loss . . . without Exception

Now that you've learned how and when to buy nothing but the best stocks, it's time for you to learn how and when to sell them. You've probably heard the sports cliché: "The best offense is a strong defense." The funny thing about clichés is they are usually true: a team that's all offense and no defense seldom wins the game. In fact, a strong defense can often propel a team to great heights.

During their heyday, when Branch Rickey was president and general manager, the Brooklyn Dodgers typically had good pitching. In the game of baseball, the combination of pitching and fielding represents the defensive side of a team and maybe 70% of the game. It's almost impossible to win without them.

The same holds true in the stock market. Unless you have a strong defense to protect yourself against large losses, you absolutely can't win big in the game of investing.

Bernard Baruch's Secret Market Method of Making Millions

Bernard Baruch, a famous market operator on Wall Street and trusted advisor to U.S. presidents, said it best: "If a speculator is correct half of the time, he is hitting a good average. Even being right 3 or 4 times out of 10 should yield a person a fortune if he has the sense to cut his losses quickly on the ventures where he has been wrong."

As you can see, even the most successful investors make many mistakes. These poor decisions will lead to losses, some of which can become quite awful if you're not disciplined and careful. No matter how smart you are, how high your IQ, how advanced your education, how good your information, or how sound your analysis, you're simply not going to be right all the time. In fact, you'll probably be right less than half the time! You positively must understand and accept that the first rule for the highly successful individual investor is . . . always cut short and limit every single loss. To do this takes never-ending discipline and courage.

Marc Mandell of *Winning on Wall Street* has been reading *Investor's Business Daily* since 1987. He likes it for its many moneymaking ideas and its emphasis on risk-management strategies. "Lose small and win big," he believes, "is the holy grail of investing."

Baruch's point about cutting losses was driven home to me by an account that I managed back in 1962. The general market had taken a 29% nose-dive, and we were right on only one of every three commitments we had made in this account. Yet at the end of the year, the account was ahead. The reason was that the average profit on the 33% of decisions that were correct was more than twice the average of the small losses we took when we were off-target.

I like to follow a 3-to-1 ratio between where to sell and take profits and where to cut losses. If you take some 20% to 25% gains, cut your losses at 7% or 8%. If you're in a bear market like 2008 and you buy any stocks at all, you might get only a few 10% or 15% gains, so I'd move quickly to cut every single loss automatically at 3%, with no exceptions.

The whole secret to winning big in the stock market is not to be right all the time, but to lose the least amount possible when you're wrong.

You've got to recognize when you may be wrong and sell without hesitation to cut short every one of your losses. It's your job to get in phase with the market and not try to get the market in phase with you.

How can you tell when you may be wrong? That's easy: the price of the stock drops below the price you paid for it! Each point your favorite brainchild falls below your cost increases both the chance you're wrong and the price you're going to pay for being wrong. So get realistic.

Are Successful People Lucky or Always Right?

People think in order to be successful, you have to be either lucky or right most of the time. Not so. Successful people make many mistakes, and their success is due to hard work, not luck. They just try harder and more often than the average person. There aren't many overnight successes; success takes time.

In search of a filament for his electric lamp, Thomas Edison carbonized and tested 6,000 specimens of bamboo. Three of them worked. Before that, he had tried thousands of other materials, from cotton thread to chicken feathers.

Babe Ruth worked so hard for his home run record that he also held the lifetime record for strikeouts. Irving Berlin wrote more than 600 songs, but no more than 50 were hits. The Beatles were turned down by every record company in England before they made it big. Michael Jordan was once cut from his high school basketball team, and Albert Einstein made an F in math. (It also took him many years to develop and prove his theory of relativity.)

It takes a lot of trial and error before you can nail down substantial gains in stocks like Brunswick and Great Western Financial when they doubled in 1961, Chrysler and Syntex in 1963, Fairchild Camera and Polaroid in 1965, Control Data in 1967, Levitz Furniture in 1970–1972, Prime Computer and Humana in 1977–1981, MCI Communications in 1981–1982, Price Company in 1982–1983, Microsoft in 1986–1992, Amgen in 1990–1991, International Game Technology in 1991–1993, Cisco Systems from 1995 to 2000, America Online and Charles Schwab in 1998–1999, and Qualcomm in 1999. These stocks dazzled the market with gains ranging from 100% to more than 1,000%.

Over the years, I've found that only one or two out of ten stocks that I've bought turned out to be truly outstanding and capable of making this kind of substantial profits. In other words, to get the one or two stocks that make big money, you have to look for and buy ten.

Which begs the question, what do you do with the other eight? Do you sit with them and hope, the way most people do? Or do you sell them and keep trying until you come up with even bigger successes?

When Does a Loss Become a Loss?

When you say, "I can't sell my stock because I don't want to take a loss," you assume that what you want has some bearing on the situation. But the stock doesn't know who you are, and it couldn't care less what you hope or want.

Besides, selling doesn't give you the loss; you already have the loss. If you think you haven't incurred a loss until you sell the stock, you're kidding yourself. The larger the paper loss, the more real it will become. If you paid $40 per share for 100 shares of Can't Miss Chemical, and it's now worth $28 per share, you have $2,800 worth of stock that cost you $4,000. You have a $1,200 loss. Whether you convert the stock to cash or hold it, it's still worth only $2,800.

Even though you didn't sell, you took your loss when the stock dropped in price. You'd be better off selling and going back to a cash position where you can think far more objectively.

When you're holding on to a big loss, you're rarely able to think straight. You get emotional. You rationalize and say, "It can't go any lower." However, keep in mind that there are many other stocks to choose from where your chance of recouping your loss could be greater.

Here's another suggestion that may help you decide whether to sell: pretend that you don't own the stock and you have $2,800 in the bank. Then ask yourself, "Do I really want to buy this stock now?" If your answer is no, then why are you holding onto it?

Always, without Exception, Limit Your Losses to 7% or 8% of Your Cost

Individual investors should definitely set firm rules limiting the loss on the initial capital they have invested in each stock to an absolute maximum of 7% or 8%. Institutional investors who lessen their overall risk by taking large positions and diversifying broadly are unable to move into and out of stocks quickly enough to follow such a loss-cutting plan. This is a terrific advantage you, the nimble decisive individual investor, have over the institutions. So use it, or lose your edge.

When the late Gerald M. Loeb of E. F. Hutton was writing his last book on the stock market, he came down to visit me in Los Angeles, and I had the pleasure of discussing this idea with him. In his first work, *The Battle for Investment Survival*, Loeb advocated cutting all losses at 10%. I was curious and asked him if he always followed the 10% loss policy himself. "I would hope," he replied, "to be out long before they ever reach 10%." Loeb made millions in the market.

Bill Astrop, president of Astrop Advisory Corp. in Atlanta, Georgia, suggests a minor revision of the 10% loss-cutting plan. He thinks that individual investors should sell half of their position in a stock if it is down 5% from their cost and the other half once it's down 10%. This is sound advice.

To preserve your hard-earned money, I think a 7% or 8% loss should be the absolute limit. The average of all your losses should be less, perhaps 5% or 6%, if you're strictly disciplined and fast on your feet. If you can keep the average of all your mistakes and losses to 5% or 6%, you'll be like the football team on which opponents can never move the ball. If you don't give up many first downs, how can anyone ever beat you?

Now here's a valuable secret: if you use charts to time your buys precisely off *sound* bases (price consolidation areas), your stocks will rarely drop 8% from a correct buy point. So when they do, either you've made a mistake in your selection or a general market decline may be starting. This is a big key for your future success.

Barbara James, an IBD subscriber who has attended several of our workshops, didn't know anything about stocks when she started investing after 20 years in the real estate business. She first traded on paper using the IBD rules. This worked so well that she finally had the confidence to try it with real money. That was in the late 1990s, when the market seemed to have only one direction—up. The first stock she bought using the IBD rules was EMC. When she sold it in 2000, she had a 1,300% gain. She also had a gain of over 200% in Gap. Ten years after her start, with the profits she made using IBD, she was able to pay off her house and her car.

And thanks to the 7% rule, Barbara can take advantage of the market once it improves. Before the market started to correct in the fall of 2007, she had bought three CAN SLIM stocks—Monolithic Power, China Medical, and St. Jude Medical. "I bought them all at exactly the right pivot point, and I got forced out of all three as the market started to correct in July and August," she says. "I am happy to lose money when it's only 7% or 8%. If it hadn't been for the sell rules, I would have lost my shirt. And I wouldn't have resources for the next bull market."

Here's what another IBD subscriber, Herb Mitchell, told us in February 2009: "Over and over again, the buy and sell rules—especially the sell rules—have been proven to work. It took me a couple of years to finally get it through my head, but then the results started to show. I spent most of 2008 on the sidelines, and I now get compliments from friends who say that they lost thousands—50% or more—in their IRA accounts while I had a 5% gain for the year. I think I should have done better, but you live and learn."

Also, there's no rule that says you have to wait until every single loss reaches 7% to 8% before you take it. On occasion, you'll sense the general market index is under distribution (selling) or your stock isn't acting right and you are starting off amiss. In such cases, you can cut your loss sooner, when the stock may be down only one or two points.

Before the market broke wide open in October 1987, for example, there was ample time to sell and cut losses short. That correction actually began on August 26. If you're foolish enough to try bucking the market by buying stocks in bearish conditions, at least move your absolute loss-cutting point up to 3% or 4%.

After years of experience with this technique, your average losses should become less as your stock selection and timing improve and you learn to make small "follow-up buys" in your best stocks. It takes a lot of time to learn to make follow-up buys safely when a stock is up, but this method of money management forces you to move your money from slower-performing stocks into your stronger ones. I call this force-feeding. (See "My Revised Profit-and-Loss Plan," pages 258–259 in Chapter 11.) You'll end up selling stocks that are not yet down 7% or 8% because you are raising money to add to your best winners during clearly strong bull markets.

Remember: 7% to 8% is your absolute loss limit. You must sell without hesitation—no waiting a few days to see what might happen; no hoping the stock will rally back; no need to wait for the day's market close. Nothing but the fact you're down 7% or 8% below your cost should have a bearing on the situation at this point.

Once you're significantly ahead and have a good profit, you can afford to give the stock a good bit more room for normal fluctuations off its price peak. Do *not* sell a stock just because it's off 7% to 8% from its peak price. It's important that you definitely understand the difference.

In one case, you probably started off wrong. The stock is not acting the way you expected it to, and it is down below your purchase price. You're starting to lose your hard-earned money, and you may be about to lose a lot more. In the other case, you have begun correctly. The stock has acted better, and you have a significant gain. Now you're working on a profit, so in a bull market, you can afford to give the stock more room to fluctuate so that you don't get shaken out on a normal 10% to 15% correction.

Don't chase your stock up too far when you're buying it, however. The key is timing your stock purchases exactly at breakout points to minimize the chance that a stock will drop 8%. (See Chapter 2 for more on using charts to select stocks.)

All Common Stocks Are Speculative and Risky

There is considerable risk in all common stocks, regardless of their name, quality, purported blue-chip status, previous performance record, or current good earnings. Keep in mind that growth stocks can top at a time when their earnings are excellent and analysts' estimates are still rosy.

There are no sure things or safe stocks. Any stock can go down at any time . . . and you never know how far it can go down.

Every 50% loss began as a 10% or 20% loss. Having the raw courage to sell and take your loss cheerfully is the only way you can protect yourself against the possibility of much greater devastating losses. Decision and action should be instantaneous and simultaneous. To be a big winner, you must learn to make decisions. I've known at least a dozen educated and otherwise intelligent people who were completely wiped out solely because they would not sell and cut a loss.

What should you do if a stock gets away from you and the loss becomes greater than 10%? This can happen to anyone, and it's an even more critical sign the stock positively must be sold. It was in more trouble than normal, so it fell faster and further than normal. In the market collapse of 2000, many new investors lost heavily, and some of them lost it all. If they had just followed the simple sell rule discussed earlier, they would have protected most of their capital. Investing is not gambling, it is investing.

In my experience, the stocks that get away from you and produce larger-than-normal losses are the truly awful selections that absolutely must be sold. Something is really going wrong with either the stock or the whole market, and it's even more urgent the stock be sold to avoid a later catastrophe.

Keep in mind that if you let a stock drop 50%, you must make 100% on your next stock just to break even! And how often do you buy stocks that double? You simply can't afford to sit with a stock where the loss keeps getting worse. Get out.

It is a dangerous fallacy to assume that because a stock goes down, it has to come back up. Many don't. Others take years to recover. AT&T hit a high of $75 in 1964 and took 20 years to come back. Also, when the S&P 500 or Dow declines 20% to 25% in a bear market, many stocks will plummet 60% to 75%.

When the S&P dives 52%, as it did in 2008, many stocks fell 80% to 90%. Who would have projected General Motors would sell for $2 a share, down from $94? The auto industry is important to the United States, but it will require a serious, top-to-bottom restructuring and will possibly have to go through bankruptcy if it is to survive and compete effectively in the new highly competitive world market. For 31 years, from 1977 to 2008, GM stock's relative price strength line declined steadily. What will GM do in the future if India or China sells cars in the United States that get 50 miles per gallon and have a much lower price?

The only way to prevent bad stock market losses is to cut them without hesitation while they're still small. Always protect your account so that you can live to invest successfully another day.

In 2000, many new investors incorrectly believed all you had to do was buy high-tech stocks on every dip in price because they would always go back up and there was easy money to be made. This is an amateur's strategy, and it almost always leads to heavy losses. Semiconductor and other technology stocks are two to three times as volatile and risky as others. So if you're in these stocks, moving rapidly to cut short every loss is even more essential. If your portfolio is in nothing but high-tech stocks, or if you're heavily margined in tech stocks, you are asking for serious trouble if you don't cut your losses quickly.

You should never invest on margin unless you're willing to cut all your losses quickly. Otherwise, you could go belly-up in no time. If you get a margin call from your broker (when you're faced with the decision to either sell stock or add money to your account to cover the lost equity in a falling stock), don't throw good money after bad. Sell some stock, and recognize what the market and your margin clerk are trying to tell you.

Cutting Losses Is Like Buying an Insurance Policy

This policy of limiting losses is similar to paying small insurance premiums. You're reducing your risk to precisely the level you're comfortable with. Yes, the stock you sell will often turn right around and go back up. And yes, this can be frustrating. But when this happens, don't ever conclude you were wrong to sell it. That exceedingly dangerous thinking will eventually get you into serious trouble.

Think about it this way: If you bought insurance on your car last year and you didn't have an accident, was your money wasted? Will you buy the same insurance this year? Of course you will! Did you take out fire insurance on your home or your business? If your home or business hasn't burned down, are you upset because you feel you made a bad financial decision? No. You don't buy fire insurance because you know your house is going to burn down. You buy insurance just in case, to protect yourself against the remote possibility of a serious loss.

It's exactly the same for the winning investor who cuts all losses quickly. It's the only way to protect against the possible or probable chance of a much larger loss from which it may not be possible to recover.

If you hesitate and allow a loss to increase to 20%, you will need a 25% gain just to break even. Wait longer until the stock is down 25%, and you'll have to make 33% to get even. Wait still longer until the loss is 33%, and you'll have to make 50% to get back to the starting gate. The longer you wait, the more the math works against you, so don't vacillate. Move immediately to cut out possible bad decisions. Develop the strict discipline to act and to always follow your selling rules.

Some people have gone so far as to let losing stocks damage their health. In this situation, it's best to sell and stop worrying. I know a stockbroker who in 1961 bought Brunswick at $60 on the way down in price. It had been the market's super leader since 1957, increasing more than 20 times. When it dropped to $50, he bought more, and when it dropped to $40, he added again.

When it dropped to $30, he dropped dead on the golf course.

History and human nature keep relentlessly repeating themselves in the stock market. In the fall of 2000, many investors made the identical mistake: they bought the prior bull market's leader, Cisco Systems, on the way down at $70, $60, $50, and lower, after it had topped at $87. Seven months later it had sunk to $13, an 80% decline for those who bought at $70. The moral of the story is: never argue with the market. Your health and peace of mind are always more important than any stock.

Small losses are cheap insurance, and they're the only insurance you can buy on your investments. Even if a stock moves up after you sell it, as many surely will, you will have accomplished your critical objective of keeping all your losses small, and you'll still have money to try again for a winner in another stock.

Take Your Losses Quickly and Your Profits Slowly

There's an old investment saying that the first loss in the market is the smallest. In my view, the way to make investment decisions is to always (with no exceptions) take your losses quickly and your profits slowly. Yet most investors get emotionally confused and take their profits quickly and their losses slowly.

What is your real risk in any stock you buy when you use the method we've discussed? It's 8%, no matter what you buy, if you follow this rule religiously. Still, most investors stubbornly ask, "Shouldn't we sit with stocks rather than selling and taking a loss?" Or, "How about unusual situations where some bad news hits suddenly and causes a price decline?" Or, "Does this loss-cutting procedure apply all the time, or are there exceptions, like when a company has a good new product?" The answer: *there are no exceptions*. None of these things changes the situation one bit. You must always protect your hard-earned pool of capital.

Letting your losses run is the most serious mistake almost all investors make. You must accept the fact that mistakes in stock selection and timing are going to be made frequently, even by the most experienced of professional investors. I'd go so far as to say that if you aren't willing to cut short and limit your losses, you probably shouldn't buy stocks. Would you drive your car down the street without brakes? If you were a fighter pilot, would you go into battle without a parachute?

Should You Average Down in Price?

One of the most unprofessional things a stockbroker can do is hesitate or fail to call customers whose stocks are down in price. That's when the customer needs help the most. Shirking this duty in difficult periods shows a lack of courage under pressure. About the only thing that's worse is for brokers to take themselves off the hook by advising customers to "average down" (buy more of a stock that is already showing a loss). If I were advised to do this, I'd close my account and look for a smarter broker.

Everyone loves to buy stocks; no one loves to sell them. As long as you hold a stock, you can still hope it might come back up enough to at least get you out even. Once you sell, you abandon all hope and accept the cold reality of temporary defeat. Investors are always hoping rather than being realistic. Knowing and acting is better than hoping or guessing. The fact that you want a stock to go up so you can at least get out even has nothing to do with the action and brutal reality of the market. The market obeys only the law of supply and demand.

A great trader once noted there are only two emotions in the market: hope and fear. "The only problem," he added, "is we hope when we should fear, and we fear when we should hope." This is just as true in 2009 as it was in 1909.

The Turkey Story

Many years ago, I heard a story by Fred C. Kelly, the author of *Why You Win or Lose*, that illustrates perfectly how the conventional investor thinks when the time comes to make a selling decision:

A little boy was walking down the road when he came upon an old man trying to catch wild turkeys. The man had a turkey trap, a crude device consisting of a big box with the door hinged at the top. This door was kept open by a prop, to which was tied a piece of twine leading back a hundred feet or more to the operator. A thin trail of corn scattered along a path lured turkeys to the box.

Once they were inside, the turkeys found an even more plentiful supply of corn. When enough turkeys had wandered into the box, the old man would jerk away the prop and let the door fall shut. Having once shut the door, he couldn't open it again without going up to the box, and this would scare away any turkeys that were lurking outside. The time to pull away the prop was when as many turkeys as one could reasonably expect were inside.

One day he had a dozen turkeys in his box. Then one sauntered out, leaving 11. "Gosh, I wish I had pulled the string when all 12 were there," said the old man. "I'll wait a minute and maybe the other one will go back." While he waited for the twelfth turkey to return, two more walked out on him. "I should have been satisfied with 11," the trapper said. "Just as soon as I get one more back, I'll pull the string." Three more walked out, and still the man waited. Having once had 12 turkeys, he disliked going home with less than 8.

He couldn't give up the idea that some of the original turkeys would return. When finally there was only one turkey left in the trap, he said, "I'll wait until he walks out or another goes in, and then I'll quit." The solitary turkey went to join the others, and the man returned empty-handed.

The psychology of normal investors is not much different. They hope more turkeys will return to the box when they should fear that all the turkeys could walk out and they'll be left with nothing.

How the Typical Investor Thinks

If you're a typical investor, you probably keep records of your transactions. When you think about selling a stock, you probably look at your records to see what price you paid for it. If you have a profit, you may sell, but if you have a loss, you tend to wait. After all, you didn't invest in the market to lose money. However, what you should be doing is selling your worst-performing stock first. Keep your flower patch free of weeds.

You may decide to sell your shares in Myriad Genetics, for example, because it shows a nice profit, but you'll keep your General Electric because it still has a ways to go before it's back to the price you paid for it. If this is the way you think, you're suffering from the "price-paid bias" that afflicts 95% of all investors.

Suppose you bought a stock two years ago at $30, and it's now worth $34. Most investors would sell it because they have a profit. But what does the price you paid two years ago have to do with what the stock is worth now? And what does it have to do with whether you should hold or sell the stock? The key is the relative performance of this stock versus others you either own or could potentially own.

Analyzing Your Activities

To help you avoid the price-paid bias, particularly if you are a longer-term investor, I suggest you use a different method of analyzing your results. At the end of each month or quarter, compute the percentage change in the price of each stock from the last date you did this type of analysis. Now list your investments in order of their relative price performance since your previous evaluation period. Let's say Caterpillar is down 6%, ITT is up 10%, and General Electric is down 10%. Your list would start with ITT on top, then Caterpillar, then GE. At the end of the next month or quarter, do the same thing. After a few reviews, you will easily recognize the stocks that are not doing well. They'll be at the bottom of the list; those that did best will be at or near the top.

This method isn't foolproof, but it does force you to focus your attention not on what you paid for your stocks, but on the relative performance of your investments in the market. It will help you maintain a clearer perspective. Of course, you have to keep records of your costs for tax reasons, but you should use this more realistic method in the longer-term management of your portfolio. Doing this more often than once a quarter can only help you. Eliminating the price-paid bias can be profitable and rewarding.

Any time you make a commitment to a security, you should also determine the potential profit and possible loss. This is only logical. You wouldn't buy a stock if there were a potential profit of 20% and a potential loss of 80%, would you? But if you don't try to define these factors and operate by well-thought-out rules, how do you know this isn't the situation when you make your stock purchase? Do you have specific selling rules you've written down and follow, or are you flying blind?

I suggest you write down the price at which you expect to sell if you have a loss (8% or less below your purchase price) along with the expected profit potential of all the securities you purchase. For instance, you might consider selling your growth stock when its P/E ratio increases 100% or more from the time the stock originally began its big move out of its initial base pattern.

If you write these numbers down, you'll more easily see when the stock has reached one of these levels.

It's bad business to base your sell decisions on your cost and hold stocks down in price simply because you can't accept the fact you made an imprudent selection and lost money. In fact, you're making the exact opposite decisions from those you would make if you were running your own business.

The Red Dress Story

Investing in the stock market is really no different from running your own business. Investing is a business and should be operated as such. Assume that you own a small store selling women's clothing. You've bought and stocked women's dresses in three colors: yellow, green, and red. The red dresses go quickly, half the green ones sell, and the yellows don't sell at all.

What do you do about it? Do you go to your buyer and say, "The red dresses are all sold out. The yellow ones don't seem to have any demand, but I still think they're good. Besides, yellow is my favorite color, so let's buy some more of them anyway"?

Certainly not!

The clever merchandiser who survives in the retail business looks at this predicament objectively and says, "We sure made a mistake. We'd better get rid of the yellow dresses. Let's have a sale. Mark them down 10%. If they don't sell at that price, mark them down 20%. Let's get our money out of those 'old dogs' no one wants, and put it into more of the hot-moving red dresses that are in demand." This is common sense in any retail business. Do you do this with your investments? Why not?

Everyone makes buying errors. The buyers for department stores are pros, but even they make mistakes. If you do slip up, recognize it, sell, and go on to the next thing. You don't have to be correct on all your investment decisions to make a good net profit.

Now you know the real secret to reducing your risk and selecting the best stocks: stop counting your turkeys and get rid of your yellow dresses!

Are You a Speculator or an Investor?

There are two often-misunderstood words that are used to describe the kinds of people who participate in the stock market: speculator and investor. When you think of the word *speculator*, you might think of someone who takes big risks, gambling on the future success of a stock. Conversely, when you think of the word *investor*, you might think of someone who approaches the stock market in a sensible and rational manner. According to these conventional definitions, you may think it's smarter to be an investor.

Baruch, however, defined *speculator* as follows: "The word speculator comes from the Latin 'speculari,' which means to spy and observe. A speculator, therefore, is a person who observes and acts before [the future] occurs." This is precisely what you should be doing: watching the market and individual stocks to determine what they're doing now, and then acting on that information.

Jesse Livermore, another stock market legend, defined *investor* this way: "Investors are the big gamblers. They make a bet, stay with it, and if it goes wrong, they lose it all." After reading this far, you should already know this is not the proper way to invest. There's no such thing as a long-term investment once a stock drops into the loss column and you're down 8% below your cost.

These definitions are a bit different from those you'll read in Webster's Dictionary, but they are far more accurate. Keep in mind that Baruch and Livermore at many times made millions of dollars in the stock market. I'm not sure about lexicographers.

One of my goals is to get you to question many of the faulty investment ideas, beliefs, and methods that you've heard about or used in the past. One of these is the very notion of what it means to invest. It's unbelievable how much erroneous information about the stock market, how it works, and how to succeed at it is out there. Learn to objectively analyze all the relevant facts about a stock and about how the market is behaving. Stop listening to and being influenced by friends, associates, and the continuous array of experts' personal opinions on daily TV shows.

For Safety, Why Not Diversify Widely?

Wide diversification is a substitute for lack of knowledge. It sounds good, and it's what most people advise. But in a bad bear market, almost all of your stocks will go down, and you could lose 50% percent or more in some stocks that will never come back. So diversification is a poor substitute for a sound defensive plan with rules to protect your account. Also, if you have 20 or 30 stocks and you sell 3 or 4, it won't help you when you lose heavily on the rest.

"I'm Not Worried; I'm a Long-Term Investor, and I'm Still Getting My Dividends"

It's also risky and probably foolish to say to yourself, "I'm not worried about my stocks being down because they are good stocks, and I'm still getting my dividends." Good stocks bought at the wrong time can go down as much as poor stocks, and it's possible they might not be such good stocks in the first place. It may just be your personal opinion they're good.

Furthermore, if a stock is down 35% in value, isn't it rather absurd to say you're all right because you are getting a 4% dividend yield? A 35% loss plus a 4% income gain equals a whopping 31% net loss.

To be a successful investor, you must face facts and stop rationalizing and hoping. No one emotionally wants to take losses, but to increase your chances of success in the stock market, you have to do many things you don't want to do. Develop precise rules and hard-nosed selling disciplines, and you'll gain a major advantage. You can do this.

Never Lose Your Confidence

There's one last critical reason for you to take losses before they have a chance to really hurt you: never lose your courage to make decisions in the future. If you don't sell to cut your losses when you begin to get into trouble, you can easily lose the confidence you'll need to make buy and sell decisions in the future. Or, far worse, you can get so discouraged that you finally throw in the towel and get out of the market, never realizing what you did wrong, never correcting your faulty procedures, and giving up all the future potential the stock market—one of the most outstanding opportunities in America—has to offer.

Wall Street is human nature on daily display. Buying and selling stocks properly and making a net profit are always a complicated affair. Human nature being what it is, 90% of people in the stock market—professionals and amateurs alike—simply haven't done much homework. They haven't really studied to learn whether what they're doing is right or wrong. They haven't studied in enough detail what makes a successful stock go up and down. Luck has nothing to do with it, and it's not a total mystery. And it certainly isn't a "random walk" or an efficient market, as some inexperienced university professors formerly believed.

It takes some work to become really good at stock selection, and still more to know how and when to sell. Selling a stock correctly is a tougher job and the one that is least understood by everyone. To do it right, you need a plan to cut losses and the discipline to do this quickly without wavering.

Forget your ego, swallow your pride, stop trying to argue with the market, and don't get emotionally attached to any stock that's losing you money. Remember: there are no good stocks; they're all bad . . . unless they go up in price. Learn from the 2000 and 2008 experience. Those who followed our selling rules protected their capital and nailed down gains. Those who did not have or follow any selling rules got hurt.

· CHAPTER ·

When to Sell and Take Your Worthwhile Profits

This is one of the most vital chapters in this book, covering an essential subject few investors handle right. So study it carefully. Common stock is just like any merchandise. You, as the merchant, must sell your stock if you're to realize a profit, and the best way to sell a stock is while it's on the way up, still advancing and looking strong to everyone.

This is completely contrary to human nature. It means selling when your stock is strong, up a lot in price, and looks like it will make even more profit for you. But when you sell like this, you won't be caught in heartrending 20% to 40% corrections that can hit market leaders and put downside pressure on your portfolio. You'll never sell at the top, so don't kick yourself when some stocks go higher after you sell.

> **If you don't sell early, you'll be late. Your object is to make and take significant gains and not get excited, optimistic, greedy, or emotionally carried away as your stock's advance gets stronger. Keep in mind the old saying: "Bulls make money and bears make money, but pigs get slaughtered."**

The basic objective of your account should be to show a net profit. To retain worthwhile profits, you must sell and take them. The key is knowing when to do just that.

Bernard Baruch, the financier who built a fortune in the stock market, said, "Repeatedly, I have sold a stock while it was still rising—and that has been one reason why I have held on to my fortune. Many a time, I might have made a good deal more by holding a stock, but I would also have been caught in the fall when the price of the stock collapsed."

When asked if there was a technique for making money on the stock exchange, Nathan Rothschild, the highly successful international banker, said, "There certainly is. I never buy at the bottom, and I always sell too soon."

Joe Kennedy, one-time Wall Street speculator and father of popular former President John F. Kennedy, believed "only a fool holds out for the top dollar." "The object," he said, "is to get out while a stock is up before it has a chance to break and turn down." And Gerald M. Loeb, a highly successful financier, stressed "once the price has risen into estimated normal or overvaluation areas, the amount held should be reduced steadily as quotations advance."

What all these Wall Street legends believed was this: you simply must get out while the getting is good. The secret is to hop off the elevator on one of the floors on the way up and not ride it back down again.

You Must Develop a Profit-and-Loss Plan

To be a big success in the stock market, you must have definite rules and a profit-and-loss plan. I developed many of the buy and sell rules described in this book in the early 1960s, when I was a young stockbroker with Hayden, Stone. These rules helped me buy a seat on the New York Stock Exchange and start my own firm shortly thereafter. When I started out, though, I concentrated on developing a set of buy rules that would locate the very best stocks. But as you'll see, I had only half of the puzzle figured out.

My buy rules were first developed in January 1960, when I analyzed the three best-performing mutual funds of the prior two years. The standout was the then-small Dreyfus Fund, which racked up gains twice as large as those of many of its competitors.

I sent for copies of every Dreyfus quarterly report and prospectus from 1957 to 1959. The prospectus showed the average cost of each new stock the fund purchased. Next, I got a book of stock charts and marked in red the average price Dreyfus paid for its new holdings each quarter.

After looking at more than a hundred new Dreyfus purchases, I made a stunning discovery: every stock had been bought at the highest price it had sold for in the past year. In other words, if a stock had bounced between $40 and $50 for many months, Dreyfus bought it as soon as it made a new high in price and traded between $50 and $51. The stocks had also formed certain chart price patterns before leaping into new high ground. This gave me two vitally important clues: buying on new highs from basing patterns was important, and certain chart patterns spelled big profit potential.

Jack Dreyfus Was a Chartist

Jack Dreyfus was a chartist and a tape reader. He bought all his stocks based on market action, and only when the price broke to new highs off sound chart patterns. He was also beating the pants off every competitor who ignored the real-world facts of market behavior (supply and demand) and depended only on fundamental, analytical personal opinions.

Jack's research department in those early, big-performance days consisted of three young Turks who posted the day's price and volume action of hundreds of listed stocks to very oversized charts. I saw these charts one day when I visited Dreyfus's headquarters in New York.

Shortly thereafter, two small funds run by Fidelity in Boston started doing the same thing. They, too, produced superior results. One was managed by Ned Johnson, Jr., and the other by Jerry Tsai. Almost all the stocks that the Dreyfus and Fidelity funds bought also had strong increases in their quarterly earnings reports.

So the first buy rules I made in 1960 were as follows:

1. Concentrate on listed stocks that sell for more than $20 a share with at least some institutional acceptance.

2. Insist that the company show increases in earnings per share in each of the past five years and that the current quarterly earnings are up at least 20%.

3. Buy when the stock is making or about to make a new high in price after emerging from a sound correction and price consolidation period. This breakout should be accompanied by a volume increase to at least 50% above the stock's average daily volume.

The first stock I bought under my new set of buy rules was Universal Match in February 1960. It doubled in 16 weeks, but I failed to make much money because I didn't have much money to invest. I was just getting started as a stockbroker, and I didn't have many customers. I also got nervous and sold it too quickly. Later that year, sticking with my well-defined game plan, I selected Procter & Gamble, Reynolds Tobacco, and MGM. They, too, made outstanding price moves, but I still didn't make much money because the money I had to invest was limited.

About this time, I was accepted to Harvard Business School's first Program for Management Development (PMD). In what little extra time I had at Harvard, I read a number of business and investment books in the library. The best was *How to Trade in Stocks*, by Jesse Livermore. From this book, **I learned that your objective in the market was not to be right, but to make big money when you were right.**

Jesse Livermore and Pyramiding

After reading his book, I adopted Livermore's method of pyramiding, or averaging up, when a stock advanced after I purchased it. "Averaging up" is a technique where, after your initial stock purchase, you buy additional shares of the stock when it moves up in price. This is usually warranted when the first purchase of a stock is made precisely at a correct pivot, or buy, point and the price has increased 2% or 3% from the original purchase price. Essentially, I followed up what was working with additional but always *smaller* purchases, allowing me to concentrate my buying when I seemed to be right. If I was wrong and the stock dropped a certain amount below my cost, I sold the stock to cut short every loss.

This is very different from how the majority of people invest. Most of them average down, meaning they buy additional shares as a stock declines in price in order to lower their cost per share. But why add more of your hard-earned money to stocks that aren't working? That's a bad plan.

Learning by Analysis of My Failures

In the first half of 1961, my rules and plan worked great. Some of the top winners I bought that year were Great Western Financial, Brunswick, Kerr-McGee, Crown Cork & Seal, AMF, and Certain-teed. But by summer, all was not well.

I had bought the right stocks at exactly the right time and I had pyramided with several additional buys, so I had good positions and profits. But when the stocks finally topped, I held on too long and watched my profits vanish. If you've been investing for a while, I'll bet you know exactly what I'm talking about. It's a problem you must tackle and solve if you want real results. When you snooze, you lose. It was hard to swallow. I'd been dead right on my stock selections for more than a year, but I had just broken even.

I was so upset that I spent the last six months of 1961 carefully analyzing every transaction I had made during the prior year. Much like doctors do postmortem operations and the Civil Aeronautics Board conducts postcrash investigations, I took a red pen and marked on charts exactly where each buy and sell decision was made. Then I overlaid the general market averages.

Eventually my problem became crystal clear: I knew how to select the best leading stocks at the right time, but I had no plan for when to sell them and take profits. I had been completely clueless, a real dummy. I was so unaware that I had never even thought about when a stock should be sold and a profit taken. My stocks went up and then down like yo-yos, and my paper profits were wiped out.

For example, the way I handled Certain-teed, a building materials company that made shell homes, was especially poor. I bought the stock in the low $20s, but during a weak moment in the market, I got scared and sold it for only a two- or three-point gain. Certain-teed went on to triple in price. I was in at the right time, but I didn't recognize what I had and failed to capitalize on a phenomenal opportunity.

My analysis of Certain-teed and other such personal failures proved to be the critical key to my seeing what I had been doing wrong that I had to correct if I was to get on the right track to future success. Have you ever analyzed every one of your failures so you can learn from them? Few people do. What a tragic mistake you'll make if you don't look carefully at yourself and the decisions you've made in the stock market that did not work. You get better only when you learn what you've done wrong.

This is the difference between winners and losers, whether in the market or in life. If you got hurt in the 2000 or 2008 bear market, don't get discouraged and quit. Plot out your mistakes on charts, study them, and write some additional new rules that, if you follow them, will correct your mistakes and let you avoid the actions that cost you a lot of time and money. You'll be that much closer to fully capitalizing on the next bull market. And in America, there will be many future bull markets. You're never a loser until you quit and give up or start blaming other people, like most politicians do. If you do what I've suggested here, it could just change your whole life.

"There are no secrets to success," said General Colin Powell, former secretary of state. "It is the result of preparation, hard work, and learning from failure."

My Revised Profit-and-Loss Plan

As a result of my analysis, I discovered that successful stocks, after breaking out of a proper base, tend to move up 20% to 25%. Then they usually decline, build new bases, and in some cases resume their advances. With this new knowledge in mind, I made a rule that I'd buy each stock exactly at the pivot buy point and have the discipline not to pyramid or add to my position at more than 5% past that point. Then I'd sell each stock when it was up 20%, while it was still advancing.

In the case of Certain-teed, however, the stock ran up 20% in just two weeks. This was the type of super winner I was hoping to find and capitalize on the next time around. So, I made an absolutely important exception to the "sell at +20% rule": if the stock was so powerful that it vaulted 20% in only one, two, or three weeks, it must be held for at least eight weeks from its buy point. Then it would be analyzed to see if it should be held for a possible six-month long-term capital gain. (Six months was the long-term capital gains period at that time.) If a stock fell below its purchase price by 8%, I would sell it and take the loss.

So, here was the revised profit-and-loss plan: take 20% profits when you have them (except with the most powerful of all stocks) and cut your losses at a maximum of 8% below your purchase price.

The plan had several big advantages. You could be wrong twice and right once and still not get into financial trouble. When you were right and you wanted to follow up with another, somewhat smaller buy in the same stock a few points higher, you were frequently forced into a decision to sell one of your more laggard or weakest performers. The money in your slower-performing stock positions was continually force-fed into your best performers.

Over a period of years, I came to almost always make my first follow-up purchase automatically as soon as my initial buy was up 2% or 2½% in price. This lessened the chance I might hesitate and wind up making the additional buy when the stock was up 5% to 10% or not add at all.

When you appear to be right, you should always follow up. When a boxer in the ring finally has an opening and lands a powerful punch, he must always follow up his advantage . . . if he wants to win.

By selling your laggards and putting the proceeds into your winners, you are putting your money to far more efficient use. You could make two or three 20% plays in a good year, and you wouldn't have to sit through so many long, unproductive corrections while a stock built a whole new base.

A 20% gain in three to six months is substantially more productive than a 20% gain that takes 12 months to achieve. Two 20% gains compounded in one year equals a 44% annual rate of return. When you're more experienced, you can use full margin (buying power in a margin account), and increase your potential compounded return to nearly 100%.

How I Discovered the General Market System

Another exceedingly profitable observation made from analyzing every one of my money-losing, out-of-ignorance mistakes was that most of my market-leading stocks that topped had done so because the general market started into a decline of 10% or more. This conclusion finally led to my discovering and developing our system of interpreting the daily general market averages' price and volume chart. It gave us the critical ability to establish the true trend and major changes of direction in the overall market.

Three months later, by April 1, 1962, following all of my selling rules had automatically forced me out of every stock. I was 100% in cash, with no idea the market was headed for a real crash that spring. This is the fascinating thing: the rules will force you out, but you don't know how bad it can really get. You just know it's going down and you're out, which sooner or later will be worth its weight in gold to you. That's what happened in 2008. Our rules forced us out, and we had no idea the market was headed for a major breakdown. Most institutional investors were affected because their investment policy was to be fully invested (95% to 100%).

In early 1962, I had finished reading *Reminiscences of a Stock Operator*, by Edwin LeFevre. I was struck by the parallels between the stock market panic of 1907, which LeFevre discussed in detail, and what seemed to be happening in April 1962. Since I was 100% in cash and my daily Dow analysis said the market was weak at that point, I began to sell short stocks such as Certain-teed and Alside (an earlier sympathy play to Certain-teed). For this, I got into trouble with Hayden, Stone's home office on Wall Street. The firm had just recommended Certain-teed as a buy, and here I was going around telling everyone it was a short sale. Later in the year, I sold Korvette short at over $40. The profits from both of these short sales were good.

By October 1962, during the Cuban missile crisis, I was again in cash. A day or two after the Soviet Union backed down from President Kennedy's wise naval blockade, a rally attempt in the Dow Jones Industrial Average followed through, signaling a major upturn according to my new system. I then bought the first stock of the new bull market, Chrysler, at 58⅞. It had a classic cup-with-handle base.

Throughout 1963, I simply followed my rules to the letter. They worked so well that the "worst"-performing account I managed that year was up 115%. It was a cash account. Other accounts that used margin were up several hundred percent. There were many individual stock losses, but they were usually small, averaging 5% to 6%. Profits, on the other hand, were awesome because of the concentrated positions we built by careful, disciplined pyramiding when we were right.

Starting with only $4,000 or $5,000 that I had saved from my salary, plus some borrowed money and the use of full margin, I had three back-to-back big winners: Korvette on the short side in late 1962, Chrysler on the buy side, and Syntex, which was bought at $100 per share with the Chrysler profit in June 1963. After eight weeks, Syntex was up 40%, and I decided to play this powerful stock out for six months. By the fall of 1963, the profit had topped $200,000, and I decided to buy a seat on the New York Stock Exchange. So don't ever let anyone tell you it can't be done! **You can learn to invest wisely if you're willing to study all of your mistakes, learn from them, and write new self-correcting rules.** This can be the greatest opportunity of a lifetime, if you are determined, not easily discouraged, and willing to work hard and prepare yourself. Anyone can make it happen.

For me, many long evenings of study led to precise rules, disciplines, and a plan that finally worked. Luck had nothing to do with it; it was persistence and hard work. You can't expect to watch television, drink beer, or party with your friends every night and still find the answers to something as complicated as the stock market or the U.S. economy.

In America, anyone can do anything by working at it. There are no limits placed on you. It all depends on your desire and your attitude. It makes no difference where you're from, what you look like, or where you went to school. You can improve your life and your future and capture the American Dream. And you don't have to have a lot of money to start.

If you get discouraged at times, don't ever give up. Go back and put in some detailed extra effort. It's always the study and learning time that you put in *after* nine to five, Monday through Friday, that ultimately makes the difference between winning and reaching your goals, and missing out on truly great opportunities that really can change your whole life.

Two Things to Remember about Selling

Before we examine the key selling rules one by one, keep these two key points in mind.

First, buying precisely right solves most of your selling problems. If you buy at exactly the right time off a proper daily or weekly chart base in the first place, and you do not chase or pyramid a stock when it's extended in price more than 5% past a correct pivot buy point, you will be in a position to sit through most normal corrections. Winning stocks very rarely drop 8% below a correct pivot buy point. In fact, most big winners don't close below their pivot point. Buying as close to the pivot point as possible is therefore absolutely essential and may let you cut the smaller number of resulting losses more quickly than 8%. A stock might have to drop only 4% or 5% before you know something could be wrong.

Second, beware of the big-block selling you might see on a ticker tape or your PC just after you buy a stock during a bull market. The selling might be emotional, uninformed, temporary, or not as large (relative to past volume) as it appears. The best stocks can have sharp sell-offs for a few days or a week. Consult a weekly basis stock chart for an overall perspective to avoid getting scared or shaken out in what may just be a normal pullback. In fact, 40% to 60% of the time, a winning stock may pull back to its exact buy point or slightly below and try to shake you out. But it should not be down 8% unless you chased it too high in price when you bought it. If you're making too many mistakes and nothing seems to be working for you, check and make sure you're not making a number of your buys 10%, 15%, or 20% above the precise, correct buy point. Chasing stocks rarely works. You can't buy when you get more excited. **So stop chasing extended stocks.**

Technical Sell Signs

By studying how the greatest stock market winners, as well as the market itself, all topped, I came up with the following list of factors that occur when a stock tops and rolls over. Perhaps you've noticed that few of the selling rules involve changes in the fundamentals of a stock. Many big investors get out of a stock before trouble appears on the income statement. If the smart money is selling, so should you. Individual investors don't stand much chance when institutions begin liquidating large positions. You buy with heavy emphasis on the fundamentals, such as earnings, sales, profit margins, return on equity, and new products, but many stocks peak when earnings are up 100% and analysts are projecting continued growth and higher price targets.

On the same day in 1999 that I sold Charles Schwab stock on a climax top run-up and an exhaustion gap, one of the largest brokerage firms in America projected that the stock would go up 50 points more. Virtually all of my successful stocks were sold on the way up, while they were advancing and the market was not affected. A bird in the hand is worth two imaginary ones in the bush. Therefore, you must frequently sell based on unusual market action (price and volume movement), not personal opinions from Wall Street. You must wean yourself from listening to personal opinions. Since I never worked on Wall Street, I never got distracted by these diversions.

There are many signals to look for when you're trying to recognize when a stock could be in a topping process. These include the price movement surrounding climax tops, adverse volume, and other weak action. A lot of this will become clearer to you as you continue to study this information and apply it to your daily decision making. These rules and principles have been responsible for most of my better decisions in the market, but they can seem a bit complicated at first. I suggest that you reread Chapter 2 on chart reading, then read these selling rules again.

In fact, most of the IBD subscribers I've met at our hundreds of workshops who have enjoyed real success with their investments have told me that they read this entire book two or three times, or even more. You probably aren't going to get it all in one reading. Some who have been distracted by all the outside noise say that they read it periodically to help them get back on the right track.

Climax Tops

Many leading stocks top in an explosive fashion. They make climax runs—suddenly advancing at a much faster rate for one or two weeks after an advance of many months. In addition, they often end in exhaustion gaps—when a stock's price opens up on a gap from the prior day's close, on heavy volume. These and related bull market climax signals are discussed in detail here.

1. **Largest daily price run-up.** If a stock's price is extended—that is, if it's had a significant run-up for many months from its buy point off a sound and proper base—and it closes for the day with a larger price increase than on any previous up day since the beginning of the whole move up, watch out! This usually occurs very close to a stock's peak.

2. **Heaviest daily volume.** The ultimate top might occur on the heaviest volume day since the beginning of the advance.

3. **Exhaustion gap.** If a stock that's been advancing rapidly is greatly extended from its original base many months ago (usually at least 18 weeks out of a first- or second-stage base and 12 weeks or more if it's out of a later-stage base) and then opens on a gap up in price from the previous day's close, the advance is near its peak. For example, a two-point gap in a stock's price after a long run-up would occur if it closed at its high of $50 for the day, then opened the next morning at $52 and held above $52 during the day. This is called an exhaustion gap.

4. **Climax top activity.** Sell if a stock's advance gets so active that it has a rapid price run-up for two or three weeks on a weekly chart, or for seven of eight days in a row or eight of ten days on a daily chart. This is called a climax top. The price spread from the stock's low to its high for the week will almost always be greater than that for any prior week since the beginning of the original move many months ago.

    In a few cases, around the top of a climax run, a stock may retrace the prior week's large price spread from the prior week's low to its high point and close the week up a little, with volume remaining very high. I call this "railroad tracks" because on a weekly chart, you'll see two parallel vertical lines. This is a sign of continued heavy volume distribution without real additional price progress for the week.

5. **Signs of distribution.** After a long advance, heavy daily volume without further upside price progress signals distribution. Sell your stock before unsuspecting buyers are overwhelmed. Also know when savvy investors are due to have a long-term capital gain.

6. **Stock splits.** Sell if a stock runs up 25% to 50% for one or two weeks on a stock split. In a few rare cases, such as Qualcomm at the end of

1999, it could be 100%. Stocks tend to top around excessive stock splits. If a stock's price is extended from its base and a stock split is announced, in many cases the stock could be sold.

7. **Increase in consecutive down days.** For most stocks, the number of consecutive down days in price relative to up days in price will probably increase when the stock starts down from its top. You may see four or five days down, followed by two or three days up, whereas before you would have seen four days up and then two or three down.

8. **Upper channel line.** You should sell if a stock goes through its upper channel line after a huge run-up. (On a stock chart, channel lines are somewhat parallel lines drawn by connecting the lows of the price pattern with one straight line and then connecting three high points made over the past four to five months with another straight line.) Studies show that stocks that surge above their *properly drawn* upper channel lines should be sold.

9. **200-day moving average line.** Some stocks may be sold when they are 70% to 100% or more above their 200-day moving average price line, although I have rarely used this one.

10. **Selling on the way down from the top.** If you didn't sell early while the stock was still advancing, sell on the way down from the peak. After the first breakdown, some stocks may pull back up in price once.

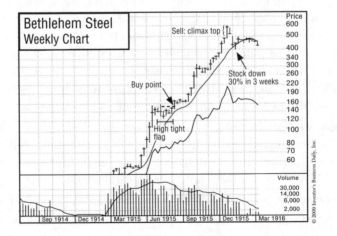

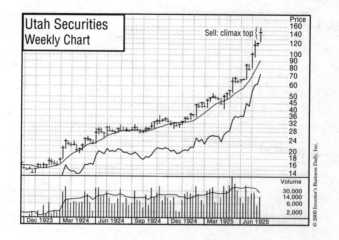

Utah Securities
Weekly Chart

Sell: climax top

Price
160
140
120
100
90
80
70
60
50
45
40
36
32
28
24
20
18
16
14

Volume
30,000
14,000
6,000
2,000

Dec 1923 | Mar 1924 | Jun 1924 | Sep 1924 | Dec 1924 | Mar 1925 | Jun 1925

© 2009 Investor's Business Daily, Inc.

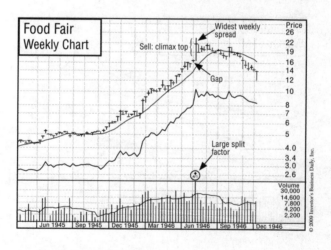

Food Fair
Weekly Chart

Widest weekly spread

Sell: climax top

Gap

Large split factor

Price
26
22
19
16
14
12
10
8
7
6
5
4.0
3.4
3.0
2.6

Volume
30,000
14,600
7,800
4,200
2,200

Jun 1945 | Sep 1945 | Dec 1945 | Mar 1946 | Jun 1946 | Sep 1946 | Dec 1946

© 2009 Investor's Business Daily, Inc.

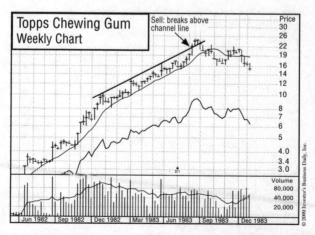

Topps Chewing Gum
Weekly Chart

Sell: breaks above channel line

Price
30
26
22
19
16
14
12
10
8
7
6
5
4.0
3.4
3.0

Volume
80,000
40,000
20,000

Jun 1982 | Sep 1982 | Dec 1982 | Mar 1983 | Jun 1983 | Sep 1983 | Dec 1983

© 2009 Investor's Business Daily, Inc.

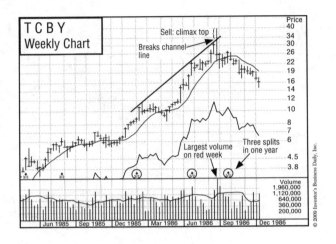

T C B Y
Weekly Chart

Sell: climax top
Breaks channel line

Largest volume on red week

Three splits in one year

Price
40
34
30
26
22
19
16
14
12
10
8
7
6
4.5
3.8

Volume
1,960,000
1,120,000
640,000
360,000
200,000

Jun 1985 | Sep 1985 | Dec 1985 | Mar 1986 | Jun 1986 | Sep 1986 | Dec 1986

© 2009 Investor's Business Daily, Inc.

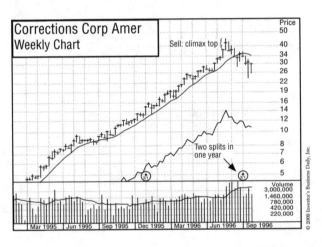

Corrections Corp Amer
Weekly Chart

Sell: climax top

Two splits in one year

Price
50
40
34
30
26
22
19
16
14
12
10
8
7
6
5

Volume
3,000,000
1,460,000
780,000
420,000
220,000

Mar 1995 | Jun 1995 | Sep 1995 | Dec 1995 | Mar 1996 | Jun 1996 | Sep 1996

© 2009 Investor's Business Daily, Inc.

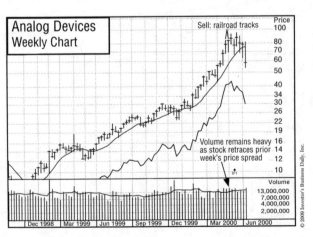

Analog Devices
Weekly Chart

Sell: railroad tracks

Volume remains heavy as stock retraces prior week's price spread

Price
100
80
70
60
50
40
34
30
26
22
19
16
14
12
10

Volume
13,000,000
7,000,000
4,000,000
2,000,000

Dec 1998 | Mar 1999 | Jun 1999 | Sep 1999 | Dec 1999 | Mar 2000 | Jun 2000

© 2009 Investor's Business Daily, Inc.

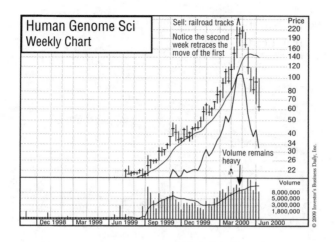

Human Genome Sci
Weekly Chart

Sell: railroad tracks

Notice the second
week retraces the
move of the first

Volume remains
heavy

Price
220
190
160
140
120
100
80
70
60
50
40
34
30
26
22

Volume
8,000,000
5,000,000
3,000,000
1,800,000

Dec 1998 | Mar 1999 | Jun 1999 | Sep 1999 | Dec 1999 | Mar 2000 | Jun 2000

© 2009 Investor's Business Daily, Inc.

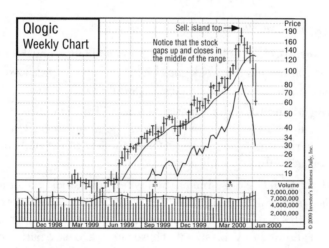

Qlogic
Weekly Chart

Sell: island top

Notice that the stock
gaps up and closes in
the middle of the range

Price
190
160
140
120
100
80
70
60
50
40
34
30
26
22
19

Volume
12,000,000
7,000,000
4,000,000
2,000,000

Dec 1998 | Mar 1999 | Jun 1999 | Sep 1999 | Dec 1999 | Mar 2000 | Jun 2000

© 2009 Investor's Business Daily, Inc.

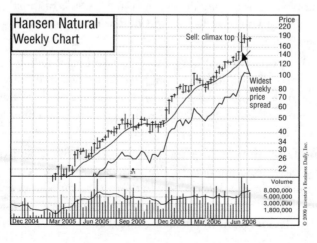

Hansen Natural
Weekly Chart

Sell: climax top

Widest
weekly
price
spread

Price
220
190
160
140
120
100
80
70
60
50
40
34
30
26
22

Volume
8,000,000
5,000,000
3,000,000
1,800,000

Dec 2004 | Mar 2005 | Jun 2005 | Sep 2005 | Dec 2005 | Mar 2006 | Jun 2006

© 2009 Investor's Business Daily, Inc.

267

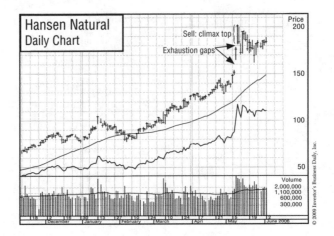

Low Volume and Other Weak Action

1. **New highs on low volume.** Some stocks will make new highs on lower or poor volume. As the stock goes higher, volume trends lower, suggesting that big investors have lost their appetite for the stock.

2. **Closing at or near the day's price low.** Tops can also be seen on a stock's daily chart in the form of "arrows" pointing down. That is, for several days, the stock will close at or near the low of the daily price range, fully retracing the day's advance.

3. **Third- or fourth-stage bases.** Sell when your stock makes a new high in price off a third- or fourth-stage base. The third time is seldom a charm in the market. By then, an advancing stock has become too obvious, and almost everyone sees it. These late-stage base patterns are often faulty, appearing wider and looser. As much as 80% of fourth-stage bases should fail, but you have to be right in determining that this is a fourth-stage base.

4. **Signs of a poor rally.** When you see initial heavy selling near the top, the next recovery will follow through weaker in volume, show poor price recovery, or last fewer days. Sell on the second or third day of a poor rally; it may be the last good chance to sell before trend lines and support areas are broken.

5. **Decline from the peak.** After a stock declines 8% or so from its peak, in some cases examination of the previous run-up, the top, and the decline may help you determine whether the advance is over or whether a normal 8% to 15% correction is in progress. You may occasionally want to sell if a decline from the peak exceeds 12% or 15%.

6. **Poor relative strength.** Poor relative price strength can be another reason for selling. Consider selling when a stock's IBD's Relative Price Strength Rating drops below 70.

7. **Lone Ranger.** Consider selling if there is no confirming price strength by any other important member of the same industry group.

Breaking Support

Breaking support occurs when stocks close for the week below established major trend lines.

1. **Long-term uptrend line is broken.** Sell if a stock closes at the end of the week below a major long-term uptrend line or breaks a key price support area on *overwhelming* volume. An uptrend line should connect at least three intraday or intraweek price lows occurring over a number of months. Trend lines drawn over too short a time period aren't valid.

2. **Greatest one-day price drop.** If a stock has already made an extended advance and suddenly makes its greatest one-day price drop since the beginning of the move, consider selling if the move is confirmed by other signals.

3. **Falling price on heavy weekly volume.** In some cases, sell if a stock breaks down on the largest weekly volume in its prior several years.

4. **200-day moving average line turns down.** After a prolonged upswing, if a stock's 200-day moving average price line turns down, consider selling the stock. Also, sell on new highs if a stock has a weak base with much of the price work in the lower half of the base or below the 200-day moving average price line.

5. **Living below the 10-week moving average.** Consider selling if a stock has a long advance, then closes below its 10-week moving average and lives below that average for eight or nine consecutive weeks, unable to rally and close the week above the line.

Other Prime Selling Pointers

1. If you cut all your losses at 7% or 8%, take a few profits when you're up 20%, 25%, or 30%. Compounding three gains like this could give you an overall gain of 100% or more. However, don't sell and take a 25% or 30% gain in any market leader with institutional support that's run up 20% in only one, two, or three weeks from the pivot buy point on a proper base. Those could be your big leaders and should be held for a potentially greater profit.

2. If you're in a bear market, get off margin, raise more cash, and don't buy very many stocks. If you do buy, maybe you should take 15% profits and cut all your losses at 3%.

3. In order to sell, big investors must have buyers to absorb their stock. Therefore, consider selling if a stock runs up and then good news or major publicity (a cover article in *BusinessWeek*, for example) is released.

4. Sell when there's a great deal of excitement about a stock and it's obvious to everyone that the stock is going higher. By then it's too late. Jack Dreyfus said, "Sell when there is an *overabundance* of optimism. When everyone is bubbling over with optimism and running around trying to get everyone else to buy, they are fully invested. At this point, all they can do is talk. They can't push the market up anymore. It takes buying power to do that." Buy when you're scared to death and others are unsure. Wait until you're happy and tickled to death to sell.

5. In most cases, sell when the percentage increases in quarterly earnings slow materially (or by two-thirds from the prior rate of increase) for two consecutive quarters.

6. Be careful of selling on bad news or rumors; they may be of temporary influence. Rumors are sometimes started to scare individual investors— the little fish—out of their holdings.

7. Always learn from all your past selling mistakes. Do your own postanalysis by plotting your past buy and sell points on charts. Study your mistakes carefully, and write down additional rules to avoid past mistakes that caused excessive losses or big missed opportunities. That's how you become a savvy investor.

When to Be Patient and Hold a Stock

Closely related to the decision on when to sell is when to sit tight. Here are some suggestions for doing just that.

Buy growth stocks where you can project a potential price target based on earnings estimates for the next year or two and possible P/E expansion from the stock's original base breakout. Your objective is to buy the best stock with the best earnings at exactly the right time and to have the patience to hold it until you have been proven right or wrong.

In a few cases, you may have to allow 13 weeks after your first purchase before you conclude that a stock that hasn't moved is a dull, faulty selection. This, of course, applies only if the stock did not reach your defensive, loss-cutting sell price first. In a fast-paced market, like the one in 1999, tech stocks that didn't move after several weeks while the general market was rallying could have been sold earlier, and the money moved into other stocks that were breaking out of sound bases with top fundamentals.

When your hard-earned money is on the line, it's more important than ever to pay attention to the general market and check IBD's "The Big Picture" column, which analyzes the market averages. In both the 2000 top and the top in the 2007–2008 market, "The Big Picture" column and our sell rules got many subscribers out of the market and helped them dodge devastating declines.

If you make new purchases when the market averages are under distribution, topping, and starting to reverse direction, you'll have trouble holding the stocks you've bought. (Most breakouts will fail, and most stocks will go down, so stay in phase with the general market. Don't argue with a declining market.)

After a new purchase, draw a defensive sell line in red on a daily or weekly graph at the precise price level at which you will sell and cut your loss (8% or less below your buy point). In the first one to two years of a new bull market, you may want to give stocks this much room on the downside and hold them until the price touches the sell line before selling.

In some instances, the sell line may be raised but kept below the low of the first normal correction after your initial purchase. If you raise your loss-cutting sell point, don't move it up too close to the current price. This will keep you from being shaken out during any normal weakness.

You definitely shouldn't continue to follow a stock up by raising stop-loss orders because you will be forced out near the low of an inevitable, natural correction. Once your stock is 15% or more above your purchase price, you can begin to concentrate on the price where or under what rules you will sell it on the way up to nail down your profit.

Any stock that rises close to 20% should never be allowed to drop back into the loss column. If you buy a stock at $50 and it shoots up to $60 (+20%) or more, even if you don't take the profit when you have it, there's no intelligent reason to ever let the stock drop all the way back to $50 or below and create a loss. You may feel embarrassed, ridiculous, and not too bright if you buy at $50, watch the stock hit $60, and then sell at $50 to $51. But you've already made the mistake of not taking your profit. Now avoid making a second mistake by letting it develop into a loss. Remember, one important objective is to keep all your losses as small as possible.

Also, major advances require time to complete. Don't take profits during the first eight weeks of a move unless the stock gets into serious trouble or is having a two- or three-week "climax" run-up on a stock split in a late-stage base. Stocks that show a 20% profit in less than eight weeks should be held through the eight weeks unless they are of poor quality without institutional sponsorship or strong group action. In many cases, stocks that advance dramatically by 20% or more in only one to four weeks are the most powerful stocks of all—capable of doubling, tripling, or more. If you own one of these true CAN SLIM market leaders, try to hold it through the first couple of times it pulls back in price to, or slightly below, its 10-week moving average price line. Once you have a decent profit, you could also try to hold the stock through its first short-term correction of 10% to 20%.

When a stock breaks out of a proper base, after its first move up, 80% of the time it will pull back somewhere between its second and its sixth week out of the base. Holding for eight weeks, of course, gets you through this first selling squall and into a resumed uptrend, and you'll then have a better profit cushion.

Remember, your objective is not just to be right but to make big money when you are right. "It never is your thinking that makes big money," said Livermore. "It's the sitting." Investors who can be right and sit tight are rare. It takes time for a stock to make a large gain.

The first two years of a new bull market typically provide your best and safest period, but they require courage, patience, and profitable sitting. If you really know and understand a company thoroughly and its products well, you'll have the crucial additional confidence required to sit tight through several inevitable but normal corrections. Achieving giant profits in a stock takes time and patience and following rules.

You've just read one of the most valuable chapters in this book. If you review it several times and adopt a disciplined profit-and-loss plan for your own investments, it could be worth several thousand times what you paid for this book. You might even make a point of rereading this chapter once every year.

You can't become a big winner in the stock market until you learn to be a good seller as well as a good buyer. Readers who followed these historically proven sell rules during 2000 nailed down most of the substantial gains they made in 1998 and 1999. A few serious students made 500% or more during that fast-moving period. Again in 2008, an even greater percentage of _Investor's Business Daily_ readers, although not every one, after much work and study were able to implement proper selling rules to protect and preserve their hard-earned capital rather than succumb to the dramatic declines in the year's third and fourth quarters.

Money Management: Should You Diversify, Invest for the Long Haul, Use Margin, Sell Short, or Buy Options, IPOs, Tax Shelters, Nasdaq Stocks, Foreign Stocks, Bonds, or Other Assets?

Once you have decided to participate in the stock market, you are faced with more decisions than just which stock to purchase. You have to decide how you will handle your portfolio, how many stocks you should buy, what types of actions you will take, and what types of investments are better left alone.

This and the following chapter will introduce you to the many options and alluring diversions you have at your disposal. Some of them are beneficial and worthy of your attention, but many others are overly risky, extremely complicated, or unnecessarily distracting and less rewarding. Regardless, it helps to be informed and to know as much about the investing business as possible—if for no other reason than to know all the things you should avoid. I say don't make it too complicated; keep it simple.

How Many Stocks Should You Really Own?

How many times have you been told, "Don't put all your eggs in one basket"? On the surface, this sounds like good advice, but my experience is that few people do more than one or two things exceedingly well. Those who are jacks-of-all-trades and masters of none are rarely dramatically successful in any field, including investing. Did all the esoteric derivatives help or harm Wall Street pros? Did experimenting with highly abnormal leverage of 50 or 100 to 1 help or hurt them?

Would you go to a dentist who did a little engineering or cabinetmaking on the side and who, on weekends, wrote music and worked as an auto mechanic, plumber, and accountant?

This is true of companies as well as people. The best example of diversification in the corporate world is the conglomerate. Most large conglomerates do not do well. They're too big, too inefficient, and too spread out over too many businesses to focus effectively and grow profitably. Whatever happened to Jimmy Ling and Ling-Temco-Vought or to Gulf+Western Industries after the conglomerate craze of the late 1960s collapsed? Big business and big government in America can both become inefficient, make many mistakes, and create nearly as many big new problems as they hope to solve.

Do you remember when Mobil Oil diversified into the retail business by acquiring Montgomery Ward, the struggling national department-store chain, years ago? It never worked. Neither did Sears, Roebuck's move into financial services with the purchases of Dean Witter and Coldwell Banker, or General Motors's takeover of computer-services giant EDS, or hundreds of other corporate diversification attempts. How many different businesses and types of loans was New York's Citigroup involved in from 2000 to 2008?

The more you diversify, the less you know about any one area. Many investors overdiversify. The best results are usually achieved through concentration, by putting your eggs in a few baskets that you know well and watching them very carefully. Did broad diversification protect your portfolio in the 2000 break or in 2008? The more stocks you own, the slower you may be to react and take selling action to raise sufficient cash when a serious bear market begins, because of a false sense of security. When major market tops occur, you should sell, get off margin if you use borrowed money, and raise at least some cash. Otherwise, you'll give back most of your gains.

The winning investor's objective should be to have one or two big winners rather than dozens of very small profits. It's much better to have a number of small losses and a few very big profits. Broad diversification is plainly and simply often a hedge for ignorance. Did all the banks from 1997 to 2007 that bought packages containing 5,000 widely diversified different real estate loans that had the implied backing of the government and were labeled triple A protect and grow their investments?

Most people with $20,000 to $200,000 to invest should consider limiting themselves to four or five carefully chosen stocks they know and understand. Once you own five stocks and a tempting situation comes along that you want to buy, you should muster the discipline to sell your least attractive investment. If you have $5,000 to $20,000 to invest, three stocks might be a reasonable maximum. A $3,000 account could be confined to two equities. Keep things manageable. The more stocks you own, the harder it is to keep track of all of them. Even investors with portfolios of more than a million dollars need not own more than six or seven well-selected securities. If you're uncomfortable and nervous with only six or seven, then own ten. But owning 30 or 40 could be a problem. The big money is made by concentration, provided you use sound buy and sell rules along with realistic general market rules. And there certainly is no rule that says that a 50-stock portfolio can't go down 50% or more.

How to Spread Your Purchases over Time

It's possible to spread out your purchases over a period of time. This is an interesting form of diversifying. When I accumulated a position in Amgen in 1990 and 1991, I bought on numerous days. I spread out the buying and made add-on buys only when there was a significant gain on earlier buys. If the market price was 20 points over my average cost and a new buy point occurred off a proper base, I bought more, but I made sure not to run my average cost up by buying more than a limited or moderate addition.

However, newcomers should be extremely careful in trying this more risky, highly concentrated approach. You have to learn how to do it right, and you positively have to sell or cut back if things don't work as expected.

In a bull market, one way to maneuver your portfolio toward more concentrated positions is to follow up your initial buy and make one or two smaller additional buys in stocks as soon as they have advanced 2% to 3% above your initial buy. However, don't allow yourself to keep chasing a stock once it's extended too far past a correct buy point. This will also spare you the frustration of owning a stock that goes a lot higher but isn't doing your portfolio much good because you own fewer shares of it than you do of your other, less-successful issues. At the same time, sell and eliminate stocks that start to show losses before they become big losses.

Using this follow-up purchasing procedure should keep more of your money in just a few of your best stock investments. No system is perfect, but this one is more realistic than a haphazardly diversified portfolio and has a better chance of achieving important results. Diversification is definitely sound; just don't overdo it. *Always set a limit on how many stocks you will own, and stick to your rules.* Always keep your set of rules with you—in a simple notebook, perhaps—when you're investing. What? You say you've been investing without any specific buy or sell rules? What results has that produced for you over the last five or ten years?

Should You Invest for the Long Haul?

If you do decide to concentrate, should you invest for the long haul or trade more frequently? The answer is that the holding period (long or short) is not the main issue. What's critical is buying the right stock—the very best stock—at precisely the right time, then selling it whenever the market or your various sell rules tell you it's time to sell. The time between your buy and your sell could be either short or long. Let your rules and the market decide which one it is. If you do this, some of your winners will be held for three months, some for six months, and a few for one, two, or three years or more. Most of your losers will be held for much shorter periods, normally between a few weeks and three months. No well-run portfolio should ever, ever have losses carried for six months or more. Keep your portfolio clean and in sync with the market. Remember, good gardeners always weed the flower patch and prune weak stems.

Lessons for Buy-and-Hold Investors Who Don't Use Charts

I've marked up the weekly charts of WorldCom in 1999, Enron in 2001, and AIG, Citigroup, and General Motors in 2007. They show 10 to 15 specific signs that these investments should clearly have been sold at that time.

Why you must always use charts...see what happens next.

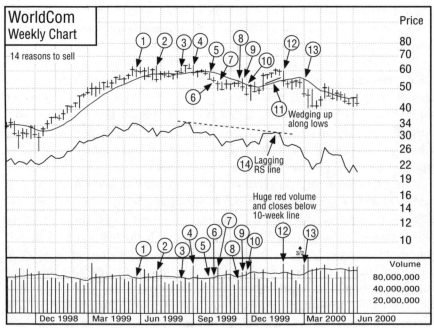

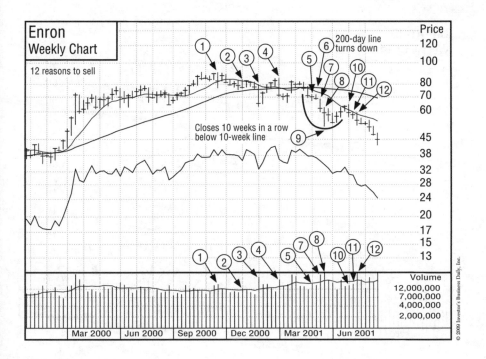

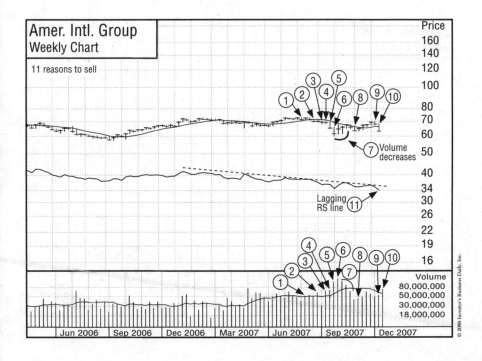

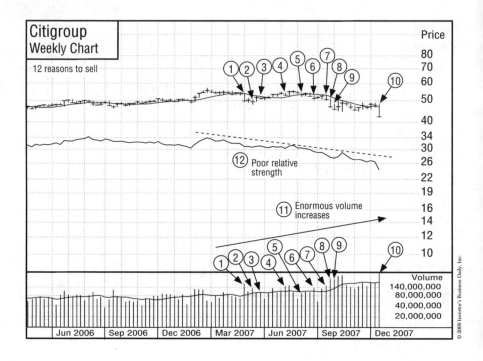

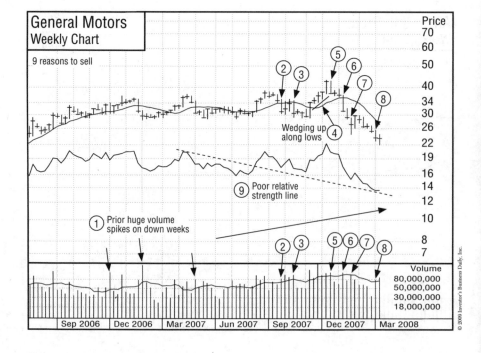

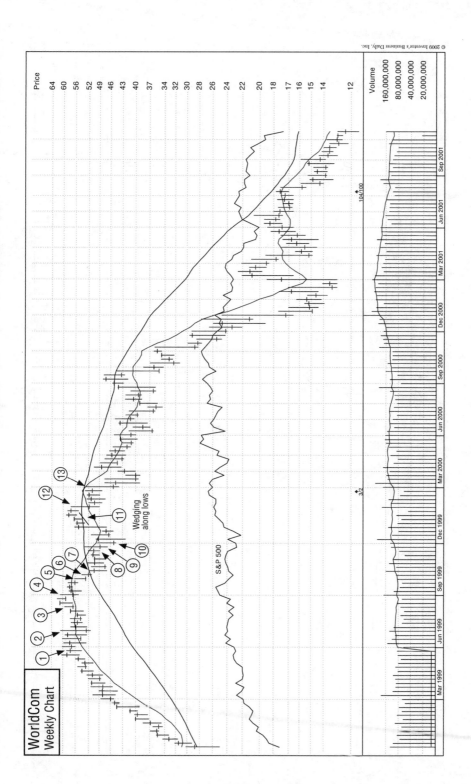

WorldCom
Weekly Chart

Price

64
60
56
52
49
46
43
40
37
34
32
30
28
26
24
22
20
18
17
16
15
14

12

S&P 500

Wedging
along lows

104/100

3/2

Volume

160,000,000
80,000,000
40,000,000
20,000,000

Mar 1999   Jun 1999   Sep 1999   Dec 1999   Mar 2000   Jun 2000   Sep 2000   Dec 2000   Mar 2001   Jun 2001   Sep 2001

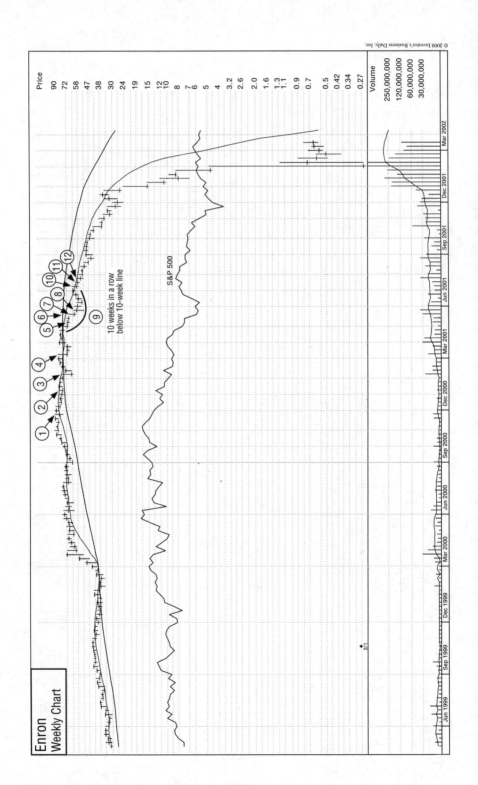

Enron
Weekly Chart

S&P 500

10 weeks in a row
below 10-week line

Price
90
72
58
47
38
30
24
19
15
12
10
8
7
6
5
4
3.2
2.6
2.0
1.6
1.3
1.1
0.9
0.7
0.5
0.42
0.34
0.27

Volume
250,000,000
120,000,000
60,000,000
30,000,000

Jun 1999   Sep 1999   Dec 1999   Mar 2000   Jun 2000   Sep 2000   Dec 2000   Mar 2001   Jun 2001   Sep 2001   Dec 2001   Mar 2002

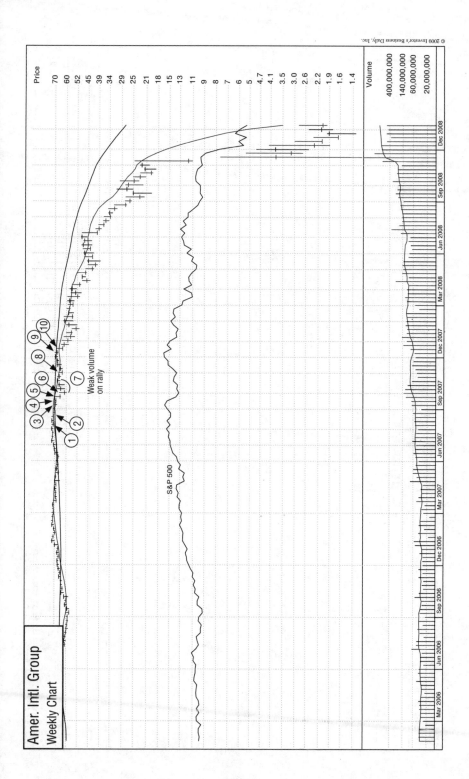

Amer. Intl. Group
Weekly Chart

Price
70
60
52
45
39
34
29
25
21
18
15
13
11
9
8
7
6
5
4.7
4.1
3.5
3.0
2.6
2.2
1.9
1.6
1.4

S&P 500

Weak volume
on rally

① ② ③ ④ ⑤ ⑥ ⑦ ⑧ ⑨ ⑩

Volume
400,000,000
140,000,000
60,000,000
20,000,000

Mar 2006 Jun 2006 Sep 2006 Dec 2006 Mar 2007 Jun 2007 Sep 2007 Dec 2007 Mar 2008 Jun 2008 Sep 2008 Dec 2008

281

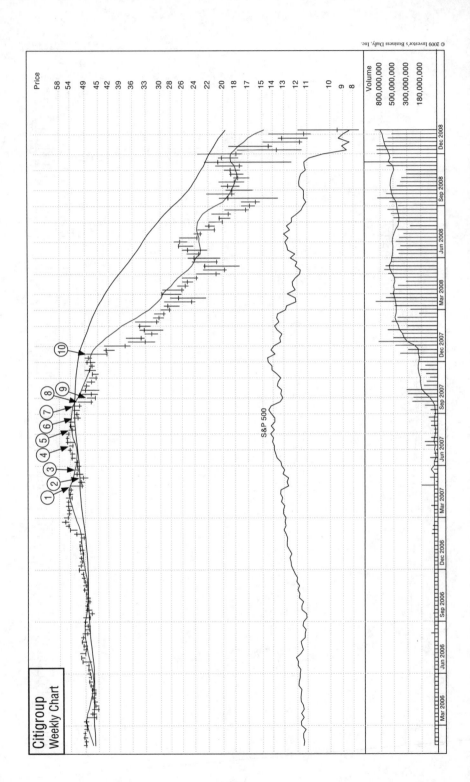

Citigroup
Weekly Chart

S&P 500

Price
58
54
49
45
42
39
36
33
30
28
26
24
22
20
18
17
15
14
13
12
11
10
9
8

Volume
800,000,000
500,000,000
300,000,000
180,000,000

Mar 2006 Jun 2006 Sep 2006 Dec 2006 Mar 2007 Jun 2007 Sep 2007 Dec 2007 Mar 2008 Jun 2008 Sep 2008 Dec 2008

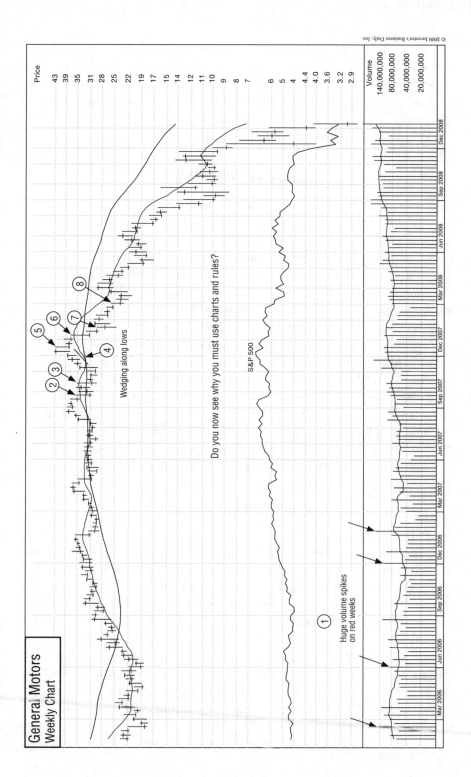

General Motors
Weekly Chart

Do you now see why you must use charts and rules?

Wedging along lows

S&P 500

Huge volume spikes
on red weeks

Price
43
39
35
31
28
25
22
19
17
15
14
12
11
10
9
8
7
6
5
4
4.4
4.0
3.6
3.2
2.9

Volume
140,000,000
80,000,000
40,000,000
20,000,000

Mar 2006   Jun 2006   Sep 2006   Dec 2006   Mar 2007   Jun 2007   Sep 2007   Dec 2007   Mar 2008   Jun 2008   Sep 2008   Dec 2008

Actually, if you looked at a longer time period, there were even more sell signals. For example, Citigroup had dramatically underperformed on a relative strength basis for the prior three years, from 2004 through 2006, and its earnings growth during that time slowed from its growth rate throughout the 1990s. It pays to monitor your investments' price and volume activity. That's how you stop losing and start winning.

Should You Day Trade?

One type of investing that I have always discouraged people from doing is day trading, where you buy and sell stocks on the same day. Most investors lose money doing this. The reason is simple: you are dealing predominantly with minor daily fluctuations that are harder to read than basic trends over a longer time period. Besides, there's generally not enough profit potential in day trading to offset the commissions you generate and the losses that will inevitably occur. Don't try to make money so fast. Rome wasn't built in a day.

There is a new form of day trading that is more like short-term swing trading (buying a stock on the upswing and selling before an inevitable pullback). It involves buying a stock at its exact pivot buy point off a chart (coming out of a base or price consolidation area) and selling it five or so days later after the breakout. Sometimes pivot points off patterns such as the cup-with-handle pattern (see Chapter 2) identified on intraday charts of five-minute intervals can reveal a stock that is breaking out from an intraday pattern. If this is done with real skill in a positive market, it might work for some people, but it requires lots of time, study, and experience.

Should You Use Margin?

In the first year or two, while you're still learning to invest, it's much safer to invest on a cash basis. It usually takes most new investors at least two to three years before they gain enough market experience (by making several bad decisions, wasting time trying to reinvent the wheel, and experimenting with unsound beliefs) to be able to make and keep significant profits. Once you have a few years' experience, a sound plan, and a strict set of both buy and sell rules, you might consider buying on margin (using borrowed money from your brokerage firm in order to purchase more stock). Generally, margin buying should be done by younger investors who are still working. Their risk is somewhat less because they have more time to prepare for retirement.

The best time to use margin is generally during the first two years of a new bull market. Once you recognize a new bear market, you should get off margin immediately and raise as much cash as possible. You must understand that when the general market declines and your stocks start sinking, you will lose your initial capital twice as fast if you're fully margined than you would if you were invested on a cash basis. This dictates that you absolutely *must* cut all losses quickly and get off margin when a major general market deterioration begins. If you speculate in small-capitalization or high-tech stocks fully margined, a 50% correction can cause a total loss. This happened to some new investors in 2000 and early 2001.

You don't have to be fully margined all the time. Sometimes you'll have large cash reserves and no margin. At other times, you'll be invested on a cash basis. At still other points, you'll be using a small part of your margin buying power. And in a few instances, when you're making genuine progress in a bull market, you may be fully invested on margin. All of this depends on the current market situation and your level of experience. I've always used margin, and I believe it offers a real advantage to an experienced investor who knows how to confine his buying to high-quality market leaders and has the discipline and common sense to always cut his losses short *with no exceptions*.

Your margin interest expense, depending on laws that change constantly, might be tax-deductible. However, in certain periods, margin interest rates can become so high that the probability of substantial success may be limited. To buy on margin, you'll also need to sign a margin agreement with your broker.

Never Answer a Margin Call

If a stock in your margin account collapses in value to the point where your stockbroker asks you to either put up money or sell stock, *don't put up money*; think about selling stock. Nine times out of ten, you'll be better off. The marketplace is telling you that you're on the wrong path, you're getting hurt, and things aren't working. So sell and cut back your risk level. Again, why throw good money after bad? What will you do if you put up good money and the stock continues to decline and you get more margin calls? Go broke backing a loser?

Should You Sell Short?

I did some research and wrote a booklet on short selling in 1976. It's now out of print, but not much has changed on the subject since then. In 2005, the booklet was the basis for a book titled *How to Make Money Selling Short*. The book was written with Gil Morales, who rewrote, revised, and updated my earlier work. Short selling is still a topic few investors understand and an endeavor at which even fewer succeed, so consider carefully whether it's right for you. More active and seasoned investors might consider limited short selling. But I would want to keep the limit to 10% or 15% of available money, and most people probably shouldn't do even that much. Furthermore, short selling is far more complicated than simply buying stocks, and most short sellers are run in and lose money.

What is short selling? Think of it as reversing the normal buy and sell process. In short selling, you sell a stock (instead of buying it)—even though you don't own it and therefore must borrow it from your broker—in the hope that it will go down in price instead of up. If the stock falls in price as you expect, you can "cover your short position" by buying the stock in the open market at a lower price and pocket the difference as your profit. You would sell short if you think the market is going to drop substantially or a certain stock is ready to cave in. You sell the stock first, hoping to buy it back later at a lower price.

Sounds easy, right? Wrong. Short selling rarely works out well. Usually the stock that you sell short, expecting a colossal price decrease, will do the unexpected and begin to creep up in price. When it goes up, you lose money.

Effective short selling is usually done at the beginning of a new general market decline. This means you have to short based on the behavior of the daily market averages. This, in turn, requires the ability to (1) interpret the daily Dow, S&P 500, or Nasdaq indexes, as discussed in Chapter 9, and (2) select stocks that have had tremendous run-ups and have definitely topped out months earlier. In other words, your timing has to be flawless. You may be right, but if you're too early, you can be forced to cover at a loss.

In selling short, you also have to minimize your risk by cutting your losses at 8%. Otherwise, the sky's the limit, as your stock could have an unlimited price increase.

My first rule in short selling: don't sell short during a bull market. Why fight the overall tide? But sooner or later you may disregard the advice in this book, try it for yourself, and find out the same hard way—just as you learn that "wet paint" signs usually mean what they say. In general, you should save the short selling for bear markets. Your odds will be a little better.

The second rule is: never sell short a stock with a small number of shares outstanding. It's too easy for market makers and professionals to run up a thinly capitalized stock on you. This is called a "short squeeze" (meaning you could find yourself with a loss and be forced to cover by buying the stock back at a higher price), and when you're in one, it doesn't feel very good. It's safer to short stocks that are trading an average daily volume of 5 to 10 million shares or more.

The two best chart price patterns for selling short are shown on the two graphs on page 288.

1. The "head-and-shoulders" top. The "right shoulder" of the price pattern on the stock chart *must* be slightly lower than the left. The correct time to short is when the third or fourth pullback up in price during the right shoulder is about over. (Note the four upward pullbacks in the right shoulder of the Lucent Technologies head-and-shoulders top.) One of these upward price pullbacks will reach slightly above the peak of a rally a few weeks back. This serves to run in the premature short sellers. Former big market leaders that have broken badly can have several upward price pullbacks of 20% to 40% from the stock's low point in the right shoulder. The stock's last run-up should cross over its moving average line. The right time to short is when the volume picks up as the stock reverses lower and breaks below its 10-week moving average line on volume but hasn't yet broken to new low ground, at which point it is too late and then becomes too obvious and apparent to most traders. In some, but not all, cases, either there will be a deceleration in quarterly earnings growth or earnings will have actually turned down. The stock's relative strength line should also be in a clear downtrend for at least 20 weeks up to 34 weeks. In fact, we found through research on model stocks over 50 years that almost all outstanding short-selling patterns occurred five to seven months after a formerly huge market leader has clearly topped.

   John Wooden, the great UCLA basketball coach, used to tell his players, "It's what you learn after you know it all that counts." Well, one know-it-all investor wrote and told us that we obviously didn't know what we were talking about, that no knowledgeable person would ever sell a stock short seven months after it had topped. Few people understand this, and most short sellers lose money because of premature, faulty, or overly obvious timing. Lucent at point 4 was in its eighth month and fell 89%. Yahoo! was in its eighth month after it had clearly topped, and it then fell 87%. Big egos in the stock market are very dangerous . . . because they lead you to think you know what you're doing. The smarter you are, the more losses ego can create. Humility and respect for the market are more valuable traits.

2. Third- or fourth-stage cup-with-handle or other patterns that have definitely failed after attempted breakouts. The stock should be picking up trading volume and starting to break down below the "handle" area. (See Chapter 2 on chart reading and failed breakouts.)

   For years, short selling had to be executed on an "uptick" from the previous trade. An uptick is any trade that is higher than the previous trade by at least a penny. (It used to be ⅛ or ¼ point or more up.) Therefore, orders should normally be entered either at the market or at a maximum, with a

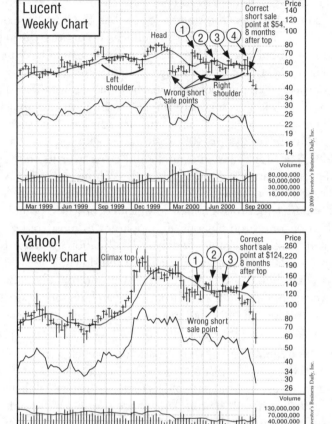

limit of $0.25 or so *below* the last price. A weak stock could trade down a point or more without having an uptick.

After a careful study, the SEC recently rescinded the uptick rule. It should and probably will be reinstated at some point, with more than a penny price increase being required—perhaps a 10- or 20-cent rally. This should reduce volatility in some equities, especially in bad, panicky markets. The uptick rule was originally created in early 1937 after the market had broken seriously in the prior year. Its purpose was to require a ⅛ or ¼ of 1 point uptick, which would be 12½ or 25 cents, to slow down the uninterrupted hammering that a stock would be subject to during severe market breaks.

One alternative to selling short is buying put options, which don't need an uptick to receive an executed trade. You could also short tracking indexes like the QQQs (Nasdaq 100), SMHs (semiconductors), or BBHs (biotech). These also do not require an uptick.

Shorting must be done in a margin account, so check with your broker to see if you can borrow the stock you want to sell short. Also, if the stock pays a dividend while you are short, you'll have to pay the dividend to the person who owned the stock you borrowed and sold. Lesson: don't short big dividend-paying stocks.

Short selling is treacherous even for professionals, and only the more able and daring should give it a try. One last warning: don't short an advancing stock just because its price or the P/E ratio seems too high. You could be taken to the cleaners.

What Are Options, and Should You Invest in Them?

Options are an investment vehicle where you purchase rights (contracts) to buy ("call") or sell ("put") a stock, stock index, or commodity at a specified price before a specified future time, known as the option expiration date. Options are very speculative and involve substantially greater risks and price volatility than common stocks. Therefore, most investors should not buy or sell options. Winning investors should first learn how to minimize the investment risks they take, not increase them. After a person has proved that she is able to make money in common stocks and has sufficient investment understanding and actual experience, then the limited use of options could be intelligently considered.

Options are like making "all or nothing" bets. If you buy a three-month call option on McDonald's, the premium you pay gives you the right to purchase 100 shares of MCD at a certain price at any time during the next three months. When you purchase calls, you expect the price of the stock to go up, so if a stock is currently trading at $120, you might buy a call at $125. If the stock rises to $150 after three months (and you have not sold your call option), you can exercise it and pocket the $25 profit less the premium you paid. Conversely, if three months go by and your stock is down and didn't perform as expected, you would not exercise the option; it expires worthless, and you lose the premium you paid. As you might expect, puts are handled in a similar manner, except that you're making a bet that the price of the stock will decrease instead of increase.

Limiting Your Risk When It Comes to Options

If you do consider options, you should definitely limit the percentage of your total portfolio committed to them. A prudent limit might be no more than 10% to 15%. You should also adopt a rule about where you intend to cut and limit all of your losses. The percentage will naturally have to be more than 8%, since options are much more volatile than stocks. If an option fluctuates three times as rapidly as the underlying stock, then perhaps 20% or 25% might be a possible absolute limit. On the profit side, you might consider adopting a rule that you'll take many of your gains when they hit 50% to 75%.

Some aspects of options present challenges. Buying options whose price can be significantly influenced by supply and demand changes as a result of a thin or illiquid market for that particular option is problematic. Also problematic is the fact that options can be artificially and temporarily overpriced simply because of a short-lived increase in price volatility in the underlying stock or the general market.

Buy Only the Best

When I buy options, which is rarely, I prefer to buy them for the most aggressive and outstanding stocks with the biggest earnings estimates, those where the premium you have to pay for the option is higher. Once again, you want options on the best stocks, not the cheapest. The secret to making money in options doesn't have much to do with options. You have to analyze and be right on the selection and timing of the underlying stock. Therefore, you should apply your CAN SLIM system and select the best possible stock at the best possible time.

If you do this and you are right, the option will go up along with the stock, except that the option should move up much faster because of the leverage.

By buying only options on the best stocks, you also minimize slippage caused by illiquidity. (Slippage is the difference between the price you wanted to pay and the price you actually paid at the time the order was executed. The more liquid the stock, the less slippage you should experience.) With illiquid (small-capitalization) stocks, the slippage can be more severe, and this ultimately could cost you money. Buying options on lower-priced, illiquid stocks is similar to the carnival game where you're trying to knock down all the milk bottles. The game may be rigged. Selling your options can be equally tricky in a thin (small-capitalization) stock.

In a major bear market, you might consider buying put options on certain individual stocks or on a major stock index like the S&P, along with selling shares of common stock short. The inability of your broker to borrow a stock may make selling short more difficult than buying a put. It is generally not wise to buy puts during a bull market. Why be a fish trying to swim upstream?

If you think a stock is going up and it's the right time to buy, then buy it, or purchase a long-term option and place your order at the market. If it's time to sell, sell at the market. Option markets are usually thinner and not as liquid as the markets for the underlying stock itself.

Many amateur option traders constantly place price limits on their orders. Once they get into the habit of placing limits, they are forever changing their price restraints as prices edge away from their limits. It is difficult to maintain sound judgment and perspective when you are worrying about changing your limits. In the end, you'll get some executions after tremendous excess effort and frustration.

When you finally pick the big winner for the year, the one that will triple in price, you'll lose out because you placed your order with a ¼-point limit below the actual market price. You never make big money in the stock market by eighths and quarters.

You could also lose your shirt if your security is in trouble and you fail to sell and get out because you put a price limit on your sell order. Your objective is to be right on the big moves, not on the minor fluctuations.

Short-Term Options Are More Risky

If you buy options, you're better off with longer time periods, say, six months or so. This will minimize the chance your option will run out of time before your stock has had a chance to perform. Now that I've told you this, what do you think most investors do? Of course, they buy shorter-term option—30 to 90 days—because these options are cheaper and move faster in both directions, up and down!

The problem with short-term options is that you could be right on your stock, but the general market may slip into an intermediate correction, with the result that all stocks are down at the end of the short time period. You will then lose on all your options because of the general market. This is also why you should spread your option buying and option expiration dates over several different months.

Keep Option Trading Simple

One thing to keep in mind is that you should always keep your investments as simple as possible. Don't let someone talk you into speculating in such seemingly sophisticated packages as strips, straddles, and spreads.

A *strip* is a form of conventional option that couples one call and two puts on the same security at the same exercise price with the same expiration date. The premium is less than it would be if the options were purchased separately.

A *straddle* can be either long or short. A long straddle is a long call and a long put on the same underlying security at the same exercise price and with the same expiration month. A short straddle is a short call and a short put on the same security at the same exercise price and with the same expiration month.

A *spread* is a purchase and sale of options with the same expiration dates.

It's difficult enough to just pick a stock or an option that is going up. If you confuse the issue and start hedging (being both long and short at the same time), you could, believe it or not, wind up losing on both sides. For instance, if a stock goes up, you might be tempted to sell your put early to minimize the loss, and later find that the stock has turned downward and you're losing money on your call. The reverse could also happen. It's a dangerous psychological game that you should avoid.

Should You Write Options?

Writing options is a completely different story from buying options. I am not overly impressed with the strategy of writing options on stocks.

A person who writes a call option receives a small fee or premium in return for giving someone else (the buyer) the right to "call" away and buy the stock from the writer at a specified price, up to a certain date. In a bull market, I would rather be a buyer of calls than a writer (seller) of calls. In bad markets, just stay out or go short.

The writer of calls pockets a small fee and is, in effect, usually locked in for the time period of the call. What if the stock you own and wrote the call against gets into trouble and plummets? The small fee won't cover your loss. Of course, there are maneuvers the writer can take, such as buying a put to hedge and cover himself, but then the situation gets too complicated and the writer could get whipsawed back and forth.

What happens if the stock doubles? The writer gets the stock called away, and for a relatively small fee loses all chance for a major profit. Why take risks in stocks for only meager gains with no chance for large gains? This is not the reasoning you will hear from most people, but then again, what most people are saying and doing in the stock market isn't usually worth knowing.

Writing "naked calls" is even more foolish, in my opinion. Naked call writers receive a fee for writing a call on a stock they do not own, so they are unprotected if the stock moves against them.

It's possible that large investors who have trouble making decent returns on their portfolio may find some minor added value in writing short-term options on stocks that they own and feel are overpriced. However, I am always somewhat skeptical of new methods of making money that seem so easy. There are few free lunches in the stock market or in real estate.

Great Opportunities in Nasdaq Stocks

Nasdaq stocks are not traded on a listed stock exchange but instead are traded through over-the-counter dealers. The over-the-counter dealer market has been enhanced in recent years by a wide range of ECNs (electronic communication networks), such as Instinet, SelectNet, Redibook, and Archipelago, which bring buyers and sellers together within each network, and through which orders can be routed and executed. The Nasdaq is a specialized field, and in many cases the stocks traded are those of newer, less-established companies. But now even NYSE firms have large Nasdaq operations. In addition, reforms during the 1990s have removed any lingering stigma that once dogged the Nasdaq.

There are usually hundreds of intriguing new growth stocks on the Nasdaq. It's also the home of some of the biggest companies in the United States. You should definitely consider buying better-quality Nasdaq stocks that have institutional sponsorship and fit the CAN SLIM rules.

For maximum flexibility and safety, it's vital that you maintain marketability in all your investments, regardless of whether they're traded on the NYSE or on the Nasdaq. An institutional-quality common stock with larger average daily volume is one defense against an unruly market.

Should You Buy Initial Public Offerings (IPOs)?

An initial public offering is a company's first offering of stock to the public. I usually don't recommend that investors purchase IPOs. There are several reasons for this.

Among the numerous IPOs that occur each year, there are a few outstanding ones. However, those that are outstanding are going to be in such hot demand by institutions (who get first crack at them) that if you are able to buy them at all, you may receive only a tiny allotment. Logic dictates that if you, as an individual investor, can acquire all the shares you want, they are possibly not worth having.

The Internet and some discount brokerages have made IPOs more accessible to individual investors, although some brokers place limits on your ability to sell soon after a company comes public. This is a dangerous position to be in, since you may not be able to get out when you want to. You may recall that during the IPO craze of 1999 and early 2000, there were some new stocks that rocketed on their first day or two of trading, only to collapse and never recover.

Many IPOs are deliberately underpriced and therefore shoot up on the first day of trading, but more than a few could be overpriced and drop.

Because IPOs have no trading history, you can't be sure whether they're overpriced. In most cases, this speculative area should be left to experienced institutional investors who have access to the necessary in-depth research and who are able to spread their new issue risks among many different equities.

This is not to say that you can't purchase a new issue after the IPO when the stock is up in its infancy. Google should have been bought in mid-September 2004, in the fifth week after its new issue, when it made a new high at $114. The safest time to buy an IPO is on the breakout from its first correction and base-building area. Once a new issue has been trading in the market for one, two, or three months or more, you have valuable price and volume data that you can use to better judge the situation.

Within the broad list of new issues of the previous three months to three years, there are always standout companies with superior new products and excellent current and recent quarterly earnings and sales that you should consider. (*Investor's Business Daily's* "The New America" page explores most of them. Past articles on a company may be available.) CB Richard Ellis formed a perfect flat base after its IPO in the summer of 2004 and then rose 500%.

Experienced investors who understand correct selection and timing techniques should definitely consider buying new issues that show good positive earnings and exceptional sales growth, and also have formed sound price bases. They can be a great source of new ideas if they are dealt with in this fashion. Most big stock winners in recent years had an IPO at some point in the prior one to eight or ten years. Even so, new issues can be more volatile and occasionally suffer massive corrections during difficult bear markets. This usually happens after a period of wild excess in the IPO market, where any and every offering seems to be a "hot issue." For example, the new issue booms that developed in the early 1960s and the beginning of 1983, as well as that in late 1999 and early 2000, were almost always followed by a bear market period.

Congress, at this writing in early 2009, should consider lowering the capital gains tax to create a powerful incentive for thousands of new entrepreneurs to start up innovative new companies. Our historical research proved that 80% of the stocks that had outstanding price performance and job creation in the 1980s and 1990s had been brought public in the prior eight to ten years, as mentioned earlier. America now badly needs a renewed flow of new companies to spark new inventions and new industries . . . and a stronger economy, millions more jobs, and millions more taxpayers. It has always paid for Washington to lower capital gains taxes. This will be needed to reignite the IPO market and the American economy after the economic collapse that the subprime real estate program and the credit crisis caused in 2008. I learned many years ago that if rates are raised, many investors will simply not sell their stock because they don't want to pay the tax and then have significantly less money to reinvest. Washington can't seem to understand this simple fact. Fewer people will sell their stocks, and the government will always get less revenue, not more. I've had many older, retired people tell me they will keep their stock until they die so they won't have to pay the tax.

What Are Convertible Bonds, and Should You Invest in Them?

A convertible bond is one that you can exchange (convert) for another investment category, typically common stock, at a predetermined price. Convertible bonds provide a little higher income to the owner than the common stock typically does, along with the potential for some possible profits.

The theory goes that a convertible bond will rise almost as fast as the common stock rises, but will decline less during downturns. As so often happens with theories, the reality can be different. There is also a liquidity question to consider, since convertible bond markets may dry up during extremely difficult periods.

Sometimes investors are attracted to this medium because they can borrow heavily and leverage their commitment (obtain more buying power). This simply increases your risk. Excessive leverage can be dangerous, as Wall Street and Washington learned in 2008.

It is for these several reasons that I do not recommend that most investors buy convertible bonds. I have also never bought a corporate bond. They are poor inflation hedges, and, ironically, you can also lose a lot of money in the bond market if you make what ultimately turns out to be a higher-risk investment in stretching for a higher yield.

Should You Invest in Tax-Free Securities and Tax Shelters?

The typical investor should not use these investment vehicles (IRAs, 401(k) plans, and Keoghs excepted), the most common of which are municipal bonds. Overconcern about taxes can confuse and cloud investors' normally sound judgment. Common sense should also tell you that if you invest in tax shelters, there is a much greater chance the IRS may decide to audit your tax return.

Don't kid yourself. You can lose money in munis if you buy them at the wrong time or if the local or state government makes bad management decisions and gets into real financial trouble, which some of them have done in the past.

People who seek too many tax benefits or tax dodges frequently end up investing in questionable or risky ventures. The investment decision should always be considered first, with tax considerations a distant second.

This is America, where anyone who really works at it can become successful at saving and investing. Learn how to make a net profit and, when you do, be happy about it rather than complaining about having to pay taxes because you made a profit. Would you rather hold on until you have a loss so you have no tax to pay? Recognize at the start that Uncle Sam will always be your partner, and he will receive his normal share of your wages and investment gains.

I have never bought a tax-free security or a tax shelter. This has left me free to concentrate on finding the best investments possible. When these investments work out, I pay my taxes just like everybody else. Always remember . . . the U.S. system of freedom and opportunity is the greatest in the world. Learn to use, protect, and appreciate it.

Should You Invest in Income Stocks?

Income stocks are stocks that have high and regular dividend yields, providing taxable income to the owner. These stocks are typically found in supposedly more conservative industries, such as utilities and banks. Most people should not buy common stocks for their dividends or income, yet many people do.

People think that income stocks are conservative and that you can just sit and hold them because you are getting your dividends. Talk to any investor who lost big on Continental Illinois Bank in 1984 when the stock plunged from $25 to $2, or on Bank of America when it crashed from $55 to $5 as of the beginning of 2009, or on the electric utilities caught up in the past with nuclear power plants. (Ironically, *17 major nations* now get or for years have gotten more of their electricity from nuclear power plants than the United States does. France gets 78% of its electricity from nuclear power.)

Investors also got hurt when electric utilities nosedived in 1994, and the same was true when certain California utilities collapsed in 2001. In theory, income stocks should be safer, but don't be lulled into believing that they can't decline sharply. In 1999–2000, AT&T dropped from over $60 to below $20.

And how about the aforementioned Citigroup, the New York City bank that so many institutional investors owned? I don't care how much it paid in dividends; if you owned Citigroup at $50 and watched it nosedive to $2, when it was in the process of going bankrupt until the government bailed it out, you lost an enormous amount of money. Incidentally, even if you do invest in income stocks, you should use charts. In October of 2007, Citigroup stock broke wide open on the *largest volume month that it ever traded*, so that even an amateur chartist could have recognized this and easily sold it in the $40s, avoiding a serious loss.

If you do buy income stocks, *never strain to buy the highest dividend yield available*. That will typically entail much greater risk and lower quality. Trying to get an extra 2% or 3% yield can significantly expose your capital to larger losses. That's what a lot of Wall Street firms did in the real estate bubble, and look what happened to their investments. A company can also cut its dividends if its earnings per share are not adequately covering those payouts, leaving you without the income you expected to receive. This too has happened.

If you need income, my advice is to concentrate on the very best-quality stocks and simply withdraw 6% of your investments each year for living expenses. You could sell off a few shares and withdraw 1½% per quarter. Higher rates of withdrawal are not usually advisable, since in time they might lead to some depletion of your principal.

What Are Warrants, and Are They Safe Investments?

Warrants are an investment vehicle that allows you to purchase a specific amount of stock at a specific price. Sometimes warrants are good for a certain period of time, but it's common for them not to have time limits. Many of them are cheap in price and therefore seem appealing.

However, most investors should shy away from low-priced warrants. This is another complex, specialized field that sounds fine in concept but that few investors truly understand. The real question comes down to whether the common stock is correct to buy. Most investors will be better off if they forget the field of warrants.

Should You Invest in Merger Candidates?

Merger candidates can often behave erratically, so I don't recommend investing in them. Some merger candidates run up substantially in price on rumors of a possible sale, only to have the price drop suddenly when a potential deal falls through or other unforeseen circumstances occur. In other words, this can be a risky, volatile business, and it should generally be left to experienced professionals who specialize in this field. It is usually better to buy sound companies, based on your basic CAN SLIM evaluation, than to try to guess whether a company will be sold or merged with another.

Should You Buy Foreign Stocks?

Yes, the best foreign stocks have excellent potential when bought at the right time and right place, but I don't suggest that you get heavily invested in them. The potential profit from a foreign stock should be a bit more than that from a standout U.S. company to justify the possible additional risk. For example, investors in foreign stocks must understand and follow the general market of the particular country involved. Sudden changes in that country's interest rates, currency, or government policy might in one unexpected action, make your investment less attractive.

It isn't essential for you to search out a lot of foreign stocks when there are more than 10,000 securities to select from in the United States. Many outstanding foreign stocks also trade in the United States, and many had excellent success in the past, including Baidu, Research In Motion, China Mobile, and América Móvil. I owned two of them in the 2003–2007 bull market. Several benefited from the worldwide wireless boom, but corrected 60% or more in the bear market that followed this bull move. There are also several mutual funds that excel in foreign securities.

As weak as our stock market was in 2008, many foreign markets declined even more. Baidu, a Chinese stock leader, dropped from $429 to $100. And the Russian market plummeted straight down from 16,291 to 3,237 once Putin invaded and intimidated the nation of Georgia.

Avoid Penny Stocks and Low-Priced Securities

The Canadian and Denver markets list many stocks that you can buy for only a few cents a share. I strongly advise that you avoid gambling in such cheap merchandise, because everything sells for what it's worth. You get what you pay for.

These seemingly cheap securities are unduly speculative and extremely low in quality. The risk is much higher with them than with better-quality, higher-priced investments. The opportunity for questionable or unscrupulous promotional practices is also greater with penny stocks. I prefer not to buy any common stock that sells for below $15 per share, and so should you. Our extensive historical studies of 125 years of America's super winners show that most of them broke out of chart bases between $30 and $50 a share.

What Are Futures, and Should You Invest in Them?

Futures involve buying or selling a specific amount of a commodity, financial issue, or stock index at a specific price on a specific future date. Most futures fall into the categories of grains, precious metals, industrial metals, foods, meats, oils, woods, and fibers (known collectively as commodities); financial issues; and stock indexes. The financial group includes government

T-bills and bonds, plus foreign currencies. One of the more active stock indexes traded is the S&P 100, better known by its ticker symbol OEX.

Large commercial concerns, such as Hershey, use the commodity market for "hedging." For example, Hershey might lock in a current price by temporarily purchasing cocoa beans in May for December delivery, while arranging for a deal in the cash market.

It is probably best for most individual investors not to participate in the futures markets. Commodity futures are extremely volatile and much more speculative than most common stocks. It is not an arena for the inexperienced or small investor unless you want to gamble or lose money quickly.

However, once an investor has four or five years of experience and has unquestionably proven her ability to make money in common stocks, if she is strong of heart, she might consider investing in futures on a limited basis.

With futures, it is even more important that you be able to read and interpret charts. The chart price patterns in commodity prices are similar to those in individual stocks. Being aware of futures charts can also help stock investors evaluate changes in basic economic conditions in the country.

There are a relatively small number of futures that you can trade. Therefore, astute speculators can concentrate their analysis. The rules and terminology of futures trading are different, and the risk is far greater, so investors should definitely limit the proportion of their investment funds that they commit to futures. There are worrisome events involved in futures trading, such as "limit down" days, where a trader is not allowed to sell and cut a loss. Risk management (i.e., position size and cutting losses quickly) is never more important than when trading futures. You should also never risk more than 5% of your capital in any one futures position. There is an outside chance of getting stuck in a position that has a series of limit up or limit down days. Futures can be treacherous and devastating; you could definitely lose it all.

I have never bought commodity futures. I do not believe you can be a jack-of-all-trades. Learn just one field as completely as possible. There are thousands of stocks to choose from.

Should You Buy Gold, Silver, or Diamonds?

As you might surmise, I do not normally recommend investing in metals or precious stones.

Many of these investments have erratic histories. They were once promoted in an extremely aggressive fashion, with little protection afforded to the small investor. In addition, the dealer's profit markup on these investments may be excessive. Furthermore, these investments do not pay interest or dividends.

There will always be periodic, significant run-ups in gold stocks caused by fears or panics brought about by potential problems in certain countries. A few gold companies may also be in their own cycle, like Barrick Gold was in the late 1980s and early 1990s. This type of commodity-oriented trading can be an emotional and unstable game, so I suggest care and caution. Small investments in such equities, however, can be very timely and reasonable at certain points.

Should You Invest in Real Estate?

Yes, at the right time and in the right place. I am convinced that most people should work toward being able to own a home by building a savings account and investing in common stocks or a growth-stock mutual fund. Home ownership has been a goal for most Americans. The ability over the years to obtain long-term borrowed money with only a small or reasonable down payment has created the leverage necessary to eventually make real estate investments possible for most Americans.

Real estate is a popular investment vehicle because it is fairly easy to understand and in certain areas can be highly profitable. About two-thirds of American families currently own their own homes. Time and leverage usually pay off. However, this is not always the case. People can and do lose money in real estate under many of the following realistic unfavorable conditions:

1. They make a poor initial selection by buying in an area that is slowly deteriorating or is not growing, or the area in which they've owned property for some time deteriorates.
2. They buy at inflated prices after several boom years and just before severe setbacks in the economy or in the particular geographic area in which they own real estate. This might occur if there are major industry layoffs or if an aircraft, auto, or steel plant that is an important mainstay of a local community closes.
3. They get themselves personally overextended, with real estate payments and other debts that are beyond their means, or they get into inviting but unwise variable-rate loans that could create difficult problems later, or they take out and live off of home equity—borrowing, rather than paying down their mortgage over time.
4. Their source of income is suddenly reduced by the loss of a job, or by an increase in rental vacancies should they own rental property.
5. They are hit by fires, floods, tornadoes, earthquakes, or other acts of nature.

People can also be hurt by well-meaning government policies and social programs that were not soundly thought through before being implemented, promoted, managed, operated, and overseen by the government. The subprime fiasco from 1995 to 2008 was caused by a good, well-intended government program that became incompetent, mismanaged, and messed up, with totally unexpected consequences that caused many of the very people the government hoped to help to lose their homes. It also caused huge unemployment as business contracted. In the greater Los Angeles area alone, many minority homeowners in San Bernardino, Riverside, and Santa Ana were dramatically hurt by foreclosures.

Basically, no one should ever buy a home unless he or she can come up with a down payment of at least 5%, 10%, or 20% on their own and has a relatively secure job. You need to earn and save toward your home-buying goal. And avoid variable-rate loans and smooth-talking salespeople who talk you into buying homes to "flip," which exposes you to far more risk. And finally, don't take out home equity loans that can put your home in a greater risk position. Also beware of getting into the terrible habit of using credit cards to run up big debts. That's a bad habit that will hurt you for years.

You can make money and develop skill by learning about and concentrating on the correct buying and selling of high-quality growth-oriented equities rather than scattering your efforts among the myriad high-risk investment alternatives. As with all investments, do the necessary research before you make your decision. Remember, there's no such thing as a risk-free investment. Don't let anyone tell you there is. If something sounds too easy and good to be true, watch out! Buyer beware.

To summarize so far, **diversification is good, but don't overdiversify. Concentrate on a smaller list of well-selected stocks, and let the market help you determine how long each of them should be held. Using margin may be okay if you're experienced, but it involves significant extra risk. Don't sell short unless you know exactly what you're doing. Be sure to learn to use charts to help with your selection and timing. Nasdaq is a good market for newer entrepreneurial companies, but options and futures have considerable risk and should be used only if you're very experienced, and then they should be limited to a small percentage of your overall investments. Also be careful when investing in tax shelters and foreign stocks only traded in foreign markets.**

It's best to keep your investing simple and basic—high-quality, growth-oriented stocks, mutual funds, or real estate. But each is a specialty, and you need to educate yourself so that you're not dependent solely on someone else for sound advice and investments.

Twenty-One Costly Common Mistakes Investors Make

Knute Rockne, the famous winning Notre Dame football coach, used to say, "Build up your weaknesses until they become your strong points." The reason people either lose money or achieve mediocre results in the stock market is they simply make too many mistakes. It's the same in your business, your life, or your career. You're held back or have reverses not because of your strengths, but because of your mistakes or weaknesses that you do not recognize, face, and correct. Most people just blame somebody else. It is much easier to have excuses and alibis than it is to examine your own behavior realistically.

When I first wrote this book, I came across lots of people who were advising: "Concentrate on your strengths, not your weaknesses." That sounded logical and reasonable in many situations. But now, after 50 years of day-to-day experience in America's amazing stock market, where every cycle thrusts forward dozens of brand-new, innovative, entrepreneurial companies that keep building our nation, I can state this:

By far the greatest mistake 98% of all investors make is never spending time trying to learn where they made their mistakes in buying and selling (or not selling) stock and what they must stop doing and start doing to become more successful. In other words, you must *unlearn* many things you thought you knew that ain't so, stop doing them, and start learning new, better rules and methods to use in the future.

The difference between successful people in any field and those who are not so successful is that the successful person will work and do what others are unwilling to do. Since the early 1960s, I have known or dealt with countless individual risk takers, from inexperienced beginners to smart professionals. What I've discovered is it doesn't matter whether you're just getting started or have many years, even decades, of investing experience. The fact is, experience is harmful if it continuously reinforces your ongoing bad habits. Success in the market is achieved by avoiding the classic mistakes most investors, whether public or professional, make.

Events in recent years should tell you it's time to educate yourself, take charge, and learn how to handle and take responsibility for your own financial future: your 401(k), your mutual funds, and your stock portfolio. These events include Bernie Madoff's theft of billions from supposedly intelligent people through his supersecretive operations, which were never transparent, as he never told anyone how he was investing their money; the public's heavy losses from the topping stock markets of 2000 and 2008; and the use of excess leverage by Wall Street firms that couldn't even manage their own money with prudence and intelligence, forcing them into bankruptcy or shotgun weddings.

You really can learn to invest with intelligence and skill. Many people have learned how to use sound rules and principles to protect and secure their financial affairs. Here are the key mistakes you'll need to avoid once you get serious and make up your mind you want better investment results:

1. Stubbornly holding onto your losses when they are very small and reasonable. Most investors could get out cheaply, but because they are human, their emotions take over. You don't want to take a loss, so you wait and you hope, until your loss gets so large it costs you dearly. This is by far the greatest mistake nearly all investors make; they don't understand that all common stocks are speculative and can involve large risks. Without exception, you should cut every single loss short. The rule I have taught in classes all across the nation for 45 years is to always cut all your losses immediately when a stock falls 7% or 8% below your purchase price. Following this simple rule will ensure you will survive another day to invest and capitalize on the many excellent opportunities in the future.

2. Buying on the way down in price, thus ensuring miserable results. A declining stock seems like a real bargain because it's cheaper than it was a few months earlier. In late 1999, a young woman I know bought Xerox when it dropped abruptly to a new low at $34 and seemed really cheap. A year later, it traded at $6. Why try to catch a falling dagger? Many people did the same thing in 2000, buying Cisco Systems at $50 on the way down after it had been $82. It never saw $50 again, even in the 5-year 2003 to 2007 bull market. In April 2009, it sold for $20.

3. Averaging down in price rather than averaging up when buying. If you buy a stock at $40, then buy more at $30 and average out your cost at $35, you are following up your losers and throwing good money after bad. This amateur strategy used in any individual stock could produce serious losses and weigh down your portfolio with a few big losers.

4. Not learning to use charts and being afraid to buy stocks going into new high ground off sound chart bases. The public generally thinks a stock making a new high price seems too high, but personal feelings and opinions are emotional and far less accurate than the market. The best time to buy a stock during any bull market is when the stock initially emerges from a price consolidation or sound "basing" area of at least seven or eight weeks. Get over the normal human desire of wanting to buy something cheap on the way down.

5. Never getting out of the starting gate properly because of poor selection criteria and not knowing exactly what to look for in a successful company. You need to understand what fundamental factors are crucial and what are simply not that important! Many investors buy fourth-rate, "nothing-to-write-home-about" stocks that are not acting particularly well; have questionable earnings, sales growth, and return on equity; and are not the true market leaders. Others overly concentrate in highly speculative or lower-quality, risky technology securities.

6. Not having specific general market rules to tell you when a correction in the market is beginning or when a market decline is most likely over and a new uptrend is confirmed. It's critical that you recognize market tops and major market bottoms if you want to protect your account from excessive giveback of profits and significant losses. You must also know when the storm is over and the market itself tells you to buy back and raise your market commitments. You can't go by your personal opinions, news, or your feelings. You must have precise rules and follow them. People wrongly think you can't time the market.

7. Not following your buy and sell rules, causing you to make an increased number of mistakes. The soundest rules you create are of no help if you don't develop the strict discipline to make decisions and act according to your historically proven rules and game plan.

8. Concentrating your effort on what to buy and, once your buy decision is made, not understanding when or under what conditions the stock must be sold. Most investors have no rules or plan for selling stocks, meaning that they are doing only half of the homework necessary to succeed. They just buy and hope.

9. Failing to understand the importance of buying high-quality companies with good institutional sponsorship and the importance of learning how to use charts to significantly improve selection and timing.

10. Buying more shares of low-priced stocks rather than fewer shares of higher-priced stocks. Many people think it's smarter to buy round lots of 100 or 1,000 low-priced shares. This makes them feel like they're getting a lot more for their money. They'd be better off buying 30 or 50 shares of higher-priced, better-quality, better-performing companies. Think in terms of *dollars* when you invest, not the number of shares you can buy. Buy the best merchandise available, not the cheapest.

Many investors can't resist $2, $5, or $10 stocks, but most stocks selling for $10 or less are cheap for a reason. They've either been deficient in the past or have something wrong with them now. Stocks are like anything else: the best quality rarely comes at the cheapest price.

That's not all. Low-priced stocks may cost more in commissions and markups. And since they can drop 15% to 20% faster than most higher-priced issues can, they also carry greater risk. Most professionals and institutions normally won't invest in $5 and $10 stocks, so these stocks do not have a top-notch following. Penny stocks are even worse. As discussed earlier, institutional sponsorship is one of the ingredients needed to help propel a stock higher in price.

Cheap stocks also have larger spreads in terms of the percentage difference between the bid and ask price. Compare a $5 stock that trades $5 bid, $5.25 ask with a $50 stock that trades $50 bid, $50.25 ask. On your $5 stock, that $0.25 difference is 5% of the bid price. On your $50 stock, that $0.25 difference is a negligible 0.5%. The difference is a factor of 10. As a result, with low-priced stocks, you tend to have much more ground to make up from your initial buy point just to break even and overcome the spread.

11. Buying on tips, rumors, split announcements, and other news events; stories; advisory-service recommendations; or opinions you hear from other people or from supposed market experts on TV. Many people are too willing to risk their hard-earned money on the basis of what someone else says, rather than taking the time to study, learn, and know for sure what they're doing. As a result, they risk losing a lot of money. Most rumors and tips you hear simply aren't true. Even if they are true, in many cases the stock concerned will ironically go down, not up as you assume.

12. Selecting second-rate stocks because of dividends or low price/earnings ratios. Dividends and P/E ratios aren't anywhere near as important as earnings per share growth. In many cases, the more a company pays in dividends, the weaker it may be. It may have to pay high interest rates to replenish the funds it is paying out in the form of dividends. Better-performing companies typically will not pay dividends. Instead, they reinvest their capital in research and development (R&D) or other corporate improvements. Also, keep in mind that you can lose the amount of a dividend in one or two days' fluctuation in the price of the stock. As for P/E ratios, a low P/E is probably low because the company's past record is inferior. Most stocks sell for what they're worth at any particular time.

13. Wanting to make a quick and easy buck. Wanting too much, too fast—without doing the necessary preparation, learning the soundest methods, or acquiring the essential skills and discipline—can be your downfall. Chances are, you'll jump into a stock too fast and then be too slow to cut your losses when you are wrong.

14. Buying old names you're familiar with. Just because you used to work for General Motors doesn't necessarily make it a good stock to buy. Many of the best investments will be newer entrepreneurial names you won't know, but, with a little research, you could discover and profit from before they become household names.

15. Not being able to recognize (and follow) good information and advice. Friends, relatives, some brokers, and advisory services can all be sources of bad advice. Only a small minority are successful enough themselves to merit your consideration. Outstanding stockbrokers or advisory services are no more plentiful than outstanding doctors, lawyers, or ballplayers. Only one out of nine baseball players who sign professional contracts ever make it to the big leagues. Most of the ballplayers coming out of college simply are not even professional caliber. Many brokerage firms have gone out of business because they couldn't manage their own money wisely. In the 2000 era, some used unbelievable leverage. You never want to make excessive use of borrowed money. That will get you into trouble.

16. Cashing in small, easy-to-take profits while holding your losers. In other words, doing exactly the opposite of what you should be doing: cutting your losses short and giving your profits more time.

17. Worrying way too much about taxes and commissions. The name of the game is to first make a net profit. Excessive worrying about taxes usually leads to unsound investment decisions in the hope of achieving a tax shelter. You can also fritter away a good profit by holding on too long in an attempt to get a long-term capital gain. Some investors convince themselves they can't sell because of taxes, but that's ego trumping judgment.

The commissions associated with buying and selling stocks, especially through an online broker, are minor compared with the money to be made by making the right decisions in the first place and taking action when needed. The fact that you pay relatively low commissions and you can get out of your investment much faster are two of the biggest advantages of owning stock over owning real estate. People can get over their head in real estate and lose money when they overstep themselves. With instant liquidity in equities, you can protect yourself quickly at low cost and take advantage of highly profitable new trends as they emerge.

18. Speculating too heavily in options or futures because you see them as a way to get rich quick. Some investors also focus mainly on shorter-term, lower-priced options that involve greater volatility and risk. The limited time period works against holders of short-term options. Some people also write "naked options" (selling options on stocks they do not even own), which amounts to taking greater risk for a potentially small reward.

19. Rarely transacting "at the market," preferring instead to put price limits on buy and sell orders. By doing so, investors are quibbling over eighths and quarters of a point (or their decimal equivalents), rather than focusing on the stock's larger and more important movement. With limit orders, you run the risk of missing the market completely and not getting out of stocks that should be sold to avoid substantial losses.

20. Not being able to make up your mind when a decision needs to be made. Many investors don't know whether they should buy, sell, or hold, and the uncertainty shows they have no guidelines. Most people don't follow a proven plan, a set of strict principles or buy and sell rules, to correctly guide them.

21. Not looking at stocks objectively. Many people pick favorites and cross their fingers. Instead of relying on hope and their own opinions, successful investors pay attention to the market, which is usually right.

How many of these describe your past investment beliefs? Poor methods yield poor results; sound methods yield sound results.

Here's some special advice just for successful intelligent men who believe they are using CAN SLIM. Stop trying to make CAN SLIM much better by adding your favorite tools, market indicators, special formulas you've created, other services, publications, opinions of experts on TV, your own opinion of the economy or market, past habits, value measurements, or other diversions that dilute results and create confusion at decision time. Follow the rules, kick the ego, stay on track.

After all of this, never feel discouraged. Remember what Rockne said: "Build up your weaknesses until they become your strong points." It takes time and a little effort to get it right, but it's worth every minute you spend on it. America offers a never-ending parade of new, growing companies. You can learn to invest with knowledge and confidence to protect your money and find and properly handle highly successful companies. **You can learn how to successfully invest in stocks.**

PART III

Investing Like a Professional

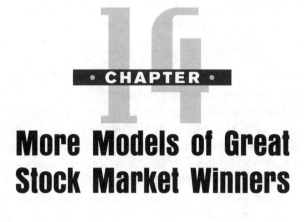

More Models of Great Stock Market Winners

Throughout this book, I've shown you and discussed many of the greatest winning stocks of the past. Now that you've been introduced to the CAN SLIM system of investing, you should know that we actually suggested some of these same companies to clients through our institutional services firm or bought them ourselves.

Regardless of your current position in life or your financial standing, it's clearly possible for you to make your dreams come true using the CAN SLIM system. You may have heard or read about the thousands of individuals who have changed their lives using this book and *Investor's Business Daily*. It really happens, and it can happen to you if you are determined and have an overpowering desire, no matter how large or small your account . . . as long as you make up your mind, work at it, and don't ever let yourself get discouraged.

This chapter will introduce you to a few early examples of success using this system. There are many, many others. In addition, it will also introduce you to more of the great winning stocks since 1952. Study this chapter closely; you'll find these patterns repeat over and over again throughout time. If you learn to recognize them early, you could get in on some future big profits, even if it takes some time.

Tracing the Growth of a Small Account

In 1961, with $10 from each of my classmates at Harvard's Program for Management Development (PMD), we started the first PMD Fund with the grand

311

total of $850. It was mostly for fun. Each classmate began with one $10 share in the fund. Marshall Wolf, then with National Newark & Essex Bank, and later an executive vice president at Midatlantic National Bank, had the thankless job of secretary-treasurer, keeping the records, informing the gang, and filing and paying taxes each year. I got the easy job of managing the money.

It's an interesting account to study because it proves you can start very small and still win the game if you stick with sound methods and give yourself plenty of time. On September 16, 1986 (some 25 years later), after all prior taxes had been paid and with Marshall having later kept some money in cash, the account was worth $51,653.34. The profit, in other words, was more than $50,000, and each share was worth $518. That is nearly a 50-fold after-tax gain from less than $1,000 invested.

The actual buy and sell records in the accompanying table illustrate in vivid detail the execution of the basic investment methods we have discussed up to this point.

Note that while there were about 20 successful transactions through 1964, there were also 20 losing transactions. However, the average profit was around 20%, while the average loss was about 7%. If losses in Standard Kollsman, Brunswick, and a few others had not been cut, later severe price drops would have caused much larger losses. This small cash account was concentrated in only one or two stocks at a time. Follow-up buys were generally made if the security moved up in price.

The account made no progress in 1962, a bad market year, but it was already up 139% by June 6, 1963, *before* the first Syntex buy was made. By the end of 1963, the gain had swelled to 474% on the original $850 investment.

The year 1964 was lackluster. Worthwhile profits were made in 1965, 1966, and 1967, although nothing like 1963, which was a very unusual year. I won't bore you with 20 pages of stock transactions. Let me just say that the next 10 years showed further progress, despite losses in 1969 and 1974.

Another period of interesting progress started in 1978 with the purchase of Dome Petroleum. All decisions beginning with Dome are picked up and shown in the second table.

Dome offers an extremely valuable lesson on why most stocks sooner or later have to be sold. While it was bought, as you can see, at $77 and sold near $98, it eventually fell below $2! History repeated itself in 2000 and 2001 when many Internet big winners like CMGI dropped from $165 to $1. Note also that the account was worn out of Pic 'N' Save on July 6, 1982, at $15, but we bought it back at $18 and $19, even though this was a higher price, and made a large gain by doing so. This is something you will have to learn to do at some point. If you were wrong in selling, in a number of cases, you'll need to buy the stock back at higher prices.

Shares	Stock	Date Bought	Price Paid	Date Sold	Price Sold	Gain or Loss
5	Bristol Myers	1/1/61	64.88	2/21/61	78.75	
7	Bristol Myers	1/4/61	67.25	2/21/61	78.75	149.87
18	Brunswick	2/21/61	53.75	3/10/61	68.00	223.35
29	Certain-teed	3/10/61	42.13	4/13/61	39.75	(104.30)
24	Stan. Kollsman	4/13/61	45.75	6/27/61	45.00	
	Stan. Kollsman		45.75	6/27/61	43.38	(82.66)
25	Endevco Corp.	4/26/61	13.00	5/25/61	17.50	102.96
10	Lockheed	6/13/61	44.88			
10	Lockheed	6/27/61	46.38			
5	Lockheed	7/25/61	48.50	8/29/61	48.25	7.55
6	Crown Cork	9/1/61	108.50			
5	Crown Cork	9/1/61	110.00	10/2/61	103.25	(100.52)
20	Brunswick	10/11/61	64.25	10/24/61	58.13	
	Brunswick			11/1/61	54.00	(223.49)
3	Polaroid	10/31/61	206.75			
3	Polaroid	11/1/61	209.00	2/21/62	180.00	(191.68)
30	Korvette	2/28/62	41.00	3/30/62	47.88	
30	Korvette	4/5/62	52.25	4/13/62	54.25	183.96
10	Crown Cork (Short)	5/28/62	99.25	5/22/62	97.25	(50.48)
30	Lockheed (Short)	6/15/62	41.25	6/2/62	39.75	(81.02)
5	Xerox	6/20/62	104.75			
5	Xerox	6/25/62	105.25	7/12/62	127.13	190.30
10	Homestake Mining	7/16/62	59.50	7/24/62	54.25	
10	Homestake Mining	7/16/62	58.75	7/24/62	54.25	(87.66)
10	Polaroid (Short)	7/31/62	105.00	7/19/62	97.88	(101.86)
30	Korvette (Short)	10/24/62	21.88	9/28/62	35.13	385.94
10	Chrysler	10/30/62	59.00			
15	Chrysler	11/1/62	60.34	1/15/63	83.63	545.40
15	RCA	1/16/63	62.50			
15	RCA	1/18/63	65.25	2/28/63	62.00	(111.02)
25	Coastal States	2/28/63	31.38	3/14/63	32.13	(8.46)
14	Chrysler	2/27/63	92.50			
8	Chrysler	3/14/63	93.00	4/16/63	109.13	300.03
25	Control Data	4/23/63	44.13	5/13/63	49.63	102.55
25	Intl. Minerals	5/6/63	52.88	5/15/63	54.88	11.47
22	Chrysler	5/13/63	54.38	6/10/63	61.75	
25	Chrysler	5/17/63	55.63	6/10/63	61.75	211.30
15	Syntex	6/11/63	89.25	9/23/63	146.13	
10	Syntex	8/7/63	114.50	9/23/63	146.13	
15	Syntex	10/9/63	149.13	10/22/63	225.00	2,975.71
15	Control Data	7/9/63	69.13	7/17/63	67.25	(59.62)
15	RCA	1/8/64	102.02	2/11/64	105.68	53.98
15	RCA	1/9/64	106.19	2/11/64	105.68	(8.49)
15	RCA	1/10/64	107.33	2/11/64	105.68	(25.54)
50	Pan Am	2/17/64	65.53	3/9/64	68.00	123.29
25	McDonnell Air	3/11/64	62.17	5/11/64	60.00	(54.26)
25	Chrysler	3/12/64	47.88	4/7/64	43.87	(100.35)
25	Chrysler	3/13/64	49.27	4/7/64	43.87	(135.06)
30	Chrysler	3/17/64	50.21	4/30/64	46.08	(123.83)
30	Consol. Cigar	3/19/64	49.35	4/20/64	47.25	(62.87)
25	Greyhound	4/7/64	55.47	5/1/64	57.63	53.88
20	Greyhound	4/8/64	58.55	5/1/64	57.63	(18.52)
15	Xerox	4/21/64	95.23	5/1/64	93.00	(33.41)
15	Xerox	4/29/64	98.53	5/5/64	95.00	(52.95)
30	Chrysler	5/13/64	52.14	7/8/64	48.75	(101.69)
50	Chrysler	5/13/64	52.32	6/11/64	46.50	(290.79)
50	Chrysler	5/13/64	52.34	6/30/64	49.00	(166.82)
50	Cerro Corp.	7/2/64	49.00	9/16/64	56.00	349.51
20	Cerro Corp.	7/6/64	50.68	9/16/64	56.00	106.50
50	NY Central RR	7/8/64	41.65	11/16/64	49.05	369.89

PMD Fund Transactions, 1961–1964

Shares	Stock	Date Bought	Price Paid	Date Sold	Price Sold	Gain or Loss
100	Dome Petroleum	12/28/78	77.00			
20	Dome Petroleum			2/26/79	97.88	
320	4/1 split on 6/6/79			10/17/80	63.00	14,226.72
300	Fluor	10/17/80	56.50	2/9/81	48.25	(3,165.82)
50	Fluor	10/17/80	56.88			
100	Pic 'N' Save	6/4/81	55.00			
300	3/1 split 6/29/81			7/6/82	15.00	(1,094.00)
100	Espey Mfg.	11/19/81	46.75	6/8/82	38.00	
50	Espey Mfg.	11/19/81	47.00	4/23/82	46.00	(1,313.16)
100	MCI Comm.	4/23/82	37.00	8/20/82	36.38	(123.50)
96	MCI Comm.	7/6/82	45.50			
	2/1 split on 9/20/82			1/3/83	38.25	2,881.92
200	Pic 'N' Save	8/20/82	18.50	7/16/84	19.25	3,892.00
45	Hewlett Packard	9/10/82	53.00	8/11/83	82.88	1,307.35
100	Pic 'N' Save	8/27/82	19.50			
185	Pic 'N' Save	1/3/83	38.13			
	2/1 split on 12/1/83			2/1/85	23.25	4,115.02
200	Price Co.	7/6/84	39.25			
326	Price Co.	2/1/85	53.75			
8	Price Co.			3/25/85	57.00	
15	Price Co.			3/20/86	43.25	
	2/1 split on 2/11/86			6/17/86	49.88	26,489.87

PMD Fund Transactions, 1978–1986

The U.S. Investing Championship

Another engaging example of the CAN SLIM principles being properly applied is the story of one of our associates, Lee Freestone. Lee participated in the U.S. Investing Championship in 1991, when he was just 24 years old. Using the CAN SLIM technique, he came in second for the year, with a result of 279%. In 1992, he gained a 120% return and again came in second. Lee was doing what David Ryan, another associate at the time, had done when he participated in the U.S. Investing Championship in prior years and won. The U.S. Investing Championship is not some paper transaction derby. Real money is used, and actual transactions are made in the market. Lee continued to invest successfully with even larger returns in the late 1990s.

So if it is followed with discipline, the CAN SLIM system has been battle-tested successfully through thick and thin from 1961 to 2009.

More Examples of Great Winners to Guide You

Graphs for an additional selected group of the greatest stock market winners follow. They are models of the most successful investments in the United States from 1952 through 2009. Study them carefully and refer to them often. They are further examples of what you must look for in the future. The thin wavy line with RS at the end shown below the prices is a relative price strength line. When the line moves up, the stock is outperforming the market. All the models show the stock's chart pattern just before the point where you want to take buying action.

If you think you're just looking at a bunch of charts, think again. What you are seeing are pictures of the price accumulation patterns of the greatest winning stocks—just before their enormous price moves began. The charts are presented in five configurations: cup-with-handle pattern, cup-without-handle pattern, double-bottom pattern, flat-base pattern, and base-on-top-of-a-base pattern. You need to learn to recognize these patterns.

Cup-With-Handle Pattern

Telex 283% increase in 27 weeks

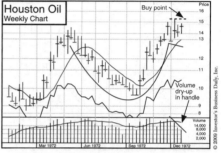

Houston Oil 1004% increase in 54 weeks

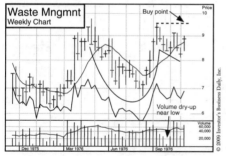

Waste Management 1180% increase in 242 weeks

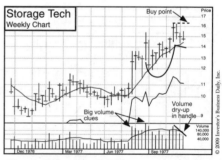

Storage Technology 371% increase in 52 weeks

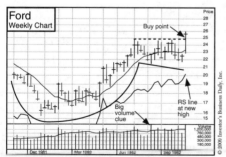

Ford 889% increase in 262 weeks

King World Prod. 588% increase in 116 weeks

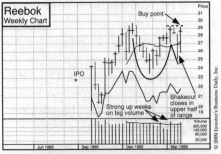

Reebok 246% increase in 18 weeks

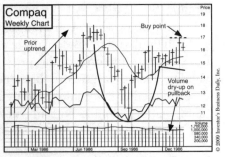

Compaq 352% increase in 46 weeks

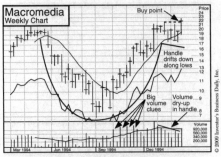

Macromedia 486% increase in 49 weeks

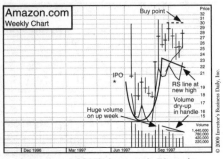

Amazon.com 3805% increase in 70 weeks

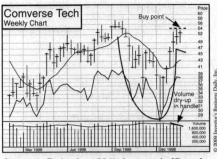

Comverse Technology 564% increase in 67 weeks

Verisign 2250% increase in 66 weeks

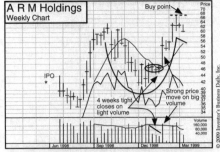

ARM Holdings 1385% increase in 57 weeks

Veritas Software 1097% increase in 62 weeks

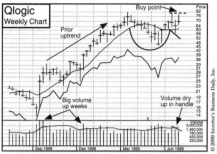

Qlogic 803% increase in 44 weeks

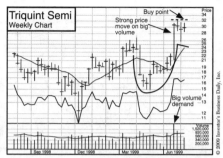

Triquint Semiconductor 1078% increase in 41 weeks

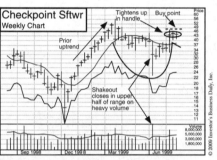

Checkpoint Software 1104% increase in 40 weeks

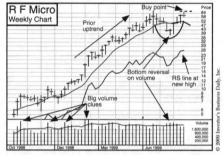

RF Micro Devices 444% increase in 36 weeks

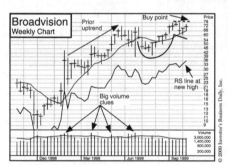

Broadvision 823% increase in 30 weeks

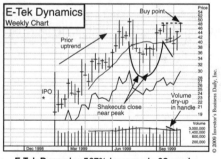

E-Tek Dynamics 507% increase in 28 weeks

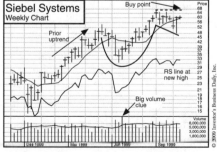

Siebel Systems 466% increase in 28 weeks

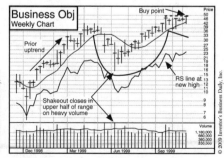

Business Objects 480% increase in 26 weeks

Microstrategy 1414% increase in 24 weeks

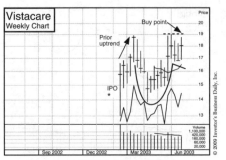

Vistacare 115% increase in 31 weeks

China Mobile 484% increase in 131 weeks

McDermott 703% increase in 128 weeks

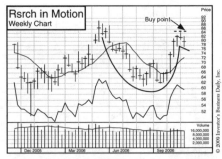

Research in Motion 382% increase in 60 weeks

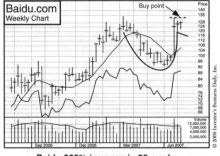

Baidu 225% increase in 25 weeks

Cup-Without-Handle Pattern

Wards 267% increase in 38 weeks

T C B Y 2189% increase in 77 weeks

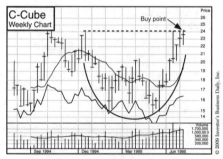

C-Cube 509% increase in 41 weeks

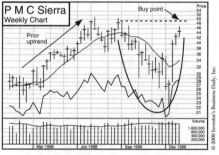

P M C Sierra 1949% increase in 70 weeks

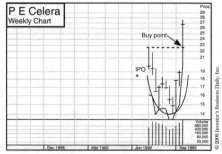

P E Celera 2281% increase in 32 weeks

Gen-Probe 122% increase in 20 weeks

Double Bottom Pattern

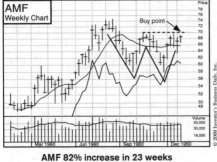

AMF 82% increase in 23 weeks

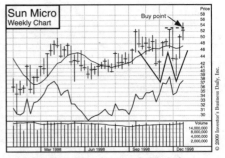

Sun Micro 701% increase in 74 weeks

Nokia 486% increase in 87 weeks

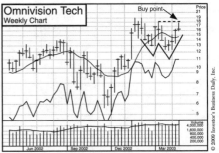

Omnivision Tech 256% increase in 39 weeks

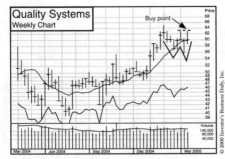

Quality Systems 177% increase in 44 weeks

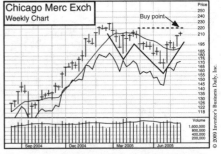

Chicago Merc. Exch. 208% increase in 132 weeks

Flat Base Pattern

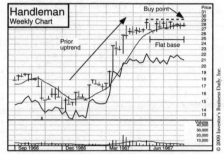

Handleman 328% increase in 139 weeks

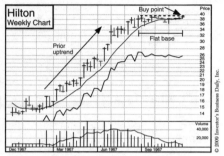

Hilton 232% increase in 60 weeks

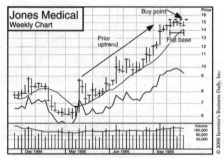

Jones Medical 447% increase in 36 weeks

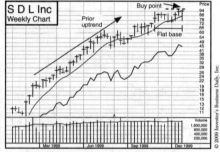

S D L Inc 814% increase in 39 week

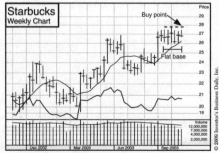

Starbucks 126% increase in 70 weeks

American Movil 730% increase in 205 weeks

Base-on-Base Pattern

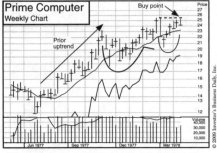

Prime Computer 1564% increase in 169 weeks

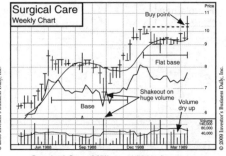

Surgical Care Affiliates 1632% increase in 150 weeks

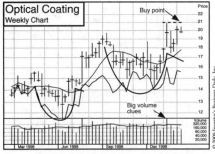

Optical Coating Labs 1957% increase in 58 weeks

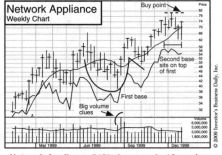

Network Appliance 517% increase in 18 weeks

· CHAPTER ·

Picking the Best Market Themes, Sectors, and Industry Groups

The majority of the leading stocks are usually in leading industries. Studies show that 37% of a stock's price movement is directly tied to the performance of the industry group the stock is in. Another 12% is due to strength in its overall sector. Therefore, roughly half of a stock's move is driven by the strength of its respective group. Because specific industry groups lead each market cycle, you can see how worthwhile it is to consider a stock's industry before making a purchase.

For the purposes of this discussion, there are three terms we will use: sector, industry group, and subgroup. A *sector* is a broad grouping of companies and industries. These include, for example, basic industries (or "cyclicals"), consumer goods and services, transportation, finance, and high technology. An *industry group* is a smaller, more specific grouping of companies; there normally are several industry groups within a sector. A *subgroup* is even more specific, dividing the industry group into several very precise subcategories.

For example, if we were to look at Viacom, it could be described as follows: Sector: Leisure and Entertainment Industry; Group: Media; and Subgroup: Radio/TV. For clarity and ease of use, industry group and subgroup names are generally combined, with the result simply being called "industry groups." For example, the industry group for Viacom is known as "Media—Radio/TV."

Why Track 197 Industry Groups?

Why does IBD divide securities into 197 industry groups rather than, say, the smaller number of groups used by Standard & Poor's? It's simple really. The stocks within a given sector do not all perform at the same rate. Even if a sector is outperforming other sectors, there may be segments of that sector that are performing extremely well and others that are lagging the market. It's important that you be able to recognize what industry group within the sector is acting the very best, since this knowledge can mean the difference between superior and mediocre results.

Early in our study of the market, we realized that many of the investment services available at the time did not adequately dissect the market into enough industry groups. It was therefore difficult to determine the specific part of a group where the true leadership was. So we created our own industry groups, breaking down the market into 197 different subcategories and providing you, the investor, with more accurate and detailed insights into the makeup of an industry. For example, the medical industry can be divided into hospital companies, generic drugs, dental, home nursing, genetics, biotech, and HMOs, plus a few other unique modern areas.

How You Can Decide Which Industry Groups Are Leading the Market

When analyzing industries, we've found that some are so small that signs of strength in the group may not be relevant. If there are only two small, thinly traded companies within a subindustry, that's not enough to consider them a group. On the other hand, there are industries with too many companies, such as chemicals and savings and loans. This excessive supply does not add to these industries' attractiveness, unless some extremely unusual changes in industry conditions occur.

The 197 industry groups mentioned earlier can be found each business day in *Investor's Business Daily*. There we rank each subgroup according to its six-month price performance so that you can easily determine which industry subgroups are the true leaders. Buyers operating on the "undervalued" philosophy love to do their prospecting in the worst-ranked groups. But analysis has shown that, on average, stocks in the top 50 or 100 groups perform better than those in the bottom 100. To increase your odds of finding a truly outstanding stock in an outstanding industry, concentrate on the top 20 groups and avoid the bottom 20.

Both *Investor's Business Daily* and the Daily Graphs Online charting services offer an additional, proprietary source of information to help you determine whether the stock you're thinking about owning is in a top-flight industry group. The Industry Group Relative Strength Rating assigns a letter grade from A+ to E to each publicly traded company we follow, with A+ being best. A rating of A+, A, or A– means the stock's industry group is in the top 24% of all industry groups in terms of price performance.

Every day I also quickly check the "New Price Highs" list in IBD. It is uniquely organized in order of the broad industry sectors with the most individual stocks that made new price highs the previous day. You can't find this list in other business publications. Just note the top six or so sectors, particularly in bull markets. They usually pick up the majority of the real leaders.

Another way you can find out what industry groups are in or out of favor is to analyze the performance of a mutual fund family's industry funds. Fidelity Investments, one of the nation's successful mutual fund managers, has more than 35 industry mutual funds. A glance at their performance provides yet another excellent perspective on which industry sectors are doing better. I've found it worthwhile to note the two or three Fidelity industry funds that show the greatest year-to-date performance. This is shown in a small special table in IBD every business day.

For William O'Neil + Co.'s institutional clients, a weekly Datagraph service is provided that arranges the 197 industry groups in order of their group relative price strength for the past six months. Stocks in the strongest categories are shown in Volume 1 of the O'Neil Database books, and stocks in the weaker groups are in Volume 2.

During a time period in which virtually all daily newspapers, including the *Wall Street Journal*, significantly cut the number of companies they covered in their main stock tables every business day and/or drastically cut the number of key data items shown daily for each stock, here's what *Investor's Business Daily* did.

IBD's stock tables are now organized in order of performance, from the strongest down to the weakest of 33 major economic sectors, such as medical, retail, computer software, consumer, telecom, building, energy, Internet, banks, and so on. Each sector combines NYSE and Nasdaq stocks so you can compare every stock available in each sector to find the best stocks in the best sectors based on a substantial number of key variables.

IBD now gives you 21 vital time-tested facts on up to 2,500 leading stocks in its stock tables each business day . . . more than virtually all other daily newspapers in America. These 21 facts are

1. An overall composite ranking from 1 to 99, with 99 best.

2. An earnings per share growth rating comparing each company's last two quarters and last three years' growth with those of all other

stocks. A 90 rating means the company has outperformed 90% of all stocks in a critical measurement, earnings growth.

3. A Relative Price Strength rating comparing each stock's price change over the last 12 months with those of all other stocks. Better firms rate 80 or higher on both EPS and RS.

4. A rating comparing a stock's sales growth rate, profit margins, and return on equity to those of all other stocks.

5. A highly accurate proprietary accumulation/distribution rating that uses a price and volume formula to gauge whether a stock is under accumulation (buying) or distribution (selling) in the last 13 weeks. "A" denotes heavy buying; "E" indicates heavy selling.

6 & 7. Volume % change tells you each stock's precise percentage change above or below its average daily volume for the past 50 days along with its total volume for the day.

8 & 9. The current and recent relative performance of each stock's broad industry sector.

10–12. Each stock's 52-week high price, closing price, and change for the day.

13–21. Price/earnings ratio, dividend yield, if the company repurchased its stock in the last year, if the stock has options, if company earnings will be reported in the next four weeks, if the stock was up 1 point or more or made a new high, if the stock was down 1 point or more or made a new low, if the stock had an IPO in the last fifteen years and has an EPS and RS rating of 80 or higher, and if a recent IBD story on the company is archived at Investors.com.

Not only does IBD follow more stocks and provide more vital data, but the table print size is much larger and easier to read.

As of this writing in February 2009, the medical sector is number one. These ratings will change as the weeks and months go by and market conditions, news, and data change. I believe these significant and relevant data for serious investors, regardless of whether they are new or experienced, are light-years ahead of the data provided by most of IBD's competitors. IBD is the #1 daily business newspaper for investors.

Considering some of the seeming disasters coming out of Wall Street and the big-city banking community in 2008, we believe we are and have been providing the American public—with our many books like the one you're reading, home study courses, more than a thousand seminars and workshops nationwide, plus *Investor's Business Daily*—a source of relevant, sound education, help, and guidance in an otherwise complex but key area that much of the investment community and Washington may not have always handled as well.

The Importance of Following Industry Trends

If economic conditions in 1970 told you to look for an improvement in housing and a big upturn in building, what stocks would you have included in your definition of the building sector? If you had acquired a list of them, you'd have found that there were hundreds of companies in that sector at the time. So how would you narrow down your choices to the stocks that were performing best? The answer: look at them from the industry group and subgroup levels.

There were actually 10 industry groups within the building sector for investors to consider during the 1971 bull market. That meant there were 10 different ways you could have played the building boom. Many institutional investors bought stocks ranging from lumber producer Georgia Pacific to wallboard leader U.S. Gypsum to building-products giant Armstrong Corp. You could have also gone with Masco in the plumbing group, a home builder like Kaufman & Broad, building-material retailers and wholesalers like Standard Brands Paint and Scotty's Home Builders, or mortgage insurers like MGIC. Then there were manufacturers of mobile homes and other low-cost housing, suppliers of air-conditioning systems, and makers and sellers of furniture and carpets.

Do you know where the traditional building stocks were during 1971? They spent the year in the bottom half of all industry groups, while the newer building-related subgroups more than tripled!

The mobile home group crossed into the top 100 industry groups on August 14, 1970, and stayed there until February 12, 1971. The group returned to the top 100 on May 14, 1971, and then fell into the bottom half again later the following year, on July 28, 1972. In the prior cycle, mobile homes were in the top 100 groups in December 1967 and dropped to the bottom half only in the next bear market.

The price advances of mobile home stocks during these positive periods were spellbinding. Redman Industries zoomed from a split-adjusted $6 to $56, and Skyline moved from $24 to what equaled $378 on a presplit basis. These are the kind of stocks that charts can help you spot if you learn to read charts and do your homework. We study the historical model of all these past great leaders and learn from them.

From 1978 to 1981, the computer industry was one of the leading sectors. However, many money managers at that time thought of the industry as consisting only of IBM, Burroughs, Sperry Rand, Control Data, and the like. But these were all large mainframe computer manufacturers, and they failed to perform during that cycle. Why? Because while the computer sector was hot, older industry groups within it, such as mainframe computers, were not.

Meanwhile, the computer sector's many new subdivisions performed unbelievably. During that period, you could have selected new, relatively unknown stocks from groups such as minicomputers (Prime Computer), microcomputers (Commodore International), graphics (Computervision), word processors (Wang Labs), peripherals (Verbatim), software (Cullinane Database), or time-sharing (Electronic Data Systems). These fresh new entrepreneurial winners increased five to ten times in price. (That's the "New" in CAN SLIM.) No U.S. administration can hold back America's inventors and innovators for very long—unless it is really stifling business and the country.

During 1998 and 1999, the computer sector led again, with 50 to 75 computer-related stocks hitting the number one spot on *Investor's Business Daily's* new high list almost every day for more than a year. If you were alert and knew what to look for, it was there to be seen. It was Siebel Systems, Oracle, and Veritas in the enterprise software group, and Brocade and Emulex among local network stocks that provided new leadership. The computer–Internet group boomed with Cisco, Juniper, and BEA Systems; and EMC and Network Appliance had enormous runs in the memory group; while the formerly leading personal computer group lagged in 1999. After their tremendous increases, most of these leaders then topped in 2000 along with the rest of the market.

Many new subgroups have sprung up since then, and many more will spring up in the future as new technologies are dreamed up and applied. We are in the computer, worldwide communications, and space age. New inventions and technologies will spawn thousands of new and superior products and services. We're benefiting from an endless stream of ingenious off-shoots from the original mainframe industry, and in the past they came so fast we had to update the various industry categories in our database more frequently just to keep up with them.

There is no such thing as "impossible" in America's free enterprise system. Remember, when the computer was first invented, experts thought the market for it was only two, and one would have to be bought by the government. And the head of Digital Equipment later said he didn't see why anyone would ever want a computer in her home. When Alexander Graham Bell invented the telephone, he was struggling and offered a half-interest in the telephone to the president of Western Union, who replied, "What could I do with an interesting toy like that?" Walt Disney's board of directors, his brother, and his wife didn't like Walt's idea to create Disneyland.

In the bull market from 2003 to 2007, two of the best leaders in 1998 and 1999, America Online and Yahoo!, failed to lead, and new innovators like Google and Priceline.com moved to the head of the pack. You have to stay in phase with the new leaders in each new cycle. Here's a historical fact to remember: only one of every eight leaders in a bull market reasserts itself as a leader in the next bull market. The market usually moves on to new leadership, and America keeps growing, with new entrepreneurs offering you, the investor, new opportunities.

A Look at Industries of the Past and What's Coming in the Future

At one time, computer and electronic stocks may outperform. In another period, retail or defense stocks will stand out. The industry that leads in one bull market normally won't come back to lead in the next, although there have been exceptions. Groups that emerge late in a bull phase are sometimes early enough in their own stage of improvement to weather a bear market and then resume their advance, assuming leadership when a new bull market starts.

These were the leading industry groups in each bull market from 1953 through 2007:

1953–1954	Aerospace, aluminum, building, paper, steel
1958	Bowling, electronics, publishing
1959	Vending machines
1960	Food, savings and loans, tobacco
1963	Airlines
1965	Aerospace, color television, semiconductors
1967	Computers, conglomerates, hotels
1968	Mobile homes
1970	Building, coal, oil service, restaurants, retailing
1971	Mobile homes
1973	Gold, silver
1974	Coal
1975	Catalog showrooms, oil
1976	Hospitals, pollution, nursing homes, oil
1978	Electronics, oil, small computers
1979	Oil, oil service, small computers
1980	Small computers
1982	Apparel, autos, building, discount supermarkets, military electronics, mobile homes, retail apparel, toys

1984–1987	Generic drugs, foods, confectionery and bakery, supermarkets, cable TV, computer software
1988–1990	Shoes, sugar, cable TV, computer software, jewelry stores, telecommunications, outpatient health care
1990–1994	Medical products, biotech, HMOs, computer peripheral/LAN, restaurants, gaming, banks, oil and gas exploration, semiconductors, telecommunications, generic drugs, cable TV
1995–1998	Computer peripheral/LAN, computer software, Internet, banks/finance, computer—PC/workstation, oil/gas drilling, retail—discount/variety
1999–2000	Internet, medical—biomed/genetics, computer—memory devices, telecommunications equipment, semiconductor manufacturing, computer—networking, fiber optic components, computer software—enterprise
2003–2007	Fertilizer, oil and gas, apparel, steel, medical, solar, Internet, home builders

As you might imagine, industries of the future create gigantic opportunities for everyone. While they occasionally come into favor, industries of the past offer less dazzling possibilities.

There were a number of major industries, mainly cyclical ones, that were well past their peaks as of 2000. Many of them, however, came back from a poor past to stronger demand from 2003 to 2007 as a result of the enormous demand from China as it copied what the United States did in the early 1900s, when we created and built an industrial world leader.

China, with its long border with Russia, witnessed firsthand the 70-year-old communist Soviet Union implode and disappear into the ash heap of history. The Chinese learned from the enormous growth and higher standard of living created in America that its model had far more potential for the Chinese people and their country. Most Chinese families want their one child to get a college education and learn to speak English. Families in India have many of the same aspirations.

Here is a list of these old-line industries:

1. Steel
2. Copper
3. Aluminum
4. Gold
5. Silver
6. Building materials

7. Autos
8. Oil
9. Textiles
10. Containers
11. Chemicals
12. Appliances
13. Paper
14. Railroads and railroad equipment
15. Utilities
16. Tobacco
17. Airlines
18. Old-line department stores

Industries of the present and future might include

1. Computer medical software
2. Internet and e-commerce
3. Laser technology
4. Defense electronics
5. Telecommunications
6. New concepts in retailing
7. Medical, drug, and biomedical/genetics
8. Special services
9. Education

Possible future groups might include wireless, storage area networking, person-to-person networking, network security, palmtop computers, wearable computers, proteomics, nanotechnology, and DNA-based microchips.

Tracking Nasdaq and NYSE Stocks Together Is Key

Groups that emerge as leaders in a new bull market cycle can be found by observing unusual strength in one or two Nasdaq stocks and relating that strength to similar power in a listed stock in the same group.

Initial strength in only one listed stock is not sufficient to attract attention to a category, but confirmation by one or two kindred Nasdaq issues can quickly steer you to a possible industry recovery. You can see this by looking at the accompanying charts of home builder Centex's OTC-traded stock from March to August of 1970, and of home builder Kaufman & Broad's NYSE-listed shares from April to August of the same year:

1. Centex's relative strength in the prior year was strong, and it made a new high three months before the stock price did.

2. Earnings accelerated (by 50%) during the June 1970 quarter.

3. The stock was selling near an all-time high at the bottom of a bear market.

4. A strong Centex base coincided with the base in Kaufman & Broad.

In the 2003 bull market, Coach (COH) was a NYSE-listed stock that we found on our weekly review of charts as it broke out of its base on February 28. It gave another buy point on April 25 when it bounced off its 10-week

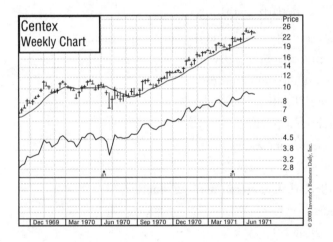

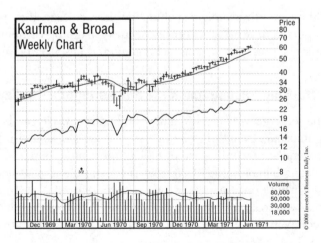

moving average price line. However, this time the new bull market had begun in earnest after a major market follow-through day in the market averages, and on April 25 two other leaders in the retail clothing industry—Urban Outfitters (URBN) and Deckers Outdoor (DECK)—broke out at the same time as the Coach move. Now there was plenty of evidence, from one NYSE stock and two Nasdaq issues in the same industry group, of a powerful new group coming alive for the new bull market that had just started. This is one more reason IBD's NYSE and Nasdaq tables are combined and the stocks are shown by industry sectors. You can spot all the leaders more easily when they're together in a group.

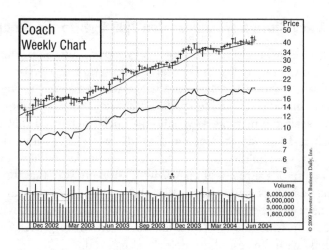

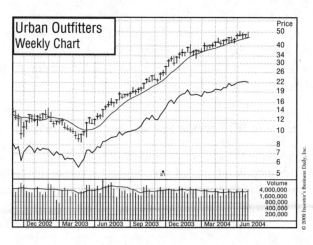

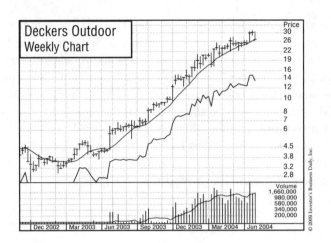

A Key Stock's Weakness Can Spill Over to the Group

Grouping and tracking stocks by industry group can also help you get out of weakening investments faster. If, after a successful run, one or two important stocks in a group break seriously, the weakness may sooner or later "wash over" into the remaining stocks in that field. For example, in February 1973, weakness in some key building stocks suggested that even stalwarts such as Kaufman & Broad and MGIC were vulnerable, despite the fact that they were holding up well. At the time, fundamental research firms were in unanimous agreement on MGIC. They were sure that the mortgage insurer had earnings gains of 50% locked in for the next two years, and that the company would continue on its merry course, unaffected by the building cycle. The fundamental stock analysts were wrong; MGIC later collapsed along with the rest of the deteriorating group.

In the same month, ITT traded between $50 and $60 while every other stock in the conglomerate group had been in a long decline. The two central points overlooked by four leading research firms that recommended ITT in 1973 were that the group was very weak and that ITT's relative strength was trending lower, even though the stock itself was not.

Oil and Oil Service Stocks Top in 1980–1981

This same "wash-over effect" within groups was also seen in 1980–1981. After a long advance in oil and oil service stocks, our early warning criteria caused our institutional services firm to put stocks such as Standard Oil of Indiana, Schlumberger, Gulf Oil, and Mobil on the "sell/avoid" side, meaning we felt they should be avoided or sold.

A few months later, data showed that we had turned negative on almost the entire oil sector, and that we had seen the top in Schlumberger, the most outstanding of all the oil service companies. Based objectively on all the historical data, you had to conclude that, in time, the weakness would wash over into the entire oil service industry. Therefore, we also added equities such as Hughes Tool, Western Co. of North America, Rowan Companies, Varco International, and NL Industries to the sell/avoid list even though the stocks were making new price highs and showed escalating quarterly earnings—in some cases by 100% or more.

These moves surprised many experienced professionals on Wall Street and at large institutions, but we had studied and documented how groups historically had topped in the past. Our actions were based on historical facts and sound principles that had worked over decades, not on analysts' personal opinions or possibly one-sided information from company officials.

Our service is totally and completely different from that of all Wall Street research firms because we do not hire analysts, make buy or sell recommendations, or write any research reports. We use supply-and-demand charts, facts, and historical precedents that now cover all common stocks and industries from the 1880s through 2008.

The decision to suggest that clients avoid or sell oil and oil service stocks from November 1980 to June 1981 was one of our institutional firm's more valuable calls at the time. We even told a Houston seminar audience in October 1980 the entire oil sector had topped. A full 75% of those in attendance owned petroleum stocks. They probably didn't believe a word we said. We were not aware at the time, or even in the several months following, of any other New York Stock Exchange firm that had taken that same negative stand across the board on the energy and related drilling and service sectors. In fact, the exact opposite occurred. Because of such decisions, William O'Neil + Co. became a leading provider of historical precedent ideas to many of the nation's top institutional investors.

Within a few months, all these stocks began substantial declines. Professional money managers slowly realized that once the price of oil had topped and the major oil issues were under liquidation, it would be only a matter of time before drilling activity would be cut back.

In the July 1982 issue of *Institutional Investor* magazine, ten energy analysts at eight of the largest and most respected brokerage firms took a different tack. They advised purchasing these securities because they appeared cheap and because they had had their first correction from their price peak. This is just another example of how personal opinions, even if they come from the highest research places or bright young MBAs from outstanding Ivy League universities, are quite often wrong when it comes to making and preserving money in the stock market.

The same situation repeated again in 2008 when we put Schlumberger on the sell/avoid list at $100 on July 3. It closed below its 10-week average and fell to $35 in eight months. Most of the oils were removed from our list on June 20th and they all slowly began their topping process as a group. Many institutions, on analysts' recommendations, bought the oils too soon on the way down because they seemed a bargain. Oil itself was midway in the process of collapsing from $147 a barrel to its eventual low of $35.

In August 2000, a survey showed many analysts had high-tech stocks as strong buys. Six months later, in one of the worst markets in many years, roughly the same proportion of analysts still said tech stocks were strong buys. Analysts certainly missed with their opinions. Only 1% of them said to sell tech stocks. Opinions, even by experts, are frequently wrong; markets rarely are. So learn to read what the market is telling you, and stop listening to ego and personal opinions. Analysts who don't understand this are destined to cause some substantial losses for their clients. We measure historical market facts, not personal opinions.

We do not visit or talk to any companies, have analysts to write research reports, or have or believe in inside information. Nor are we a quantitative firm. We tell our institutional subscribers who have teams of fundamental analysts to have their analysts check with their sources and the companies concerned to decide which of our rather unusual ideas based on historical precedent may be sound and right fundamentally and which are possibly not right. Institutions have always had a prudent personal responsibility for the stocks they invest in. We make our mistakes too, because the stock market is never a certainty. But when we make mistakes, we correct them rather than sit with them.

The Bowling Boom Tops in 1961

Beginning in 1958 and continuing into 1961, Brunswick's stock made a huge move. The stock of AMF, which also made automatic pinspotters for bowling alleys, gyrated pretty much in unison with Brunswick. After Brunswick peaked in March 1961, it rallied back to $65 from $50, but for the first time, AMF did not recover along with it. This was a tip-off that the entire group had made a long-term top, that the rebound in Brunswick wasn't going to last, and that the stock—as great as it had been—should be sold.

One practical, commonsense industry rule is to avoid buying any stock unless its strength and attractiveness are confirmed by at least one other important stock in the same group. You can get away without such confirmation in a few cases where the company does something truly unique, but these situations are very few in number. From the late 1980s to the late 1990s, Walt Disney fell into this category: a unique high-quality entertainment company rather than just another filmmaker in the notoriously unsteady, less-reliable movie group.

Two other valuable concepts turned up as we built historical models in the stock market. The first we named the "follow-on effect," and the second, the "cousin stock theory."

The "Follow-On Effect"

Sometimes, a major development takes place in one industry and related industries later reap follow-on benefits. For example, in the late 1960s, the airline industry underwent a renaissance with the introduction of jet airplanes, causing airline stocks to soar. A few years later, the increase in air travel spilled over to the hotel industry, which was more than happy to expand to meet the rising number of travelers. Beginning in 1967, hotel stocks enjoyed a tremendous run. Loews and Hilton were especially big winners. The follow-on effect, in this case, was that increased air travel created a shortage of hotel space.

When the price of oil rose in the late 1970s, oil companies began drilling like mad to supply the suddenly pricey commodity. As a result, higher oil prices fueled a surge not only in oil stocks in 1979, but also in the stocks of oil service companies that supplied the industry with exploration equipment and services.

The roaring success of small- and medium-sized computer manufacturers during the 1978–1981 bull market created follow-on demand for computer services, software, and peripheral products in the market resurgence of late 1982. As the Internet took off in the mid-1990s, people discovered an insatiable demand for faster access and greater bandwidth. Soon networking stocks surged, with companies specializing in fiber optics enjoying massive gains in their share prices.

The "Cousin Stock" Theory

If a group is doing exceptionally well, there may be a supplier company, a "cousin stock," that's also benefiting. As airline demand grew in the mid-1960s, Boeing was selling a lot of new jets. Every new Boeing jet was outfitted with chemical toilets made by a company called Monogram Industries. With earnings growth of 200%, Monogram stock had a 1,000% advance.

In 1983, Fleetwood Enterprises, a leading manufacturer of recreational vehicles, was a big winner in the stock market. Textone was a small cousin stock that supplied vinyl-clad paneling and hollow-core cabinet doors to RV and mobile home companies.

If you notice a company that's doing particularly well, research it thoroughly. In the process, you may discover a supplier company that's also worth investing in.

Basic Conditions Change in an Industry

Most group moves occur because of substantial changes in industry conditions.

In 1953, aluminum and building stocks had a powerful bull market as a result of pent-up demand for housing in the aftermath of the war. Wallboard was in such short supply that some builders offered new Cadillacs to gypsum board salespeople for just letting them buy a carload of their product.

In 1965, the onrush of the Vietnam War, which was to cost $20 billion or more, created solid demand for electronics used in military applications and defense during the war. Companies such as Fairchild Camera climbed more than 200% in price.

In the 1990s, discount brokerage firms continued to gain market share relative to full-service firms as investing became more and more mainstream. At that time, a historical check proved that Charles Schwab, one of the most successful discount brokerage firms, had performed as well as market leader Microsoft during the preceding years—a valuable fact few people knew then.

Watch for New Trends as They Develop

In our database research, we also pay attention to the areas of the country where corporations are located. In our ratings of companies as far back as 1971, we assigned extra points for those headquartered in Dallas, Texas, and other key growth or technology centers, such as California's Silicon Valley. Recently, however, California's high-cost, high-tax business environment has caused a number of companies to move out of the state to Utah, Arizona, and the Southwest.

Shrewd investors should also be aware of demographic trends. From data such as the number of people in various age groups, it's possible to predict potential growth for certain industries. The surge of women into the workplace and the gush of baby boomers help explain why stocks like The Limited, Dress Barn, and other retailers of women's apparel soared between 1982 and 1986.

It also pays to understand the basic nature of key industries. For example, high-tech stocks are 2½ times as volatile as consumer stocks, so if you don't buy them right, you can suffer larger losses. Or if you concentrate most of your portfolio in them, they could all come down at the same time. So, be aware of your risk exposure if you get overconcentrated in the volatile high-tech sector or any other possibly risky area.

Sometimes Defensive Groups May Flash General Market Clues

It's also important for investors to know which groups are "defensive" in nature. If, after a couple of bull market years, you see buying in groups such as gold, silver, tobacco, food, grocery, and electric and telephone utilities, you may be approaching a top. Prolonged weakness in the utility average could also be signaling higher interest rates and a bear market ahead.

The gold group moved into the top half of all 197 industries on February 22, 1973. Anyone who was ferreting out such information at that time got the first crystal-clear warning of one of the worst market upheavals up to that point since 1929.

60% or More of Big Winners Are Part of Group Moves

Of the most successful stocks from 1953 through 1993, nearly two out of three were part of group advances. So remember, the importance of staying on top of your research and being aware of new group movements cannot be overestimated.

• CHAPTER •

How I Use IBD to Find Potential Winning Stocks

Why We Created *Investor's Business Daily*

For decades, professional money managers were the only ones who had access to the in-depth data that are critical to finding winning stocks. In effect, they had a monopoly on relevant investment information. That's why I started *Investor's Business Daily* in April 1984: to bring the needed information to all investors, small or large, new or experienced.

Known for its investing capabilities as far back as the early 1960s, William O'Neil + Co. built the first computerized daily stock market database in the United States to track and compare stock performance. Detailed tracking uncovered key insights into what produces stock market winners, particularly their characteristics *before* they make a major price move.

Much of this information is now available through *Investor's Business Daily*, which offers everyone—professional and individual investors alike—a better opportunity to grow and profit from the detailed data. Because our primary concern is understanding and interpreting the national economy using our comprehensive database, *Investor's Business Daily* is a vital information provider first and a newspaper second.

If you're serious about becoming a more successful investor, it is positively within your grasp. If you can commit to studying the time-tested, historically proven strategies outlined in this book, being disciplined, and focusing on daily and weekly learning, you're more than halfway there. IBD's proprietary research tools are the other half of the equation. For many of you, this means familiarizing yourself with data, methods, and concepts very different from those you're accustomed to hearing, seeing, and using.

For example, according to our historical study of all the greatest winning stocks, if you'd been relying on P/E ratios, you would have missed almost every major winner for decades. The information in IBD is based on the characteristics of the most successful companies of all time before their major price moves. Following these valid model examples of success has helped me and many others achieve success since the 1960s.

Investor's Business Daily began in April 1984 with only 15,000 subscribers. In the years prior to our launch, the *Wall Street Journal* grew steadily to reach its peak of 2.1 million domestic circulation by our 1984 introduction date. Since that time, *Investor's Business Daily* has increased its market share over many years. In key high-population areas such as southern California, Florida, and Long Island, New York, IBD has a larger than normal number of readers. While many of our readers were former *Wall Street Journal* subscribers, there is little current duplication of readership, since several surveys show that only 16% of IBD subscribers also take the *Journal*.

How *Investor's Business Daily* Is Different

So what is it exactly that distinguishes IBD from other sources? Let's take a closer look.

- **IBD makes it easier to search for winning stocks.** With more than 10,000 publicly traded stocks to choose from, IBD provides performance lists and proven proprietary fundamental and technical ratings and rankings that help you narrow your choices to only the very best opportunities.

- **It offers quicker, easier, and more accurate and reliable ways to interpret the general market.** The key elements of the day's trading action are explained in IBD's "The Big Picture" column to give you a sound perspective on the health of the overall market and improve your timing of buy and sell decisions. In tough markets like 2000–2003 and 2007–2009, this is critical information.

- **It provides you with valuable investing education and support.** IBD's entire focus is on solid database research and extensive historical model building to serve as examples—facts, not personal opinions. There are a multitude of sources outlined in this chapter that can help you learn and understand how the market really works, based on years of historical precedent.

A New, Better Way to Find Winning Stocks

At *Investor's Business Daily*, we've developed an entirely different way to search for winning stocks. That's because after more than four decades of historical research, we know top stocks show definite signs of strength before they become exceptional winners. That confuses people who prefer a bargain—the low-priced, unknown stocks they hope will take off and surprise us all. As we've said, cheap stocks are cheap for a reason: they have deficiencies that don't allow the stock to progress. For a stock to move higher, it needs earnings growth and strong sales, plus several other factors that demonstrate it's emerging as a new leader. If you catch such a stock at the early stages, you will be able to capitalize on its enormous progress.

Remember, the greatest winners of all time, like Cisco Systems and Home Depot, began their biggest price moves after they'd gained leadership in earnings, sales growth, and the other factors described in this book. Some of the critical data you need to start your search can be found in the IBD stock tables.

The unique IBD ratings are a way to spot potential winners before they take off, so it's important that you review these ratings daily. IBD's stock tables are different from anything you'll see anywhere else. Proprietary *SmartSelect* Corporate Ratings speak volumes about each stock's performance and how a stock compares to all the others in our database. The elements in these ratings, which are numbered 1 through 6 in the accompanying chart, are explained in detail here.

┌ **IBD Composite Rating**
  ┌ **Earnings Per Share Growth Rating**
    ┌ **Relative Price Strength Rating**
      ┌ **Sales+Profit Margins+Return On Equity**
        ┌ **Accumulation/Distribution (last 3 mos)**

				52-wk High	Stock	Dividend % Yield	Symbl	Close Price	Chg	Vol% Chg	Vol 1000	P E
▼	▼	▼	▼	▼								

Common stocks above $10 for Friday, March 27, 2009

⑤①②③④   **1. MEDICAL**   ⑥

59	1	87	E	B	-49.4	AMAGPhrm	**AMAG**	36.84	+.10	-55	167	..0
90	88	76	B	B	30.6	Abaxis	**ABAX**	17.72	-.93	-4	267	31
85	84	67	A	D	-60.8	AbbotLa	3.4 r **ABT** ●	46.58	+.13	-5	11m	14⅛
48	50	33	D	D	79.0	AbraxisBn	**ABII**	44.38	-.88	-42	13	99
65	5	93	E	B	-35.7	AcordaTh	**ACOR**	25.11	-1.16	-22	509	..0
75	90	43	B	C	47.5	Aetna	.2 r **AET**	24.50	+.08	-14	6.2m	6⅛

The IBD *SmartSelect*® Corporate Ratings

The one line of information in the IBD *SmartSelect* Corporate Ratings is much more powerful and meaningful than anything you'll find in standard price tables. These ratings, which have been proven to be the most predictive measurements of a stock's possible future value, will narrow your search from over 10,000 stocks to the top investment prospects.

You'll find these ratings are like a condensed statistical summary financial report that looks at the fundamental strength or weakness of a stock. They are also a well-rounded evaluation of each company's general health. Most importantly, along with daily and/or weekly charts, these ratings will help you find better stocks. Let's examine each element.

Earnings per Share Rating Indicates a Company's Relative Earnings Growth Rate

Strong earnings growth is essential to a stock's success and has the greatest impact on its future price performance. The first absolutely vital component of the *SmartSelect* ratings is the Earnings per Share (EPS) rating, which is labeled 1 in the chart.

The EPS rating calculates the growth and stability of each company's earnings over the last three years, giving additional weight to the most recent few quarters. The result is compared with those of all other common stocks in the price tables and is rated on a scale from 1 to 99, with 99 being the best.

Example: An EPS rating of 90 means that a company's bottom-line earnings results over the short and the long term are in the top 10% of the roughly 10,000 stocks being measured.

This one number gives you the relative earnings performance for publicly held companies and the possible prospects for their stocks. It's an objective measure you can use to compare the audited results of one company to those of any other; for example, the earnings growth of IBM to that of Hewlett-Packard, Lockheed, Loews Companies, Wal-Mart, or Apple. Earnings estimates are not used in the calculation because they are personal opinions, which, as you know, might be wrong and do change.

Since earnings power and earnings growth are the most basic measures of a company's success, the EPS rating is invaluable for separating the true leaders from the poorly managed, deficient, and lackluster companies in today's tougher worldwide competition.

The EPS rating is also more meaningful than the widely followed Fortune 500 lists that rank corporations by company size. Size alone rarely guarantees innovation, growth, or profitability. Large companies that are between 50 and 100 years old may have a well-known brand image, but often they are losing market share to younger, more innovative companies that have created newer, better products. Consider the decline of some of our auto companies and their unions, Alcoa, Eastman Kodak, International Paper, Xerox, CBS, Gannett, and Citigroup.

Relative Price Strength Rating Shows Emerging Price Leaders

Since we've learned that the best stocks are superior price performers even before their major moves, you should look for stocks with price leadership. The Relative Price Strength (RS) rating shows you which stocks are the best price performers, measuring a stock's performance over the previous 12 months. That performance is then compared with the performance of all other publicly traded companies and given a 1 to 99 rating, with 99 being best. Look at the column labeled 2 in the chart example.

Example: An RS rating of 85 means the stock's price movement has outperformed 85% of all other common stocks in the last year. The greatest winning stocks since 1952 and even much earlier showed an average RS rating of 87 when they broke out of their first price consolidation areas (bases). In other words, the greatest stocks were already outperforming nearly 90%, or nine out of ten, of all other stocks in the market *before* they made their biggest price gains.

Even in poor markets, a Relative Price Strength rating that breaks below 70 can forewarn you of a possible problem situation. On the sell side, however, we have a ton of sell rules that can lead you to sell most stocks sooner and more effectively than relying on a deteriorating relative strength line that is calculated using the past 12 months' price action. When you compare these fact-based performance ratings to the old, unscientific methods, which were typically based on faulty personal opinions, beliefs, academic theories, stories, promotions, egos, tips, and rumors, it becomes inarguable that IBD's unique factual ratings can give you a more clearheaded edge up in the complex market.

You Need Both Strong EPS and Strong RS Ratings

The implications of both the Earnings per Share rating and the Relative Price Strength rating are considerable. So far, you've been able to determine the top leaders in earnings and relative price strength. The vast majority of superior stocks will rank 80 or higher on *both* the EPS and the RS ratings *before* their major moves. Since one of these is a fundamental measurement and the other is a marketplace valuation, insisting on both numbers being strong should, in positive markets, materially improve your selection process.

Of course, there's no guarantee that a company's terrific past or current record won't suddenly turn sour in the future. That's why you must always use a loss-cutting strategy, such as the sell rules discussed in Chapters 10 and 11. It's also prudent and essential to check the stock's daily or weekly chart to see if it's in a proper base or if it's extended in price too far above its most recent area of consolidation. (For a review of common chart patterns to watch for, refer back to Chapter 2.)

As previously discussed, models of the best-performing companies over the last century showed that earnings growth for the last three years and percent increase in earnings per share for the latest two or three quarters were the two most common fundamental characteristics.

Having hard data like these available to you naturally begs the question, why would you ever invest your hard-earned dollars in a sluggish stock that sports a 30 EPS rating or a 40 RS rating when there are literally thousands of companies with higher ratings, including hundreds with superlative numbers?

It's not that companies with poor ratings can't perform. It's just that a greater percentage of them turn out to be disappointments. Even when a low-rated company has a decent price move, you'll find that the better-rated stocks in the same industry have probably done much better.

In a way, the combination of the EPS rating and the RS rating is similar to A. C. Nielsen's viewer ratings for TV shows. Who wants to continue sponsoring a TV show that gets poor ratings?

Now, pretend for a minute you're the manager of the New York Yankees. It's off-season, and you're going to pick new players for next year's team. Would you trade for, recruit, or sign only .200 hitters? Or would you select as many .300 hitters as possible? The .300 hitters cost you more money; their P/Es are higher, and they sell nearer to their price high. It's true the .200 hitters are available at a cheaper price, but how many games will you win with nine players in your lineup averaging .200? When the bases are loaded in the ninth inning and the score is tied, who would you rather see step up to the plate: a .200 hitter or a .300 hitter? How often does an established .200 hitter blossom into a batting champion?

Selecting and managing a portfolio of stocks is no different from baseball when it comes to performance. To win consistently and finish first in your division, you need a roster of the very best players available—those with proven records of excellence. You won't do as well in your investing if you insist on buying poorer performers and "cheaper stocks," or those with some positive features but three or four little-noticed defects, in the hope of "discovering" a winner. Every little detail separates winners from losers. Hope never works in the market unless you start with a high-quality stock that's begun to build steam. It's the "steam" (earnings, sales, and price and volume strength) that is the key prerequisite for future growth. Don't be fooled by bargain-basement thinking or buy stocks on the way down because they look cheap. Replace your hopes and fallible personal opinions with proven, measurable facts.

It's also interesting to note that these practical, no-nonsense ratings have helped to wake up corporate board members and put pressure on management teams producing second-rate results. A consistently low IBD relative performance rating should be a serious wake-up call to any top management team or board of directors.

Strong Sales, Profit Margins, and Return on Equity Are a Big Clue

Cutting costs may boost a company's earnings for a quarter or two, but powerful, sustained profit increases require healthy sales growth. It's also important to buy companies that make the most of their sales growth. How much profit do they generate from each dollar of sales? How well do they use their capital? The Sales + Profit Margins + Return on Equity (SMR®) rating combines these important fundamental factors and is the fastest way to identify truly outstanding companies with real sales growth and profitability. These are factors that are widely followed by the better analysts and portfolio managers. The SMR rating is on an A to E scale, with A and B being the best. In most cases, you want to avoid stocks with an SMR rating of D or E. See the column labeled 3 on the chart on page 342.

Example: An SMR rating of A puts a stock in the top 20% of companies in terms of sales growth, profitability, and return on equity. During the brief rally that followed the Nasdaq's bear market plunge from March to May 2000, SDL Inc. shot ahead as a leading performer. The maker of components for fiber-optic networks broke out to new highs just as the market confirmed a new uptrend, the most ideal situation for buying a stock. SDL Inc. ran up 112% in just eight weeks. Among its many strong qualities was an SMR rating of A.

For those who may not have always checked your stocks' return on equity, it's important. The table on page 347 of past leaders shows their ROEs.

Accumulation/Distribution—The Influence of Professional Trading on Stocks

Professional investors wield a huge amount of influence over a stock's price. Thus, it's essential that you buy the better stocks that mutual funds are buying and that you sell or avoid the ones they may be selling on a heavy basis. Trying to go against this monumental amount of trading will only hurt your results. A quick, efficient way to keep track of the end result of professional trading is to use IBD's Accumulation/Distribution Rating (the column labeled 4 on the chart on page 342), which is based on daily price and vol-

ROE of Past Leaders

Stock name	Return on equity at the time	Year an up move started	Percent increase to peak
Pic 'N' Save	28.7%	1976	2950%
Home Depot	27.8%	1982	958%
Price Co	55.4%	1982	1086%
Liz Claiborne	42.4%	1984	715%
The Limited	42.3%	1985	451%
This Can't Be Yogurt	41.2%	1985	2073%
Merck	19.8%	1985	870%
Microsoft	40.5%	1986	340%
Cisco	36.3%	1990	74445%
Intl. Game Tech	22.9%	1991	1691%
Nokia	30.9%	1998	8620%
Qlogic	18.8%	1998	3345%
America Online	36.3%	1998	481%
Charles Schwab	29.4%	1998	434%
Coach	43.1%	2002	625%
Chicago Mercantile Exchange	28.2%	2002	915%
Nextel Intl.	56.1%	2003	368%
Google	87.8%	2003	536%
Southern Copper	47.6%	2004	369%
C B Richard Ellis	26.4%	2004	220%
Hansens	43.6%	2004	751%

ume changes. It tells you if your stock is under accumulation (professional buying) or distribution (professional selling). This thoroughly tested, complex, and proprietary formula is highly accurate and is not based on simple up/down volume calculations. Stocks are rated on an A to E scale, with each letter representing the following:

A = heavy accumulation (buying) by institutions

B = moderate accumulation (buying) by institutions

C = equal (or neutral) amount of buying and selling by institutions

D = moderate distribution (selling) by institutions

E = heavy distribution (selling) by institutions

When a stock receives an A or B rating in *Investor's Business Daily*, it means that the stock is being bought on balance. However, this does not guarantee that it will go up. The buying activity is being picked up, but maybe the funds are buying into a questionable position, and what they are doing could be wrong. In some cases, stocks rated as D should be avoided. I would not buy a stock with an E rating. Later, however, if and when the market improves, it could change. C-rated stocks may be OK.

You needn't feel you've missed out on the trading action if you spot heavy buying or selling. Many funds take weeks or even months to complete their positions in a stock or rid themselves of those positions, which gives you time to capitalize on that action. However, be sure to check a daily or weekly stock chart to see if the stock is in the early, beginning stage of a move or if it is overextended in price and too risky or late to more safely buy.

Composite Rating: An Overview

The rating in the first column of the IBD stock tables is the *SmartSelect* Composite Rating, which combines all four *SmartSelect* ratings into a summary rating for quick review of overall performance. Look at the column labeled 5 (page 342). The *SmartSelect* Composite Rating formula is simple:

- Because of the impact of earnings and previous price performance on stock price, double weighting is given to both the Earnings per Share and the Relative Price Strength ratings. This weighting may change somewhat in the future as we continue to improve our ratings. Normal weight is given to the Industry Group Relative Strength, SMR, and Accumulation/Distribution ratings.

- The percent off the stock's 52-week high is also used in the *SmartSelect* Composite Rating.

- The results are then compared to the entire database, and a 1 to 99 rating (with 99 being best) summarizes the five most predictive measurements we've just discussed.

For some stocks, the *SmartSelect* Composite Rating may be higher than the four individual *SmartSelect* ratings. This is because the formula is weighted and includes the stock's percent off its 52-week high.

When you review the stock tables, this simple rating gives you an enormous time-saving edge. Work your way down the columns and look for *SmartSelect* Composite Ratings of 80 or better to spot the potential strong opportunities when you are in an uptrending general market.

The next step is to review all four individual *SmartSelect* ratings: EPS, RS, SMR and Accumulation/Distribution. With a quick scan of the stock tables, you're now that much closer to being sure you are selecting better stocks.

Volume Percent Change Tracks the Big Money Flow

Another important measurement IBD created is Volume Percent Change (see the column labeled 6 on page 342). Most newspapers and information providers on TV and the Web provide only a stock's trading volume for the day, which doesn't tell the entire, meaningful story. Based on the volume information they provide, how would you know whether the volume for all the stocks in your portfolio and those you're considering for purchase is normal, abnormally low, or abnormally high?

In order to know this, you'd have to keep in your head or on paper what the average daily volume is for each stock under review. Instead, you can rely on IBD to keep track of this key measure of supply and demand for you. IBD was the first to provide investors with a Volume Percent Change measure that monitors what the normal daily trading level for every stock has been over the most recent 50 trading days. It pays to always have the most relevant facts, not just a bunch of numbers.

Stocks trade at many different volume levels, and any major change in volume can give you extremely significant clues. One stock may trade an average of 10,000 shares a day, while another trades 200,000 shares a day, and still another trades 5 million shares a day. The key is not how many shares were traded, but whether a particular day's volume activity is or is not unusually above or below average. For example, if a stock with an average trading volume of 10,000 shares suddenly trades 70,000 shares, while its price jumps one point, the stock has increased in price on a 600% increase in volume—generally a positive sign as long as other market and fundamental measurements are constructive.

If this happens, the Volume Percent Change column will show a +600%, which quickly alerts you to possible emerging professional interest in the stock. (In this case, the stock is trading 600% above its normal volume, and if the price is up substantially all of a sudden; this can be a major tip-off.) Volume Percent Change is like having a computer in your pocket to carefully monitor the changing supply and demand for every single stock. Where else can you get such preeminently critical data?

Almost all daily newspapers have cut out essential information in their stock tables. This includes the *Wall Street Journal*, which no longer even shows a stock's trading volume in its daily stock tables.

Volume Percent Change is one of the main reasons so many specialists on the floor of the New York Stock Exchange, professional portfolio managers, top-producing stockbrokers, and savvy individual investors use and refer to IBD's stock tables. There is no better way to track the flow of money into and out of companies, if you know how to utilize these data. If price is all you look at when you check your stocks, you're like a piano player who plays with only one hand, uses only one finger, has never heard of a chord or foot pedal, or doesn't read sheet music, so he never knows when to speed up, get loud, or get softer.

Investor's Business Daily is more than a newspaper. It's also a gigantic radar set that monitors every variable that's important to the successful investor. And it lays all the information out for you daily, both in print and electronically, with the version that's available on the Internet.

The electronic version lets you have the information sooner—within hours after the market closes. Investors who like to prepare for the next trading day find this especially convenient. Others prefer a paper they can carry with them, make notes on, and use as a valuable guidebook.

How to Use *Investor's Business Daily*

Whether she uses the print or the electronic version (or both), each reader probably has a different way of reading the paper. My preference is to start with the front page and then proceed page by page to the end.

Front Page Comes First

The first feature I check on the front page is the short, quick market summaries at the top, above the paper's nameplate. These show price and volume changes for the S&P 500 index, the Dow Jones Industrials, and the Nasdaq, plus brief, two-line comments on market highlights. Brief notes on fixed income, currency, and commodities are also shown.

For example, the comment under NYSE volume reads, "Volume above average, up from previous day." In 40 seconds I look at these briefs to make sure I didn't miss anything important from the day's action.

S&P 500 INDEX	DOW JONES IND.	NYSE VOL. (MIL)	NASDAQ	NASDAQ VOL. (MIL)
845.85	8063.07	1,619	1546.24	2,549
+13.62 (+1.6%)	+106.41 (+1.3%)	+230 (+16.5%)	+31.19 (+2.1%)	+324 (+14.6%)
MasterCard, Akamai explode on upside	GM, Wal-Mart Stores lead blue chip rally	Volume above average, up from previous day	50-day line retaken; chips up for fourth day	Best upside volume since Nov. 21 low

"IBD's Top 10" Stories

The second thing I read on page 1 is "IBD's Top 10," a quick, time-saving way to stay informed. In briefs of only seven to nine lines each, the ten most important new stories are summarized. Today, for example, the number two story tells how same-store sales were down last month at most retail chains, but Wal-Mart's were not only up but better than expected. In the number three spot is "Senate Nears Vote On Stimulus," an update on Congress's efforts to come up with an economic recovery plan.

The Big Picture

The third feature I always check on page A1 is the "The Big Picture" column at the bottom. It's a fairly short but excellent summary of market action and key developments. Inside the column is "Market Pulse," a valuable box that notes leaders that were up in volume for the day and those that were down. The pulse also lets you know whether the market's in an uptrend or a declining phase.

"The Big Picture" column is one of IBD's most highly read features. Dedicated readers have repeatedly told us it has helped them immeasurably in dissecting the general market. In fact, more than a thousand have given testimonials on how it has helped them raise cash when the market began getting difficult or determine when it was starting a major uptrend.

THE BIG PICTURE

Stocks Back Off, But Close With Gains For 3rd Week

BY DONALD H. GOLD
INVESTOR'S BUSINESS DAILY

Stocks ended the week with losses across the board on disappointing economic data and some dour comments from the country's biggest bankers.

The Nasdaq and NYSE composite each tumbled 2.6%, the S&P 500 fell 2% and the Dow lost 1.9%. Losers hounded winners by about 3-to-1.

Volume fell on both major exchanges, providing a bit of relief.

What's more, there were no great collapses by the market's best stocks, and few fell substantially in high volume.

MARKET PULSE

Friday's action:
Profit-taking pushes market lower, but volume also drops

Current outlook:
Market in confirmed rally

Distribution days:
1 for S&P 500, Nasdaq, Dow, NYSE composite

Leaders down in volume:
Accenture^ACN   Longtop
Financial Technologies^LFT
ViaSat^VSAT   Tetra Tech^TTEK

of 2% or 2.6% would be an awful lot. But the market is still volatile.

treated, and rose as the market climbed. No distribution days were logged.

The market closed at or very near the day's high twice, once Monday and again Thursday.

The distribution-day count has fallen for the Nasdaq and S&P 500, to one from two.

Why? The market has climbed more than 10% from the March 16 session, the first distribution day since the March 12 follow-through. As the market rises farther from that bad day, that distribution is less dangerous to the overall uptrend.

Somewhat troubling, the IBD 100 only climbed 4.4% for the

far above average in the morning, but had cooled off by day's end.

Monro Muffler Brake^MNRO fell 7% in busy trade. The chain of service centers and tire shops ended a three-week winning streak.

In economic news, February personal income fell 0.2%, a bit worse than expected. Personal spending rose 0.2%, following January's 1% increase.

The personal consumption expenditure deflator, said to be the Fed's favorite inflation guide, rose 1% in February, higher than expected. Core PCE gained 1.8% in February, topping forecasts.

The Reuters/University of Michigan final index of consumer senti-

© 2009 Investor's Business Daily, Inc.

Top Stories

Finally, I glance at the headlines on the main two front-page stories. I'm a headline reader: if a story is on a subject I want to know about, I read it; if not, I skip it and go to the next page.

The top stories will often show charts or tables. The one I'm looking at has a table of 15 retailers. It shows sales changes for the month plus same-store results and estimates for the future. This quickly tells me three companies in the field are doing excellently, but many others aren't.

To The Point

Page 2 saves a busy executive or investor time. Titled "To The Point," it provides some 50 business briefs, arranged by industry sector, and short summaries on the nation, the world, and the economy. I can quickly scan each headline and read the briefs I'm interested in. There's also a column called "Trends and Innovations" that I always try to read to learn about the new things that keep being invented in today's society.

In the middle is a feature that's particularly valuable to the investor: a half-dozen short stories about companies that reported earnings after the close and how the market reacted in after-hours trading. This is a fast way to make sure you didn't miss anything after the market close.

Leaders & Success

"Leaders & Success" on page A3 is a unique feature that's been in the paper since we started. I always read "Wisdom to Live By"—the short two- or three-line quotes from famous people at the top of the page.

Many people find inspiration on this page. It's about people who have been immensely successful: what they did and how they did it, what they believed in and how they overcame the problems they faced along the way.

10 Secrets To Success

Another element on the page is called IBD's "10 Secrets To Success." A lot of parents teach this to their kids by having them read these little short stories. The 10 secrets start with "How You Think Is Everything: Always Be Positive. Think Success, Not Failure. Beware of a Negative Environment." The second is "Decide upon Your True Dreams and Goals: Write Down Your Specific Goals and Develop a Plan to Reach Them." The third is "Take Action: Goals Are Nothing without Action. Don't Be Afraid to Get Started. Just Do It." The fourth is "Never Stop Learning: Go Back to School or Read Books. Get Training and Acquire Skills." And so on, until you get to the last one, which is "Be Honest and Dependable; Take Responsibility: Otherwise, Nos. 1–9 Won't Matter."

Below the list, one of the 10 secrets is discussed in detail each day. Parents find this is something their children don't get in school, and they use it to help them learn the basic principles of how to succeed in life.

Rounding out the "Leaders & Success" page are two profiles of outstanding people, past and present, and how they succeeded.

Internet & Technology

The next page focuses on "Internet & Technology." Some investors don't spend much time here. But if tech stocks are leading the market, you want to read this section to be on top of the discussions. We have a bureau in Silicon Valley staffed by experienced reporters who've been with us many years. The page they put together is designed not only for investors but for anyone in the tech industry—computer programmers, engineers, systems people, and others.

We have a subscriber who works at a big outfit the government uses to research how inventions might be applicable to defense efforts. One of the firm's top researchers has found that our writers get their facts straighter and understand the technologies better than those on most of the business magazines. We also have CEOs of computer software companies that subscribe to IBD.

Your Weekly Review

There is a feature in the first section called "Your Weekly Review." It includes a table of 35 stocks showing strong weekly gains and a chart on each one. It also includes a story on some of the companies. In a recent story, Paul Whitfield tells how the stocks of Netflix, Edwards Life Sciences, Matrix Initiative, and McDonald's are all acting in a superior way accompanied by interesting news.

Inside Real Estate

The next page I turn to is "Inside Real Estate." I don't normally read this, but somebody who is interested in the real estate market certainly should.

The New America

Next is "The New America" page, devoted to young, entrepreneurial companies. One company gets extensive treatment each day. At the top of the page, we sometimes have short briefs under the heading "AfterMarket." The one I'm looking at is headlined "Neutral Tandem Soars on Q4 Results." It notes that "telecom gear maker Neutral Tandem gapped up 11% in more than seven times average volume" and then quotes what ana-

THE NEW AMERICA

KINROSS GOLD CORP. *Toronto, Ontario*

Rising Prices And New Mines Drive Growth For Canadian Gold Miner

BY MARILYN ALVA
INVESTOR'S BUSINESS DAILY

Gold is looking shiny from a couple of angles.

It's seen as a hedge against economic hardship and a good investment when inflation returns.

Though volatile, shares of major gold miners have performed relatively well as gold prices have risen the past few years.

One of them is Canada's **Kinross Gold**™, which has benefited from rising production and prices.

Three new mining projects started or expanded last year in Russia, Brazil and Washington state are expected to boost Kinross' production by 32% this year vs. 2008, to between 2.4 million and 2.5 million gold equivalent ounces.

Kinross is boosting production at a time when supply is shrinking. Global production of gold – a finite resource – has been declining for years as mines mature and supply

Work at Washington state's Buckhorn mine, one of three growth projects that has helped Kinross Gold.

Kinross Gold	
kinross.com	
Ticker	KGC
Share price	Near 18
52-month sales	$1.41 bil
5-year profit growth rate	n.a.

IBD SmartSelect Corporate Ratings	
Composite Rating	97
Earnings Per Share	64
Relative Price Strength	64
Industry Group Rank	1
Sales+Profit Margins+ROE	B
Accumulation/Distribution	B+
Top Investors.com for more details	

in the face of the global meltdown, ranging between $700 and $1,000 an ounce the past year. Since mid-January, prices have risen to above $900 an ounce from the mid-$800 range.

"We're in a deflationary environment now, but if inflation kicks up, gold prices will likely push up to $1,000 or more," analyst Bridges said.

Gold, he says, could continue to rise if investors lose confidence in

forecast for 2009 to $1,000 an ounce.

However, gold stocks might dull some even if prices stay high. Bridges warns. When investors have enough confidence that the economy is under control and moving in the right direction, money will likely flow back into other types of stocks, he says, putting pressure on gold equities. But that could take a while.

For now, growth in demand for gold as an investment has somewhat offset slowing demand for gold jewelry – particularly in India, a big jewelry-consuming nation hit by a plummeting stock market.

Low Costs Help

Kinross is one of the lowest-cost producers in the industry. That gives it good insurance against volatile, low gold prices," Burt said. Lower fuel costs also help.

In the third quarter, Kinross' cost of sales per ounce of gold equivalent lysts are saying. When these tidbits of unusual activity catch my attention, I'll check them out on my computer and view a chart to see how the stock really looks.

You never know how many ideas you're going to pick up from reading IBD. But in each issue, there will be several you'll want to check out. It takes no time at all to go to your PC, punch in the symbol that appears in the paper right alongside the first mention of the company's name, and check into the history of the stock, its earnings, and a few other key basics. Some of the best portfolio managers in the country quickly check out stocks this way to decide which companies they want to focus on or get more information about. It's a good way to add to your watch list.

Mutual Funds & ETFs

On the first page of the "Mutual Funds & ETFs" section, there are two information boxes I usually check. They zero in on growth funds with excellent records. The boxes show these funds' largest holdings in the latest quarter, along with their top new buys and sells. New buys may be of interest. We also show how the funds have performed relative to the market in each of the last five years. After you've taken the paper for a while, you'll know which are the better funds. One way you can judge is by noting their top positions. If the fund has three or four of the better leaders, I know the managers really know what they're doing.

I don't normally look at our mutual fund tables, but I will frequently check one or two fund families that I know are outstanding to get a feel of how they're doing. We cover far more funds and include more data in our tables than most daily publications. Many papers have sharply cut the num-

Mutual Fund Performance

36 Mos Performance Rating/Fund	4 Wk Net % Chg	Asset NAV Value/Chg	36 Mos Performance Rating/Fund	4 Wk Net % Chg	Asset NAV Value/Chg	36 Mos Performance Rating/Fund	4 Wk Net % Chg	Asset NAV Value/Chg	36 Mos Performance Rating/Fund	4 Wk Net % Chg	Asset NAV Value/Chg
For Thursday, March 19, 2009			B– Hllncome b	0	5.70 +.05	C+ Growth	0	15.47n –.03	C IncFd Am	0	11.66n –.04
—A—			E IntlGrowth	+2	9.15 +.04	B– Income	0	21.50n +.03	D InvCo Am	+1	18.70n –.05
			E IntlVal	+4	8.70 +.10	**Amer Cent A**			D+ Mutual	–1	17.02n –.05
Access Capital Strat			D+ Lrg Cp Grow	+1	15.01 –.15	$ 3.9 bil 800–345–2021			C– New Pers	+2	17.04n +.03
$ 536 mil 617–236–7274			A– Muni CA	–1	10.02 +.09	A+ Divers Bd	+1	10.29	A+ US Gov Sec	+1	14.17n –.01
Commirvmnt +1 9.58n			D+ Muni Natl	0	9.00 +.07	C+ Equity Inc	0	5.35 –.02	D Wash Mut	–1	18.06n –.13
Advance Cap I			A– Muni NY	–1	9.24 +.07	C+ StrAltpMod	+1	4.60 –.03	**American Funds A**		
$ 574 mil 800–345–4783			B+ Qual Bond	–1	8.95 –.01	**Amer Cent Adv**			$ 456 bil 800–421–4120		
B– Retire Inc	–1	7.35n –.02	E Wealth Appr	+2	7.21 –.96	$ 1.6 bil 800–345–2021			D– AMCAP	+3	11.24 –.02
AdvisorOne Funds			**Alliance Brnstn Adv**			A Infftn Adj	+3	10.98n +.05	C Balanced	+1	12.54 –.08
$ 542 mil 866–811–0225			$ 2.8 bil 800–221–5672			**Amer Cent Instl**			B Bd Fd Am	–1	10.56 –.01
E Amerigo N	+3	7.75n –.03	E IntlVal	+4	8.87n +.10	$ 5.2 bil 800–345–2021			C+ CapIncBldr	0	37.73 –.01
AIM Funds A			E Wealth Appr	+2	7.22n –.96	A+ Divers Bd	+1	10.29n	C– CapWld G&I	+3	23.60 +.06
$ 17.2 bil 800–959–4246			**Alliance Brnstn B**			C+ EquityIncoma	0	6.36n –.02	A– CapWrldB&I	+2	18.34 +.18
E BasicValue b	+2	11.60 –.21	$ 2.0 bil 800–221–5672			C– StrAlloMod	+1	4.66n –.03	C– EuroPac Gr	+3	25.62 +.11
E CapDvlp b	+2	9.21 –.06	D+ Bal Wealth b	+1	7.77n –.13	**Amer Cent Inv**			0+ Fundmntl	+3	23.03 +.09
C Charter b	+1	10.52 –.12	**Alliance Brnstn C**			$ 34.8 bil 800–345–2021			D Gr Fd Amer	+3	19.39 +.91
E Constlam b	–6	14.93 –.17	$ 3.2 bil 800–221–5672			C+ 1ChoicsMod	–1	8.18n –.04	B– High Inc Muni	0	12.01 +.05
C– Develp Mkts m	+6	15.23 +.10	D+ Bal Wealth x	+1	7.76n –.13	C+ Balanced	0	11.37n –.09	C+ High Income	–2	7.71 +.02
C+ Energy b	+8	25.29 +.88	B GlobIBond	–1	6.58+.02	B CAHi Yld	–1	8.45n+.05	C IncFd Amer	0	11.74 –.04
D Euro Grwth m	+2	18.15 –.05	**Alliance Brnstn I**			A– CA LgTmHsFi	–1	10.23n+.05	A Interm Bond	0	12.75 –.02
C– GlbHlthCare b	–8	18.42 –.35	$ 2.7 bil 800–221–5672			A CA TxFreeBd	–1	10.76n +.05	C IntlGr&Inc	+3	21.15 +.07
D– GlbSmMidGr	+3	10.16 –.04	E GlbREsIII x	+5	4.89n –.11	A+ Divers Bd	+1	10.29n	D– InvCo Am	+2	18.78 –.04
C– Intl Growth	+2	17.30 –.03	E IntlValue	+4	8.76 +.11	D– EquityGrow	–2	13.19n –.18	A LtdTax Ex	–1	14.71 +.07
D Lrg Cap Gr b	–2	7.54 –.01	B+ Intmd Dur	–1	13.32n –.02	C+ EquityInc	0	5.35n –.02	C– Mutual	+1	17.17 –.04
C MidCore Eq b	–1	14.60 –.14	**Allianz A**			C Giftrust	+4	15.92n –.14	D New Econ	+3	14.70 –.06
A– Muni Bond b	0	7.55 +.05	$ 4.7 bil 800–426–0107			A+ Ginnie Mae	+1	10.67n +.01	C New Pers	+2	17.31 +.03
E Real Estate b	+5	10.32 –.55	E NFJ Div Val x	–1	7.50 –.17	B GlbI Gold Eq	+5	15.93n+.94	C+ New World	+4	29.09 +.13
D Sml Cap Gr b	+2	15.49 –.07	D+ NFJ IntlVal x	+4	12.11 +.04	A– Govt Bond	+1	11.26n –.01	E ShrTermBd	0	9.89 –.02
A+ US Govt	+2	9.09 –.02	C– NFJ SmlCpVal	–1	16.25 +.03	C– Growth	+1	15.35n –.09	E Sm Cp Wrld	+2	18.% +.06

ber of funds they follow. Besides current activity, we include the four-week percentage change and a 36-month performance ranking for each fund. We also include the phone number for each fund family.

A couple of tables in the fund section are unique. One shows how big-cap growth funds are doing compared with small-cap growth funds. The other compares growth funds to value funds. This is important for you to know in any market: Are growth stocks leading, or are value stocks? Are big caps leading, or are small caps? Here you have the answers at a glance. In the edition I have, growth is leading.

Leading Fund Sectors

You also need to know the broad, overall sectors that are in demand. So, on Fridays we have two tables showing the top industry and sector funds. On other days, different fund types are displayed. If you're interested in what industries are doing well, you can see here that gold has been doing well in

BIG-CAP GROWTH FUNDS VS. SMALL-CAP GROWTH FUNDS			
Funds in Big-Cap Index:	**Largest positions of funds in Big-Cap Index:**		
Amer Century Ultra Inv	MastrCd	IBM	RepnSvc	ExxonMb:
Marsico 21st Century	Micrslt	Apple Inc	Cisco	HomeDp
Fidelity Blue Chip Growth	WalMrt	PeopUtd	WellsFg	EntpsPrd
Rs Large Cap Alpha A	AbbotLabs	Mnsnto	ProctGm	Visa n
Vanguard Growth Index	Costco	Qualcm	PhilMor n	HewlttPk

GROWTH FUNDS VS. VALUE FUNDS			
Funds in Growth Index:	**Largest positions of funds in Growth Index:**		
Rs Large Cap Alpha A	Haemonetic	SilgnHld	CHRobn	ProctGm
Vanguard Growth Index	SouthwstEn	FLIR Systms	WalMrt	PhilMor n
Lkcm Small Cap Equity Instl	Micrslt	IBM	RepbSvc	OSI Pharmac
Federated Kaufmann K	AbbotLabs	PeopUtd	WstCnn	PSS World
Franklin Small Mid Cap Gr A	FstSolar	DresserR	PrecCast	Allergan

When the line is heading up, Big-Cap Growth Funds are outperforming Small-Cap.
APR JUL OCT JAN 2009

When the line is heading up, Growth Funds are outperforming Value Funds.
APR JUL OCT JAN 2009

Top Industry & Sector Funds

Best % change in last 4, 8 & 12 weeks on a total return basis.
★ indicates fund is on 3 different weeks' lists.

Mutual Fund		% Change	$ Net Assets
Best % Change Last 4 Weeks:			
Amer Cent Inv Glbl Gold Eq	★	+ 9	719 mil
Van Eck Intl Gold A	★	+ 9	436 mil
Tocqueville Gold	★	+ 9	555 mil
Fidelity Sel Med Eq & Sys		+ 8	1.1 bil
First Eagle Gold A		+ 7	726 mil
Fidelity Sel Medcl Dlvry		+ 7	265 mil
Best % Change Last 8 Weeks:			
US Glob Inv WrldMineral		+ 31	292 mil
Van Eck Intl Gold A	★	+ 29	436 mil
USAA Prcs Metals	★	+ 28	879 mil
Tocqueville Gold	★	+ 27	555 mil
Rydex Investor Prec Metals	★	+ 26	149 mil
Oppenheimer A Gold&SpMin		+ 25	1 bil
Best % Change Last 12 Weeks:			
USAA Prcs Metals	★	+ 56	879 mil
Van Eck Intl Gold A	★	+ 56	436 mil
Amer Cent Inv Glbl Gold Eq	★	+ 55	719 mil
Rydex Investor Prec Metals	★	+ 54	149 mil
Tocqueville Gold	★	+ 51	555 mil
Frank/Tmp Fr A Gold & Prec		+ 50	878 mil

Top Industry & Sector Funds

Best % change in last 16 & 39 weeks on a total return basis.
★ indicates fund is on 3 different weeks' lists.

Mutual Fund		% Change	$ Net Assets
Best % Change Last 16 Weeks:			
Van Eck Intl Gold A	★	+ 40	436 mil
Amer Cent Inv Glbl Gold Eq	★	+ 39	719 mil
USAA Prcs Metals	★	+ 37	879 mil
Fidelity Sel Gold		+ 36	1.7 bil
Evergreen A PreciousMtl		+ 35	420 mil
Tocqueville Gold	★	+ 34	555 mil
Oppenheimer A Gold&SpMin		+ 34	1 bil
Gamco AAA Gold		+ 32	367 mil
Frank/Tmp Fr A Gold & Prec		+ 31	878 mil
DWS Scudder S Gold & Prec		+ 30	227 mil
Rydex Investor Prec Metals	★	+ 29	149 mil
US Glob Inv GlbGoldMtl		+ 26	154 mil
Best % Change Last 39 Weeks:			
Eaton Vance A WW HlthSci		+ 1	887 mil
Frank/Tmp Fr A Biotch Dsc		+ 1	291 mil
Fidelity Sel Biotechnlgy		— 1	1.2 bil
Putnam A GlbHlthCre		— 10	996 mil
Vanguard Health Care		— 10	10.8 bil
Blackrock A HealthSciOp		— 10	418 mil
Fidelity Sel Pharm		— 13	166 mil
First Eagle Gold A		— 14	726 mil
Schwab Health Care		— 14	523 mil
FBR SmFinl Inv		— 15	180 mil
Fidelity Sel Med Eq & Sys		— 16	1.1 bil
ICON Healthcare		— 17	147 mil

© 2009 Investor's Business Daily, Inc.

the last 4-week, 8-week, 12-week, and 16-week periods. The medical field shows well in the longer, 39-week table.

Issues & Insights

At the back of the first section, you'll find our editorial pages, titled "Issues & Insights." We have an outstanding staff of a half-dozen highly experienced writers turning out up to six editorials a day. I do not write these. Wes Mann, our distinguished and talented editor, who has been with IBD from the beginning, is in charge of this key area and is assisted in the important role it plays for IBD readers and the nation by Terry Jones, who has also been with IBD since its start-up 25 years ago. Terry came to us from *BusinessWeek*. I'll normally read two or three of the editorials after checking the headlines and summary paragraphs to see if I'm interested in the subject.

We also have columns from guest writers plus syndicated columnists "On the Left" and "On the Right," so you get different points of view. On the right, I always respect the work of Thomas Sowell and Victor Davis Hanson. Both are older, experienced observers with great insight. Sowell, from Stanford's Hoover Institute, is in my view the best, most accurate economist and historian in America. He has a book out entitled *Applied Economics: Thinking beyond Stage One*, one of 42 books he has written. From Washington, we run columns by conservative Charles Krauthammer and liberal David Ignatius, who is well informed on international issues.

But the first thing I look at each day in "Issues & Insights" is the cartoon. We have the best editorial cartoonist in the nation, Michael Ramirez. He won a Pulitzer Prize for *Investor's Business Daily* in 2008—the second time he had received this prestigious award.

IBD also has an extensive public polling operation, conducting monthly surveys on economic confidence, presidential leadership, and major national issues year-round and daily tracking polls in election years. In 2008, for the second presidential election in a row, the IBD/TIPP poll not only came closest to the final margin between Barack Obama and John McCain, but was right on the money. These feats, tantamount to hitting a bullet with a bullet, have earned the IBD/TIPP poll, conducted by TechnoMetrica Market Intelligence, the honor of being America's most accurate.

Making Money

In the "Making Money" section, starting on page B1, we try to cover the relevant facts, skills, and rules you need if you are to be a successful investor. We view *Investor's Business Daily* as an educational medium. We don't tell people what to buy. We don't recommend stocks or tout "10 stocks that are going to go up tomorrow." We just explain time-tested rules based on models of successful stocks in all of past history and provide sound techniques and methods for managing your portfolio wisely.

We also give classes and several levels of paid workshops, from beginning to very advanced, on investing; in addition, we have a chart school, have several books out, including this fourth edition of the one you're reading, and offer a home study course. We view our mission as being to teach anyone who wants to learn how to become a better investor and protect himself so he doesn't get hurt in bear markets.

NYSE + Nasdaq Stocks On The Move

The first thing I read on page B1 is the "NYSE + Nasdaq Stocks On The Move" tables—a feature that's in no other publication. We have a massive computer database that each day screens for those stocks that had the greatest increase in trading volume over and above their average daily volume in the last three months. This isolates the true demand for securities you would not otherwise notice. On these lists, you'll find many new, innovative companies with names you may not know. But if they appear frequently, you'd better find out what they're doing or making. They could be the next Microsoft or Apple.

In this current issue, Visa is on the NYSE list. It was up 4.6 points on a volume increase to 239% more than normal for the credit card company. Visa just reported earnings during a bearish period. There were also a few medical stocks on the lists.

In addition to price and volume change, the tables show the same company variables IBD shows in its main stock tables. For example, IBD shows the Earnings per Share rank of Visa as 99, meaning its earnings growth rate in the last three years and in recent quarters puts it in the top 1% of all companies in our database. This doesn't mean the stock's going to go up. But it certainly means it has characteristics worth checking if you're hunting for entrepreneurial stocks that might outperform in a future better market.

We boldface those names on this list that have Earnings per Share and Relative Strength ratings of 80 or higher, meaning they're in the top 20% of all stocks based on those measurements. The stocks with stronger records are the ones you want to investigate.

Below the list of stocks that advanced for the day is a list of stocks that were down in price. They too are ranked by percentage increase in volume. You can judge the market environment and how well our new government is doing by how many stocks are on the upside versus how many are on the downside. In the example shown, the table has eight NYSE stocks on the upside versus 30 on the downside, meaning there were more stocks that day with greater-than-normal volume that dropped in price than that increased

NYSE + Nasdaq Stocks on the Move

Stocks with high volume vs. 50-day avg., reflecting heavy institutional action. 80 EPS & 80 RS or better are **boldfaced**.

SMARTSELECT® COMPOSITE RATING (NYSE)

EPS Rnk	Rel Str	Acc Dis	52-Wk High	NYSE Stock	Stock Symbol	Closing Price	Chg	Vol (1000s)	Vol% Chg
94	99	76 B-	89.84	Visa n o	V	53.74	+4.61	24,135	+239
94	94	75 B-	37.40	Aeropostl o	ARO	22.81	+1.68	4,176	+53
96	86	87 C	29.11	AtmosEngy o	ATO	25.40	+0.77	810	+42
91	95	95 B-	87.88	CmpsMn o	CMP	63.45	+1.57	969	+30
92	96	72 B	105.1	NobleEnr o	NBL	53.44	+1.47	3,044	+18
99	99	98 B	59.45	ScOmMra o	SQM	29.30	+0.72	1,134	+15
97	91	74 D+	60.00	ITCHldgs	ITC	42.57	+0.80	552	+15
99	91	94 B+	52.00	MedcoHlth o	MHS	48.50	+1.77	3,832	+10
48	45	57 C+	40.75	I D E X Corp o	IEX	21.51	-1.56	2,874	+399
80	83	70 B-	50.04	RegalBel	RBC	31.07	-1.92	1,689	+345
57	53	49 C+	35.81	SonocoP o	SON	20.47	-3.22	2,433	+247
90	80	68 B-	30.95	BurgerK o	BKC	20.51	-1.35	4,775	+230
79	59	63 D+	63.77	CocaCFmsa	KOF	33.49	-1.10	540	+203
72	59	55 D	34.53	Unilever o	UN	21.10	-0.87	7,453	+162
98	94	93 B	171.4	TerraNit	TNH	122.5	-4.55	228	+158
90	78	96 B	32.50	FamlyDlr o	FDO	26.63	-1.68	9,139	+126
55	77	35 E	86.91	Credicorp o	BAP	37.61	-0.54	895	+123
90	84	81 C+	65.54	ChrchDwt o	CHD	52.50	-1.45	1,319	+113
98	93	77 B-	73.73	NovNrdk o	NVO	52.73	-0.85	525	+102
76	98	42 B-	83.81	ContiRes n o	CLR	21.09	-0.90	2,779	+94
76	91	61 D	68.09	RoperInd	ROP	39.50	-0.75	1,572	+88
75	59	57 C+	34.89	Unilever Plc	UL	20.74	-0.58	2,042	+86
19	42	8 D-	99.46	Orix	IX	21.27	-1.21	256	+82
81	53	82 D	31.26	BrklyWR o	WRB	24.55	-0.51	2,617	+70
98	98	71 B-	81.59	NwOriEd o	EDU	52.00	-2.00	894	+65
84	63	76 C+	92.13	Exelon o	EXC	57.11	-0.57	6,002	+64
95	89	93 B-	67.44	Sunoco o	SUN	41.12	-3.79	6,913	+63
84	78	69 D-	50.00	AON o	AOC	36.45	-0.96	5,307	+63

SMARTSELECT® COMPOSITE RATING (Nasdaq)

EPS Rnk	Rel Str	Acc Dis	52-Wk High	Nasdaq Stock	Stock Symbol	Closing Price	Chg	Vol (1000s)	Vol% Chg
98	99	86 B	23.00	NeutTand n	TNDM	17.74	+1.77	1,583	+818
85	82	82 D+	45.00	Blkboard o	BBBB	29.01	+4.68	1,951	+532
99	96	95 B-	31.05	TowrGp o	TWGP	26.78	+1.80	1,860	+382
99	91	90 A-	64.47	ShireLtd o	SHPGY	46.14	+0.57	1,763	+179
88	85	86 C+	41.56	RossSts o	ROST	30.63	+2.38	5,257	+135
99	75	99 B-	85.40	MyriadGn o	MYGN	83.61	+0.50	1,469	+62
99	95	99 D+	45.07	LifePtnrs	LPHI	38.91	+2.47	196	+52
99	96	91 B-	73.59	Biognldec o	BIIB	53.28	+0.53	4,843	+31
94	99	91 B-	144.3	Priceline o	PCLN	72.67	+1.91	1,779	+29
98	75	89 B	47.96	AlexionPhr o	ALXN	39.18	+1.36	1,046	+23
97	75	99 C+	24.08	Crucell o	CRXL	20.60	+0.62	373	+23
99	92	98 B+	33.84	HMS Hld o	HMSY	34.12	+0.99	430	+18
86	89	80 C	106.3	Itron Inc o	ITRI	60.72	+0.53	842	+15
99	85	95 C+	49.06	Allegiant o	ALGT	34.38	+1.38	637	+15
98	95	86 A-	36.95	Synaptics o	SYNA	25.84	+0.59	1,804	+14
96	91	98 D+	33.43	Thoratec o	THOR	27.17	+0.63	1,775	+12
84	75	97 C+	61.24	FuelSys o	FSYS	27.04	+1.29	785	+10
91	98	61 D+	50.00	ConcurTch o	CNQR	22.77	-2.46	8,955	+788
94	84	90 B-	44.32	DollarTree o	DLTR	35.03	-6.72	12,381	+476
44	72	32 D	60.24	Varian o	VARI	26.91	-2.04	1,091	+302
99	89	89 C	47.94	QualtySys o	QSII	35.23	-1.88	1,975	+299
94	82	97 A	29.21	MultFnElc o	MFLX	19.02	-1.00	646	+297
88	72	72 B	44.10	PanAmSlvr o	PAAS	16.60	-1.45	5,480	+255
80	76	57 C	42.58	Dentsup o	XRAY	26.88	-0.57	5,920	+194
81	82	62 B-	80.60	Dionex	DNEX	49.52	-1.22	408	+180
38	48	22 D	64.22	AdvsrBrd	ABCO	16.59	-1.07	303	+150
99	82	96 A-	39.29	Athenahlt n o	ATHN	35.38	-1.82	1,166	+134

in price. This zeroes in on the daily supply and demand for leading securities. It was a bearish day.

I've found this computer screen to be valuable. For it to fail to pick up a new big leader is almost impossible. But you've got to do your own homework to understand some of these names you might not know. IBD also tries to cover these companies in our various columns.

How's The Market?

Page B2 is titled "How's The Market?" It is loaded with absolutely crucial data. We present the four key general market indexes—the NYSE composite, Nasdaq, S&P 500, and Dow Jones Industrials—in large, easy-to-read charts. We stack them one on top of the other so you can compare them and see which indexes are stronger and if one index diverges from the others at some point. At this time, we note that while all the indexes were in a negative trend in January, the Nasdaq was down only 2%, less than the others, implying it is the leader at this stage in a difficult market.

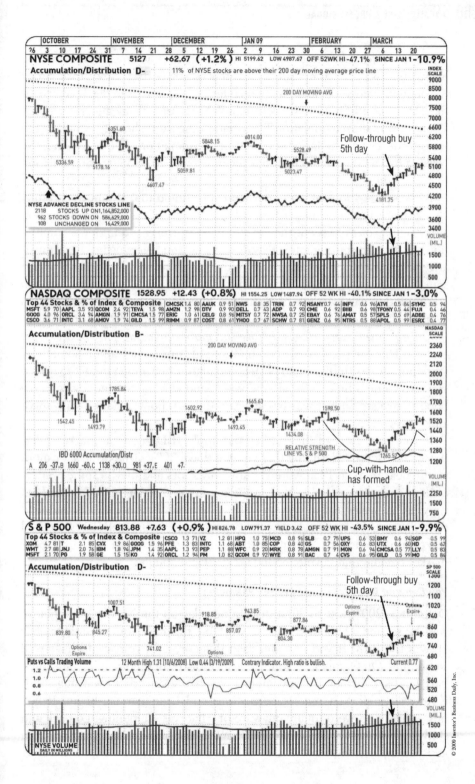

We also have relative strength lines, moving average lines, and a line just below the NYSE Composite chart that displays the New York Stock Exchange advance-decline line, which let's you quickly see day by day over the last six months if more stocks on the NYSE were advancing or declining. There's even an Accumulation/Distribution measure showing which of the major indexes has the largest amount of accumulation. At this reading, the Nasdaq had a "B–," meaning it has recently enjoyed stronger accumulation than the others.

B2 is a page I look at every day, and you should too. I want to carefully check the recent price and critical volume activity of the leading indexes on a day-by-day basis to see if they're still in an uptrend and under accumulation or if they're shifting into a new downtrend and behaving in a highly negative way. Don't neglect the daily volume; it's the key that can tell you if something is going wrong. If you study and learn to interpret the general market indexes correctly, which can take some time, you will learn how to avoid most of the serious declines *because the increased distribution always shows up in the early stages, before the more damaging part of a decline evolves*. This can preserve a good bit more of your money and is something it's definitely worth striving to perfect, no matter how much time it may take you. How much time, after all, did you spend earning the money you now hope to invest? So is it worth your time to learn how to skillfully preserve and protect it?

If you learn to read the market and apply IBD's general market rules, there's no excuse for finding that you are down 30%, 40%, or 50% or more in any bear market. I know most public investors and maybe some readers of the paper were possibly hurt in the market correction of 2008. But IBD supplied the rules and information. If readers did their homework and read the "The Big Picture" column, they should have seen that IBD's method picked up the adverse activity in the earlier stages of the emerging bear market decline that developed in late 2000 and 2008.

You Can and Must Learn to Spot the Following

October 3, 2007, was the first distribution day on the Nasdaq, October 11 was the second, October 15 and 16 were the third and fourth, and October 19 was the fifth. If you saw and read this correctly, you would have sold something. On October 24 you had a sixth distribution day, and you should have cut back further. By November 1, you had seven crucial warnings. This is how all important market corrections and bear markets begin. If you missed this and were totally unaware of what was happening, go back and study all the market-top charts in Chapter 9 until they make sense to you and you understand what you must look for in the future. Many investors have discovered they need to take charge, get serious, and learn the basics of sound, successful investing. You can do far better in the future.

IBD Mutual Fund Index

There is another unique feature on page B2 you can't find in other daily publications—the "IBD Mutual Fund Index," where we pick two dozen leading growth funds and show their composite performance in a graphic display. I use this as a supplementary index because it is in a way a giant advance-decline line of some of the better funds with a combined 1,000 to 2,000 or more stocks owned among the 24 funds. When I've seen a classic, well-formed cup-with-handle pattern in this index, preceded by a strong prior uptrend to the pattern, the index and the market have almost always moved up.

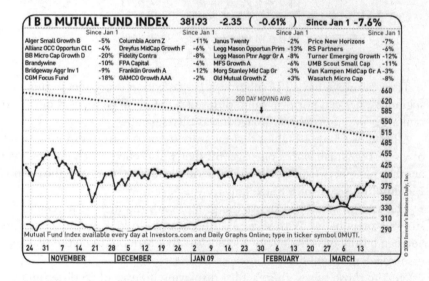

| I B D MUTUAL FUND INDEX | 381.93 | -2.35 | (-0.61%) | Since Jan 1 -7.6% |

	Since Jan 1		Since Jan 1		Since Jan 1		Since Jan 1
Alger Small Growth B	-5%	Columbia Acorn Z	-11%	Janus Twenty	-2%	Price New Horizons	-7%
Allianz OCC Opportun Cl C	-4%	Dreyfus MidCap Growth F	-6%	Legg Mason Opportun Prim	-13%	RS Partners	-6%
BB Micro Cap Growth D	-20%	Fidelity Contra	-8%	Legg Mason Ptnr Aggr Gr A	-8%	Turner Emerging Growth	-12%
Brandywine	-10%	FPA Capital	-4%	MFS Growth A	-6%	UMB Scout Small Cap	-11%
Bridgeway Aggr Inv 1	-9%	Franklin Growth A	-12%	Morg Stanley Mid Cap Gr	-3%	Van Kampen MidCap Gr A	-3%
CGM Focus Fund	-18%	GAMCO Growth AAA	-2%	Old Mutual Growth Z	+3%	Wasatch Micro Cap	-8%

Mutual Fund Index available every day at Investors.com and Daily Graphs Online; type in ticker symbol 0MUTI.

| 24 | 31 | 7 | 14 | 21 | 28 | 5 | 12 | 19 | 26 | 2 | 9 | 16 | 23 | 30 | 6 | 13 | 20 | 27 | 6 | 13 |
| NOVEMBER | | | | | | DECEMBER | | | | JAN 09 | | | | | FEBRUARY | | | | MARCH | |

© 2009 Investor's Business Daily, Inc.

IBD's 197 Industry Sub-Group Rankings

On this jam-packed page, we also have IBD's "197 Industry Sub-Group Rankings." This list shows a composite rating for each sub-group and each sub-group's change from the previous day, plus where the group ranked three and six weeks and seven months ago. The top 20 and bottom 20 sub-groups are circled because they represent the best- and worst-performing industries.

By now, you should know I am not going to own anything in the bottom 20 because we've proven over many years that these industries are going to be having a lot of trouble. On the other hand, we know that most of the leading areas of a positive market will show up in the top 20.

| Rank | | | | | Subgroup % Chg | Daily |
| 3 | 6 | 7 | | | Comp. | Since | % |
This Wk	Wks Ago	Wks Ago	Mo Ago	Industry Name	Rating	Jan 1	Chg
1	60	38	78	Metal Ores–Gld/Silvr	90	+4.1	+1.7
2	2	8	83	Comml Svcs–Schools	95	+8.1	+0.4
3	8	12	57	Medical–Genetics	..	+16.4	+0.9
4	4	10	98	Coml Svcs–Scrty	90	–4.7	+0.1
5	18	20	80	Medical–Ethical Drgs	89	+1.7	+0.6
6	15	33	23	Telecom–Wirlss Eqp	90	–2.2	+1.7
7	3	2	134	Comptr Sftwr–Mdcl	94	–7.3	–1.4
8	7	4	133	Utility–Water Supply	89	+0.3	+0.6
9	12	14	43	Medical–Biomed/Bth	89	+5.2	+1.3
10	28	54	112	Fnancepbl Inv Fdbnd	..	+14.2	+0.3
11	6	9	118	Insrnce–Prp/Cas/Titl	81	–9.7	+1.1
12	1	1	197	Trnsprttin–Airlne	67	–22.8	+3.7
13	10	19	104	Retail/Whlsle–Food	84	–0.4	+0.2
14	17	26	77	Utility–Elctric Pwr	87	+0.3	+0.7
15	16	21	45	Utility–Gas Dstribtn	88	+1.6	+1.3
16	14	22	94	Rtail/Whlsle–At/Prts	85	–4.0	+2.7
17	72	89	101	Oil&Gas–Trnsprt/Pip	87	+16.4	+1.0
18	35	106	145	Oil&Gas–Rfing/Mkt	90	+15.9	–0.1
19	24	48	191	Mdical–Hlth Mnt Org	92	+10.5	+3.6
20	13	5	99	Cmml Svcs–Cnsltng	90	–6.8	+0.7

The reason we have 197 subgroups is that within every sector, there are segments that can perform quite differently. Medical genetics is our third-ranking group. Seven months ago it was fifty-seventh.

All told, we have 10 tables that measure industries from different points of view. Two small boxes on page B2 that I also check each day give you another perspective on which industries are leading. One shows the "Top 10 Fidelity Industry Funds Since Jan. 1."

The second small box shows the groups with the highest percentage of stocks at new highs. With several different ways to look at market sectors, you can hardly miss the one or two sectors that turn out to be the real leaders in each new bull market.

Next to those boxes, there's a list displaying indexes of 28 different market sectors and how each performed for the day.

IBD Industry Themes

On page B3, we have another way of keeping track of industries—a daily column called "IBD Industry Themes." In every market, there are certain leading themes. Investors may be buying medical stocks, for example, or technology stocks. So what are the themes in the current market?

We also have a column on New York and Nasdaq stocks and one for the long-term investor. Another three columns (on page B5) include "The Base Reader," which analyzes various chart patterns, "The Income Investor," and "International Leaders," covering the foreign markets. I don't read all these

Groups Highest % Of Stocks At New High

Tobacco	11%
Retail/Wholesale-Food	11%
Finance-Mortgage&Rel Svc	9%
Computer Software-Medical	8%
Retail-Home Frunshngs	7%
Retail/Wholesale-Auto/Prts	6%
Retail-Super/Mini Markets	5%
Internet-Network Sltns	5%
Computer-Integrated Syst	5%
Retail-Clothing/Shoe	2%

Top 10 Fidelity Industry Funds Since Jan. 1

1.	Wireless	+17%
2.	Netwk&Infr	+11%
3.	Telecommun	+10%
4.	Gold	+8%
5.	Electronics	+7%
6.	Natural Gas	+7%
7.	Energy Svcs	+6%
8.	Commequip	+5%
9.	Computers	+4%
10.	Natural Res	+4%

Market Indexes list sorted by % gain in last 3 months. (★ on left, top 4 indexes since Jan. 1 on right, top 4 indexes yesterday.)

Since Jan 1	3 Month % Change	Index	Value	Change	Yesterday's % Change
+ 8.30% ★	+21.51%	Gold Index	91.31	+ 3.97	+4.55% ★
+ 9.71% ★	+ 9.95%	High-Tech Index	323.42	+ 2.95	+0.92% ★
- 4.42% ★	- 1.23%	Amex Composite	1335.74	+ 8.01	+0.60% ★
- 5.93% ★	- 4.44%	Nasdaq OTC Comp	1483.48	- 7.74	-0.52%
- 9.44%	- 7.31%	IBD New America Index	161.96	- 2.13	-1.30%
-11.01%	- 7.68%	Value Line Index	1250.09	- 4.17	-0.33%
-11.00%	- 7.77%	New Issues Index	220.72	- 1.56	-0.70%
-11.14%	- 7.99%	S&P Midcap 400	478.33	- 2.82	-0.59%
- 9.36%	- 9.52%	Senior Growth Index	394.71	- 3.19	-0.80%
-11.17%	- 9.89%	Dow Jones Utility	329.33	+ 2.77	+0.85% ★
-12.37%	-10.23%	Defensive Index	872.86	- 5.95	-0.68%
- 9.83%	-11.11%	Consumer Index	604.03	- 3.83	-0.63%
-11.29%	-11.19%	Medical/Healthcare	2870.64	-102.20	-3.44%
-13.20%	-11.44%	S&P 500	784.04	-10.31	-1.30%
-14.24%	-12.11%	N.Y.S.E. Composite	4937.22	-38.08	-0.77%
-17.26%	-13.76%	Russell 2000	413.26	- 4.37	-1.05%
-15.67%	-13.99%	Dow Jones Industrials	7400.80	-85.78	-1.15%
-19.19%	-15.30%	S&P 600	217.16	- 2.50	-1.14%
-19.16%	-15.90%	U.S. Defense Index	494.43	- 7.06	-1.41%
-25.44%	-22.01%	Dow Jones Trans	2637.27	+ 4.79	+0.18%
-26.77%	-24.14%	N.Y.S.E. Finance	2818.02	-116.34	-3.96%
-29.17%	-26.86%	Bank Index	279.23	-25.81	-8.46%
-33.63%	-30.90%	Insurance Index	220.72	- 9.74	-4.23%

Today's general market highlights:

Energy dominated Thursday's list of top-performing groups. Crude jumped $3.47 to $51.61 a barrel, continuing oil's recent rally. Production cuts and oil companies' reduced investments have pinched supply, countering lower global demand.

© 2009 Investor's Business Daily, Inc.

columns. But I do read the headlines, and if a quick glance tells me a column is talking about some situation I'm interested in, I'll read it.

2,500 Leading Stocks (NYSE + Nasdaq Research Tables)

A powerhouse element we've added recently is the way we organize and display our one-of-a-kind stock tables. We call them "Research Tables" because we have a boatload of data on each company. IBD follows up to 2,500 stocks, combining New York and Nasdaq stocks in one table, whereas some of our competitors carry only 1,000 stocks and have nothing close to the critical ratings and data we provide for each company.

Right off the bat, you'll see that our "2,500 Leading Stocks" tables starting on page B3 are organized in order of the strongest of 33 broad economic sectors. Almost everyone else's tables are organized alphabetically. For decades, Americans used the stock tables in their local newspaper or in one of our financial competitors just to look up where their stocks closed yesterday: "Was my General Motors up, or was it down?" While it's nice to be able to check how your stock did, these days you can get quotes anywhere on the Web. What *we're* doing is making the tables an advanced research lab to help you discover the next big leading stock you'll want to invest in. Here's what we're able to do with how *we* display the tables.

This particular issue confirms what we saw in other tables: that the "Medical" sector is number one. Then we show every one of the stocks in the medical field, listed alphabetically. Each has a composite rating, which goes from 0 to 99, with 99 being the very best. This is an overall rating that considers key individual ratings. (Of course, this current rating could decline if our government succeeds in its attempt to rewrite all the rules and decide how it wants to run our entire medical system.)

If you spot a stock that looks interesting, we have given you the stock symbol, and you can go to Investors.com and check out the chart or other vital facts and figures, using a handy checklist to flesh out what you've uncovered in the tables.

As I scan the tables, I look for stocks that are boldfaced. Here, too, we boldface anything that's up one point or more or is making a new high in price. I'm mainly interested in keeping track of price movements so I don't miss anything that might turn out to be a huge new leader. The boldfaced stocks can be scanned very quickly, and if you're using charts, you may already be aware of the patterns of some of the ideas you notice in the tables. For example, if you go through a number of charts every week, looking for sound patterns with strong fundamentals, and you scan the bold-faced stocks in the tables daily, you'll see a bolded stock whose chart you were impressed with start to move up.

When I spot unusual activity by high-ranked stocks, I tend to write down the symbol at the top of the B1 page. When I get through scanning the tables, I may have eight or ten symbols that I'll check out because they look interesting based on their price activity and high ratings. You can go right to Investors.com or Daily Graphs Online and evaluate the chart to see if the stock is acting right or acting poorly.

So rather than using the tables just to find out how my stocks did yesterday, I'm using them to screen for potential ideas that might become super leaders at some point in the future. For any serious investor, this is almost a necessity if you are going to improve your performance.

"You Can Do It Too"

At the top of page B4, we have something called "You Can Do It Too." These are short quotes by investors who have written to tell us they've done well and what their main observations were. I realize there are a number of people who probably aren't so successful or who haven't done their homework, didn't follow rules, or didn't have any system. Many of these quotes, however, are inspiring.

It's interesting that more than 1,000 people have written to tell us that they've finally figured out how to put it all together to achieve outstanding results. I say "finally" because it takes some time and effort to get truly superior results. There are no free lunches in the stock market. But once you understand and apply yourself, you could in time become financially independent. Would that be a worthy goal for you to strive for and achieve?

"Stocks in the News"

A section that I also check every day is what I call the "mini-charts" in the "NYSE Stocks in the News" and "Nasdaq Stocks in the News" sections. We used to show 20 or more charts in this screen, but we've now limited it to 10 because we've refined and improved the sorting mechanism. And what we've learned is that, once you're in any future bull market, these two lists will materially outperform the S&P 500 and any new names on the charts will be well worth your checking.

If you're in a bear market, don't expect these lists to work. Three out of every four stocks will be going down in such an environment, and growth situations can have significant corrections. But if you know you're in an uptrending market, and this is confirmed by the "The Big Picture" column, these mini-charts—each of which is packed with 20 key statistics—can be a source of high-probability new ideas. They won't all work. But when you're in a positive market, you follow up on the ideas that work. Sooner or later, if you're patient, a market will develop into a strong bull market. And when that happens, these are definitely screens you want to check out thoroughly. If you do your homework, you then have a better chance of materially improving your performance.

Over time, I've found that the first six or seven sectors in our stock tables will contain most of the new leaders. I've also found that just

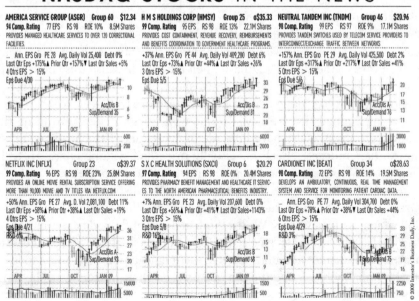

NASDAQ STOCKS IN THE NEWS

because some of the sectors in the back half haven't been leaders recently doesn't mean that some of them won't later possibly become turnarounds. Lower-ranked and poor-performing sectors in this issue are Computer— Hardware, Savings & Loans, Apparel, Machinery, Media, Steel, Real Estate, and Semiconductors.

These rankings can shift over a period of weeks or months. But it pays to know what's leading now and which names within each sector have the best fundamental and market-action variables. That's where you want to concentrate your research.

These tables may take a little time to get used to. But after a few weeks, you'll know where your stocks are listed. To make it easier, we also have a table that lists all of IBD's 197 subindustries and tells you which of the 33 broad sectors each subindustry belongs to.

One thing that most of us fail to do, but that I would highly encourage you to do, is read the box (usually on page B7) that explains the various ratings and measures and how they're computed and used. By doing this, you will understand how best to utilize these advanced, very sophisticated tables that could hold the key to dramatic success or improvement in your future.

Below the how-to-read box is a short list of "do's and don'ts"—in other words, what you should be doing to avoid the classic errors people sometimes make when they're investing without doing their due diligence.

IBD Timesaver Table

The "IBD Timesaver Table" on the same page is a feature many busy people like to use because it picks up all the high-ranking stocks that were up or down in price in a short table that includes volume and some other rankings. I always check this and take particular note of the "Stocks Down" list. I want to be aware of the stocks that have been hit hard because this could affect others in the same industry. If a stock shows up repeatedly on this list, it could be that it has topped and is headed for more trouble.

I've mentioned that we have 10 different ways you can zero in on the leading groups. We also have little sector charts under the heading "Leading Market Indexes." Each has a daily price and volume chart. Hi-tech, Junior Growth, Leisure, and Consumer Sectors now top the list.

Alongside, we have the "New Highs" list. This list has also been reorganized. We weren't interested in just showing which stocks made new highs and which made new lows. We list them in order of the industry sectors that had the largest number of stocks making new price highs. When you get into a strong bull market and find that, say, the medical sector continues to lead, it will probably be among the top one, two, or three sectors with the most stocks making new highs.

IBD TIMESAVER TABLE

Combined summary of key price action for NYSE & Nasdaq highest-rated stocks, a quick and easy snapshot for busy investors. Stocks up at least 1 point or making new highs, and stocks down 1 point or making new lows are boldfaced. Sorted by Composite Rating, IBD's single most useful fundamental and technical gauge.

SMARTSELECT® COMPOSITE RATING
— EARNINGS PER SHARE
— RELATIVE PRICE STRENGTH
— INDUSTRY GROUP RELATIVE STRENGTH
— SALES+PROFIT MARGINS+ROE
— ACCUMULATION/DISTRIBUTION

STOCKS UP

Comp	EPS	RPS	Ind	Sls	Acc	52-wk High	Stock & Symbol	Close Price	Chg	Vol% Chg	Vol 1000	P E
99	99	86	A	A	B–	40.3	Ebix rEBIX	24.67	+3.86	+273	309	10
99	97	94	A–	A	C+	27.2	Netease rNTES	22.23	+1.14	+180	3.2m	13o
99	97	85	A+	A	C+	57.6	GileadSci GILD	45.43	+1.00	–6	8.7m	20o
99	96	98	A	A	A– NH	ScherPlg SGP	24.21	+1.89	+142	49m	13o
99	95	98	A	A	B NH	HMSHld HMSY	35.33	+1.45	+77	725	44o
99	92	84	A	A	D+	81.4	Cephalon CEPH	66.32	+1.92	–5	1.8m	13o
99	77	99	A+	B	A–	33.5	AmItPastan AIPC	32.09	+1.37	–1	427	14o
98	99	97	A–	A	A– NH	NeutTandn TNDM	20.96	+.08	+151	1.1m	28
98	99	86	A–	A	B+	382	Baidu rBIDU	172.7	+3.26	–32	1.7m	36o
98	99	75	A	A	D+	77.4	Celgene CELG	48.20	+1.04	+14	6.9m	30o
98	94	95	B+	B	C+	18.7	BeaconRfg BECN	12.65	+1.27	+169	1.7m	10o
98	93	83	A–	B	D+	52.0	MedcoHlth MHS	40.98	+2.26	+4	4.5m	17o
98	92	98	A–	A	B–	38.2	Shandalnt rSNDA	36.31	+1.21	+23	1.0m	13o
98	88	97	A–	A	B–	67.0	EdwdLfSci rEW	61.40	+2.33	+23	759	23o
98	88	97	A+	A	B+	31.0	CmptrPr CPSI	27.75	+1.54	+71	328	19
98	87	91	A	A	B–	48.7	Teva TEVA	35.39	+1.09	+18	8.1m	16o
98	87	87	A+	A	C+	62.4	GenProbe rGPRO	44.86	+1.21	–29	515	23o
98	72	98	A–	A	B	35.9	CardioNetn BEAT	28.63	+1.55	+197	905	77o
98	45	98	A	B	B NH	Pegsys rPEGA	17.23	+.85	+197	566	57
97	89	95	A	B	D–	39.1	EmergMedS EMS	31.35	+1.70	–13	174	15

STOCKS DOWN

Comp	EPS	RPS	Ind	Sls	Acc	52-wk High	Stock & Symbol	Close Price	Chg	Vol% Chg	Vol 1000	P E
97	99	80	B–	B	B+	58.0	PowellInds POWL	32.53	–2.60	+12	102	12
97	94	63	B	A	A–	42.6	NasdaqOMX NDAQ	22.27	–1.66	+12	4.4m	11o
96	99	76	B	A	B–	89.8	Visan V	52.05	–2.04	+35	12m	21o
95	96	79	C	A	B–	87.9	CmpsMn CMP	53.43	–8.24	+100	2.3m	10o
94	95	76	B–	A	C	145	Mnsnto rMON	79.11	–2.58	+3	9.0m	18↑
93	90	79	B	A	C+	66.2	Stericycle SRCL	48.42	–2.16	+55	1.8m	27o
92	88	74	B–	B	B	66.8	Syngenta SYT	37.52	–3.47	+233	2.6m	11o
86	92	70	B+	B	C	66.9	PrefrmLn PLPC	39.00	–3.00	+225	18	12
84	82	47	B	A	B+	526	CMEGrp rCME	198.2	–2.80	+7	1.6m	11o
84	67	69	B+	B	B	69.2	PhillD PHI	42.61	–5.14	+88	339	10x
82	78	71	C+	B	B–	100	OcciPet rOXY	54.69	–1.77	–4	8.8m	6o
75	94	39	B	A	D–	67.7	AlliancDta rADS	30.78	–1.72	0	2.3m	6o
75	30	83	A	B	C+	355	FairfxFnl FFH	241.0	–5.51	–27	48	3o
73	77	40	C+	A	C+	95.2	Contango rMCF	36.64	–1.66	–31	105	5o
65	40	66	B+	B	D+	168	ArdGpA ARDNA	91.69	–3.27	–73	0.3	11k
63	80	52	C–	C	B–	713	WashPost WPO	344.3	–10.61	+4	42	10
63	69	60	B–	D	C+	13972z	BrkHaA BRKA	83950	–2150	–23	1	13
62	45	51	A	B	C	249	Blackrck BLK	108.0	–3.20	–17	710	16o
57	69	59	B–	D	D–	4700	BerkHaB BRKB	2742	–39.00	–20	37	13
55	39	66	B–	B	E	1975	Seaboard SEB	933.0	–6.00	–36	0.7	7

When high technology was leading in the bull market of the 1990s, the computer sector was number one for a year and a half. Stocks like Cisco and Dell were constantly on the new-high list. If you knew what you were looking for, and you understood the significance of a stock's displaying new highs in a bull market, maybe you too could have participated when these stocks were going up 10 times or more. There's a lot you can learn by studying past markets. We are historians.

In other words, it's hard *not* to notice the real action and the real leaders in the market. They are as obvious as the elephant that jumps into the bathtub and splatters water all over the place. When a whole sector is moving, the sheer volume and broad-based activity cannot be hidden. We saw this in the energy sector from 2004 to 2007, when virtually all oil and gas stocks were moving up dramatically.

At some point, all sectors change. And when they do, the 10 different ways we have to pick up leaders and laggards will point you in a direction where you can say, "Those stocks are no longer leading the way they did before." If you just go on emotions and your attachment to a stock, you can get into a lot of trouble. You need precise measurements to tell you if this sector or that security is really behaving properly.

Company Earnings Reports

IBD's earnings reports feature stock symbols, industry groups, percent above or below consensus estimates, and EPS and Relative Strength Ratings. Earnings growth greater than 25%, a key characteristic of winning stocks, is boldfaced. The whole line is boldfaced when EPS growth is more than 25%, EPS Rating more than 85, and earnings are stronger than expected. Arrows indicate acceleration or deceleration in earnings or sales growth compared with the prior quarter. Data reported may be derived from 6-, 9- or 12-month reports. All earnings represent the current quarter. Foreign companies are not reported. Nonrecurring items may be excluded from earnings per share. Unique circumstances are taken into account for many industry groups. Sales may not apply for certain industries. Real estate investment trusts may reflect EPS or funds from operations.

Company Name	Symbol	Industry	Closing Price	Curr Qtr Erns	Prior Yr's Qtr Erns	EPS %Chg	Under /Over Est %	Sales (Mil)	Sales % Chg	EPS Rtg	Rel Str Rtg

94 Ups

Company Name	Symbol	Industry	Closing Price	Curr Qtr Erns	Prior Yr's Qtr Erns	EPS %Chg	Under /Over Est %	Sales (Mil)	Sales % Chg	EPS Rtg	Rel Str Rtg
Hill–rom Holdings	HRC	Medical–Systems/Eqp	12.71	0.25 vs	0.22	+13.6↓	+25	352	+3.0↓	63	15
Horace Mann Educ	HMN	Insrnce–Prp/Cas/Titl	9.92	0.51 vs	0.49	+4.1↓	+16	221	-0.2	86	70
I Two Technologies	ITWO	Comptr Sftwr–Entr	7.48	r0.31 vs	0.26	+19.2↓	+41	63.8	+0.8	64	43
IMS Health	RX	Comml Svcs–Hlthcre	15.49	0.50 vs	0.43	+16.3↓	0.0	581	-4.1	81	71
Infinity Ppty&Cslty	IPCC	Insrnce–Prp/Cas/Titl	39.44	1.78 vs	1.16	+53.5↑	+109	200	-25	73	86
Isilon Systems Inc	ISLN	Elec–Smicondctr Mfg	2.89	-0.04 vs	-0.11	..	..	31.8	+19↓	38	40
Kellogg	K	Food–Msc Prparation	43.68	0.47 vs	0.44	+6.8↓	-6.0	2933	+5.0↓	76	73
Knoll Inc	KNL	Hsholdoffic Furnitr	7.37	0.52 vs	0.42	+23.8↓	+27	276	-2.0	92	25
Luminex	LMNX	Medical–Systems/Eqp	21.97	0.05 vs	-0.08	+163↓	-17	28.2	+31↓	67	97
Mastercard Inc Cl A	**MA**	**Financial Srvcs–Misc**	**159.8**	**1.87 vs**	**0.89**	**+110↑**	**+15**	**1225**	**+14↓**	**99**	**71**
Maximus	MMS	Cmml Svcs–Cnsltng	37.89	r0.67 vs	0.56	+19.6↑	+1.5	180	+1.7↓	56	95
Mednax Inc	MD	Mdcal–Outpnt/Hm Cr	37.26	0.85 vs	0.80	+6.3↑	+9.0	298	+19↑	73	68
Merit Medical Syst	MMSI	Medical–Products	16.77	0.20 vs	0.17	+17.6↓	0.0	58.0	+6.7↓	78	88
Metavante Tech	MV	Fnancial Srvcs–Misc	16.48	0.36 vs	0.28	**+28.6**	-2.7	433	+6.2↑	79	68
Micros Systems Inc	MCRS	Cmptr–Intgrtd Syst	15.09	0.37 vs	0.34	+8.8↓	+5.7	238	-2.5	88	38
Microtune Inc	TUNE	Elec–Smicondctr Mfg	1.79	0.04 vs	0.03	**+33.3**	+100	24.0	+5.5↓	39	27
Micrus Endovasculr	MEND	Medical–Products	9.61	-0.07 vs	-0.28	..	..	18.3	-0.1	53	56
Multi Fineline Elec	MFLX	Elec–Cmpnent/Cntr	19.02	0.56 vs	0.54	+3.7↓	+9.8	217	+18↓	82	97
N C R	NCR	Cmptr–Intgrtd Syst	10.44	0.58 vs	0.54	+7.4↓	+7.4	1421	-6.6	82	19
National Bkshrs VA	NKSH	Banks–Southeast	18.15	0.52 vs	0.46	+13.0	+4.0	14.9	-1.1	72	86
Neutral Tandem Inc	**TNDM**	**Telecom–Services**	**17.74**	**0.25 vs**	**0.06**	**+317↑**	**+32**	**34.9**	**+41↑**	**99**	**86**
Newbridge Bancorp	NBBC	Banks–Southeast	2.18	-0.53 vs	-0.67	..	..	32.0	-16	13	11
Nutrition 21	NXXI	Cosmetics/Persnl Cre	.19	0.01 vs	-0.06	**+117**	..	12.9	-1.1	31	28

© 2009 Investor's Business Daily, Inc.

One last thing: earnings are what drive a stock, and the rate of earnings improvement is more important than the P/E ratio. So, you want to make sure you check the "Company Earnings Reports" that come out at certain times during a quarter. You can discover a company that's suddenly showing much better earnings than in the past.

It helps to be up on stocks that come through with better-than-expected earnings—what the Street refers to as "earnings surprises." What we have learned to watch for are stocks whose earnings estimates are constantly being raised and that show an acceleration in their percentage rate of increase in earnings quarter by quarter. As mentioned earlier, the bigger the earnings increase, the better. And we don't fall into the trap of eliminating any stock just because its P/E ratio looks high.

To wrap up the paper, we cover more futures and options than most publications. There's a column on the bond market, several interest-rate charts and tables, and no fewer than 36 charts on commodities futures.

Key Commodity Futures

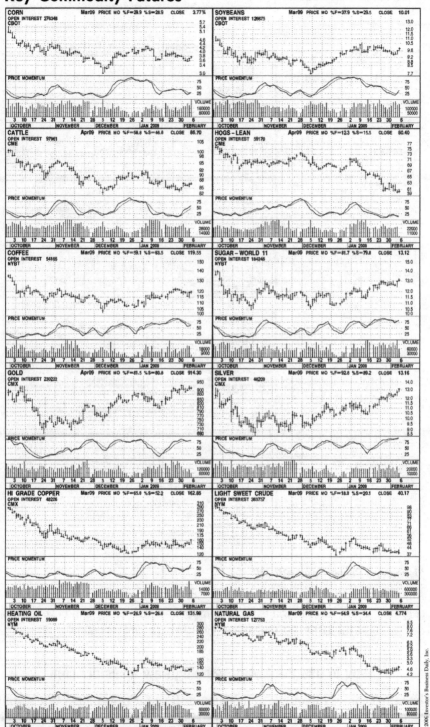

369

Money Rates

Prime Rate: 3.25
Base interest rate charged by major U.S. commercial banks on loans to corporations.

Discount Rate:
Primary..0.50
Secondary..1.00
Rate charged by Federal Reserve System on loans to depository institutions

Broker Call Loan Rate: 2.00
Rate charged on short-term loans to brokerage dealers backed by securities.

Federal Funds Target Rate: 0.00-0.25
Rates on overnight loans among financial institutions.

Certificates of Deposit:
1 months..0.87
3 months..1.37
6 months..1.82
1 year...2.27
Interest rate paid by dealers for certificates of deposit based on the duration of the security.

Jumbo CDs:
1 month...0.87
3 months..1.46
6 months..1.94
1 year...2.39

London Interbank Offered Rate:
3 months..1.24
6 months..1.77
1 year...2.09
The average of rates paid on dollar deposits.

Treasury Bill Auction Results:
3-months (as of Feb. 2)...........................0.270
6-months (as of Feb. 2)...........................0.390
Average discount rate for Treasury bills in minimum units on $10,000.

Treasury Bill:
1-year, (as of Feb. 2)..............................0.49
Annualized rate on weekly average basis, yield adjusted for constant maturity.

For Friday, February 6, 2009

Bonds Summary

	Domestic		All Issues	
	Fri	Thu	Fri	Thu
Issues traded	2	1	2	1
Advances	2	1	2	1
Declines	0	0	0	0
Unchanged	0	0	0	0

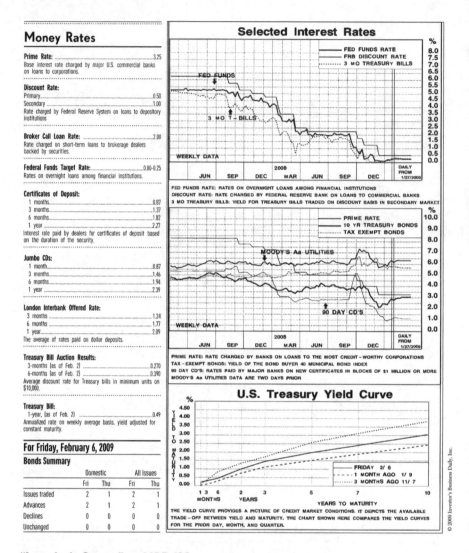

"Investor's Corner" and IBD 100

Among other IBD features, "Investor's Corner" is a popular daily educational column for anyone who wants to learn more about investing. And every Monday we show the IBD 100, with charts on 100 high-ranked potential prospects.

How to Use the Award-winning New Investors.com

Investors.com is the online companion to *Investor's Business Daily's* print edition. Like the newspaper, it helps you quickly and confidently apply the investing strategy outlined in this book. Whether you have just a few minutes each day or you're investing full-time, you can develop an effective routine that fits your schedule using the tools and features found on Investors.com.

We discussed the ways *Investor's Business Daily* starts the research process with an efficient assessment of the market, industry groups, and stocks. Here are some additional ways to dig deeper in your research with IBD's specially designed screening tools and charts.

If you're reading this book to hone your investing skills, going through these tools in the following manner will help you develop an easy daily system for reviewing the market, top industries, and, finally, the top stocks.

The IBD Stock Research Tool on the home page of Investors.com is structured to let you do just that from one central location. As you can see from the graphic on this tool, you can use it to follow "Market Direction" and to "Find," "Evaluate," and "Track" leading stocks. Following this approach will help you find the best stocks, will let you know the right time to buy and sell, and could materially improve your results.

The key is to take some time to become familiar with the investing tools and features on Investors.com. The CAN SLIM chapters in this book will help you understand the rationale for IBD's investing tools, which are programmed to search for companies with the performance characteristics typical of emerging stock market winners.

Market Direction

As discussed, three out of four stocks usually follow the overall market trend, whether it's up or down. That's why it's critical for you to learn to follow, not fight, the market. Within the "Market Direction" tab, you'll find links to features that will help you do just that.

Start by taking another look at the "The Big Picture" and "Market Pulse" to see what stage the market is currently in. You can also click on the "Indexes" link to view the latest charts for each of the major indexes. The charts are updated throughout the trading day with a 20-minute delay.

For timely analysis of the market action as it happens, read the "Markets Update," featuring intraday reports. You'll find concise insights that put the day's events into perspective, plus highlights of leading stocks making a big move.

IBD TV: "Market Wrap" Regularly watching the IBD "Market Wrap" video is a good way to stay on top of the market and improve your analytical skills. Available hours after the close each trading day, this short video uses charts to visually show you how the market and leading stocks are acting, and what trends and potential buy points to look out for.

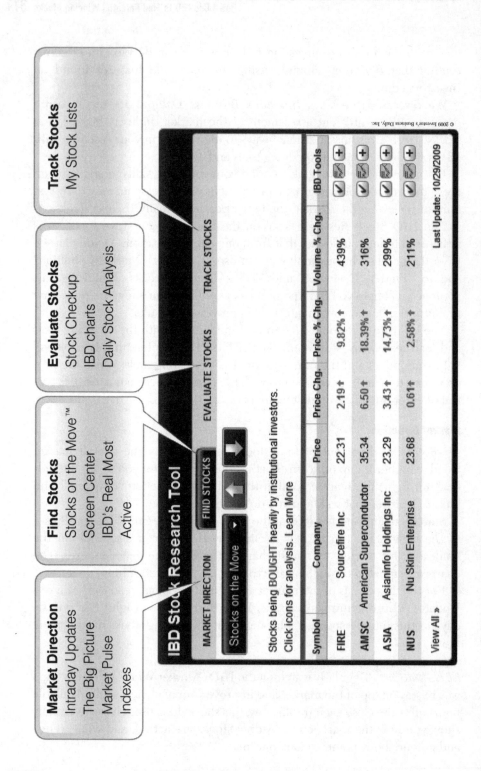

Market Direction
Intraday Updates
The Big Picture
Market Pulse
Indexes

Find Stocks
Stocks on the Move™
Screen Center
IBD's Real Most
Active

Evaluate Stocks
Stock Checkup
IBD charts
Daily Stock Analysis

Track Stocks
My Stock Lists

IBD Stock Research Tool

MARKET DIRECTION | FIND STOCKS | EVALUATE STOCKS | TRACK STOCKS

Stocks on the Move ▸

Stocks being BOUGHT heavily by institutional investors. Learn More
Click icons for analysis.

Symbol	Company	Price	Price Chg.	Price % Chg.	Volume % Chg.	IBD Tools
FIRE	Sourcefire Inc	22.31	2.19 ↑	9.82% ↑	439%	
AMSC	American Superconductor	35.34	6.50 ↑	18.39% ↑	316%	
ASIA	Asianinfo Holdings Inc	23.29	3.43 ↑	14.73% ↑	299%	
NUS	Nu Skin Enterprise	23.68	0.61 ↑	2.58% ↑	211%	

View All »

Last Update: 10/29/2009

Find Stocks

Once you've reviewed the current market conditions, use the "Find Stocks" tab to look for new investing ideas. Here you'll find a wide range of idea-generating screens in addition to those in the IBD print edition.

"Stocks on the Move™"–Learn What the Institutions May Be Buying and Selling as It Happens This is the online version of the IBD print edition feature. As we've mentioned earlier, just looking at typical most-active lists won't give you the whole picture. You need to know about the emerging institutional trades that are beginning to show promise.

These stocks will appear on this radar screen, which is updated continuously throughout the trading day. You can quickly spot the stocks that institutions may be moving into—or out of—in a major way as it happens. Remember that institutional buyers who are taking a position in a stock usually buy in huge quantities, which may create major volume in the stock.

Nearly every winning stock will show this type of activity at the onset of its price advance. You don't want to miss this screen if you are searching for emerging leaders. Remember that not all the stocks shown on this list will be winners. It's important to check further to make sure the stock's chart looks sound and the ratings show leadership potential. This is a good way to spot the breakout of a stock as it is happening or shortly thereafter.

Intraday Volume Percent Change–Another Way to Spot Possible Winners A key element of the online version of "Stocks on the Move" is the *intraday* volume percent change. As we've seen, a stock needs support from institutional buying to propel it further. Volume percentage changes on an intraday basis will tell you—as it is happening—if a stock is trading above or below its average daily volume of the last 50 trading days. That's a sign of institutional buying (or selling) and a key component of "Stocks on the Move." You can also get the intraday volume percent change for any stock you're looking at on the "Stock Quotes" page of Investors.com.

"Screen Center" Click on the "Screen Center " link to pull up the latest "Screen of the Day." Each day, there's a different list that sorts the entire stock database looking for potentially superior stocks based on important performance criteria.

To access additional stock lists, click on "Screen Center" in the drop-down menu within the "Stock Research" tab on the Investors.com home page. You'll find more possible ideas from lists including "CAN SLIM Select," "IBD 100," "Sector Leaders," "Tech Leaders," and "Long-Term Investor." This is a quick way to find leaders and the better possible ideas in different categories. You can then check weekly or daily charts on these potential ideas plus earnings and sales data to pick the best ones to add to your watch list.

Most Active—NYSE and Nasdaq This daily column (also found in the print edition) highlights breakouts and basing patterns in the best institutional-quality stocks experiencing unusually heavy trading volume. You'll also find a discussion of potential buy points that indicate the best time to make initial and secondary purchases. This column will also flag potentially negative action as stocks reach their peaks.

Evaluate Stocks

Next, let's look at how you can evaluate any stocks you already own or are thinking of buying. There are many questions that should first be answered:

- Is this the right stock to own? Or are there better ones in its group?
- Is the stock in a leading industry group or a laggard one?
- If you own the stock, have you held it too long?
- If the stock looks fundamentally strong and you want to invest in it, is it too soon or too late?
- Are we in a bull market or a bear market?

These are just a few questions that need to be answered before you make your move. Two IBD investing tools—"IBD Stock Checkup®" and "IBD Charts"—will help you sort through the stock-picking puzzle.

"IBD Stock Checkup®" "IBD Stock Checkup" evaluates and compares more than 6,000 publicly traded companies and assigns a composite rating and a pass, neutral, or fail grade to put your ideas in the proper perspective. It's essentially a statistical summary report made up of several components, including

- Composite Rating
- Performance Within Group
- Group Leaders
- IBD Stock Checklist—with a pass, neutral, or fail grade

● **Red Light, Green Light**

For the composite rating and most of the components listed in "IBD Stock Checkup," you'll see a green (pass), yellow (neutral), or red (fail) icon. This is a quick and easy way to see if your stock passes muster in that particular category based on time-tested CAN SLIM criteria.

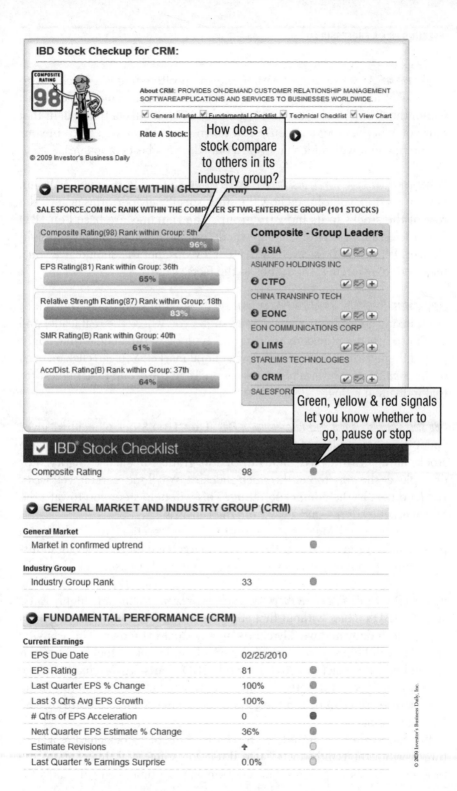

IBD Stock Checkup for CRM:

COMPOSITE RATING 98

About CRM: PROVIDES ON-DEMAND CUSTOMER RELATIONSHIP MANAGEMENT SOFTWAREAPPLICATIONS AND SERVICES TO BUSINESSES WORLDWIDE.

☑ General Market ☑ Fundamental Checklist ☑ Technical Checklist ☑ View Chart

Rate A Stock: ➤

How does a stock compare to others in its industry group?

© 2009 Investor's Business Daily

⊙ PERFORMANCE WITHIN GROUP (CRM)

SALESFORCE.COM INC RANK WITHIN THE COMPUTER SFTWR-ENTERPRSE GROUP (101 STOCKS)

Composite Rating(98) Rank within Group: 5th	**96%**
EPS Rating(81) Rank within Group: 36th	65%
Relative Strength Rating(87) Rank within Group: 18th	83%
SMR Rating(B) Rank within Group: 40th	61%
Acc/Dist. Rating(B) Rank within Group: 37th	64%

Composite - Group Leaders

❶ ASIA   ☑ ✉ ➕
ASIAINFO HOLDINGS INC

❷ CTFO   ☑ ✉ ➕
CHINA TRANSINFO TECH

❸ EONC   ☑ ✉ ➕
EON COMMUNICATIONS CORP

❹ LIMS   ☑ ✉ ➕
STARLIMS TECHNOLOGIES

❺ CRM   ☑ ✉ ➕
SALESFOR...

Green, yellow & red signals let you know whether to go, pause or stop

☑ IBD° Stock Checklist

Composite Rating	98	⊙

⊙ GENERAL MARKET AND INDUSTRY GROUP (CRM)

General Market

Market in confirmed uptrend		⊙

Industry Group

Industry Group Rank	33	⊙

⊙ FUNDAMENTAL PERFORMANCE (CRM)

Current Earnings

EPS Due Date	02/25/2010	
EPS Rating	81	⊙
Last Quarter EPS % Change	100%	⊙
Last 3 Qtrs Avg EPS Growth	100%	⊙
# Qtrs of EPS Acceleration	0	⊙
Next Quarter EPS Estimate % Change	36%	⊙
Estimate Revisions	✦	○
Last Quarter % Earnings Surprise	0.0%	○

Composite Rating As we discussed earlier, the composite rating is a quick way to know whether you should move ahead or not. With the color-coded icons within the "IBD Stock Checklist" (see page 375), it's like a traffic light that tells you whether to go (green), slow down (yellow), or stop (red) in your research, and it will guide you toward only the very best companies.

Performance Within Group—Buy the Best Stocks in the Top Groups In the "Performance Within Group" section, you can see how the stock specifically performs against the rest of the stocks in its industry group. The rankings are based on IBD *SmartSelect* ratings. This will help you determine if you're making the right choices. It's easy to be swayed by news or TV tips, but this should give you a major edge by forcing you to stick to the facts.

Group Leaders—Pointing You Toward Real Potential Leadership No matter what you've bought or are thinking about buying, this screen shows you where the real leadership is. These are the stocks exhibiting the type of performance that might propel them further in an uptrending general market. You can click on each of the *SmartSelect* ratings to see which stocks in the group rank highest for that individual rating.

"IBD Stock Checklist" Is Your Stock Pass, Neutral, or Fail? The "IBD Stock Checklist" gives you a thorough review of the fundamental and technical strength of each stock, along with a pass, neutral, or fail grade for each category. For example, at the very top of the stock checklist, you'll see a green, yellow, or red icon next to the composite rating. This will help steer you toward the true market leaders—and away from the laggards.

In the "General Market and Industry Group" section, you'll also get a pass, neutral, or fail grade for the general market and for the relevant industry group. Do not buy stocks when the general market flashes a red signal.

IBD Charts Show You the Right Time to Buy or Sell You never want to buy any highly rated stock in IBD's tables without first checking a chart, and it pays to regularly review both daily and weekly charts on any stocks you own. This is a vital step that will help you spot emerging trends and track a stock's movement so you know the exact time to buy or sell. IBD charts are designed to make it easier and faster for both new and experienced chart readers to get the real picture. You can obtain these daily and weekly charts that are free on Investors.com.

For those who are intimidated by charts, think of a stock chart as a "picture worth a thousand words." It will tell you some vital things about the progress (or lack of progress) of any company. In time, you will find your

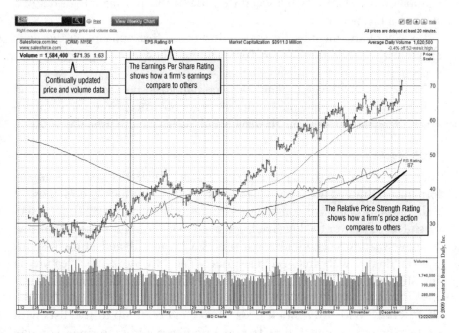

review is quite automatic. Daily charts can also help you spot possible future winners. IBD daily charts include the following:

- Up days in price in blue; down days in red
- Continually updated price and volume data
- EPS and RS ratings
- Relative Price Strength line
- 50- and 200-day moving averages of price

Refer again to Chapter 2 to learn to recognize chart patterns. You may also want to consult the "IBD University" section of Investors.com for a course on chart analysis. Also remember that the majority of stocks tend to follow the overall trend of the market, so be sure to check current market conditions, as discussed earlier, to confirm that your overall timing is correct.

Weekly Charts—Tip-Off to Institutional Trading IBD weekly charts will help you gauge institutional buying. Since mutual funds typically take days, if not weeks (and sometimes longer), to build (or unload) their positions, any heavy volume on the chart may tell you if they're possibly moving into or out of a stock in a major way.

Weekly charts include the same information that appears on the daily charts, with the addition of shares outstanding. These charts span nearly two years of price and volume movements.

To capture the biggest gains, it's important that you use both daily and weekly charts, since they offer different views on a stock. You will get more exact timing indications from the dailies and the big picture from the weeklies.

Track Stocks

Once you've evaluated and purchased a stock, it's crucial that you track its performance. "Buy and hold" is a dangerous strategy, as *all* stocks—even those of well-known, established companies—can be volatile and risky. To be a successful investor over the long haul, you need to keep all your losses small and to know when to sell and take your profits. Chapters 10 and 11 discuss how you can do that with time-tested sell rules. The "My Stock Lists" feature on Investors.com will help you stay organized so you can apply them effectively.

"My Stock Lists" With "My Stock Lists," you can create up to five lists with up to 50 stocks on each list. To stay organized and save time, you can

create different lists for different purposes. For example, you could create a "My Portfolio" list for the stocks you own, a list of "Stocks in Bases" for leading stocks that are currently forming a base, and a "Near a Buy Point" list for stocks that are approaching a proper buy point. It's important that you review and manage your lists regularly, adding and deleting stocks as needed.

To help you track the performance of your stocks, the "My Biggest Price Movers" feature automatically alerts you to the stocks on your lists that are making the biggest price moves, up or down.

"My Stock Lists" also gives you one-click access to "IBD Stock Checkup," IBD charts, and IBD archives for each stock. Use IBD archives to read what IBD has written about the companies you're watching; it can provide valuable insight into the story behind the stock. Use "IBD Stock Checkup" and IBD charts to continually evaluate both the stocks you own and those you're watching.

● **"My Routine": Create Your Own Custom Investing Routine**

"My Routine" gives you one-click access to your favorite tools and features from virtually any page on Investors.com. It's a convenient, time-saving way to go through your investing "to do" list quickly.

Here's a sample routine you could set up to follow market direction and find, evaluate, and track your stocks.

1. "The Big Picture"
2. "Screen Center"
3. "Stock Checkup"
4. IBD Charts
5. "My Stock Lists"

☼ Hi, Justin	My IBD »	Sign Out
▾ My Routine		Modify »
The Big Picture	IBD Alerts Plus	
My Stock Lists	Fund Center	
Stocks On The Move	eTables	
Industry Groups	Screen Center	
Custom Screen Wizard	Stock Checkup	
▸ My Biggest Price Movers	My Stock Lists »	

© 2009 Investor's Business Daily, Inc.

eIBD—The Online Version of the Newspaper

We just talked about the unique elements of *Investor's Business Daily*. The paperless online version, *e*IBD, allows you to get that same information in IBD—and more—just hours after the market. So that advantage gives you a critical head-start on tomorrow's market. Here's how it works:

Say you're reading an article on the latest Apple innovation. Just put your cursor over the AAPL ticker symbol in the article, and instantly you get a window showing Apple's mini chart, a stock quote, and IBD's Stock Checkup Rating—all in one place. So it's a chance to size up a stock very quickly.

From there, you have one-click access to the research on Investors.com if you want to look further into a stock.

And the Intelligent Search feature helps to find any articles or data on stocks you're following—so if you type AAPL, it'll direct you to all the places we talk about Apple.

Equally handy is that this electronic version of the paper can be saved to your desktop or mobile device, printed, translated to another language or listened to via audio. The choice is up to you.

Continuing Education—The Key to Investing Success

"IBD University" For most investors, not a day goes by without questions. The "IBD University" section of Investors.com provides a complete stock investment course to help you improve your knowledge and skill. It outlines every aspect of buying and selling stocks, along with chart reading and many other important topics. The lessons are free, and you can take them at your own pace anywhere you have an Internet connection.

IBD TV: Daily Stock Analysis The "Daily Stock Analysis" video reviews the technical and fundamental strength of a current leading stock. Watching this every day will give you new investing ideas—and help you improve your own chart-reading and analytical skills. You can also read the "Daily Stock Analysis" column for a summary of key points discussed in the video.

"Investor's Corner"—Find Answers to Your Questions You can search the archives of the "Investor's Corner" column to quickly find detailed answers to beginning, intermediate, and advanced questions on a wide range of investing topics.

"IBDextra!" Monthly Newsletter The "IBDextra!" newsletter provides exclusive videos, articles, and stock lists to help you follow current market conditions, improve your investing skills, and get the most out of IBD's features and tools. The newsletter is free when you register on Investors.com.

● **IBD TV: Watch Your Results Improve**

IBD TV offers a unique way to reinforce and master the strategies outlined in this book.

The *IBD Market Wrap* and *Daily Stock Analysis* videos show you, on a daily basis, how to apply CAN SLIM in the current market conditions. We also produce special video and audio analysis as needed to help you navigate major market events, such as the financial crisis in 2008.

The key is to tune in regularly. Make IBD TV a part of your routine and you'll see your investing skills and confidence improve significantly. For the latest videos, visit www.investors.com/IBDtv.

Tap into the IBD Community

Since we started publication in 1984, IBD has helped countless people achieve financial success. It has created a vibrant community of investors who proactively share their ideas and knowledge, both online and offline. Here are two ways you can get involved in and benefit from the IBD community.

IBD Meetups

Each month, like-minded investors meet to share stock ideas and benefit from members' knowledge and experiences. Through discussing your individual investing strengths and trading mistakes, IBD Meetup gives you an opportunity to hone your CAN SLIM investing skills with the support of others, and ultimately, learn how to make more money. IBD's Meetup program is the largest investing Meetup organization in the world.

Look for officially sponsored IBD Meetup groups in your city by visiting www.investors.com/Meetup. No other newspaper, magazine or online service provides such a comprehensive educational opportunity.

IBD Forums

IBD Forums is the official online message board for IBD and CAN SLIM investors. On IBD Forums, you can post, read, and reply to messages on a wide variety of investing and other related topics. You can register for free on Investors.com.

· CHAPTER ·

Watching the Market
and Reacting to News

Tape Reading Is Emotional

Ticker tape watching or being glued to your PC or watching the market on a TV channel all day can get dangerously emotional. Sometimes a stock keeps rising to the point where everyone—including you—is convinced it's going "straight through the roof." That's when discipline is most needed because the stock is probably topping. When a stock's merits are so obvious that it looks fantastic to everyone, you can be sure almost everyone who can buy it has already done so. Remember, majority opinion is rarely right in the stock market.

Winners in the stock market need perspective, discipline, and self-control above all else. Those who continually sit in front of the moving ticker tape that shows many stocks as they change prices or their PC monitoring hundreds of stocks changing prices risk making emotional decisions.

Is the Stock in a Base or Is It Too Extended?

There's an easy way to keep your head if you're keeping your eye on the tape or on your PC.

When you see activity that impresses you, always refer to a weekly chart to see if the stock is building a base or if it is extended too far past its buy or pivot point. If it is extended, leave it alone; it's too late. Chasing stocks, like crime, doesn't pay.

If the stock is building a base, then apply the CAN SLIM system. Are current earnings up a meaningful amount? Is the three-year earnings record good? Use IBD's checklist for all the other CAN SLIM criteria.

More than half the stocks that look inviting on the tape will fail the CAN SLIM test and prove to be deficient, mediocre investments. However, sooner or later, convincing market action will point you to a golden opportunity that meets all your criteria for a possible star performer.

Scan Chart Books Weekly and List Your Buy Points

Another way to use market action productively is to review a comprehensive online or printed chart book or charts from a special screen every week and list stocks that meet your technical and fundamental criteria. Then jot down the buy point at which you would consider buying each stock. Also note the average daily volume for each stock on your prospect list so that you can easily verify any noteworthy increases in volume.

Keep this shopping list with you every day for the next couple of weeks as you watch the market. In time, one or two of the stocks on your list will begin to approach your buy point. This is the time to get ready to buy—when the stock trades at your buy point, you anticipate the day's volume will be at least 50% above average and the general market direction is positive. The more demand there is for a stock at the buy point, the better.

Tape and market watchers expect the pace of activity to slow down around lunchtime in New York (12 p.m. to 1 p.m. Eastern). They also know the market frequently shows its true colors in the last hour of the day, either coming on and closing strong, or suddenly weakening and failing to hold the gains established earlier in the session.

Don't Buy on Tips and Rumors

I never buy stocks on tips, rumors, or inside information. Doing so simply isn't sound. Of course, tips, rumors, and inside information are what most people are looking for. However, I should remind you again that what most people believe and do in the market doesn't work very well. Beware of falling into the typical market traps.

Certain advisory services and columns in some business newspapers are fed by Street gossip, rumors, and tips, along with planted personal opinions or inside information. These services and columns, in my opinion, are unprofessional and unsophisticated. There are far sounder and safer methods of gathering information.

Bernard Baruch stressed the importance of separating the facts of a situation from tips, "inside dope," and wishful thinking. One of his rules was to beware of barbers, beauticians, waiters, or anyone else bearing such gifts.

Watch for Distortion around the End of the Year and in Early January

A certain amount of distortion can occur in optionable stocks around option expiration dates. There's also a significant amount of year-end distortion in stocks during December and sometimes through January and early February.

Year-end is a tricky time for anyone to buy stock, since numerous trades are based on tax considerations. Many low-grade losers will suddenly seem strong, while former leaders lie idle or start to correct. In time, this misleading activity dissipates and the true leaders reemerge.

General market sell-offs also occasionally start after the beginning of a new year, which further adds to the difficulty. Fake-out action can occur with one big "up" day followed by a big "down" day, only to be followed by another big "up" day. There are times when I'd rather take a vacation in January. The January effect, where small- and mid-cap stocks get a boost during January, can be a misleading and spurious indicator. At best, it "works" for only a brief period.

It's important that you stick with your rules and don't get sidetracked by questionable, less-reliable indicators, of which there are many.

Interpret and React to Major News

When domestic or foreign news of consequence hits the street, capable market sleuths are sometimes less concerned with whether the news is good or bad than they are with analyzing its effect on the market. For example, if the news appears to be bad but the market yawns, you can feel more positive. The tape is telling you that the underlying market may be stronger than many people believe. On the other hand, if highly positive news hits the market and stocks give ground slightly, the tape analyst might conclude the underpinnings of the market are weaker than previously believed.

Sometimes the market overreacts to or even counteracts favorable or disappointing news. On Wednesday, November 9, 1983, someone ran a full-page ad in the *Wall Street Journal* predicting rampant inflation and another 1929-type depression. The ad appeared during the middle of an intermediate correction in the market, but its warnings were so overblown that the market immediately rebounded and rallied for several days.

There's also a difference between a market that retreats in the face of news that's scary but easy to understand and explain, and one that slumps noticeably on no apparent news at all.

Experienced market investigators have long memories. They keep records of past major news events and how the market reacted. The list would include President Eisenhower's heart attack, the Cuban missile crisis, the Kennedy assassination, an outbreak of war, the Arab oil embargo, expectations of government actions such as wage and price controls, 9/11, war in the Mideast and, more recently, in early September 2008, when subprime real estate news got worse and the market expected a very liberal president to be elected.

Old News versus New News

After it's been repeated several times, both good news and bad news become old news.

Old news will often have the opposite effect on the stock market from what it had when the news first broke.

This, of course, is the opposite of how propaganda and disinformation work in totalitarian dictator-controlled countries. There, the more often a lie or distortion is repeated to the masses, the more it may become accepted as truth. Here, when news becomes widely known or anticipated, it's "discounted" by experienced individuals in the marketplace, blunting the effect of its release—unless, of course, the news keeps getting worse than expected.

To market neophytes, news can be paradoxical and confusing. For example, when a company releases a bad quarterly earnings report, its stock may go up in price when this is reported. When this occurs, it's often because the news was known or anticipated ahead of time, and a few professionals may decide to buy or to cover short sales once all the bad news is finally out. "Buy on bad news" is what some wily institutions use as a guide. Others believe they should step in and provide support for their large positions at difficult times.

Analyzing Your National News Media

How the national news is edited and presented or suppressed dramatically affects the economy and public confidence. It can also influence public opinion of the government, elections, our presidents, and our stock market.

Several excellent books have been written on the subject of analyzing our national news. Humphrey Neill, author of the 1931 classic *Tape Reading and Market Tactics*, also wrote *The Art of Contrary Opinion*. It carefully examines the way identical news stories are reported quite differently in the headlines of different newspapers and how that can be misleading to stock owners and the public. Neill developed contrarian theories based on how frequently conventional wisdom or consensus opinion expressed in the national media turns out to be ill-conceived or just plain wrong.

In 1976, media expert Bruce Herschensohn wrote *The Gods of Antenna*, which tells how some TV networks manipulate the news to influence public opinion. Another book on the subject is *The Coming Battle for the Media*, written in 1988 by William Rusher.

One of the most outstanding studies on the subject is *The Media Elite*, written by Stanley Rothman and Robert Lichter in 1986. Rothman and Lichter interviewed 240 journalists and top staffers at three major newspapers (the *New York Times*, the *Wall Street Journal* and the *Washington Post*), three news magazines (*Time*, *Newsweek* and *U.S. News & World Report*), and the news departments of four TV networks (ABC, CBS, NBC, and PBS). On average, 85% of these top national journalists were found to be liberal and to have voted the Democratic ticket in national elections in 1964, 1968, 1972 and 1976. Another survey showed only 6% of national journalists to have voted Republican.

A Freedom Forum poll reinforced *The Media Elite* when it documented that 89%—9 out of 10—of Washington reporters and bureau chiefs voted for Clinton in 1992 and 7% voted for the first George Bush.

More recently, Tim Groseclose of UCLA and Stanford and Jeff Milyo of the University of Chicago published "A Measure of Media Bias." They counted the number of times a news outlet quoted certain think tanks and compared this with the number of times members of Congress cited the same think tanks when speaking from the floor.

Comparing the citation patterns enabled them to construct an ADA (Americans for Democratic Action) score for each media outlet. They found that *Fox News Special Report* was the only right-of-center news outlet in their sample. The most liberal was *CBS Evening News* followed by the *New York Times*, the *Los Angeles Times*, *USA Today*, *NBC Nightly News*, and ABC's *World News Tonight*.

More surprising was the astonishing degree that your mainstream media in these surveys are far more liberal than the general voting public.

In the 1984 presidential election, Mondale vs. Reagan, the ABC, CBS, and NBC prime-time news programs from Labor Day to Election Day were taped and dissected by Maura Clancy and Michael Robinson. They focused only on reports in which spin for or against each candidate was definite. *Public Opinion* magazine found Reagan got 7,230 seconds of bad press and only 730 of good, while Mondale enjoyed 1,330 seconds of good press and 1,050 seconds of bad.

Leading up to Reagan's reelection run, the Institute for Applied Economics surveyed how the network news treated economic news during the strong recovery in the last half of 1983. It discovered that nearly 95% of the economic statistics were positive, yet 86% of the networks' stories were primarily negative.

Emmy Award winner Bernard Goldberg spent nearly 30 years with CBS News. His book *Bias* documents in detail how network television has provided one-sided news with little balance or fairness. This is a book all young people in America should read to be well informed.

Goldberg tells how journalists decide what news they want to cover and the slant they want to impart. More damaging, they determine what news to minimize or keep quiet. They take sides and assign labels to people.

MSNBC's Chris Matthews, a leading media figure, was a speechwriter for Jimmy Carter. The late Tim Russert of NBC was a political advisor to New York's governor, Mario Cuomo. ABC's Jeff Greenfield was a speechwriter for Robert Kennedy, PBS's Bill Moyers was Lyndon Johnson's press secretary, and ABC news anchor George Stephanopoulos was Clinton's communications director.

To succeed, as individual investors and a free nation, we must learn to separate facts from the personal political opinions and strong agenda-driven biases of the majority of the national media. This could be the number one problem in our country today.

In addition to one-sided bias in the national media, freedom can be jeopardized by either infiltration or propaganda designed to undermine the nation and its people. This is intended to confuse national issues; pit one group against another; stir up class envy, fear and hatred; and tear down or demean certain key people or established institutions.

The most questionable practice of the one-sided media is how they select which stories and facts to cover and continually promote. Even more important are the critically relevant stories and facts they choose not to cover because those stories or facts don't support their agenda or the slant they want the story to have.

In late 2008, public fear the recession then under way might become like the Great Depression of the 1930s escalated. Most Americans weren't even born then and know little about the period. Here are three outstanding books about the 1930s and early 1940s every American should read:

Since Yesterday, The 1930s in America by Frederick Allen, gives a good account of what happened in that period. *The Life & Death of Nazi Germany*, by Robert Goldston, covers Hitler and the rapid rise of the Nazis from the late 1920s to the end of World War II. *Masters of Deceit* by former FBI Director J. Edgar Hoover, covers how communism functions and operates. A well-informed and aware nation will protect and defend its freedoms.

It's Not Like 1929, It's 1938

I've overlayed a chart of the Nasdaq Composite Index from the "Anything Goes 1990s" through March 2009 over the Dow Jones Industrials in the

Roaring 1920s and the Depression era of the 1930s. They are almost exact duplicates. The Nasdaq was used because it trades more volume now than the NYSE and represents more entrepreneurial new America companies that have driven our markets in recent years. The Nasdaq from September 1998 to the wild peak in March 2000 actually soared 2.5 times the Dow's 1928–1929 climax run-up. The Nasdaq dot-com bubble was like the tulip bulb mania of 1636 in Holland. The Nasdaq declined 78% whereas the Dow's 1929 crash declined 89%.

The reason history repeats in this amazing manner is the market is made up of supply and demand and millions of people acting almost 100% on human emotions. It's crowd psychology: human hopes, desires, fears, pride, and ego behind so many decisions. Human nature is pretty much the same today as it was in 1929. These two periods happened 70 years apart, about a lifetime. So, few people today know what happened then. Like now, the banks had excessive loans, then to farmers, plus stocks were bought on excessive leverage. Unemployment at the Depression lows in 1932 peaked at 25% but was still 20% in 1939 just before WWII began.

The rally from the 1932 low to the 1936–1937 peak lasted the same amount of time as our Nasdaq rally back from the low of 2002 to 2007 . . . and then both fell around 50% to 60%.

History is now on the march, but it's not like 1929, it's like 1938.

So, what was happening leading up to 1938?

**Nasdaq Composite February 1992–March 2009 compared
to Dow Jones Industrials November 1921–December 1942.**

The Nazi party in 1930 won 107 seats in the Reichstag. Hitler became Chancellor of Germany in January 1933. He already had his storm troopers and the Hitler youth. Only months later, the Reichstag gave Hitler all its constitutional powers. By July, all other political parties were outlawed. Hitler kept saying he was only interested in peace. His speeches were grandiose promises that enthralled the German people.

By 1938, Britain and France negotiated with Hitler and tried to appease him by making concessions. Britain believed they had a peace agreement with Hitler, "Peace in our time." The crowds cheered. In Parliament, Churchill said, "We've suffered a defeat." No one believed him. He was booed. World War II began in 1939. Germany rolled over France in only a few weeks.

Today, Iran is a key sponsor of terrorist organizations and will have nuclear weapons very soon plus the missile ability to deliver them. Have we learned anything from history in the 1930s? Will we repeat Neville Chamberlain's mistaken belief in a phony agreement on a piece of paper?

I'm including two editorials by Thomas Sowell, whom I mentioned earlier in Chapter 16. His work always shows important facts and wisdom.

Roman Empire Outlasted U.S., But It Too Fell

December 9, 2008

THOMAS SOWELL

Will the horrors unleashed by Islamic terrorists in Mumbai cause any second thoughts by those who are so anxious to start weakening the American security systems currently in place, including government interceptions of international phone calls and the holding of terrorists at Guantanamo?

Maybe. But never underestimate partisan blindness in Washington or in the mainstream media where, if the Bush administration did it, then it must be wrong.

Contrary to some of the more mawkish notions of what a government is supposed to be, its top job is the protection of the people. Nobody on 9/11 would have thought that we would see nothing comparable again in this country for seven long years.

Many people seem to have forgotten how, in the wake of 9/11, every great national event—the World Series, Christmas, New Year's, the Super Bowl—was under the shadow of a fear that this was when the terrorists would strike again.

They didn't strike again here, even though they have struck in Spain, Indonesia, England and India, among other places. Does anyone imagine that this was because they didn't want to hit America again?

Could this have had anything to do with all the security precautions that liberals have been complaining about so bitterly, from the interception of international phone calls to forcing information out of captured terrorists?

Too many people refuse to acknowledge that benefits have costs, even if that cost means only having no more secrecy when making international phone calls than you have when sending e-mails, in a world where computer hackers abound. There are people who refuse to give up anything, even to save their own lives.

A very shrewd observer of the deterioration of Western societies, British writer Theodore Dalrymple, said: "This mental flabbiness is decadence, and at the same time a manifestation of the arrogant assumption that nothing can destroy us."

There are growing numbers of things that can destroy us. The Roman Empire lasted a lot longer than the United States has lasted, and yet it too was destroyed.

Millions of lives were blighted for centuries thereafter, because the barbarians who destroyed Rome were incapable of replacing it with anything at all comparable. Neither are those who threaten to destroy the United States today.

The destruction of the United States will not require enough nuclear bombs to annihilate cities and towns across America. After all, the nuclear destruction of just two cities was enough to force Japan to surrender—and the Japanese had far more willingness to fight and die than most Americans have today.

How many Americans are willing to see New York, Chicago and Los Angeles all disappear in nuclear mushroom clouds, rather than surrender to whatever outrageous demands the terrorists make?

Neither Barack Obama nor those with whom he will be surrounded in Washington show any signs of being serious about forestalling such a terrible choice by taking any action with any realistic chance of preventing a nuclear Iran.

<u>Once suicidal fanatics have nuclear bombs, that is the point of no return. We, our children and our grandchildren will live at the mercy of the merciless, who have a track record of sadism.</u>

There are no concessions we can make that will buy off hate-filled terrorists. What they want—what they must have for their own self-respect, in a world where they suffer the humiliation of being visibly centuries behind the West in so many ways—is our being brought down in humiliation, including self-humiliation.

Even killing us will not be enough, just as killing Jews was not enough for the Nazis, who first had to subject them to soul-scarring humiliations and dehumanization in their death camps.

This kind of hatred may not be familiar to most Americans but what happened on 9/11 should give us a clue—and a warning.

The people who flew those planes into the World Trade Center buildings could not have been bought off by any concessions, not even the hundreds of billions of dollars we are spending in bailout money today.

They want our soul—and if they are willing to die and we are not, they will get it.

False Solutions and Real Problems

March 17, 2009

THOMAS SOWELL

Someone once said that Senator Hubert Humphrey, liberal icon of an earlier generation, had more solutions than there were problems.

Senator Humphrey was not unique in that respect. In fact, our present economic crisis has developed out of politicians providing solutions to problems that did not exist—and, as a result, producing a problem whose existence is all too real and all too painful.

What was the problem that didn't exist? It was a national problem of unaffordable housing. The political crusade for affordable housing got into high gear in the 1990s and led to all kinds of changes in mortgage lending practices, which in turn led to a housing boom and bust that has left us in the mess we are now trying to dig out of.

Usually housing affordability is measured in terms of how much of the average person's income it takes to cover either apartment rent or a monthly mortgage payment.

There were certainly places here and there where it took half a family's income just to put a roof over their heads. Many such places were in coastal California but there were a few others, here and there, on the east coast and elsewhere.

But, vast areas of the country in between—"flyover country" to the east coast and west coast elites—had housing prices that took no larger share of the average American's income than in the decade before the affordable housing crusade got under way.

Why then a national crusade by Washington politicians over local problems? Probably as good an answer as any is that "It seemed like a good idea at the time." How are we to be kept aware of how compassionate and how important our elected officials are unless they are busy solving some problem for us?

The problem of skyrocketing housing prices was all too real in those places where this problem existed. When you have to live on half your income because the other half goes for housing, that's a real downer.

Almost invariably, these severe local problems had local causes—usually severe local restrictions on building homes. These restrictions had a variety of politically attractive names, ranging from "open space" laws and "smart growth" policies to "environmental protection" and "farmland preservation."

Like most wonderful-sounding political slogans, none of these lofty goals was discussed in terms of that one four-letter word that people do not use in polite political society—"cost."

No one asked how many hundreds of thousands of dollars would be added to the cost of an average home by "open space" laws, for example. Yet empirical studies have shown that land-use restrictions added at least a hundred thousand dollars to the average home price in dozens of places around the country.

In some places, such as coastal California, these restrictions added several hundred thousand dollars to the price of the average home.

In other words, where the problem was real, local politicians were the cause. National politicians then tried to depict this as a national problem that they would solve.

How would they solve it? <u>By pressuring banks and other lenders to lower their requirements for making mortgage loans, so that more people could buy houses. The Department of Housing and Urban Development gave the government-sponsored enterprise Fannie Mae quotas for how many mortgages it should buy that were made out for people with low to moderate incomes.</u>

Like most political "solutions," the solution to the affordable housing "problem" took little or no account of the wider repercussions this would entail.

Various economists and others warned repeatedly that lowered lending standards meant more risky mortgages. Given the complex relationships among banks and other financial institutions, including many big Wall Street firms, if mortgages started defaulting, all the financial dominoes could start falling.

These warnings were brushed aside. Politicians were too busy solving a national problem that didn't exist. In the process, they created very real problems. Now they are offering even more solutions that will undoubtedly lead to even bigger problems.

For more information on how politicians in our government were the real cause behind our worst financial crisis since 1938, Thomas Sowell has authored a short easy to read, but historically invaluable book entitled, *The Housing Boom and Bust*. It's a must read for all investors, consumers, and voters affected by the resulting mess of the 2008 massive financial market meltdown.

Sowell's latest (2010) master stroke, *Intellectuals and Society*, examines the track record of intellectuals in the things they have advocated and surprisingly how often they have been proved not only wrong, but grossly and disastrously wrong in their prescriptions for the ills of society—and how little their views have changed in response to empirical evidence of the disasters their views caused.

18

·CHAPTER·

How You Could Make Your Million Owning Mutual Funds

What Are Mutual Funds?

A mutual fund is a diversified portfolio of stocks managed by a professional investment company, usually for a small management fee. Investors purchase shares in the fund itself and make or lose money based on the combined profits and losses of the stocks within the fund.

When you purchase a mutual fund, what you're buying is long-term professional management to make decisions for you in the stock market. You should probably handle a mutual fund differently from the way you handle individual stocks.

A stock may decline and never come back in price. That's why you must *always* have a loss-cutting policy. In contrast, a well-selected, diversified domestic growth-stock fund run by an established management organization will, in time, always recover from the steep corrections that naturally occur during bear markets. The reason mutual funds come back is that they are broadly diversified and generally participate in each recovery cycle in the U.S. economy.

How to Become a Millionaire the Easy Way

Mutual funds are outstanding investment vehicles if you learn how to use them correctly. However, many investors don't understand how to manage them to their advantage.

The first thing to understand is that the big money in mutual funds is made by owning them through several business cycles (market ups and downs). This means 15, 20, or 25 years or longer. Sitting tight for that long requires enormous patience and confidence. It's like real estate. If you buy a house, then get nervous and sell out after only three or four years, you may not make anything. It takes time for your property to appreciate.

Here's how I believe you, as a shrewd fund investor, should plan and invest. Pick a diversified domestic growth fund that performed in the top quartile of all mutual funds over the last three or five years. It will probably have an average annual rate of return of about 15% or 20%. The fund should also have outperformed many other domestic growth-stock funds in the latest 12 months. You'll want to consult a reliable source for this information. Many investment-related magazines survey fund performance every quarter. Your stockbroker or library should have special fund performance rating services so you can get an unbiased review of the fund you're interested in purchasing.

Investor's Business Daily rates mutual funds based on their 36-month performance records (on a scale from A+ to E) and also provides other performance percentages based on different time periods. Focus your research on mutual funds with an A+, A, or A− performance rating in IBD. During a bear market, growth fund ratings will be somewhat lower. The fund you pick does not have to be in the top three or four in performance each year to give you an excellent profit over 15 years or more.

You should also reinvest your dividends and capital gains distributions (profits derived from a mutual fund's sales of stocks and bonds) to benefit from compounding over the years.

The Magic of Compounding

The way to make a fortune in mutual funds is through compounding. Compounding occurs when your earnings themselves (the performance gains plus any dividends and reinvested capital) generate more earnings, allowing you to put ever-greater sums to work. The more time that goes by, the more powerful compounding becomes.

In order to get the most benefit from compounding, you'll need a carefully selected growth-stock fund, *and* you'll need to stick with it over time. For example, if you purchase $10,000 of a diversified domestic growth-stock fund that averages about 15% a year over a period of 35 years, here is an approximation of what the result might be, compliments of the magic of compounding:

First five years: $10,000 might become $20,000

Next five years: $20,000 might become $40,000

Next five years: $40,000 might become $80,000

Next five years: $80,000 might become $160,000

Next five years: $160,000 might become $320,000

Next five years: $320,000 might become $640,000

Next five years: $640,000 might become **$1.28 million!**

**Suppose you also added $2,000 each year and let it compound as well.
Your total could possibly then come to more than $3 million!**

Now, how much more do you think you'd have if you also bought a little extra during every bear market of 6 to 12 months while the fund was temporarily down 30% or more from its peak?

Nothing's ever guaranteed in this world, and, yes, there are always taxes. However, this example is representative of how the better growth funds have performed over the last 50 years, and what could happen to you if you plan and invest in mutual funds correctly. Over any 20- to 25-year period, your growth fund should average two to three times what a savings account would return. It's definitely possible.

When Is the Best Time to Buy a Fund?

Anytime is the best time. You'll never know what the perfect time is, and waiting will usually result in your paying a higher price. You should focus on getting started and becoming regular and relentless about building capital that can compound over the years.

How Many Funds Should You Own?

As time passes, you may discover you'd like to develop an additional long-term program. If so, do it. In 15 years, you might have hefty amounts in two or even three funds. However, don't overdo it. There's no reason to diversify broadly in mutual funds. Individuals with multimillion-dollar portfolios could spread out somewhat further, allowing them to place sums into a more diverse group of funds. To do this correctly, you need to make some attempt to own funds with different management styles. For example, you could divvy up your money among a value-type growth fund, an aggressive growth fund, a mid- to large-cap growth fund, a small-cap fund, and so on. Many fund organizations, including Fidelity, Franklin Templeton, American

Century, and others, offer funds with varied objectives. In most cases, you have the right to switch to any other fund in the family at a nominal transfer fee. These families offer you added flexibility of making prudent changes years later if you want an income or balanced fund.

Are Monthly Investment Plans for You?

Programs that automatically withhold money from your paycheck are usually sound if you deposit that money in a carefully selected, diversified domestic growth-stock fund. However, it's best to also make a larger initial purchase that will get you on the road to serious compounding all that much quicker.

Don't Let the Market Diminish Your Long-Term Resolve

Bear markets can last from six months to, in some rare cases, two or three years. If you're going to be a successful long-term investor in mutual funds, you'll need the courage and perspective to live through many discouraging bear markets. Have the vision to build yourself a great long-term growth program, and stick to it. Each time the economy goes into a recession, and the newspapers and TV are saying how terrible things are, consider *adding* to your fund when it's 30% or more off its peak. You might go so far as to borrow a little money to buy more if you feel a bear market has ended. If you're patient, the price should be up nicely in two or three years.

Growth funds that invest in more aggressive stocks should go up more than the general market in bull phases, but they will also decline more in bear markets. Don't be alarmed. Instead, try to look ahead several years. Daylight follows darkness.

You might think that buying mutual funds during periods like the Great Depression would be a bad idea because it would take you 30 years to break even. However, on an inflation-adjusted basis, had investors bought at the exact top of 1929, they would have broken even in just 14 years, based on the performance of the S&P 500 and the DJIA. Had these investors bought at the top of the market in 1973, they would have broken even in just 11 years. If, in addition, they had dollar cost averaged throughout these bad periods (meaning they had purchased additional shares as the price went down, lowering their overall cost per share), they would have broken even in half the time.

The 1973 drop in the Nasdaq from the peak of 137 would have been recovered in 3½ years, and as of February 2009, the Nasdaq average had recovered from 137 to 1,300. Even during the two worst market periods in history, growth funds did bounce back, and they did so in less time than you'd expect. In other words, if you took the absolutely worst period of the twentieth century, the Great Depression, and you bought at the top of the market, then dollar cost averaged down, at worst, it would have taken you seven years to break even, and over the following 21 years, you would have seen your investment increase approximately eight times. This is compelling evidence that dollar cost averaging into mutual funds and holding them for the long haul could be smart investing.

Some people may find this confusing, since we have said that investors should never dollar cost average down in stocks. The difference is that a stock can go to zero, while a domestic, widely diversified, professionally managed mutual fund will find its way back when the market eventually gets better, often tracking near the performance of benchmarks like the S&P 500 and the Dow Jones Industrial Average.

The super-big gains from mutual funds come from compounding over a span of many years. Funds should be an investment for as long as you live.

They say diamonds are forever. Well, so are your funds. So buy right and sit tight!

Should You Buy Open- or Closed-End Funds?

"Open-end" funds continually issue new shares when people want to buy them, and they are the most common type. Shares are normally redeemable at net asset value whenever the present holders wish to sell.

A "closed-end" fund issues a fixed number of shares. Generally, these shares are not redeemable at the shareholder's option. Redemption takes place through secondary market transactions. Most closed-end fund shares are listed for trading on exchanges.

Better long-term opportunities are found in open-end funds. Closed-end funds are subject to the whims and discounts below book value of the auction marketplace.

Should You Buy Load or No-Load Funds?

The fund you choose can be a "load" fund, where a sales commission is charged, or a "no-load" fund. Many people prefer no-loads. If you buy a fund with a sales charge, discounts are offered based on the amount you invest. Some funds have back-end loads (sales commissions that are charged when withdrawals are made, designed to discourage withdrawals) that you may also want to take into consideration when evaluating a fund for purchase. In any event, the commission on a fund is much less than the markup you pay to buy insurance, a new car, a suit of clothes, or your groceries. You may also be able to sign a letter of intent to purchase a specified amount of the fund, which may allow a lower sales charge to apply to any future purchases made over the following 13 months.

Few people have been successful in trading no-load growth funds aggressively on a timing basis, using moving average lines and services that specialize in fund switching. Most investors shouldn't try to trade no-load funds because it's easy to make mistakes in the timing of buy and sell points. Again, get aboard a mutual fund for the long term.

Should You Buy Income Funds?

If you need income, you may find it more advantageous *not* to buy an income fund. Instead, you should select the best fund available and set up a withdrawal plan equal to 1½% per quarter, or 6% per year. Part of the withdrawal will come from dividend income received and part from your capital. If you selected the fund correctly, it should generate enough growth over the years to more than offset annual withdrawals of 6% of your total investment.

Should You Buy Sector or Index Funds?

Steer away from funds that concentrate in only one industry or area. The problem with these funds is that sectors go into and out of favor all the time. Therefore, if you buy a sector fund, you will probably suffer severe losses when that sector is out of favor or a bear market hits, unless you decide to sell it if and when you have a worthwhile gain. Most investors don't sell and could end up losing money, which is why I recommend not purchasing sector funds. If you're going to make a million in mutual funds, your fund's investments should be diversified for the long term. Sector funds are generally not a long-term investment.

If you are conservative, it may be OK for you to pick an index fund, where the fund's portfolio closely matches that of a given index, like the S&P 500. Index funds have outperformed many actively managed funds over the long run. I tend to prefer growth funds.

Should You Buy Bond or Balanced Funds?

I also don't think most people should invest in bond or balanced funds. Stock funds generally outperform bond funds, and when you combine the two, you're ultimately just watering down your results. However, someone who is in retirement might want to consider a balanced fund if less volatility is desired.

Should You Buy Global or International Funds?

These funds might provide some diversification, but limit the percentage of your total fund investment in this higher-risk sector to 10% or 15%. International funds can, after a period of good performance, suffer years of laggard results, and investing in foreign governments creates added risk. Historically, Europe and Japan have underperformed the U.S. market.

The Size Problem of Large Funds

Asset size is a problem for many funds. If a fund has billions of dollars in assets, it will be more difficult for the fund manager to buy and sell large positions in a stock. Thus, the fund will be less flexible in retreating from the market or in acquiring meaningful positions in smaller, better-performing stocks. For this reason, I'd avoid most of the largest mutual funds. If you have one of the larger funds that's done well over the years, and it is still doing reasonably well despite having grown large, you should probably sit tight. Remember, the big money is always made over the long haul. Fidelity Contrafund, run by Will Danoff, has been the best-managed large fund for a number of years.

Management Fees and Turnover Rates

Some investors spend a lot of time evaluating a fund's management fees and portfolio turnover rates, but in most cases, such nitpicking isn't necessary.

In my experience, some of the best-performing growth funds have higher turnover rates. (A portfolio turnover rate is the ratio of the dollar value of buys and sells during a year to the dollar value of the fund's total assets.) Average turnover topped 350% in the Fidelity Magellan Fund during its three biggest performance years. CGM Capital Development Fund, managed by Ken Heebner, was the top-performing fund from 1989 to 1994. In two of those years, 1990 and 1991, it had turnover rates of 272% and 226%, respectively. And Heebner's superior performance even later in CGM Focus fund was concentrated in 20 stocks that were actively managed.

You can't be successful and on top of the market without making any trades. Good fund managers will sell a stock when they think it's overvalued, when they are worried about the overall market or a specific group, or when they find another, more attractive stock to purchase. That's what you hire a professional to do. Also, the institutional commission rates that funds pay are extremely low—only a few cents per share of stock bought or sold. So don't be overly concerned about turnover rates. It's the fund's overall performance over several years that is key.

The Five Most Common Mistakes Mutual Fund Investors Make

1. Failing to sit tight for at least 15 years or more
2. Worrying about a fund's management fee, its turnover rate, or the dividends it pays or buying new funds or last year's #1 fund
3. Being affected by news in the market when you're supposed to be investing for the long term
4. Selling out during bad markets or switching funds too often
5. Being impatient and losing confidence too soon

Other Common Mistakes

Typical investors in mutual funds tend to buy the best-performing fund after it's had a big year. What they don't realize is that history virtually dictates that in the next year or two, that fund will probably show much slower results. If the economy goes into a recession, the results could be poorer still. Such conditions are usually enough to scare off those with less conviction and those who want to get rich quick.

Some investors switch (usually at the wrong time) to another fund that someone convinces them is much safer or that has a "hotter" recent performance record. Switching may be OK if you have a really bad fund or if you're in the wrong type of fund, but too much switching quickly destroys what must be a long-term commitment to the benefits of compounding.

America's long-term future has always been a shrewd investment. The U.S. stock market has been growing since 1790, and the country will continue to grow in the future, in spite of wars, panics, and deep recessions. Investing in mutual funds—the right way—is one way to benefit from America's growth and to secure your and your family's long-term, 20-plus-year financial future.

How to Use IBD to Buy ETFs

To be perfectly honest, I'm not a big fan of exchange-traded funds because I think you can make more money by focusing on the market leaders. But because ETFs had become so wildly popular with not only individual investors but also asset managers, we started covering ETFs in February 2006.

ETFs are basically mutual funds that trade like a stock, but offer transparency, tax efficiency, and lower expenses.

While mutual funds set their prices or net asset value (NAV) once a day, the prices of ETFs jump up and down throughout the day, just like a stock price. Anything you can do with a stock, you can do with an ETF, such as selling short and trading options.

ETFs are more tax-friendly than mutual funds because of what happens under the hood. When market makers need to create or redeem shares, they round up the underlying stocks and trade them with the provider for new ETF shares. They do the opposite to redeem ETF shares for the underlying stocks. No money changes hands because the shares are traded in-kind.

Unlike mutual funds, ETFs are not affected by shareholder redemptions. If too many investors pull money out of mutual funds, fund managers may be forced to sell the stocks they hold to raise cash, thereby incurring a taxable event. ETFs keep trading to a minimum, so there are few taxable gains.

ETFs charge management fees of anywhere from 0.10% to 0.95%. That's considerably smaller than those of mutual funds, which charge 1.02% on average.[1]

However, with a good mutual fund, you're getting a top-notch manager who makes investment decisions for you. An ETF requires that you pull the buy and sell triggers.

Don't kid yourself that the diversification in an ETF will somehow protect you. Take the SPDR Financial Sector (XLF). In the banking meltdown in 2008, this ETF plunged 57%.

The SPDR (SPY), which tracks the S&P 500, was the first U.S.-listed ETF. It started trading on the Amex in 1993. The Nasdaq 100, known today as PowerShares QQQQ Trust (QQQQ), and the Diamonds Trust (DIA), which tracks the Dow Jones Industrial Average, were both launched in the late 1990s.

Today, there are ETFs tracking not only benchmark indexes, but also bonds, commodities, currencies, derivatives, carbon credits, investment strategies such as low-P/E stocks, and more. In 2007 and 2008, ETF launches were what IPOs were to the Internet bubble. Providers floated ETFs based on esoteric indexes that diced sectors into ridiculous slices such as Wal-Mart suppliers, spin-offs, companies with patents, those that don't do any business with Sudan, and those engaged in "sinful" activities like gambling, alcohol, and tobacco.

---

[1] *Investment Company Fact Book* (Investment Company Institute, 2008).

ETFs have changed the way many people trade, although not always for the better. They offer average investors access to foreign markets such as India, which limits foreign investors. They also let you trade commodities and currencies without having to open a separate futures or foreign exchange trading account. And the advent of inverse ETFs lets those with accounts that prohibit shorting to put on a short position by buying long.

Since February 2004, ETFs have accounted for from 25% to as much as 44% of the monthly trading volume on the NYSE Arca.

Top-Down Selection

IBD lists the 350 ETFs with the highest 50-day average volume and categorizes them by U.S. Stock Indexes, Sector/Industry, Global, Bonds/Fixed Income, and Commodities and Currencies. Within each category, they're listed by our proprietary Relative Strength rating in descending order. Ranking ETFs by RS highlights the leaders within each category and helps you compare them. The tables also list year-to-date return, Accumulation/Distribution rating, dividend yields, the prior day's closing price, the price change, and the change in volume versus the daily average.

Aside from reading IBD's ETF coverage, monitor the "Winners & Losers" table on the exchange-traded funds page. Every day it lists the leaders and laggards over a given time period, which is rotated daily:

Monday: one-week percentage change

Tuesday: one-month percentage change

Wednesday: three-month percentage change

Thursday: six-month percentage change

Friday: twelve-month percentage change

Owning Both Mutual Funds and a Stock Portfolio

Many smart investors own both funds and stocks. If you have learned how to manage your stock portfolio with skill using all the CAN SLIM buy and sell rules, you should be showing improved, superior results during each bull market and moving out of most stocks in the early phase of each bear market.

Institutional Portfolio Ideas

The 31-year performance graph from inception of our weekly Leaders and Laggards Institutional Service is shown in this chapter. It proves what is potentially possible over a long period if you concentrate on innovative new entrepreneurial leaders that have a unique new product that's better, faster, or cheaper than others in their field . . . and you face up to and eliminate your laggards and possible mistakes before they are allowed to deteriorate into huge losses.

Here are 10 charts of many of the better performers with annotations showing key facts known at the time each stock was first added to our service in, around, and following the general market follow-through of the March 12, 2009 market bottom.

You'll note, half of these stocks, after the third or fourth worst market collapse in 100 years, had an average P/E ratio over 45, 6 of these innovators had an average return on equity of 45%, and all 10 averaged having their IPO in just the last 12 years.

Most averaged earnings up 40% in their latest quarter plus powerful earnings growth in the prior two or three years. All had unique industry leading products. So, you see . . . the winner's secret is to always insist on and combine outstanding fundamentals together with sound chart patterns under accumulation during an uptrending general market.

The 2008 bear market was twice as long and deep as typical bears. The S&P 500 fell 58% in 17 months. Nearly all stocks were therefore coming up off the bottom of 50% to 80% or 90% declines. So, Amazon, Vistaprint, Priceline, Baidu, and Ctrip were all "potential deep cup-with-handle bases," just starting up the right side of a cup, somewhat like Xerox in June 1962.

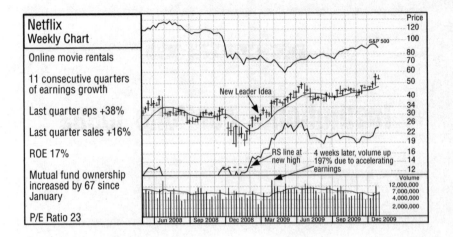

Netflix
Weekly Chart

Online movie rentals

11 consecutive quarters of earnings growth

Last quarter eps +38%

Last quarter sales +16%

ROE 17%

Mutual fund ownership increased by 67 since January

P/E Ratio 23

Chart annotations: S&P 500 • New Leader Idea • RS line at new high • 4 weeks later, volume up 197% due to accelerating earnings

Price axis: 120, 100, 80, 70, 60, 50, 40, 34, 30, 26, 22, 19, 16, 14, 12

Volume axis: 12,000,000 / 7,000,000 / 4,000,000 / 2,000,000

Time axis: Jun 2008 | Sep 2008 | Dec 2008 | Mar 2009 | Jun 2009 | Sep 2009 | Dec 2009

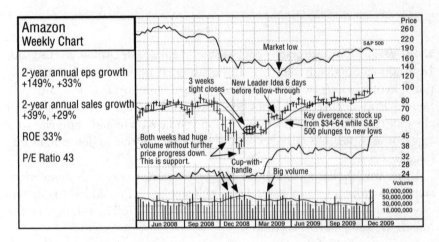

Amazon
Weekly Chart

2-year annual eps growth +149%, +33%

2-year annual sales growth +39%, +29%

ROE 33%

P/E Ratio 43

Chart annotations: Market low • S&P 500 • 3 weeks tight closes • New Leader Idea 6 days before follow-through • Key divergence: stock up from $34-64 while S&P 500 plunges to new lows • Both weeks had huge volume without further price progress down. This is support. • Cup-with-handle • Big volume

Price axis: 260, 220, 190, 160, 140, 120, 100, 80, 70, 60, 45, 38, 32, 28, 24

Volume axis: 80,000,000 / 50,000,000 / 30,000,000 / 18,000,000

Time axis: Jun 2008 | Sep 2008 | Dec 2008 | Mar 2009 | Jun 2009 | Sep 2009 | Dec 2009

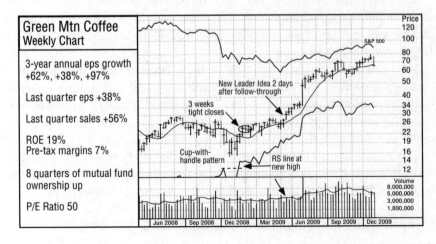

Green Mtn Coffee
Weekly Chart

3-year annual eps growth +62%, +38%, +97%

Last quarter eps +38%

Last quarter sales +56%

ROE 19%
Pre-tax margins 7%

8 quarters of mutual fund ownership up

P/E Ratio 50

Chart annotations: S&P 500 • New Leader Idea 2 days after follow-through • 3 weeks tight closes • Cup-with-handle pattern • RS line at new high

Price axis: 120, 100, 80, 70, 60, 50, 40, 34, 30, 26, 22, 19, 16, 14, 12

Volume axis: 8,000,000 / 5,000,000 / 3,000,000 / 1,800,000

Time axis: Jun 2008 | Sep 2008 | Dec 2008 | Mar 2009 | Jun 2009 | Sep 2009 | Dec 2009

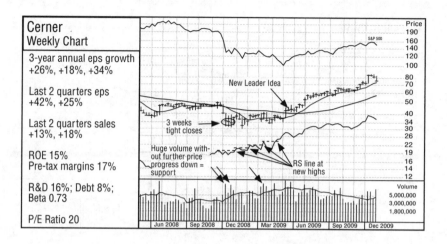

Cerner
Weekly Chart

3-year annual eps growth
+26%, +18%, +34%

Last 2 quarters eps
+42%, +25%

Last 2 quarters sales
+13%, +18%

ROE 15%
Pre-tax margins 17%

R&D 16%; Debt 8%;
Beta 0.73

P/E Ratio 20

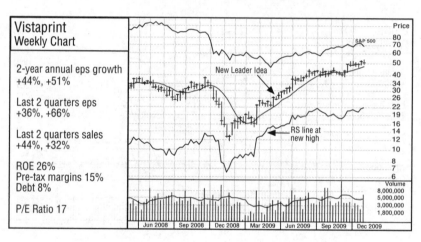

Vistaprint
Weekly Chart

2-year annual eps growth
+44%, +51%

Last 2 quarters eps
+36%, +66%

Last 2 quarters sales
+44%, +32%

ROE 26%
Pre-tax margins 15%
Debt 8%

P/E Ratio 17

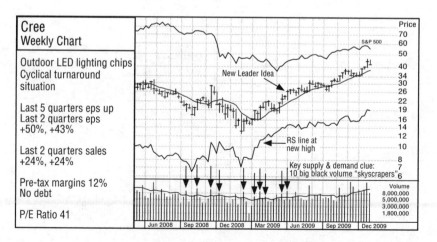

Cree
Weekly Chart

Outdoor LED lighting chips
Cyclical turnaround
situation

Last 5 quarters eps up
Last 2 quarters eps
+50%, +43%

Last 2 quarters sales
+24%, +24%

Pre-tax margins 12%
No debt

P/E Ratio 41

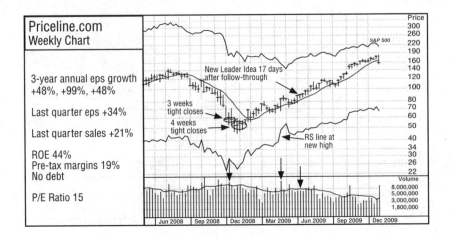

Priceline.com
Weekly Chart

3-year annual eps growth
+48%, +99%, +48%

Last quarter eps +34%

Last quarter sales +21%

ROE 44%
Pre-tax margins 19%
No debt

P/E Ratio 15

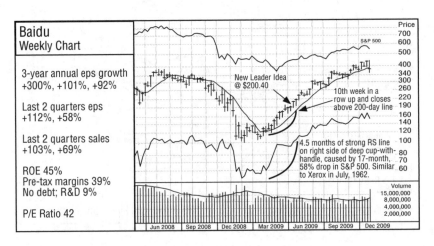

Baidu
Weekly Chart

3-year annual eps growth
+300%, +101%, +92%

Last 2 quarters eps
+112%, +58%

Last 2 quarters sales
+103%, +69%

ROE 45%
Pre-tax margins 39%
No debt; R&D 9%

P/E Ratio 42

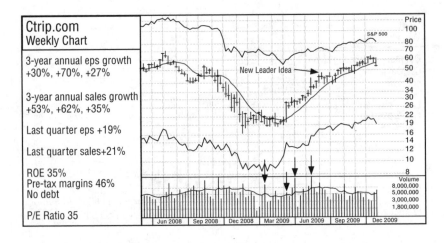

Ctrip.com
Weekly Chart

3-year annual eps growth
+30%, +70%, +27%

3-year annual sales growth
+53%, +62%, +35%

Last quarter eps +19%

Last quarter sales+21%

ROE 35%
Pre-tax margins 46%
No debt

P/E Ratio 35

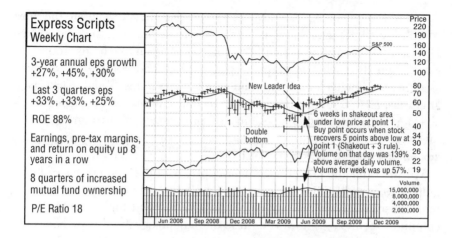

Express Scripts
Weekly Chart

3-year annual eps growth
+27%, +45%, +30%

Last 3 quarters eps
+33%, +33%, +25%

ROE 88%

Earnings, pre-tax margins, and return on equity up 8 years in a row

8 quarters of increased mutual fund ownership

P/E Ratio 18

New Leader Idea

6 weeks in shakeout area under low price at point 1. Buy point occurs when stock recovers 5 points above low at point 1 (Shakeout + 3 rule). Volume on that day was 139% above average daily volume. Volume for week was up 57%.

Double bottom

Institutional Investors: An Overview

In 1929, the public was heavily involved in stocks, speculating with 10% cash and 90% margin. This is one reason why so many people got hurt when the market collapsed . . . they had too much debt.

However, margin debt as a percentage of market capitalization of NYSE stocks also reached an extreme level at the end of March 2000.

Banks in 1929 also had huge mortgage debt. This time around, banks had lower-quality mortgage debt. However, this subprime debt was strongly mandated and pursued by our key politicians in government from 1995 on, something they don't want to admit as they investigate and blame everyone else rather than take responsibility for their major role in creating the subprime loan 2008 financial crisis. Great government intention—catastrophic results.

The First Datagraph Books Evolve into WONDA

The first product we developed for institutional investors was the O'Neil Database Datagraph books, which contain extremely detailed charts on thousands of publicly traded companies. They were the first of their kind and represented an innovation in the institutional investment world.

We were able to produce these books at timely weekly intervals, updating them at market close every Friday. These comprehensive books were delivered to institutional money managers over the weekend in time for Monday's market open. This quick turnaround (for its time) was achieved not only because of the equity database we compiled and maintained on a daily basis, but also because of our high-speed microfilm plotting equipment. In 1964, this costly computer machinery was so new no one knew how to get a graph out of it. Once this barrier was cleared, it was possible to turn out complex, updated graphs through an automated process, at the rate of one per second.

Today, the technology has advanced so far that we can generate the most complex stock datagraphs with hardly a second thought, and the O'Neil Database books became a mainstay at many leading mutual funds around the globe. Initially, each Datagraph displayed price and volume information, along with a few technical and fundamental data items. Today, each Datagraph displays 96 fundamental and 26 technical items, and these are available for more than 8,000 stocks in 197 proprietary industry groups. This means an analyst or portfolio manager can quickly compare any company to any other, either in the same industry or in the entire database.

We still offer the O'Neil Database books, with their 600 pages of Datagraphs, to our institutional clients as part of our overall institutional investment business. With the advent of the Internet and highly sophisticated computer technology, however, these old-technology, hard-copy books are being replaced by our most innovative flagship service, WONDA. WONDA stands for William O'Neil Direct Access, and it provides institutional clients with a direct interface to the O'Neil Database. The O'Neil Database now contains more than 3,000 technical and fundamental data items on more than 8,000 U.S. stocks, and WONDA allows users to screen and monitor the database using any combination of these data items.

We originally developed WONDA as an in-house system to manage our own money. In the 1990s, after years of real-time use and refinement, the service was rolled out as the newest William O'Neil + Co. service, available to the professional and institutional community.

Because WONDA was conceived and created by our in-house portfolio managers and computer programmers, the service was designed with the serious institutional money manager in mind. Institutional money managers must frequently make rapid decisions while under pressure, and WONDA offers a wide range of features that allows instantaneous access to and monitoring of crucial stock data and related information as the market is moving.

Some of our institutional clients who use WONDA say they can "practically print money" with the system. These clients run the gamut from very conservative value-type managers to hedge fund managers. Clearly, no computer system can print money, but that type of comment from some of our biggest and best institutional clients points out the functionality and effectiveness of WONDA.

Interpreting Dome Petroleum's Datagraph

The accompanying Datagraph of Dome Petroleum is marked up to highlight a few of the ways we interpret and use this display of fundamanetal and technical information. We suggested Dome to institutions in November

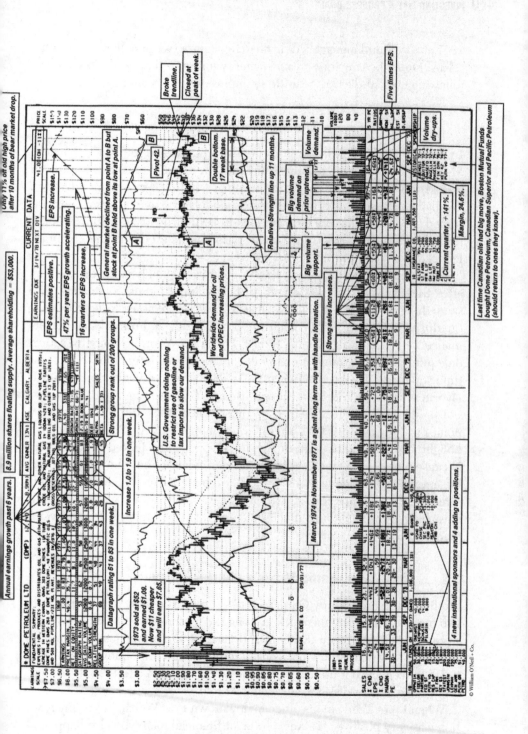

© William O'Neil + Co.

1977 at $48. Fund managers didn't like the idea, so we bought the stock ourselves. Dome became one of our biggest winners at that time. This and the following case studies are real-life examples of how it's actually done.

The Pic 'N' Save Story

In July 1977, we suggested a stock no institution would touch: Pic 'N' Save. Most money managers felt the company was entirely too small because it traded only 500 shares a day, so we began purchasing it several months later. We had successful historical computer models of Kmart in 1962, when it traded only 1,000 shares a day, and Jack Eckerd Drug in April 1967, when it traded 500 shares a day, so we knew, based on its excellent fundamentals, Pic 'N' Save could become a real winner.

Precedent was with us. Both Kmart and Eckerd had become big winners after they were discovered. Average daily volume increased steadily. The same thing occurred with Pic 'N' Save. This little, unknown company, headquartered in Carson, California, turned in a steady and remarkable performance for seven or eight years. In fact, Pic 'N' Save's pretax margins, return on equity, annual earnings growth rate, and debt-to-equity ratio were at that time superior to those of other, more widely accepted institutional growth favorites—such as Wal-Mart Stores—that we had also suggested.

I've always thought of finding an outstanding stock and buying it every point on the way up. That's almost what happened with Pic 'N' Save. We bought it almost every point or two for several years. I liked the company because it gave a way for families of meager means to buy the necessities of life at exceptionally low prices. All told, we bought Pic 'N' Save on 285 different days and held it for 7½ years. When we finally sold it, while it was still advancing, our sale did not affect the market. Early purchases showed more than a 10-fold gain.

Radio Shack's Charles Tandy

We first uncovered Tandy Corp. in 1967, but we were able to convince only two institutions to buy the stock. Among the reasons given for not buying it were that it didn't pay a dividend and Charles Tandy was just a promoter. (Qualcomm was another stock considered to be too promotional from 1996 to 1998. We picked it up straight off the weekly chart in late 1998. It became the leading winner of 1999, advancing 20-fold.)

When I met Tandy in his office in downtown Fort Worth, Texas, my reaction was very positive. He was a brilliant financial man who also happened to be an outstanding salesman. He had innovative incentives, departmental financial statements, and highly detailed daily computer reports on sales of every item in every store by merchandise type, price, and category. His automated inventory and financial controls were almost unbelievable for that time.

After the stock tripled, Wall Street analysts started to acknowledge its existence. There were even a few research reports noting Tandy as an undervalued situation. Isn't it strange how far some stocks have to go up before they begin to look cheap to everyone?

The Size Problem in Portfolio Management

Many institutions think size is a problem. Because they manage billions of dollars, there never seem to be enough big-capitalization stocks they can buy.

Let's face it: size is definitely an obstacle. It's easier to manage $10 million than $100 million; it's easier to manage $100 million than $1 billion; and $1 billion is a piece of cake compared to running $20 billion or $30 billion. The size handicap simply means it's harder to buy or get rid of a huge stock holding in a small- or medium-sized company.

However, I believe it's a mistake for institutions to restrict their investments solely to large-cap companies. In the first place, there definitely aren't enough outstanding ones to invest in at any given time. Why buy a slow-performing stock just because you can easily acquire a lot of it? Why buy big-caps with earnings growing only 10% to 12% a year?

From 1981 to 1987, in the Reagan years, more than 3,000 dynamic, up-and-coming companies incorporated or had initial public offerings. This was a first, and was due mainly to several cuts in the capital gains tax during the early 1980s. Many small- to mid-sized entrepreneurial concerns became enormous market leaders that drove the unprecedented technology boom and expansion of new jobs in the 1980s and 1990s. Most were small, unknown companies, but you'll recognize them now as some of the greatest winning companies of that period. Here is a partial list of the thousands of ingenious innovators that reignited growth in America until the March 2000 market top.

Adobe Systems, Altera, America Online, American Power Conversion, Amgen, Charles Schwab, Cisco Systems, Clear Channel Communications, Compaq Computer, Comverse Technology, Costco, Dell Computer, Digital Switch, EMC, Emulex, Franklin Resources, Home Depot, International Game Technology, Linear Technology, Maxim Integrated Products, Micron Technology, Microsoft, Novell, Novellus Systems, Oracle, PeopleSoft, PMC-Sierra, Qualcomm, Sun Microsystems, UnitedHealth Group, US Healthcare, Veritas Computer, Vitesse Semiconductor, Xilinx.

As mentioned earlier, our government should lower the capital gains tax again and shorten the holding period to six months to help fuel a new cycle of entrepreneurial start-up companies and jobs.

Today's markets are more liquid than past markets, with volume of many medium-sized stocks averaging 500,000 to 5,000,000 shares a day. In addition, significant block crossing between institutions also aids liquidity. The institutional manager handling billions of dollars would be best advised to broaden his prospects to the 4,000 or more innovative companies available. This is better than restricting activities to the same few hundred large, well-known, or legal-list-type companies. And today, a huge number of international entrepreneurial stocks are available.

A sizable institution would probably be better off owning 500 companies of all sizes than 100 large, mature, slow-moving companies. Pension funds can address size problems of their own by spreading their money among several different managers with different investment styles. However, size isn't the number one problem for institutional investors. Frequently, it's their investment philosophies and methods that keep them from fully capitalizing on the potential of the market. Superior performance comes from fresh ideas, not from the same old overused, stale names or last cycle's favorites. For example, the super tech leaders of 1998 and 1999 will probably be replaced by many new consumer leaders in the twenty-first century.

Bottom Buyers' Bliss

Many institutions buy stocks on the way down, but bottom fishing isn't always the best way to achieve superior performance. It can place decision makers in the position of buying stocks slowly deteriorating or whose growth is decelerating.

Other money management groups use valuation models that restrict investments to stocks in the lower end of their historical P/E ranges. This approach works for a number of unusually capable, conservative professionals, but over time, it rarely produces superior results. Several major Midwest banks that use this approach have lagged in performance.

Too many analysts have a P/E hang-up. They want to sell a stock with a P/E that's up and buy one if its P/E is down. Fifty years of models of the most successful stocks show low or "reasonable" P/Es do not cause huge increases in price. Those who buy low P/Es probably missed every big stock market winner of the last half century.

Most of those who concentrate on the undervalued theory of stock selection may lag today's better managers. Sometimes these undervalued situations get more undervalued or lag the market for a long time. In the market free-fall in late 2008 and early 2009, I noticed several value funds that were down about as much as some of the growth funds, which is unusual.

Comparing Growth versus Value Results

Over the previous 12 business cycles, it's been my experience the best money managers during a cycle produced average annual compounded total returns of 25% to, in a few rare cases, 30%. This small group consisted of either growth-stock managers or managers whose most successful investments were in growth stocks plus a few turnaround situations.

The best undervalued-type managers in the same period averaged only 15% to 20%. A few had gains of over 20%. Most typical investors haven't prepared themselves enough to average 25% or more per year, regardless of the method used.

Value funds will do better in down or poor market periods. Their stocks typically haven't gone up a large amount during the prior bull market periods, and so they will correct less. Therefore, people who want to prove the value case will pick a market top as the beginning point of a 10-year period to compare value with growth investing. This is an unfair comparison in which value investing may "prove" more successful than growth-stock investing. The reality is if you look at the situation fairly, growth-stock investing usually outperforms value investing over most periods. I am also not convinced over- and under-weighting relative to the S&P 500 Index is as wise as some managers believe.

Weaknesses of the Industry Analyst System

Another widely used expensive and ineffective practice is to hire a large number of analysts and divvy up coverage by industry.

The typical securities research department has an auto analyst, an electronics analyst, an oil analyst, a retail analyst, a drug analyst, and on and on. But this setup is not efficient and tends to perpetuate mediocre performance. What does an analyst who is assigned two or three out-of-favor groups do? Recommend the least bad of all the poor stocks she follows?

On the other hand, the analyst who happens to follow the year's best-performing group may recommend only two or three winners, missing many others. When the oil stocks boomed in 1979 and 1980, all of them doubled or tripled. The best shot up five times or more.

The theory behind dividing up research is to allow them to be an expert on an industry. In fact, Wall Street firms may hire a chemist from a chemical company to be their chemical analyst and a Detroit auto specialist to be their auto analyst. These individuals may know the nuts and bolts of their industries, but in many cases, have little understanding of the general market and what makes leading stocks go up and down. Maybe this explains why virtually every analyst appearing on CNBC after September 2000 continued to recommend buying high-tech stocks on their way to 80% to 90% declines. People lost a lot of money if they followed this free advice on TV. A similar repeat performance occurred in 2008, when some fundamental analysts recommended buying oils and banks on their way down since they looked cheap. They then got a lot cheaper. An analyst's job should be to make money for clients.

Firms like to advertise they have more analysts, the largest department, or more top-ranked "all-star" analysts. I'd rather have five good analysts who are generalists than 60 or 70 who are confined to limited specialties. What are your chances of finding 60 or more analysts who are outstanding at making money in the market or finding moneymaking ideas?

The shortcomings of Wall Street analysts were never made plainer to investors than during the 2000 bear market. While the market continued to sell off and become the worst bear market since 1929, and former high-flying tech and Internet stocks were being decimated, Wall Street analysts continued to issue "buy" or "strong buy" recommendations on these stocks.

In October 2000, one major Wall Street firm ran full-page ads calling the market "One of the Ten Best Times to Own Stocks" in history. As we now know, the market continued to plummet well into 2001 and 2002, making that period one of the *worst* times in history to own stocks! It was not until many of the tech and Internet high-flyers were down 90% or more from their peaks that these analysts finally changed their tune—many days and many dollars late!

A December 31, 2000, *New York Times* article on analysts' recommendations quoted Zacks Investment Research as follows: "Of the 8,000 recommendations made by analysts covering companies in the Standard & Poor's 500 Index, only 29 now are sells." In the same article, Arthur Levitt, chairman of the Securities and Exchange Commission, stated: "The competition for investing banking business is so keen that analysts' sell recommendations on stocks of banking clients are very rare." A mutual fund manager quoted by the *Times* said: "What passes for research on Wall Street today is shocking to me. Instead of providing investors with the kind of analysis that would have kept them from marching over the cliff, analysts prodded them forward by inventing new valuation criteria for stocks that had no basis in reality and no standards of good practice." *Vanity Fair* also ran an interesting article on the analytical community in August 2001. Clearly, at no time in the history of the markets has the phrase caveat emptor had more meaning for investors, both institutional and individual alike.

The implementation of SEC Rule FD, governing fair disclosure of material company information to both institutional and individual investors, in 2000 has restricted the ability of major brokerage research analysts to receive inside information from a company before it is released to the rest of the Street. This further reduced any advantage that can be gained by listening to most Wall Street analysts. We prefer to deal only with facts and historical models rather than opinions about supposed values. Many research analysts in 2000 and 2001 had not been in the business for 10 years or longer and therefore had never experienced the terrible bear markets of 1987, 1974–1975, and 1962.

On still another subject, many large money-management groups probably deal with entirely too many research firms. For one thing, there aren't that many strong research inputs, and dealing with 20 or 30 firms dilutes the value and impact of the few good ones. Confusion, doubt, and fear created by conflicting advice at critical junctures may prove to be expensive. It would be interesting to know how many analysts have been highly successful in their own investments. This is the ultimate test.

Financial World's Startling Survey of Top Analysts

A *Financial World* article dated November 1, 1980, also found that analysts selected by *Institutional Investor* magazine as the best on Wall Street were overrated and overpaid, and they materially underperformed the S&P averages. As a group, the "superstar" analysts failed on two out of three stock picks to match either the market or their own industry averages. They also seldom provided sell recommendations, limiting most of their advice to buys or holds. The *Financial World* study confirmed research we performed in the early 1970s. We found only a minority of Wall Street recommendations were successful. We also concluded during a period where many sell opinions were in order, just 1 in 10 reports made a sell suggestion.

Database Power and Efficiency

On any day, most institutional money managers receive a stack of research reports. Trudging through them in search of a good stock is usually a waste of time. If lucky, they may spot 1 in 20 that's right to buy.

In contrast, managers with access to WONDA can rapidly screen all the companies in our database. If the defense industry pops up as one of the leading industries, they can call up 84 different companies whose primary business is in that area. The typical institution might look at Boeing, Raytheon, United Technologies, and two or three other big, well-known names. Since WONDA provides more than 3,000 technical and fundamental variables on each of the 84 companies stretching back a number of years, as well as the ability to display these variables quickly on identical graphic displays, it's possible for an institutional money manager to identify in 20 minutes the 3 or 4 companies in the entire group that show outstanding characteristics and are worthy of more detailed research. It's a vital time-saver some of America's very best money managers relentlessly use.

In other words, there are ways for an institution's analysts to spend their time far more productively. Yet, not all research departments are organized to take advantage of such advanced and disciplined procedures.

How well has this approach worked? In 1977, we introduced an institutional service called New Stock Market Ideas and Past Leaders to Avoid (NSMI). Now titled New Leaders and Laggards Review, it is published every week, and its documented, 31-year long-term performance record is shown on the accompanying graph. These performance returns were audited and verified by one of the top independent accounting firms in America.

Over the last 30 years, positive selections outperformed *avoids* 307 to 1, and positive picks outran the S&P 500 stocks more than 41-fold. Compounding over the 30 years' time helps make a superior long-term record like this possible. For the entire 30 years ended 2008, stocks to avoid made a teeny 19% gain. Institutions could have improved their performance just by staying out of the stocks on our avoid list. As a service to our institutional clients, we provide them with computerized quarterly performance reports for every *positive* and *avoid* suggestion made in the New Leader Ideas service. How many competing firms provide the actual percent performance of all of their ideas over an extended period?

By having massive factual data on every firm and proven historical precedent chart models over more than 100 years, we're able to discover a stock beginning to improve or get in trouble earlier—without ever visiting or talking to the company. It may be naïve to believe companies are always going to tell you when they are beginning to have problems. By using our own factual data and historical precedent research, we discourage reliance on tips, rumors, and analysts' personal opinions. We don't need such information. We also do not have investment banking clients or market-making activities. Nor do we manage money for other people or hire research analysts to prepare long written research reports. So those areas of potential bias or underperformance are nonexistent.

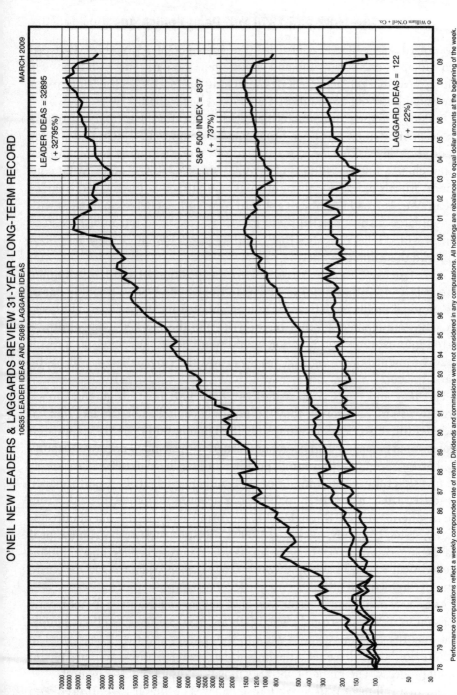

O'NEIL NEW LEADERS & LAGGARDS REVIEW 31-YEAR LONG-TERM RECORD

10635 LEADER IDEAS AND 5089 LAGGARD IDEAS

MARCH 2009

© William O'Neil + Co.

LEADER IDEAS = 32895
(+ 32795%)

S&P 500 INDEX = 837
(+ 737%)

LAGGARD IDEAS = 122
(+ 22%)

Performance computations reflect a weekly compounded rate of return. Dividends and commissions were not considered in any computations. All holdings are rebalanced to equal dollar amounts at the beginning of the week. Percent gains and losses are calculated for all issues that remain on the "LEADER IDEAS" or "LAGGARD IDEAS" at the end of the week.

Performance results do not represent actual trading, and they may not reflect the impact that material economic and market factors might have had on the investment decision-making process if actually managing client money. The above does not imply comparable future performance. It should be recognized there is substantial speculative risk in most common stocks.

417

The 1982 and 1978 Full-Page Bullish Ads

We don't try to call every short-term or intermediate correction. Our primary focus is on recognizing and acting upon the early stages of each new bull or bear market. This includes searching for market sectors and groups that should be bought and those that should be avoided.

In early 1982, we placed a full-page ad in the *Wall Street Journal* stating the back of inflation had been broken and the important stocks had already made their lows. That May, we mailed out two wall charts to our institutional clients: one of defense electronics stocks, and the other of 20 consumer growth stocks we thought might be attractive for the bull market ahead. We also made a point of going to New York and Chicago to meet with several large institutions. In these meetings, we stated our bullish posture and provided a list of names that could be purchased after these organizations did their due diligence.

The stance we took was counter to the position of most institutional research firms at that time, as well as to the negative news flooding out of the national media each day. Most investment firms were downright bearish. They anticipated another big down leg in the market. They also projected interest rates and inflation would soar back to new highs as a result of government borrowing that would crowd the private sector out of the marketplace.

The fear and confusion created by these judgments frightened many large investors. As a result, they did not fully capitalize on the fact that we had identified two leading groups for the coming bull market. It appeared professional managers had been bombarded with so much negative "expert" Wall Street input that they found positive findings hard to believe. As for us, we invested fully in the summer of 1982 and enjoyed our best performance up to that time. From 1978 to 1991, our account increased 20-fold. From the beginning of 1998 through 2000, our firm's account, run out of our separate holding company, increased 1,500%. Results such as this remind us it may be an advantage *not* to be headquartered in rumor-filled and emotion-packed Wall Street. I have never worked one day on Wall Street in my entire time in the investment field.

As a savvy individual investor, you have a gigantic advantage in not having to listen to different, strongly held opinions. You can see from this example that majority opinions seldom work in the market and that stocks seem to require doubt and disbelief—the proverbial "wall of worry"—to make meaningful progress. The market contrarily moves to disappoint the majority.

Our first full-page *Wall Street Journal* ad was in March 1978. It predicted a new bull market in small- to mid-sized growth stocks. We had written the "Grab The Bull By The Horns" ad weeks ahead of time and waited to run it until the time was right. The right time came when the market was making new lows, which caught investors by surprise. Our only reason for placing the ad was to document in print what our position was at that point, so institutional investors could have no question about it later. We were also one of the few firms to tell its accounts they should avoid or sell tech stocks and raise cash in March, April, and September 2000.

It is at these extremely difficult market turning points an institutional firm can be of most value. At such times, many people are either petrified with fear or carried away with excessive fundamental information.

Institutional Investors Are Human

If you don't think fear and emotion can ride high among professional investors after a prolonged decline, think again. I remember meeting with the top three or four money managers of one important bank at the bottom of the 1974 market. They were as shell-shocked, demoralized, and confused as anyone could possibly be. (The ordinary stock at that time was down 75%.) About the same time, I recall visiting another top manager. He too was thoroughly worn out and, judging from the peculiar color of his face, suffering from market sickness. Yet another top fund manager in Boston looked as if he'd been run over by a train. (Of course, all of this is preferable to 1929, when some people jumped out of office buildings in response to the devastating market collapse.)

I also recall a high-tech seminar in 1983 in San Francisco, attended by 2,000 highly educated analysts and portfolio managers. Everyone was there, and everyone was ebullient and self-confident. That marked the exact top for high-tech stocks.

I also remember a presentation we gave to a bank in another large city. All its analysts were brought in and sat around an impressive table in the boardroom, but not one analyst or portfolio manager asked any questions during or after the presentation. It was the strangest situation I've ever been in. Needless to say, this institution consistently performed in the lower quartiles compared to its more alert and venturesome competitors. It's important to communicate and be open to new ideas.

Years ago, one medium-sized bank for which we did consulting work insisted we give them recommendations only from among the stocks it carried on its limited approved list. After consulting with the bank's managers each month for three months and telling them there was nothing on their approved list that met our qualifications, we had to honorably part company. A few months later, we learned key officials in that trust department had been relieved of their jobs as a result of their laggard performance.

We provided product to another Midwest institution, but it was of doubtful value because the institution had a cast-in-concrete belief that any potential investment had to be screened to see if it passed an undervalued model. The best investments rarely show up on any undervalued model, and there's probably no way this institution will produce first-rate results until it throws out the model. This isn't easy for large organizations to do. It's like asking a Baptist to become a Catholic or vice versa.

Some large money-management companies with average records tend to fire the head of the investment department and then look for a replacement who invests pretty much the same way. Naturally, this doesn't solve the problem of deficient investment methods. Security Pacific Bank in Los Angeles was an exception to this rule. In July 1981, it made a change in its top investment management. It brought in an individual with a completely different approach, a superior investment philosophy, and an outstanding performance record. The results were dramatic and were accomplished almost overnight. In 1982, Security Pacific's Fund G was ranked number one in the country.

Penny-Wise and Performance-Foolish

Some corporations put too much emphasis on saving management fees, particularly when they have giant funds to be managed. It's usually an actuary who convinces them of the money their pension fund can save by shaving the fee by ¼ of 1%.

If corporations have billions of dollars to be managed, it makes sense for them to increase their fees and incentives so they can hire the best money managers in the business. The better managers will earn the extra 0.25% or 0.50% ten times over. The last thing you ever want is cheap advice in the stock market. If you were going to have open-heart surgery, would you look for the doctor who'll charge the absolute least?

How to Select and Measure Money Managers

Here are a few tips for organizations that want to farm out their funds to several money managers.

In general, portfolio managers should be given a complete cycle before their performance is reviewed for the purpose of deciding whether to change managers. Give them from the peak of one bull market period to the peak of the next or from the trough of one cycle to the trough of another. This will usually cover a three- or four-year period and allow all managers to go through both an up market and a down market. At the end of this period, the bottom 20% of managers in performance should be replaced. Thereafter, every year or two, the bottom 5% or 10% over the most recent three- or four-year period should be dropped. This avoids hasty decisions based on disappointing performance over a few short quarters or a year. Given time, this process will lead to an outstanding group of proven money managers. Because this is a sound, longer-term, self-correcting system, it should stay that way. Then it won't be necessary to pay as many consultants to recommend changes in personnel.

In selection of managers, consideration should be given to their latest three- to five-year performance statistics as well as to a more recent period. Diversification among the types, styles, and locations of managers should be considered. The search should be widespread and not necessarily limited to one consultant's narrow, captive universe or stable of managers.

The corporate or pension fund client with money to be managed also has to be careful not to interfere at critical junctures—deciding, for example, when a greater proportion of the portfolios should be either in stocks or in bonds or that undervalued stocks should be emphasized.

Cities and counties that have funds to invest must be extremely careful. Few of their personnel are highly experienced in the investment field. These inexperienced people can easily be talked into investing in bonds that are promoted as being safe but that later cause enormous losses. This happened, of course, in 2008 with AAA subprime loans in real estate mortgage packages.

Clients can also interfere by directing where commissions should go or insisting that executions be given to whomever does them most cheaply. The latter, while a well-meaning attempt to save money, commonly results in forcing upon a money manager someone who provides either poorer executions or no research input of real value. This handicap costs the portfolio money, as it pays ½ point or more (or its decimal equivalents) on trades that are executed by less expert people.

Daily Graphs Online becomes MarketSmith®

In 1973, a friend suggested that we produce a weekly chart book to help retail investors find growth stocks with CAN SLIM characteristics. Our weekly Daily Graphs® books were a tremendous success because they helped investors cull through thousands of potential investments quickly and efficiently. We still print them, but in 1998 Daily Graphs moved online with applications such as Charting, Custom Screens, Industry Groups, Option Guide, and Mutual Fund Center.

In early 2010, Daily Graphs Online will again transform itself into MarketSmith. MarketSmith graphs stay true to the original Daily Graphs

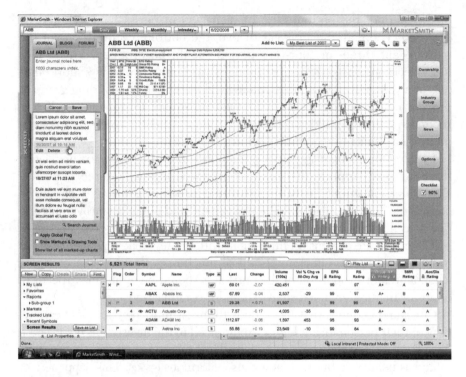

design. But we've taken the tool a few steps beyond the expected. We engaged one of the country's premier Web site design firms to help us create a research tool that was robust enough for the sophisticated user and yet intuitive enough for the novice investor.

MarketSmith gives users access to several proprietary ratings and rankings such as Relative Strength Rank, Earning Per Share Rank, Sales-Margins-Return on Equity (SMR) Rating, and the Composite Rating using the same institutional quality data that William O'Neil + Company provides to professional money managers through the WONDA platform.

We've integrated a checklist feature to help remind an investor how any stock rates against important financial benchmarks.

MarketSmith has a visually intuitive stock and mutual fund database screening module. Investors can search over 7,000 stocks and 9,000 mutual funds to find those that meet specific fundamental and technical criteria.

MarketSmith users who belong to investment clubs or attend IBD Meetups can share database screens and stock lists and blog about their own market observations and experiences. IBD subscribers have exclusive access to IBD content such as the IBD news stories and the IBD 100.

We've designed MarketSmith so it can run on a Mac or PC, and there's even a MarketSmith iPhone application for when you are away from your desk.

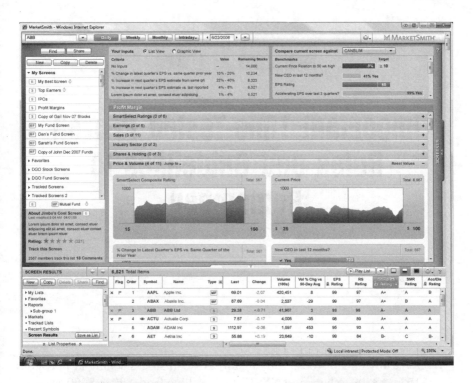

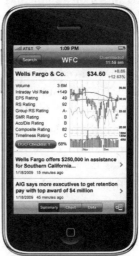

MarketSmith is the ultimate stock research tool that takes the information and knowledge that you gain from reading this book and brings it to life. As you gain experience and learn to effectively use MarketSmith, you can truly become an investing master.

Important Time-Tested Proven Rules and Guidelines to Remember

1. Don't buy cheap stocks. Buy mainly Nasdaq stocks selling at between $15 and $300 a share and NYSE stocks selling from $20 to $300 a share. The majority of super stocks emerge from sound strong chart bases of $30 and up. Avoid the junk pile below $10.

2. Buy growth stocks where each of the last three years' annual earnings per share have been up at least 25% and the next year's consensus earnings estimate is up 25% or more. Many growth stocks will also have annual cash flow of 20% or more above EPS.

3. Make sure the last two or three quarters' earnings per share are up a huge amount. Look for a minimum of 25% to 30%. In bull markets, look for EPS up 40% to 500%. (The higher, the better.)

4. See that each of the last three quarters' sales are accelerating in their percentage increases or the last quarter's sales are up at least 25%.

5. Buy stocks with a return on equity of 17% or more. The outstanding companies will show a return on equity of 25% to 50%.

6. Make sure the recent quarterly after-tax profit margins are improving and are near the stock's peak after-tax margins in prior quarters.

7. Most stocks should be in the top six or more broad industry sectors in IBD's daily "New Price Highs" list or in the top 10% of IBD's "197 Industry Sub-Group Rankings."

8. Don't buy a stock because of its dividend or its P/E ratio. Buy it because it's the number one company in its particular field in terms of earnings and sales growth, ROE, profit margins, and product superiority.

9. In bull markets, buy stocks with a Relative Price Strength rating of 85 or higher in *Investor's Business Daily's SmartSelect* ratings.

10. Any size capitalization will do, but the majority of your stocks should trade an average daily volume of several hundred thousand shares or more.

11. Learn to read charts and recognize proper bases and exact buy points. Use daily and weekly charts to materially improve your stock selection and timing. Long-term monthly charts can help, too. Buy stocks when they initially break out of sound and proper bases with volume for the day 50% or more above normal trading volume.

12. Carefully average up, not down, and cut every single loss when it is 7% or 8% below your *purchase price*, with absolutely no exceptions.

13. Write out your sell rules that determine when you will sell and nail down a worthwhile profit in your stock on the way up.

14. Make sure that one or two better-performing mutual funds have bought your stock in the last reporting period. You also want your stocks to have increasing institutional sponsorship over the last several quarters.

15. The company should have an excellent, new, superior product or service that is selling well. It should also have a big market for its product and the opportunity for repeat sales.

16. The general market should be in an uptrend and be favoring either small- or big-cap companies. (If you don't know how to interpret the general market indexes, read IBD's "The Big Picture" column every day.)

17. Don't mess around with options, stocks trading only in foreign markets, bonds, preferred stocks, or commodities. It doesn't pay to be a "jack-of-all-trades" or overdiversify or have too much asset allocation. Either avoid options outright or restrict them to 5% or 10% of your portfolio.

18. The stock should have ownership by top management.

19. Look mainly for "new America" entrepreneurial companies (those with a new issue within the last eight or even up to 15 years) rather than too many laggard, "old America" companies.

20. Forget your pride and your ego; the market doesn't care what you think or want. No matter how smart you think you are, the market is always smarter. A high IQ and a master's degree are no guarantee of market success. Your ego could cost you a lot of money. Don't argue with the market. Never try to prove you're right and the market is wrong.

21. Read *Investor's Corner* and "The Big Picture" in IBD daily. Learn how to recognize general market tops and bottoms. Read up on any company you own or plan to buy; learn and understand its story.

22. Watch for companies that have recently announced they are buying back 5% to 10% or more of their common stock. Find out if there is new management in the company and where it came from.

23. Don't try to buy a stock at the bottom or on the way down in price, and don't average down. (If you buy the stock at $40, don't buy more if it goes down to $35 or $30.)

Key Reasons People Miss Buying Great Winning Stocks

1. Disbelief, fear, and lack of knowledge. Most big winners are newer companies (with IPOs in the last eight or 15 years). Everyone knows Sears and General Motors, but most people are simply unaware of or unfamiliar with the hundreds of new names that come into the market every year. The new America names are the great growth engine of America, creating innovative new products and services plus most of the new technology. (A chart service is one easy way to at least be aware of the basics of price, volume, sales, and earnings trends of all these compelling younger entrepreneurial companies.)

2. P/E bias. Contrary to conventional wisdom, the best stocks rarely sell at low P/Es. Just as the best ballplayers make the highest salaries, the better companies sell at better (higher) P/Es. Using P/Es as a selection criterion will prevent you from buying most of the best stocks.

3. Not understanding that the real leaders start their big moves by selling near or at new price highs, not near new lows or off a good amount from their highs. Investors like to buy stocks that look cheap because the stocks are lower than they were a few months ago, so they buy stocks on the way down. They think they are getting bargains. They should be buying stocks that are on the way up, just making new price highs as they emerge from a proper base or price consolidation area.

4. Selling too soon, either because they get shaken out or because they are too quick to take a profit, and psychologically having a hard time buying back a stock at a higher price if necessary. They also sell too late, letting a small loss turn into a devastating one by not cutting all their losses at 8%.

One Final Thought

You can definitely become financially independent once you learn to save and invest properly. But you first have to get serious and make up your mind to work at it and never let yourself get discouraged, regardless of circumstances. My parting advice: have courage, be positive, and don't ever give up. Great opportunities occur every year in America. Get yourself prepared, study, learn, and go for them. What you'll find is that little acorns can, over time, grow into giant oaks, and that with persistence and hard work, anything is possible. You can do it, and your own determination to succeed is the most important element. When you get off the track and make mistakes, which all of us do, re-read this book, attend a workshop or seminar, or take a home-study course and get back on track . . . there are no overnight successes in the stock market.

**Success in a free country is simple.
Get a job, get an education, and learn to save and invest wisely.
Anyone can do it. You can do it.**

Success Stories

Over the course of 25 years and counting, *Investor's Business Daily* has heard from countless readers who have experienced life-changing financial success because of the CAN SLIM and IBD method. The following is a small sample of the thousands of success stories we've received over the years from people of all ages and experience levels. It's a powerful testament to the fact that with a little hard work, patience, and dedication, anyone can learn to follow this system to improve their results.

Market Timing

"IBD is a proven and no-nonsense approach to investing. This system has helped me find the big winners in a market rally, and more importantly, it has helped me avoid the big losses in a market downturn. This, in turn, has allowed me to retire in my early fifties, spend more time with my family, work on my hobbies and interests, and generally lead a very happy life."

Michael A., Florida, Retired

"I shared IBD's 'Big Picture' recommendation to trim equity holdings and raise cash in December 2007 with my 'smart friends' (attorney and financial services manager). I reiterated the fact that IBD had had the same market call in January 2000. While my friends and colleagues were chasing financials (see falling knife), my wife and I were able to buy quality CAN SLIM stocks at proper breakpoints. Suffice it to say that my wife and I have had a

429

great year being in cash for most of 2008. Thanks, IBD! Rest assured, you may have two more subscribers on the way!!!"

Ken C., California, Financial Advisor

"I've been a follower of IBD for around 17 years. A serious follower for the last four years. In 2007, I achieved a return of +56% in my trading account, and I broke even in 2008 by staying out of the market for most of the year. The system has never failed me. The paper's content, format, and teachings have only gotten better over the years."

Eric M., Illinois, Engineer

"I have been a reader of IBD since 2005 and have profited immensely from it. Also, I have attended more than five IBD workshops from level 1 to level 3, and each has made me a better disciplined investor. The CAN SLIM system, a system that works great whether in good times or bad times."

Rajesh S., Texas, Electrical Engineer

"I'd like to take a moment to thank IBD for the 'Big Picture' and the 'Market Outlook.' I'm a federal employee with a 401(k) plan called the Thrift Savings Program. We are limited to five basic funds. The government or 'G' Fund is invested in government securities and is our safe haven. The 'C' Fund is our S&P 500 stock fund, the 'F' Fund is our commercial bond fund, the 'S' Fund is our small-cap fund, and finally the 'I' fund is our international fund. By using the 'Big Picture' and 'Market Outlook,' I was able to follow the general market trend and move all of my retirement funds out of the market and into a cash position in the 'G' fund. While most of my coworkers suffered huge losses in the market and the market in general lost over 35%, my total return for 2008 was up 4%. I simply check the 'Big Picture' every day and move my money either into or out of the market using 'Market Outlook' information. Again, thanks for your hard work."

Brian D., Florida, Supervisory Special Agent

No Opinions, Only Facts

"In describing IBD, I would say it is without doubt one of the best sources of information for investors that is available for the money. You don't get any 'Wall Street' spin on the markets from IBD. It gives you the straight stuff. By that, I mean IBD tells you the truth about the markets, economy, political events, etc., that affect the markets, whether positive or negative. That is huge in this climate because there is a lot of 'Financial Nonsense' being fed to investors by too many unreliable sources these days. IBD tells investors the truth. You can count on it!"

Steve C., Texas, Ophthalmologist

"IBD and Investors.com let you focus on what the market is actually doing at any given moment, allowing you not to have to listen to all the noisy fortune tellers on the tube."

Norm D., California, Individual Investor

"IBD is a tremendous time-saver. I make it a part of my daily process to read IBD every business day, even if I do not read anything else. It is a great way to quickly get a feel for the general market direction, continue to remain educated, and learn about the secrets of success that keeps me motivated. Where else can you get that in about 15 minutes a day? It is an extraordinary publication!"

George M., California, Executive

"To me, *Investor's Business Daily* is an outstanding market analysis resource because it is based on objective empirical research that cuts through pundit opinions and personal emotions in buying and selling stock. Its greatest strength is its direct, clear-thinking presentation of market-relevant news that leaves often confused approaches of other publications behind."

Allen A., Connecticut, Ph.D.

CAN SLIM

"Just studying IBD and CAN SLIM shows that if you really apply yourself properly, you can succeed. You don't have to be at the mercy of so-called experts who really aren't. I don't like the intimidation tactics or the pressure tactics of the money managers. There are no guarantees in investing, but with IBD and CAN SLIM, the odds are on your side."

Carol T., Massachusetts, Anesthesiologist

"I have been trading stocks full time since 2003, thanks largely to William O'Neil's *How to Make Money in Stocks* and IBD. I have reread the book many times and am rereading it again. It is full of different-color marks, as each time I read it I find something new and useful. I must say, *How to Make Money in Stocks*, the IBD subscription, and the online tools are essential to successful stock trading. Just like people grab their family photo albums from the house on fire, if I were to pick just one thing to assure my continued success in stock trading, it would be William O'Neil's *How to Make Money in Stocks*."

Slav F., California, Stock Trader

Proven Rules

"*Investor's Business Daily* is a source for useful and accurate information about how the market works. I have found that following the buy and sell rules works. If you follow those seemingly simple but at times hard to follow rules, you will make money."

Herb M., Michigan, Individual Investor

"It was only when I started properly applying the IBD sell rules that I realized the power to not only cut losses short, but stay away when conditions are not good for making money. A day without IBD is a day of missed opportunity."

Dennis H., Florida, Retired Broker

"William O'Neil taught me the two rules that form the cornerstone of my investing plan: (1) keep your losses small, and (2) average up, never down. Those two simple rules have kept me out of a lot of trouble. When I have strayed from them, it inevitably cost me money. Thank you, Bill, for all you have done for the average investor."

Peter M., California, Executive

Investor Education at Its Best

"I have gone to great lengths to learn about investing. I attended business school as an undergraduate and graduate student, and worked for a retail brokerage firm and for a small-cap research firm that supported institutional clients. Even after all this experience, it wasn't until I read *How to Make Money in Stocks* that I began to understand how to succeed in the market."

Andrew M., New York, Vice President

"My students were participating in the Stock Market Game and struggling with losses. Then they started using *Investor's Business Daily*. IBD helped my students reverse big losses and win third place in the Stock Market Game. IBD has helped motivate my students to get great information in an easy-to-use format. It's given them the tools to research and make investment decisions, and become their own independent investors."

Stephen D., New York, High School Teacher

"I've been a subscriber to *Investor's Business Daily* since 1991. This is investor education at its best. I fired my broker two weeks after I got IBD. I told him I didn't need him anymore. I trade over 150,000 shares each year. I used to have no savings, but because of IBD, my net worth is well over 1 million dollars. I run it as a business. I'm just an average guy, I'm not a genius, but I study a lot and use IBD. That's how I succeed. It's more than a newspaper; it's a working document."

George G., Georgia, Pilot Trainer

"My stock life before IBD had no direction. I had no idea there was anything to learn. Life after IBD opened my eyes, and my mind. I don't ever expect to stop learning!"

Marilyn W., Ohio, Retired

"Investing without IBD is like trying to live without water. IBD will give you the proper structure to make informed and assessed decisions about the general market or a particular stock issue, intelligently. I have taught the principles of the paper to several hundred of my college students over the past four years, and they have had fantastic results. They do not invest without it, and neither do I."

James D., Florida, College Instructor

"Spend a year learning everything there is to learn in IBD. It's like getting your doctorate in investing without going to four schools. It's the easiest, quickest way to become a savvy investor, regardless of how much you have to invest."

Julie P., Colorado, Author, Nutritionist

"I have been subscribing to IBD since first studying stocks about 1990 and would not do without it. I read it every day, and it is like my right hand."

Averie M., Florida, Retired

"Over my 18 years of teaching junior high, high school, and college, I have used a wide variety of texts, videos, Web sites, newspapers, magazines, computers, and board games in teaching my students about investing. Without question, IBD has been the most exciting and pertinent resource I have ever used on the basis of student success in investing as well as student motivation to use the resource."

Mike S., Texas, Teacher

Real Performance

"I figure I've made more money in stocks using IBD as my daily resource than I've made as a CPA over the last 10 years."

Robert F., Illinois, CPA

"With Bill O'Neil's guidance, I was able to reach my goal. I now can enjoy and support my 12-year-old twin sons, trading stocks as a single, work-at-home Dad. Bill's stock wisdom allowed me to grow and protect my hard-earned money plus enabled me to live a more rewarding lifestyle."

Tim K., California, Chief Investment Officer

"I've been reading IBD since its inception. I started with $5,000, and three years later, it escalated to $50,000. Why? Because of IBD. Need I say more?"

Fred B., New York, Arbitrator

"Since I started using CAN SLIM and IBD, and now Investors.com, I was able to make 359% on my original investment! IBD has so many features that help me find the great stocks. I'm grateful for all the work you do to help investors."

Kathleen P., California, Individual Investor

"I subscribed to *Investor's Business Daily* for the first time after I retired. I started using it for my stock portfolio because I wasn't happy with my brokers. With them, my portfolio was racking up losses. With IBD's help, over time I was able to get my portfolio back in the green with 20% and 30% gains. I took a portfolio of $400,000 to $700,000 thanks to IBD. I love IBD. I talk it up wherever I go."

Don R., Washington, Restaurant Owner

"For more than ten consecutive years, we've realized a compounded 57% annual return. CAN SLIM and IBD played a preeminent role in that success."

Florence R., Texas, Investor

"I started investing more than ten years ago. I was not very consistent until I was introduced to *Investor's Business Daily*. I've been profitable ever since."

Ash M., Hawaii, Business Owner

"After reading IBD, learning the CAN SLIM investing system, and reading IBD founder Bill O'Neil's books, I've become successful enough to be a stay-at-home Dad. Thanks to IBD and CAN SLIM, my dreams have come true."

Eric K., Illinois, Individual Investor

"I have been reading IBD since the late 1990s. I've employed the CAN SLIM rules, and they allowed me to comfortably retire last May. This is the only paper I read for financial investment advice. I continue to recommend IBD to all my investor friends."

Frederick D., Michigan, Retired

"How about an investor up over 130% in 2008? *Investor's Business Daily* is where I look to make it happen!!!"

John B., Illinois, Real Estate Broker

"By following IBD's rules, I have quadrupled my account since May 2003. IBD has also helped me remain flat this year in a severe bear market. The best thing is that the rules are very easy to learn and follow, and I have lost money only when I tried to put my own 'wrinkles' on them."

Edward K., Arizona, Retired Doctor

"Thanks to *Investor's Business Daily* and Mr. O'Neil's CAN SLIM, my 401(k) is still +10%. I have continually kept my losses at less than or equal to 8%. This with taking 20–25% gains with the occasional larger take has resulted in investment success. Thank you."

Don B., Michigan, Retired Anesthesiologist

"Starting in 1999 with $5K in savings and $7K in wedding presents, I used the CAN SLIM system to make over seven figures by 2008."

Jonathan S., Tennessee, Individual Investor

"I am glad to say I have kept almost all of my profits from the 2003 bull run thanks to your publication. . . . IBD is an excellent data source about the markets and can help individuals and professionals make better decisions about how to invest their money."

Bruce W., California, Attorney

"With my knowledge from IBD, I have experienced excellent performance in my investing from the late 1990s to October 2007."

Bob K., Hawaii, Mechanical Engineer

"Between the dot-com bust and 9/11, my portfolio lost nearly half its value over two years. Though I subscribed to the *Wall Street Journal* at the time, it did not prevent my loss. I subscribed to *Investor's Business Daily* and found it much more informative on investing. Soon, I found myself reading IBD rather than the *WSJ*. It was more to the point and was tailored to individual stocks rather than worldviews and mutual funds. I have never looked back. Using the knowledge I gained from IBD on reading stock charts and trends, I bought into stocks for triple-digit gains among many other double-digit-gain stocks. IBD has paid for itself many times over with what I have learned from CAN SLIM and other resources available. Thanks, IBD! I will be a lifetime subscriber."

Kenneth G., Michigan, Utility Planner

"I believe in results: I made my monthly salary in three days using IBD. I'm a believer! I've looked at several investing sources. IBD and Investors.com are the only ones that made me more money than I spent learning it."

Kent J., California, Manager

"I sold a business, and after a couple of years with GS money management, I decided that I must manage my money myself. It wasn't long before we realized that IBD is the only daily publication that sincerely wants to help people make money in the market. That's why we're so loyal to the paper. We don't look at any other sources of information of any kind because it only confuses the issue. It's tough to shut down those media inputs. IBD has been wonderful for us. It works very well, and every year we're doing better because we see the results in the portfolio. In our second year using IBD we had a 26% gain, and it's only gone up substantially since there."

Michael D., California, Retired

"In 2006 I used a number of newly acquired CAN SLIM skills to buy into Hansen Natural and to pyramid and force-feed my growing position to the point where I had nearly 80% invested in HANS. Following CAN SLIM principles, I sold my entire position May 11, 2006, for near perfect timing. This one trade made my year and enough to cover for lean years the following two years. I would not have traded with this success without using IBD."

Joseph S., Pennsylvania, Executive

"Investor's Business Daily is one of the best things that has happened to our family from a financial point of view."

Roger D., Iowa, Teacher

Tools That Work

"The 'Big Picture' keeps me focused on proper interpretation of general market averages. I also use the IBD 100 for confirmation that stocks I might be interested in are seen in the same light by the experts at IBD. I like the entire B section: 'Stocks on the Move' shows where the action is; industry group rankings let me know where to focus research; the stock research tables grouped by leaders make it easy to see what stocks are leading. I could keep going. The A section is excellent for keeping up on important news. The paper is so well organized."

Mark R., Washington, Individual Investor

"I love reading the IBD newspaper—the 'Big Picture,' 'IBD's Top 10' news stories, and many more. It keeps me focused on what's happening with the stock market and the economy. While IBD provides a superior wealth of information for finding good stocks, this newspaper is also an excellent space- and time-saver. It makes it so easy to take anywhere I go. Thanks to the IBD staff for their great work."

Paul C., Maryland, Investor

"The IBD 100 is the foundation of my portfolio. It provides a list of stocks that I assess from a fundamental and technical basis. The quality of the stocks maximizes the probability of a trade."

Steve M., Colorado, Equity Trading Manager

"The 'Big Picture,' 'Investor's Corner,' 'NYSE & NASDAQ Stocks in the News,' along with the *'Market Wrap'* and *'Daily Stock Analysis'* videos, 'Stock Checkup,' and 'IBD University' at Investors.com, are the features I use the most to help me stay on top of the market, select strong stocks, and learn to become a better stock investor. All are invaluable."

Alex J., California, Student

"I read the 'Big Picture' first because it is the starting point for getting a feel for how the market is going. Once you have that information, you can make informed decisions on how to proceed with investing decisions. IBD is the premier investing document that provides everything for everyone, from the beginning investor to the most advanced investor. Taking full advantage of all of the many features will give you the best chance of success."

Cliff B., Texas, Retired U.S. Air Force

The Confidence to Win

"IBD changed my life in that it gave me full confidence as a self-directed investor, and it presented the right information that has allowed me to grow and preserve my portfolio. What began as an education blossomed into a passion, and this was the real life change for me."

Mary L., Tennessee, Realtor

"I'm a beginning investor who knew nothing about the stock market. Through Bill O'Neil's *How to Make Money in Stocks, 24 Essential Lessons*, and the excellent coverage, education, and tips provided in IBD and Investors.com, I find myself more knowledgeable than most people I know who've been investing for years."

Kim P., California, Individual Investor

"William O'Neil enabled me to do something even my CPA was not able to do: master my finances."

Mike H., Florida, CPA

"I got started in the market in 1990 after reading I believe it was your second edition, and what it did for me is truly unbelievable. You really explain every aspect of the market so well. I also have been a subscriber to *Investor's Business Daily* since that year and spend two hours per day on it. Thanks for helping to make me secure in investments."

Ruth B., California, Individual Investor

"Using *Investor's Business Daily*—both the newspaper and Investors.com, along with the Daily Graphs and my own research—I am extremely confident of continuing to make money in the markets."

Daryl T., Texas, Computer Programmer

"IBD and Investors.com have been a tremendous teacher & tool for me. IBD is one of the few resources I've found that not only gives information in an understandable way but also includes instruction on deciphering information that makes sense. Thank you for taking the intimidation out of investing!"

Sherrie C., Nevada, Investor

"IBD and CAN SLIM empower me with the information I need to manage my money more successfully. I'm in charge of my money, so it's important that I understand how to invest it. And IBD is so good for that. Knowledge is power, and that's why I read IBD."

Carol M., Oregon, Planning Commissioner

Oldies but Goodies

The third edition of *How to Make Money in Stocks* featured IBD readers who achieved investing results or shared how they learned to use the IBD and CAN SLIM system. We thought we should reprint a few of these comments in hopes they might provide helpful insights for you.

Labor Day, 2001

Dear Mr. William O'Neil and *Investor's Business Daily*,

As a huge enthusiast of *Investor's Business Daily* and all of your written material, I can't write enough explaining how much your works have changed my life.

I first came across *How to Make Money in Stocks* in the fall of 1997 through reading reviews of it on Amazon.com. I was living and teaching in Guatemala at the time, and was looking to get involved in investing and the stock market. Consequently, I ordered *How to Make Money in Stocks* and a few other books, but it was your book, based on historical research, that intrigued me the most. I reasoned that you had seen both great times and rough times in your over 40 years of trading, while most other books had research based only from the 1990s. In addition to that, you used both technical and fundamental analysis rather than concentrating on just one method. The other books I read advocated either one analysis or the other.

I was further convinced that your system of trading was for me when you wrote how David Ryan and Lee Freestone had won U.S. Investing Championships using the CAN SLIM system.

What complements *How to Make Money in Stocks* perfectly is *Investor's Business Daily*. I had clipped out the coupon in the back of your book for a free two-week subscription to IBD, and when I received the paper for the first time, the whole system made sense to me. Finding the CAN SLIM stocks was so much easier to do using IBD, and the paper had so many other great articles, including 'Leaders & Success,' 'The New America,' 'Stocks in the News,' and my favorite, 'Investor's Corner,' that further enhanced my insights into trading. I immediately subscribed to it, even though $180 was a lot for me at the time. Then, even though the paper would arrive in Guatemala three days late each day, I could still use its valuable information for research.

I read everything I could in the paper and decided to use it in my profession of teaching. That year, as I was teaching English as a Second Language in Guatemala, I also taught one class of fifth-grade gifted and talented students.

I introduced them to IBD, and they ate it up. These students, and my other students later, especially loved the stock tables because each stock is graded like they are graded, using 1–99 and A through E or F. Students were always coming up to me and saying things like, 'Look at this one! It's got a 99, 99, and AAA.' I have even taught my students to look for cups with handles, and they have enjoyed the challenge of that, too.

I moved back to Denver in the summer of 1998 and continued using IBD both personally and professionally. I had the same success here, with many of the same student reactions as I did in Guatemala. Then, last year, during the 2000–2001 school year, I taught a sixth- through eighth-grade after-school business club. Using IBD, I helped my students participate in the *Denver Post* annual stock market competition. One team, a group of two Ethiopian boys and one boy from the Philippines, all of whom had only been in America for a year, won second prize in the state! In fact, the only problem I've had using IBD in my classroom is when these students fought over who got IBD's 'Your Weekend Review' section on Fridays.

As a result of this success utilizing IBD in my classroom, I have a lot of other ideas for using IBD in education. If you ever think about creating a curriculum outreach program, I'd love to share them with you. There is so much in IBD that would be great for schools!

As far as my own investing, I still read IBD daily and subscribe to Daily Graphs Online. I am more confident now and strongly feel that when this bear slowly turns itself into a bull, I will be able to find and buy, at the pivot point, the next Qualcomm, JDSU, or Qlogic. (The pivot point took me about three years to completely appreciate!) At first, I was the typical beginner with no discipline. I would cheat on the CAN SLIM rules, simply buying anywhere and anytime regardless of what the chart showed. I also bought Internet stocks simply because they were Internet stocks. And I tried many other methods looking for instant profit and success. All in all, during my first two years of investing, I 'nickeled and dimed' my account to very low points, dragging my ego down with it.

Finally, I disciplined myself and made a CAN SLIM checklist. I swore that I wouldn't violate any of the system's rules. As a result, my successes have increased. And even though the market during the last year and a half has been rough, I did make a few nice trades, such as with Techne, Skechers, International Gaming, and Direct Focus. I have read and reread Chapter 11 [When to Sell and Take Your Profit] in *How to Make Money in Stocks* about 20 times so that I can remain focused for the next rally. I'll be shooting for the stars like you did from 1962 to 1963.

In conclusion, I would also like to express my appreciation for your love and respect of America. I have taught and traveled in many countries, and it is easy to say that America isn't perfect, but I feel, as you do, that if you work hard in America, great things will come. My father came to America as a poor, young immigrant in 1950 and has built up a great mason business, all through hard work. He always told me that if you work hard and remain positive, you can achieve anything you want. I feel that you and IBD express this same sentiment every day. And believe it or not, I bought my father a subscription to IBD for his birthday, and now he loves it, quotes from it, and reads it every day!

Most importantly, however, I want to thank you for the great work you do and the great information you print daily. It is greatly appreciated!

Sincerely,

David C., Investor

I started studying the market in March 1999.

After six months with a broker and no results, I went to the library, found *Investor's Business Daily*, and decided to learn to invest on my own. I started last September with $50K. When I sold everything in March after reading your latest book, I had $174K. Made most of my money on cup-with-handle formations and reading your book, *How to Make Money in Stocks*. I am a minister and want to use the money to start churches here in Illinois. My goal is to start 13 churches in the next few years. Thanks so very much for sharing your strategy with others.

Dr. Larry R., Pastor

In addition to success stories, we also receive letters from readers that provide extraordinary insight. The following is from one of our readers whose background, as a civil engineer in the former Soviet Union, gave an interesting perspective to contrasting economic systems. We ended up creating a series of articles from this reader to share her insight.

Perspective of a Russian Immigrant (No. 4)

Svetlana Kunin
12/08/2009

I look at the people who support the transformation of America in disbelief: They are destroying the very land that gave them so much opportunity.

Groomed, well-fed and educated, comfortably living in a prosperous society, they need a mission to give meaning to their lives. These "fighters for the less-fortunate among us" glaze over the fact that hundreds of millions of people from around the world desperately try to come to this country for all it offers, regardless of their economic status, race, class, or gender.

Immigrants rightly see this country as the best place to obtain a decent life for themselves and their families.

When I immigrated to America in 1980, I was overwhelmed with the amount of food and goods available at any store, at the numerous charitable organizations helping the needy, and even the government programs that helped people to obtain necessary skills to find a job.

Later, I realized that the country was in the midst of a deep recession. Compared to where I came from, it seemed like the pinnacle of prosperity.

As a secular Soviet Jew, my first Christmas in America was amazing. The proud display of religious symbols was a celebration not only of the holiday, but of a population free to express their beliefs without fear of oppression.

I understand why at the beginning of the 20th century Jewish immigrants in America wrote many beautiful Christmas songs; these songs were born out of grateful hearts. Churches and synagogues coexist without issues. Nobody is forced to practice or not practice a religion.

Soon, however, I noticed darker aspects underlying life in America. Political correctness had seeped into everything like cancer. Under the pretense of multicultural diversity, suppression and intolerance of uniquely American traditions such as liberty, private property, and e pluribus unum (out of many, one), became not only acceptable, but necessary in supposedly enlightened society.

Under the pretext of helping the needy, liberals eliminate people's drive to better themselves and their families. Instead, they obsess about events of the past and exacerbate the victim mentality in the very people they claim to help.

The stranglehold of political correctness has only grown stronger. I see in today's governmental policies a replication of the very things I escaped from.

In the USSR, representatives of the Communist party—partorgs (literally: party organizers)—were ingrained into every aspect of civilian, official, and military life. These political organizers controlled public order by observing the behavior and speech of every citizen.

People who wanted a more secure and privileged life found it necessary to join the propaganda machine. In order to survive, citizens were silent out of fear of retaliation by the authorities.

Government-controlled medical care and poorly compensated medical personnel stimulated corruption at every level of service. People had to resort to bribery in order to get the help they needed, and underpaid medical personnel were open to the payouts.

Those who could not pay had to beg for help. The only hospitals comparable to American hospitals were in Moscow and a few other cities, where government officials were treated. In the rest of the country, medical care was substandard. This was the reality of free health care for everyone.

No one can dispute that America has issues with its medical system, and here too, some people struggle to get the help they need. But the solution to the problem is not more bureaucratic control. The quality of medical care will inevitably decline for everyone.

I came to this country in the middle of a recession, and I saw the economy revive and prosper when the government eased the tax burden on people and businesses. People were free to use their talents without the interference of central planning. Today the opposite is taking place, and we see the opposite results because central planning results in wasteful spending, corruption, and the suppression of initiative.

I am afraid these transformers of America are destroying the future of our children. I hope the free spirit of America triumphs.

• ACKNOWLEDGMENTS •

I want to recognize and express my thanks for the following dedicated people who assisted in this current edition. Wes Mann, IBD's editor, provided his insights and editing, Justin Nielsen helped significantly with the tables and charts, and my assistant Deirdre Abbott Casey worked with the many manuscript changes.

The following individuals made other key efforts in making the book possible: Andy Ansryan, Ates Arkun, Matt Galgani, Chris Gessel, Dayna Grund, Jonathan Hahn, Trang Ho, Brian Lawlor, Sarah Lawrence, Susan McKnight, Adrienne Merrick-Tagore, Anne Morein, Zarzand Papikyan, Sarah Schneider, Kathy Sherman, Tina Simpkins, Kate Stalter, Cuong Van, Diana Wada, Mike Webster, and Christina Wise.

I also want to thank Mary Glenn, Ruth Mannino, and their fine staff at McGraw-Hill.

• ABOUT THE AUTHOR •

William J. O'Neil is one of Wall Street's most seasoned and successful veterans. At age 30, he bought his own seat on the Big Board with profits made in the stock market and founded William O'Neil + Co., Inc., a leading institutional investment research organization based in Los Angeles. The firm's current clients are over 600 of the top institutional investment firms in the world. Mr. O'Neil is also the founder of *Investor's Business Daily* and its companion Web site, Investors.com.

Get 10 Free Issues

Also Available in Digital Version

You've Read the Book. Now You Can Take Action!

Investor's Business Daily has helped investors be more successful for 25 years. IBD gives you vital data to help you make better investing decisions and improve your results.

IBD helps you zero in on leading stocks in leading industries and shows you how to get the most out of IBD's top-performing Investing Strategy.

Plus, IBD gives you:

- Top Stock Lists
- Proprietary Stock Ratings
- Exclusive Market Analysis
- Industry-leading Investor Education
- **And, you'll get access to the powerful investing tools and personalized features on IBD's web site, Investors.com.**

Try 10 FREE Issues of IBD

Call 1.800.831.2525

to get your free trial

(Hours: 5:30am - 4:30pm PT, Monday - Friday / 7:00am - 3:30pm PT, Saturday)

INVESTOR'S BUSINESS DAILY   **INVESTORS.com**

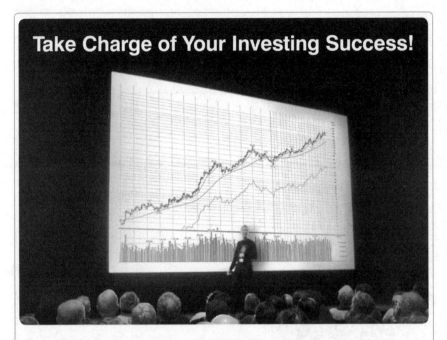

Don't miss these other great books from the *How to Make Money in Stocks* series!

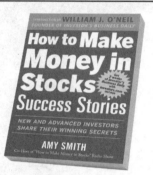

This essential guide reveals how top investors have applied the powerful CAN SLIM® Investment System—showing you how to replicate their success and generate outsized returns.

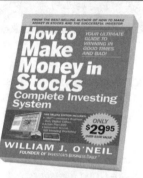

This book/DVD combo provides one month access to the tools and features of *Investor's Business Daily*® online and investors.com; a three-hour workshop with IBD experts; and the entire content of the national bestselling *How to Make Money in Stocks*.

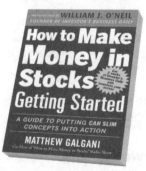

Introduces beginners to the winning CAN SLIM® Investment System, focusing on the basic rules and routines they need to draw greater profits than ever. Comes with free trial subscription to *Investor's Business Daily*®.